Acta Universitatis Upsaliensis
Uppsala Studies in Cultural Anthropology
9

Dualism and Hierarchy in Lowland South America

Trajectories of Indigenous Social Organization

by
Alf Hornborg

UPPSALA 1988

Distributed by
ALMQVIST & WIKSELL INTERNATIONAL
STOCKHOLM, SWEDEN

Printed edition of doctoral dissertation presented to the Faculty of Arts, Uppsala University 1986.

The publication of this book has been financially supported by Magn. Bergvalls Stiftelse and the Department of Cultural Anthropology, Uppsala University.

Abstract:

Hornborg, A., 1988. Dualism and Hierarchy in Lowland South America: Trajectories of Indigenous Social Organization. Acta Univ. Ups., *Uppsala Studies in Cultural Anthropology* 9. 304 pp. Uppsala. ISBN 91-554-2166-0.

The study is based on a comparative analysis of published ethnographic data on the social organization of 48 indigenous cultures in lowland South America. Each culture is analyzed according to a uniform matrix focussing on data pertaining to kin terminology, local group size, patterns of affiliation, hierarchy, alliance, and external relations. Kin terminologies are discussed in terms of the ways in which they deviate from a fundamental two-line (Dravidian) structure of kin classification. Some characteristic correlations are established between various parameters pertaining to social organization, suggesting a logical typology of South American lowland societies as well as some transformational trajectories which may be responsible for this variation.

To account for the specific mechanisms of cultural transformation, the book offers a restatement of the structuralist position in anthropology. Structural change is seen as the result of a dialectical interaction between a surmised socio-structural reality and a population's various attempts to conceptualize and formulate that reality. The indeterminate relationship between model and reality generates shifts of emphasis through series of logically contiguous permutations. The data from lowland South America suggest various trajectories which appear to be immanent in Dravidian classification: parallel affiliation, alternating generations, Crow-Omaha kin equations, unilateral and oblique marriage preferences, dual organization, and concepts of social hierarchy based on birth order.

The theoretical concerns transcend the geographical context, addressing not only anthropological epistemology and the problem of structural transformation, but also some traditional anthropological controversies such as idealism versus materialism, functionalism versus evolutionism, alliance versus descent, and the theory of prescriptive alliance.

A. Hornborg, Department of Cultural Anthropology, Uppsala University, Trädgårdsgatan 18, S-752 20 Uppsala, Sweden.

ISBN 91-554-2166-0
ISSN 0348-5099

Printed in Sweden by
Borgströms Tryckeri, Motala 1988

To Anne-Christine,
Sara and Christoffer

Contents

List of Tables

List of Figures

Preface

Through the years a number of people have contributed – knowingly or unknowingly – to the course of this inquiry. My interest in South America, structural transformation, and the origins of social stratification dates back to my first encounter with anthropology, at Lund University's then newly started Department of Social Anthropology in the mid-1970:s. For generous guidance and encouragement during those early years, I wish to thank Jonathan Friedman and Kajsa Ekholm-Friedman. At the turn of the decade, I transferred to the Department of Cultural Anthropology at the University of Uppsala. I am particularly grateful to Anita Jacobson-Widding, Jan Ovesen, and Kaj Århem for encouragement and support ever since. My subsequent focus on dual organization was inspired by the writings of Claude Lévi-Strauss, David Maybury-Lewis, and Tom Zuidema, but I owe its extension to the analysis of kin nomenclatures to the invaluable guidance of Kaj Århem and to the reading of Rodney Needham, Louis Dumont, and Peter Rivière.

I gratefully acknowledge the support of the Swedish Council for Research in the Humanities and Social Sciences, which enabled me to spend three months in Peru in 1981. While in Peru, I had the opportunity to meet a number of Americanists who all in some measure – great or small – influenced my studies. Of these, I am particularly indebted to Tom Zuidema, Juan Ossio, and Salvador Palomino. I also gratefully recall conversations with Monica Barnes, Alejandro Camino, Frédéric Engel, Ann Kendall, Patricia Lyon, Tom Moore, Jaime Regan, Johan Reinhard, John Rowe, Charlotte Seymour-Smith, and Michael Shott. All have helped in some way, if only with a bibliographic reference, the address of a colleague, or a useful caution. For her hospitality and assistance during my stay in Lima, I also want to thank my hostess, Sra. Doris Lavaggi. For taking the time to answer my letters requesting advice of various kinds, I wish to thank Daniel Gade, Jack Ives, Donald Lathrap, Claude Lévi-Strauss, John Murra, Patricia Netherly, and Peter Rivière. Among Scandinavian Americanists, I have valued the advice of Niels Fock, Anna-Britta Hellbom, Sven-Erik Isacsson, and Harald and Sarah Skar.

For invaluable assistance in locating rare literature, I am indebted to Åsa Henningsson of the University Library in Uppsala, Ingrid Friberg at the Ethnographical Museum of Gothenburg, and Kajsa Andersson of the City Library of Västervik.

The task of polishing my English was efficiently carried out by Theodosia Gray, to whom I remain deeply grateful.

I would like to thank my parents for continuous moral support, and my wife Anne-Christine and two children, Sara and Christoffer, for putting up with me during these years.

Finally, I wish to acknowledge my debt to the many ethnographers whose experiences in the lowlands of South America form the subject matter of this book. Their perceptions of alternative ways of organizing human society are more than invaluable documents. To anyone concerned with finding a viable mode of existence for mankind, they are a major inspiration.

Yxnevik in March 1986

Alf Hornborg

Preface to the published edition

Although unaltered in terms of fundamental arguments and conclusions, the thesis has profited from some suggestions offered by Dr. Peter Rivière while publicly examining it in May 1986. Dr. Rivière also directed my attention to several useful contributions (Dumont 1966, Korn 1973, Ortiz 1969, Trautmann 1981), some arguments of which have been incorporated and referred to in this final version. For his many penetrating and stimulating comments, I extend my profound gratitude. The responsibility for any remaining shortcomings is, of course, entirely my own.

I wish to thank Anchylin Århem for improving the aesthetic dimension of this book by carefully redrawing all the figures.

Finally, my heartfelt thanks to Magn. Bergvalls Stiftelse and to the Department of Cultural Anthropology, University of Uppsala, for making publication possible.

Yxnevik in January 1988

Alf Hornborg

Chapter 1
Introduction

This book deals with the relationship between the ideas a population holds about its social structure, and its actual social organization. By "ideas," I mean systems of classification, conscious or subconscious. By "social organization," I mean the way in which a human population reproduces itself through exchanges of goods, services, and people.

The problem of social classification vis-à-vis social organization raises the basic philosophical question of whether we can speak of society as an objective reality apart from the way in which human beings conceptualize it, or if you will, if a social *science* is at all possible. I believe that structures of exchange do have an objective existence, which can be more or less successfully perceived by the participants themselves or by the social scientist. Anthropology as a discipline focuses in large measure on the relation between a culture's models of social reality and that reality in an objective sense. This relationship between model and reality has in itself become an object of the anthropologists' own professional models. Throughout this book, we shall be concerned with avoiding linear cause-and-effect models of the role of ideas (i.e. ideology, cosmology, classification, etc.) in social systems, in favour of a dialectical approach. Human reflection on a collective level is neither the epiphenomenal frosting on a materialist layer-cake, nor the essence of an Hegelian cosmos. Rather, it is an information-processing subsystem comparable with analogous subsystems at other levels of integration in living systems, e.g. the central nervous system of the organism or the genetic code of a particular species.

As information-processing subsystems, such cultural codes simultaneously reflect and control. Like the human mind or the DNA molecule, a cultural code is the product of its own history. It reflects not only some of the external conditions of the system as a whole, but also the internal contradictions generated in the process of its own consolidation. In its confrontation with inconsistent conditions, it is continually faced with the prospect of losing its internal consonance. To maintain consonance, ideological systems, much as individual minds, are constantly forced to reinterpret and reorganize. Cultures, therefore, generally maintain a number of parallel and only partially congruent images of their own behaviour. By superimposing such parallel perspectives on each other, I believe we may come closer to approximating the essential features of a particular social structure.

To emphasize the reverse relation, i.e. the actively "structuring" aspect of cultural codes, we can resort to the concepts of social "templates" or "programmes" suggested by general systems theorists (Miller 1965:204, 224). Much as a single biological genotype can be variably transduced into different phenotypes, there is no immediate correspondence between classification and social organization. For anthropologists studying kinship-organized societies, this relationship has long been the focus of inquiries into the social correlates of different systems of kin classification. In our survey of lowland South American social organization, we shall be particularly concerned with the way in which separate societies may codify a similar form of organization in terms of different systems of rules and categories, or inversely, with how differently they may "enact" a similar system of classification.

My aims are comparative and analytical. By juxtaposing partially congruent images emphasizing different aspects of more or less continent-wide structural themes, I believe we can postulate probable sequences in the accretion, replacement, and transformation of such models over time.

Two decades ago, Irving Goldman spoke of South America as an "anthropological *terra incognita*" (1963:1), where "both kinds of study, the survey of traits and the intensive study of a society, are eminently justifiable." A decade later, Pat Lyon (1974) still found reason to subtitle her anthology, "Ethnology of the Least Known Continent," and in her introduction she deplores the difficulties involved in assembling material for detailed comparison. Indeed, few wide-scale attempts have been made towards this end. Early efforts to characterize socio-structural variation in the Amazon Basin (Steward 1946a, 1948a; Lévi-Strauss 1963d/1952/; Oberg 1973/1955/) suffer from the dearth of ethnographic data, particularly on social classification. The expansion of South American ethnography in recent decades has produced relatively few comparative ventures dealing with social organization. These have generally been restricted either to a single linguistic family (e.g. Maybury-Lewis 1967, 1971a, 1979a; Rivière 1977; Ramos & Albert 1977; Schwerin 1982) or to a small number of societies or parameters (e.g. Rivière 1973; Jackson 1975a, 1984; Dietschy 1977; Dreyfus 1977; Kaplan 1977, 1981; Kensinger 1979a; Århem 1981:273-303; J. Shapiro 1985; Kelly 1985). Nevertheless, they jointly represent a renewed interest in isolating common denominators of structural variation in lowland South American societies, and have yielded many new, vital insights. Recently, some very useful attempts at wider synthesis (Rivière 1984, J. Shapiro 1984) may announce a stronger momentum for comparative studies.

South America, next to Australia the most isolated continent in the world in Pre-Columbian times, provides us with somewhat of a laboratory situation. Most important, it gives us a unique opportunity for reconstructing the ideological correlates of a transition from egalitarian reciprocity to strict hierarchy. In fact, the original impetus toward this comparative venture derived from some intriguing suggestions by Claude Lévi-Strauss (1944:40; 1957; 1963c:105-106) and Tom Zuidema (1964:21-23, 26-28; 1965) on the issue of whether the hierarchical development of Andean social organization was associated with a permutation of dual systems of classification surviving into the ethnographic present in the Amazon Basin. My intention was to assemble, in a single volume, both a comprehensive summary of the ethnography on hierarchical ideologies in the South American lowlands, and an investigation of relevant highland-lowland parallels. I initially turned my attention to the most conspicuous aspect of such parallels: the spatial representation of social organization as expressed in site layouts, ritual, and other forms of symbolism. Much as the logic of terminological kin equations determines the trajectories whereby systems of classification (and often, in effect, forms of social organization) are transformed, I assumed that other symbolic codes (such as the conceptual grids by which social dimensions are plotted in physical space) are also subject to their own semantic logic. In the architectural and ritual recognition of social space, we may discern how a particular symbolic "grammar" is used to mediate between contradictory aspects of social organization, alleviating the cognitive dissonance generated by the emergence of hierarchy in a society where the system of classification is emphatically dualistic. The symbolic recognition of such contradictions not only facilitates social change, but also encodes the different structural options of a society, granting it a certain reversibility over time.

Thanks to the Swedish Council for

Research in the Humanities and Social Sciences, I was able to spend July through September of 1981 in Peru, acquainting myself with several Pre-Columbian sites, relevant literature, and the Peruvianist anthropologists whom I was able to reach. Some of the ideas developed in this context were later presented in a paper (Hornborg 1982) delivered at the 44th International Congress of Americanists in Manchester.

As I penetrated deeper into the ethnographic literature, however, I realized that in order to understand the nature of dualism and hierarchy in the lowlands, it was necessary consistently to juxtapose the relatively sparse data on hierarchy with the entire context of kin classification, affiliation, marriage rules, and relations with the outside. In the process, I became more and more intrigued by the tantalizing congruities and redundancies intertwining systems of social classification throughout lowland South America.

A particularly obvious problem was how to define "dual organization." I soon realized that ethnographers of the South American lowlands approached dual organization in a bewildering variety of ways. Lévi-Strauss (1945:38) had called dual organization "one of the main problems of South American sociology." In the use of a two-section (or two-line) kin terminology among the cognatic Nambikwara, he had seen "a theoretical possibility, as well as . . . a practical ability" for moiety formation (ibid., 39). This perspective is reiterated by Oberg (1973:205) for the Upper Xingú tribes, by Goldman (1963:288) for the Cubeo, and by Århem (1981:299) for the Makuna. Needham (1958b:210; 1960b:23, note 1; cf. Maybury-Lewis 1967:216) coined the term "two-section system" for a "form of dual organization" lacking exogamous moieties, and instead suggested (1967:45) that the terminology developed from moiety systems. Displeased with the "two-section" designation, "since it confuses the formal properties of a terminology with the contingent features of a type of social organization," Needham (1966b:142, note 2) instead suggests that we call it a "two-line terminology of symmetric alliance." Maybury-Lewis (1960b:42) rejects Lévi-Strauss' hypothesis of alliance reciprocity as the foundation for dual organization on the grounds that symbolic dualism is a more widespread phenomenon than exogamous moieties. He notes (1979b: 224), however, that the two-section terminology of the Sherente is "perfectly adapted to their obsolescent moieties." Rivière (1973:4) similarly mentions societies the two-line relationship terminologies of which "form a consistent fit" with grosser social units such as moieties, and Kensinger (1979b:82) writes that two-line terminologies may be "used to express the social categories created by . . . social groups." However, Rivière (1973:5) adds that the description "dual organization" is always inappropriate for societies lacking unilineal descent groups. By contrast, Chagnon (1968:57, note 4) asserts that dual organization is "implied" in the kinship terminology of the Yanomamö, even though they lack named moieties. In the same vein, Siskind (1973:199, note 3) remarks that the kin terminology of the Sharanahua "analyzes easily as a perfect moiety and brother-sister exchange structure," C. Hugh-Jones (1977a:96) finds Barasana kin terms "consistent with a 'dual organization' marriage system," and Dole (1979:29) observes that "a moiety structure is suggested" by the kin terminology of the Amahuaca. Similarly, Jackson (1975b:328) attributes to Rivière the position that "all lowland South American societies have an underlying two-section terminology, *moieties*, and a principle of direct exchange" (italics mine), and suspects (1975a:8) that the Tikuna have a Dravidian terminology because of their "strong moiety system" (ibid.), which, however, they themselves do not acknowledge (Kracke 1984:123, note 6). Diametrically opposed to these interpretations are the struggles of Basso (1973:90), Kaplan (1972, 1973, 1975), and Schwerin

(1982:2, 7) wholly to dissociate the concept of dual organization from discussions of two-line terminologies.

I realized that instead of a static typology of kin terminologies we have to recognize a spectrum of variants on the two-section pattern. At one end there are those systems which we may call Dravidian. These represent the simplest and most consistent codification of bilateral cross-cousin marriage (symmetric alliance): the cross/parallel distinction is extended indefinitely (Scheffler 1971), and cross-collaterals are consistently equated with affines (Buchler & Selby 1968:233; Kaplan 1975:127-128, note 1). These systems, in fact, rarely feature dual organization. Towards the other end there are a number of variants on bifurcate merging, Iroquois-type systems, where the cross/parallel distinction is inconsistently extended and the presence of distinct affinal terms produces an attenuated two-line structure only. At this end of the spectrum, we find various reflections of unilateral affiliation, such as when Ego's FZ or MB is classified as "kin" and one of his parents as "affine" (W. Shapiro 1970; cf. C. Hugh-Jones 1977a:95; Århem 1981:37, 341; Kensinger 1984:229). If we keep in mind that Rivière uses "social structure" in the sense of "social rules," we can only agree with his observation (1984: 103) that if "in Lowland South America we have so many examples of one basic structure, . . . it is still incumbent upon us to explain why the elementary structure of reciprocity gives rise to different social structures" (cf. Kaplan 1981:164; 1984:151).

As I came increasingly to focus on these problems, the range of lowland cultures embraced by my comparison expanded to almost 50. By and by, I realized that the comparative problems raised in the lowland synthesis in itself would suffice for a thesis, and that I would have to postpone the highland-lowland comparison until a later date. Accordingly, a major part of this book (Part II) is devoted to a survey of social classification and social organization in lowland South America. As we have indicated, this survey is intended to be part of a wider research programme designed to investigate how dualistic and hierarchical principles of social classification have been articulated in indigenous South America. Ethnohistorical and contemporary sources on indigenous Andean culture are particularly rich in information of this nature, but for reasons of space we have been compelled to omit such material from the present volume.

In several instances (e.g. the controversial Apinayé and Sherente), specific cultures have occasioned lengthy analyses interspersed with the data. There are also separate conclusions for each linguistic family. and a general summary (Part III) suggesting trajectories of socio-structural transformation which may account for some of the variation in lowland South American social organization. In Part IV, we shall return to the theoretical issues raised in Part I, supporting our conclusions with statistical information derived from the ethnographic sample. The final synthesis (Table 58) presented in Chapter 23 is meant to incorporate the various structural congruities discussed throughout Part IV. In concentrated form, it illustrates the eclectic approach which follows from the conviction that there are generally several equally valid ways of describing reality.

Part I
Theoretical and Methodological Points of Departure

In this section, we formulate the fundamental problems guiding our inquiry. Though raised by the reading of ethnographical accounts of lowland South American social organization, many of these issues transcend the geographical context. We discuss the concept of "social structure" in relation to various models of society (emic or etic, morphological or processual), and the shortcomings of linguistic metaphors in accounting for socio-structural transformation. We juxtapose separate but functionally congruent codifications of social behaviour, suggesting that the congruities thus isolated represent relatively invariant features of behaviour. Our foremost example is the pervasive phenomenon of direct exchange, or symmetric alliance. Finally, we sketch the implications of our approach for several traditional anthropological controversies such as idealism versus materialism, functionalism versus evolutionism, alliance versus descent, and prescriptive versus preferential marriage rules. A fundamental and illustrative issue to which we continually return is the relationship between the terminological dualism inherent in two-line systems of kin classification and the corporate dualism of exogamous moieties.

Chapter 2
Code, Behaviour, and Structure in Social Systems

". . . We are led to conceive of social structures as entities independent of men's existence, and thus as different from the image which men form of them as physical reality is different from our sensory perceptions of it and our hypotheses about it."
– C. Lévi-Strauss (1963d:121)

Social Structure

A common source of confusion in anthropology is the socio-structural congruity of differently expressed rules and categories. To take an example particularly relevant to South America, it appears that an identical, symmetric alliance structure could be produced by either (a) a rule encouraging sister exchange continued over the generations, (b) a Dravidian, two-line kin nomenclature defining as marriageable the category of "opposite-sex affines of Ego's generation." or "opposite-sex children of parent's same-sex affines," (c) a rule enjoining marriage with the bilateral cross-cousin, genealogically specified (i.e. the child of a cross-sex sibling of Ego's parent), or (d) a rule prescribing marriage into the opposite exogamous moiety. This functional convergence of distinct rules, in terms of organizational potential, indicates that it would be inadvisable to claim, as has e.g. Leach (1954:4), that social structure is a set of ideas. Systems of rules and categories do have semantic and logical structures which can be analyzed in their own terms, but the locus of "*social* structure" must instead be the behavioural correlates of these rules, in reference to actual, often unconscious alignments and regularities in communication and exchange. The definition of "social

structure" advocated here could be phrased as *objective regularities in the flow of energy, matter, and information between people.* Such objective regularities can obviously be visualized in different ways by different peoples, or by the same people on different occasions. Regional, historical, and contextual variability are all aspects of this general phenomenon of culture.

Lévi-Strauss returns again and again (e.g. 1969:119) to the analytical opposition between what he calls the "method of relations" and the "method of classes" in kin classification. Discussing dual organization, he suggests that the rule of bilateral cross-cousin marriage and exogamous moiety institutions represent "different stages in the growing awareness" of a common structure of reciprocity (ibid., 101). This is a crucial point, because it locates an element of the process whereby social groups and categories emerge, i.e. of the formation of a given structure of social organization, *beyond* the human faculty of classification (cf. Lévi-Strauss 1963d:121).

Such an approach is not universally accepted. In a critique of Durkheim and Mauss' theory of the socio-structural foundations of primitive classification, Needham (1963: xxvi) suggests that "a causal interpretation . . . should rather be that where correspondences between social and symbolic forms are found it is the social organization which is itself an aspect of the classification." However, although a far from exhaustive account of the relation between society and cosmology, Durkheim and Mauss' perspective has considerable merit. Lévi-Strauss' useful concept of "codification" represents a direct development of their approach, recognizing that systems of classification in part constitute the attempts of people to phrase (or rationalize) an observed, pre-existent reality in terms of behavioural rules. Needham, on the other hand, has concentrated on the reverse aspect of the dialectical relation between classification and organization, analyzing social structures in terms of their derivation from systems of rules and categories. He holds that "there is no un-categorized social action," since "behaviour reflects ideas, and ideas . . . are expressed in categories" (Needham 1967:48). For simplification, we might characterize these two approaches as inclining toward either "social determinism" (Durkheim and Mauss) or "mental determinism" (Needham). As no element of a truly dialectical relation can be said to have primacy over the other, it is obvious that neither position is sufficient.

Structures and Models

With Kroeber (quoted in Lévi-Strauss 1963f: 278), we prefer to maintain the general meaning of "structure" by which it can be applied to "a physiology, any organism, all societies and all cultures, crystals, machines – in fact everything that is not wholly amorphous." Systems of classification and of social organization both have "structures", in the sense of specific patterns of relationships connecting their different components (semantic categories or actual people.) Lévi-Strauss, however, chooses to equate "social structure" with "model," letting "social relations" signify what is in fact the *behavioural* structure of a society (ibid., 279). His definition of social structure as "models which are built up after (empirical reality)" is difficult to reconcile with his views on dual organization referred to earlier, where models corresponding to bilateral cross-cousin marriage and exogamous moieties "both have their origin in the apprehension, by primitive thought,

of those completely basic *structures* on which the very existence of culture rests" (Lévi-Strauss 1969:101; italics mine.) Apparently, we are to understand that native models of social structure represent the imperfect apprehension not of regularities in social behaviour, but of *yet deeper mental models*, submerged in the human unconscious. In locating the underlying structures of human society in less accessible levels of the human mind, Lévi-Strauss never really grants "society" the status of a scientific object. The interaction between conscious and unconscious models, which is offered as the very mechanism of social transformation, is confined to the realm of the mental. Insofar as we may presume that "those completely basic structures" of the mind are invariant, this perspective seems incapable of accounting for structural change. In our view, the social reality imperfectly encoded in native models must be assumed to lie at the mutable level of social *behaviour* rather than that of thought.

Lévi-Strauss' definition of social structure as a mental model has been reiterated by British structuralists such as Leach (1954:4-5) and Maybury-Lewis (1967:293). The latter concludes that there can be no talk of the "real" structure of a society (ibid., 295), but only of perspectives or hypotheses. But there is a crucial difference between saying that our *perception* of social structure can only amount to a model, and saying that social structure *is* a model. If we want to talk about our *models* of social structure, we would do well to call them just that, reserving the concept of social structure for the epistemologically inaccessible, real-world phenomenon of ordered relationships in social systems. If it can never be fully grasped, social structure must at least be assumed.

Structure and Language

The notion that social structure should be sought in the human mind was inspired by linguistics (Lévi-Strauss 1963b:33–34). In the study of language, it has been useful to distinguish between actual speech (Saussure's "*parole*") and the system of unconscious rules according to which speech is organized ("*la langue*"). These levels correspond to a more general distinction between behaviour and codes applicable to all forms of human communication. Different disciplines attempt to formulate the codes relevant to different forms of communication, but are all constrained by the fact that codes can only be induced from actual behaviour. Musical theory can only be constructed from the experience of music, semiotics from the study of how symbols are actually used in art, myth, and ritual, and so on. In the case of language, there is a hierarchy of such codes corresponding to different levels of integration in human speech. The behavioural manifestations at each such level of integration serve as the set of "signs" to be integrated at the next. Phonemes are organized by a phonological code into words, as are letters of the alphabet by rules of orthography. Words are organized by lexicological and syntactic codes into sentences, and sentences by logic into messages (i.e. speech.) All these codes, which are necessary to human communication, belong to the unconscious. Lévi-Strauss' application of this distinction between code and behaviour to the level of social interaction has inspired the structuralist tenet that regularities in social organization can be attributed to yet another assumed, unconscious code. According to this scheme, social structure, like the structure of language, would be reducible to properties of the human mind.

It certainly seems justifiable to treat social behaviour as a highly organized form of communication. Inasmuch as social roles and relations can be visualized as being composed of sets of messages, social interaction would represent a level of integration higher than that of speech. But here are the limits of the linguistic metaphor. Whereas phonemes, words, sentences, and messages involve an exchange of information only, the total phenomenon of social organization is simultaneously a material process of reproduction. Flows of goods, services, and people follow patterns which may be more or less consistent with the cognitive patterns which we may describe as cultural (or social) codes. It is reasonable to let "social structure" denote such patterned processes of reproduction, rather than mental representations of them. The patterned processes unfold as products of specific norms, but in a sense independently of this code. Fundamental regularities will be generated which are *unintentional* in the sense that they are not an aspect of the code. The potential autonomy (or even opacity) of behavioural processes vis-à-vis codes cannot be accommodated in the linguistic metaphor.

Another flaw in the linguistic analogy is the fact that whereas *la langue* is definitely unconscious, social behaviour is generally allegedly "explicable" in terms of conscious emic models. This is not to deny that there may be unconscious, abstract "deep structures" of classification of which the conscious model is but a specification, or even that the conscious model may be a collective rationalization of less conscious motives which must be suppressed in order to maintain cognitive consonance. In this sense, the cultural code consists of both conscious and unconscious elements. But an important distinction between speech and social behaviour is that whereas the former is more or less taken for granted (i.e. the various codes of expression are acquired at a level of learning which does not involve reflective thought), the latter is constantly the object of self-reflection and re-interpretation. As interpretation automatically becomes an active determinant of behaviour, there is a dialectic between code and behaviour the immediacy of which is not paralleled in language. Whereas speech is dialectical in the sense that the speaker will allow contextual feedback continually to determine his *use* of the code, which even includes choosing among various sub-codes, the codes and sub-codes themselves remain relatively invariant. In the long run, of course, even *la langue* is not merely the instrument of speech but also, unconsciously, its product. But even if the relative autonomy of the behavioural context is, to a degree, applicable also to language, there is a great difference in terms of the immediacy of feedback.

If the code, up to a point, is the *product* of contexts determining what people *are compelled* to do or to express, we can only assume that the source of these compulsions are structures at the level of behaviour. If systems have structures at both the level of code and the level of behaviour, it is meaningless to debate the locus of *the* structure of a system. I have only argued that the term "social structure" should be used for behavioural structures, and for this purpose I have found it necessary to argue for their very existence. Admittedly, however, taken by itself the question of whether objective structures of social organization are to be envisaged as embedded in the unconscious or as external to the human mind is largely a philosophical issue, since in neither case are they amenable to verification. The achievements of Lévi-Strauss' methodology suggest that much of the analytical work should follow the same lines, whichever philosophical position is adopted. The most satisfying solution would be to refuse to phrase the issue in terms of "either – or." Lévi-Strauss himself suggests (1969: xxx) that the "duplication" by cultural models of natural mechanisms is "permitted by the emergence of certain cerebral structures which themselves belong to nature." This perspective converges admirably with Gregory Bateson's (1973: 461) profound warning not to "separate mind from the structure in which it is immanent, such as human relationship, the human society, or the ecosystem." Problems appear when this dual nature of "structure" is not properly handled, as when the relative

autonomy of either its mental or behavioural aspects is neglected or even denied. The issue is crucial to several topics of anthropological debate, where different perspectives will yield radically different conclusions. One such issue is the definition and implications of prescriptive marriage systems. Another, related problem concerns whether the opaque aspects of social behaviour (e.g. the expansive properties of matrilateral cross-cousin marriage) really can be assumed to be encoded, albeit unconsciously, in the human mind? Most important, however, is the potential either perspective has for accounting for structural transformation. If the congruities shared by a series of conscious models are simply thought to approximate universal structures of the human mind rather than an elusive social reality, the point of orientation is fixed and unresponsive, and there can be no dialectical movement.

Structure and Process

Attempts by general systems theorists (e.g. Miller 1965) to merge the vocabularies of biologists and social scientists, as students merely of different levels of integration in living systems, reveal the nature of the ambiguity surrounding the concept of "structure." In biology, the analytical distinction between "structure" and "process," i.e. morphology and physiology, has been challenged by Bertalanffy, who points out that it derives from "a static conception of the organism" (ibid., 211). In reality, "the organism is the expression of an . . . orderly process . . . sustained by underlying structures," and morphology "a momentary cross-section through a spatio-temporal pattern." The unfortunate separation of static and dynamic aspects of living systems has been difficult to apply to the study of societies. Social structure has been morphologically defined by Radcliffe-Brown (1952:191) as a collection of social roles and all the relations interconnecting them, retaining its continuity over time. "Social physiology," on the other hand, i.e. "the mechanisms which maintain a network of social relations in existence," includes "every kind of social phenomenon" such as "morals, law, etiquette, religion, government, and education" (ibid., 195). Radcliffe-Brown's reasons for assembling this mixture of categories and institutions appears to stem from the notion that physiology (i.e. process) in a living system *serves to* maintain its structure, a very misleading dichotomy indeed. Living systems *are* structured processes, the relative stability of which over time is maintained by information-storing subsystems (codes, templates, programmes) which simultaneously reflect and reproduce these processes. Actually, all of Radcliffe-Brown's phenomena of "social physiology" except one (government) constitute such information. By including government in his list, which for *his* purposes also might have embraced lawyers, priests, and scientists, Radcliffe-Brown reminds us that much of the ideological codification in complex societies has become the work of specialists and special-interest groups.

It may well be that the misleading distinction between morphology and physiology is responsible for the widespread disavowal of a concept of real-world "social structures" in anthropology. While anatomists may find it useful to distinguish the static, concrete arrangement of organs and tissues as a literal embodiment of a biological process, the social scientist in search of analogous structures would have to look at "the arrangement of streets, houses, and other buildings" (A.H. Leighton, quoted in Miller 1965:210). This analogy gives us an idea of how incomplete a picture of biological systems sheer morphology can produce. The very fact that such study can be pursued after the death of an organism (or the abandonment of a city; cf. the archaeological study of ruins), i.e. after the system as a reproductive process has ceased to exist, indicates that any cognate notion of social structure should be dismissed. Similarly unacceptable are attempts to define social structures in terms merely of constituent groups, rather than of the vital metabolic flows we think of as communication and exchange.

To describe an organism in terms of its morphological structure is to present a very incomplete picture. Yet the tangible, material nature of biological systems would seem to provide some justification for the study of morphology. But this concreteness is altogether relative to the position of the student. Living systems at all levels of integration consist primarily of *organization* (i.e. relationships, structure), and the "material" parts which are thus organized upon closer scrutiny also dissolve into organization. Human beings perceive biological systems as more material than social systems because they can observe the former from without, from a higher level of integration, while being confined to conceptualizing the latter from within. In reality, both types of system consist of analogous processes of matter-energy conversion organized by information, and there is no reason to consider one more "material" than the other. It would be a grave mistake to draw the conclusion, from the fact that a social structure will never rest in our hands like a dissected rodent, that it exists only in our minds.

The Interpretation of Social Structure

"The traditional differences of (human cultures) . . . in many ways resemble the different equivalent modes in which physical experience can be described."
– Niels Bohr (quoted in Lévi-Strauss 1963g:364)

From the assumption that social structure does exist as an objective reality, we can predict that the emic recognition of this reality will vary in terms of the level at which it is perceived. Systems of social classification, rules and categories are codifications of the aspects of social structure which have been *recognized* by the participants. This implies that different rules may co-exist as different interpretations of the same structure, and even replace each other over time. Hence, rules which at one time accompanied a given behavioural pattern, and which would enlighten us as to the explanation, or rationale, of the appearance of that pattern, may disappear entirely and be superseded by other rules with slightly different structural implications. This, we suggest, is a fundamental mechanism of transformation in social systems (Fig. 1).

The contemporary rules and categories presented to field-workers as the rationale of social organization are no more than the native's own interpretation of his social structure. In this light, the distinction between emic and etic (i.e. participant's and observer's) models begins to fade. The native and the field-worker are in a similar position, both interpreters of a pre-existing order. The parallel is even more apparent if we consider the anthropologist or sociologist struggling to understand his *own* society. Emic models ("norms" or "conscious models" in the terminology of Lévi-Strauss), though they "furnish an important contribution to an understanding of the structures," may be "just as remote from the *unconscious reality*" as those stemming from the anthropologist's own culture (Lévi-Strauss 1963f: 282, italics mine.) Here, Lévi-Strauss clearly illustrates his conviction that social structures are real, but again chooses to locate them in the participant's unconscious. This would be equivalent to considering the structure of an organism real only in the sense that it is encoded in its DNA molecules. On the contrary, much as the phenotype carries some information not contained in the genotype, social organization should be partially opaque to mental models.

Dual Organization

" . . . The dual system does not give rise to reciprocity, but merely gives it form. . . . . . The essential thing, as we see it, is not dual organization but the principle of reciprocity of which it constitutes, in some way, the codification."
– C. Lévi-Strauss (1969:70,72)

The socio-structural congruity of different systems of classification, and their interchangeability over time, poses problems for the analyst who wishes to reconstruct the original rationale of a particular feature of social organization. To exemplify, we shall return to the phenomenon of dual organization. Lévi-Strauss (1969:101) characterizes dual organization (exogamous moieties) as a codification, more coherent and rigid and representing a more complete and definitive awareness, of the same structure towards which bilateral cross-cousin marriage is an "attempt," or tendency. Bilateral cross-cousin marriage, in turn, is a genealogical specification of the marriageable category in a society where a principle of sister exchange (direct exchange, symmetric alliance) is obeyed over the generations. The exchange of sisters is the simplest possible form of alliance, and the immediate reciprocity inherent in this type of marriage explains why it is an explicit ideal in so many societies all over the world. It is reasonable to hypothesize that sister exchange was an archaic rule, which over time has been supplemented with isomorphic but differently phrased codifications of the same structure of exchange. Two-line kin terminologies, rules explicitly enjoining bilateral cross-cousin marriage, and systems of exogamous moieties all represent such emic elaborations of the same social structure.

In an attempt to account for moiety systems among the Central Gê, Maybury-Lewis (1967:298) defines their dual organization simply by observing that "every aspect of the social life of its members is ordered according to a single antithetical formula." This approach leads Maybury-Lewis to assume that *exogamous* moiety systems among the Gê are simply a special subset of those societies of Eastern Brazil which are organized according to a binary mental matrix. Among the Bororo, the Sherente, the Western Shavante, and possibly the Eastern Timbira, the pervasive "antithetical formula" would have permeated social organization to the point where it even ordered the fundamental structures of alliance. Probably deterred by the kind of "conjectural history" conducted by early evolutionists such as Rivers, who saw traces of exogamous moiety systems in any bifurcate merging system of kin classification (1968:83, 88), Maybury-Lewis (1960b:42) appears unwilling to treat the general phenomenon of dual organization among the Gê as the codification of a kin-affine polarity historically generated by an ideal of direct exchange. Such an approach, however, has several advantages. By tracing the corporate dualism of the Gê to the ideal of direct exchange, our account of dual organization would be phrased in terms of sociology rather than psychological idiosyncracy. It would also provide a solution to Maybury-Lewis' problem of "why dual organization is mainly found in more 'primitive' societies" (1960b: 42), as the introversion inherent in direct exchange suggests social systems at lower levels of integration. But whereas Lévi-Strauss penetrates the dualistic cosmological surface in pursuit of underlying socio-structural principles, Maybury-Lewis views the dual cosmology itself as the core. This difference in approach illustrates precisely the aforementioned disagreement between Durkheim/Mauss and Rodney Needham.

Relations or Classes

The difficulties in establishing which of several congruent rules is primary can be exemplified in a number of other cases as well. For instance, the corporate name-hold-ing groups of the Krĩkatí, which maintain their integrity through all three ceremonial moiety systems, are not fully *recognized* by the Krĩkatí themselves. Rather, name transmission is conceptualized in terms of relations between individual name-givers and name-receivers. Lave (1979:30) says that "they describe formal friend relationships in terms of links between individual name-givers and name-receivers, although it would be equally accurate to talk about a tie of formal friendship linking two name-holding groups," and finds it "puzzling that the Krĩkatí do not make use of the corporate properties of name-holding groups in characterizing their own society." Similarly, Kracke (1984:119) shows how a system of exogamous clans and moieties among the Kagwahiv could be reproduced by a functionally congruent system of name transmission, "even without full understanding on the part of the participants" (cf. ibid., 123, note 6, for similar conclusions for the Tukuna.) A given structure can be recognized in terms of either relations or classes, and again it appears that egocentric relationship categories may be prior to the codification of corporate groups.

In the same vein, Basso (1973:89-90) notes that affinal exchange between two Kalapalo kin groups is often repeated over "several consecutive generations." Nevertheless, the two groups are regarded as being related "on the basis of specific and individual alliances only, rather than in terms of some generalized definition by which they are conceived as 'spouse-exchangers' before the fact." Basso concludes that "Kalapalo kin groups which give each other marriage partners are *distinctively different* from units or categories defined in terms of such exchange, such as is often the case with clans, lineages, and moieties" (ibid, italics mine.) In fact, this "distinctive difference" between systems where direct exchange between two groups is phrased in terms of kin nomenclature (*ifandaw* = potential spouses, a category including all opposite-sex cross-cousins), and systems where the same exchange relationship is codified as a rule of moiety exogamy, is at the level of classification only. The social structure remains the same in both cases. Should someone object that relations of direct exchange among the Kalapalo are only temporary, in comparison with rigid moiety institutions, I would argue that the temporal duration of a process of exchange is of no relevance to its structure. While it lasts, direct exchange between two groups of Kalapalo generates the same structure as that found in exogamous moiety systems. Moiety exogamy, on the other hand, is probably a much more ephemeral state of affairs than is suggested by the elaborate ideological and ceremonial superstructure with which moiety divisions are reified. The dimension of time is here relevant only to the extent that a structure of direct exchange requires a minimal measure of continuity in order for its dualistic character to become sufficiently apparent to achieve emic recognition in the institution of moieties.

Alternating Generations

The Kalapalo case illustrates once again the potential congruity of emic rules employing a method of relationships on the one hand, and those applying a method of classes, on the other. We shall mention two additional examples of the kind of problem deriving from the congruity of different emic models. These final examples both originate from Kaplan's (1977) comparative comments on the symposium "Social Time and Social Space in Lowland South American Societies," held in Paris in 1976. Kaplan (ibid., 388-389) notes that "a principle of alternate generations . . . may take its form from different sources, as the examples of the Cuiva, the Cashinahua, the Matsiguenga and the Timbira illustrate: from the relationship terminology, from naming or ceremonial systems, or through a particular system of marriage alliance." Here, again, are three

different means of conceptualizing a similar structural feature. It will be seen that two of these models, the terminology of the Cuiva and the transmission of names among the Timbira, are classifications which give us no immediate indications as to the behavioural rationale of alternation. Among the Cashinahua and the Matsiguenga, on the other hand, the alternating mode of classification is demonstrably linked to rules of marriage, residence, and affiliation, in a sense which closely complies with the type of explanation offered by Lévi-Strauss (1969: 219; 1973c:109-111). While relationship terminologies or systems of ceremonial name transmission may codify cycles of structural alternation in social systems, the logical rationale of such alternation can be phrased either in terms of the cyclical merging of a unilocal rule of residence with a non-congruent ("disharmonic") ideology of affiliation in a system of bilateral cross-cousin marriage, or in terms of patrilateral cross-cousin marriage. The former explanation seems to fit the data on the Cashinahua, who combine uxorilocality and patrilineal moieties (Kensinger 1977:235-236), while the latter can be applied to the Matsiguenga (Casevitz 1977).

Lévi-Strauss (1969:219) has shown that systems of alternating generations result "from a system of patrilateral marriage just as much as from a double patrilineal and matrilineal dichotomy." In a later context (1973c:110-111), he suggests that alternation might also be associated with sex (i.e. parallel) affiliation, and speaks of this tripartite congruity as "a phenomenon of convergence." A logical next step would be to suggest how one of these alternative models may have been derived from another. A conceivable hypothesis is that patrilateral cross-cousin marriage in particular instances may derive from bilineal/ "disharmonic" or parallel principles. If there are two or more uxorilocal groups between which men are exchanged, and simultaneously an ideology of patrifiliation, there might well be a conscious stress on the value of a male Ego's return to his father's natal household. This is accomplished by his marrying a FZD. An alternative understanding of the same rule would be to note that principles of parallel affiliation make FZD a closer relative than MBD (cf. Scheffler & Lounsbury 1971:175) and thus, if an ideal of close marriage prevails, the preferred spouse. Patrilateral cross-cousin marriage is certainly not a prerequisite for classification by alternating generations, but a possible trajectory of disharmonic systems which is equally compatible with, and may reinforce, the emergent alternation. It is difficult, finally, to draw a line between disharmonic systems ("double descent") and parallel affiliation. Among the Gê, the matrilineal continuity of uxorilocal residence is generally the concern of females, while the patrilineal continuity of ceremonial life is incumbent on males. The cyclical merging of matrilineal and patrilineal continuities may result from parallel affiliation just as much as from double descent. Dumont (1966) maintains that a principle of alternating generations does not require any culturally explicit bilineality, but may simply represent the recognition of a structural epiphenomenon generated by symmetric alliance (cf. Korn 1973:111, 121-123). Trautmann (1981:188-200, 233-237, 436), in fact, shows how alternation may be derived from the extension of "crossness" into grandkin categories in Dravidian terminologies. Bilineality and alternation would thus be alternative, not necessarily co-existent codifications of symmetric alliance. This position, although a modification of Lévi-Strauss', exemplifies the same general approach.

Uxorilocal Residence

Our final example is "what superficially appears to be one phenomenon, but obviously is not: that of uxorilocality" (Kaplan 1977: 393; cf. Rivière 1984:40-41). The arrangement whereby women remain in their natal households while men are exchanged can apparently derive from, and be phrased in terms of, a number of different rules. Kaplan (1977:393-394) notes that the focus may be on (a) the mother-daughter unit (Bororo, Txicáo), (b) the female sibling set (Canela), (c) the co-resident male affines (Yanoama), or even (d) the male sibling set (Barama River Caribs). It is conceivable that all of these valued relationships could be developed to satisfaction within a single uxorilocal society, but it is probable that different societies will tend to emphasize the significance particularly of one or two of these. In terms of explicit ideals, or of the rationale offered for the practice of uxorilocality, there may thus be considerable variation. Once again, however, the real-life structure by which men are exchanged between localized lines of women remains constant, as a regularity of organization in relation to which all the different emic models are congruent.

All these examples suggest that an exclusive pre-occupation with the specifics of emic models may lead to an over-emphasis on variation, and to the unwarranted conclusion that different sets of rules and categories necessarily imply different origins for various instances of a similar social structure. More important than speculating about chronological succession, however, is to articulate various native models in cross-cultural, comparative sequences and analyze their various permutations in terms of organizational potential. Comparison necessarily requires an element of "etic" reductionism (cf. Kensinger 1984:243).

Structural Transformation

We have proposed a model of social systems which is consistent with the approach of general systems theory to lower-level units such as organisms and cells. The analogy is founded on the analytical division of a reproductive process into an *informational*

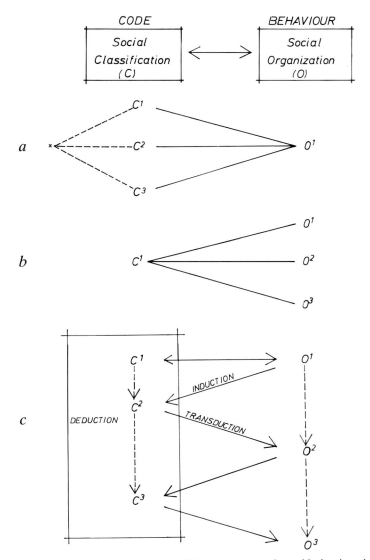

Fig. 1. Some postulated relationships between code and behaviour in social systems.

(a) A single structure of social organization (O) can be apprehended in terms of several emic systems of classification (C). An etic representation of the structural congruity (x) of several systems of classification (C^1, C^2, C^3) may correspond more concisely to the behavioural realities of social organization (O^1) than any one of the emic models.

(b) A single system of classification (C^1) can be transduced into several different forms of organization (O^1, O^2, O^3).

(c) The indeterminate relationship between code and behaviour is the basis for dialectical interaction yielding structural transformation. A shift in emphasis from one emic model (C^1) to another (C^2), whether generated by deduction or by renewed induction from O^1, may stimulate slightly different strategies of behaviour, resulting in social change (O^2, O^3. . .). The box represents that segment of reality which is directly accessible to ethnographers, i.e. a series of structurally contiguous permutations of social classification.

27

component, on the one hand, and actual organization of matter and energy, on the other. Codification, of course, involves a certain expenditure of matter and energy, but the crucial point is that the information-carrying subsystem (code, template, programme) at once regulates and reflects the total process of reproduction of which it is but a part, or aspect.

Much as the genotype and phenotype are indeterminately related, the levels of classification and social organization maintain a relative autonomy vis-à-vis each other. Systems of classification will undergo a continuous struggle towards internal, cognitive consonance, while some aspects of organization will remain obscure or opaque to the system of classification. A particular structure of social organization may be conceptualized in different ways, varying with cultures, periods, and even speech contexts. As one such mode of conceptualizing social structure for some reason comes increasingly to replace another, there may be a transition of emphasis, which in turn may stimulate new strategies of behaviour, i.e. social change. Transformation at the behavioural level, of course, may be followed by further transformation at the level of classification, and so on (Fig. 1). In the dialectical interaction between code and behaviour (here: classification and social organization) lies the mechanism of structural transformation. In concentrating each on a different aspect of this dialectic, the early French structuralists (Durkheim, Mauss) were more prone to emphasize the primacy of social organization, while British structuralists (Leach, Needham, Maybury-Lewis) have tended to take classification as the point of departure.

Alliance or Descent

" . . . Both ideas are given together, and spring from one another: no kin without alliance, no alliance without kin."
– L. Dumont (1953a:37)

"Consanguinity and affinity are related as chicken and egg." – T.R. Trautmann (1981:60)

Turning again to ethnographical examples, the evidence for a transition of emphasis, such as has been hypothesized here, is particularly clear among groups of the Yanoama linguistic family. Comparing the sub-groups Sanumá and Yanomam, Ramos and Albert (1977:87) note striking differences in terms of the relative emphasis on descent or alliance as principles of social organization. While the Yanomam seem to be organized entirely in terms of alliance, i.e. with an emphasis on solidarity and proximity between affines, the Sanumá adhere to a rigid codification of patrilineal descent, which extends even beyond the community. Dumont (1961:25) suggested that "descent theory" and "alliance theory" could be taken as "particular cases of a more general, and more complex, theory." In refining Lévi-Strauss' (1969:47) distinction between "true endogamy" and "functional endogamy," Kaplan (1973:567) addresses a problem the consideration of which may provide us with a better understanding of the relation between descent and alliance. Lévi-Strauss distinguished between "true" endogamy as a "positive formula of being obliged to marry within a group defined by certain concrete characteristics," and "functional" endogamy as, in fact, "a function of exogamy, or the counterpart of a negative rule" (1969:47). To exemplify the latter, Lévi-Strauss says that cross-cousins "are not so much relatives who must inter-marry, as they are the first persons among relatives between whom marriage is possible once parallel cousins are classified as brothers and sisters." Kaplan's concept of "group" endogamy corresponds to Lévi-Strauss' "true" endogamy, but his "functional" endogamy is further subdivided into "genealogical" endogamy and "alliance" endogamy. The distinction Kaplan adds is between "the obligation to choose as spouse an individual who is related to Ego in some particular way" (e.g. to marry MBC/ FZC, or to marry within the immediate kindred), and the obligation to reaffirm a former alliance (i.e. to replicate the marriage of one's parents.) "It might well be," she adds (Kaplan 1973:568), " . . . that the latter form ideologically implies the former, and both entail what Lévi-Strauss has termed 'true' endogamy," but the distinctions are nevertheless important, as "each has considerably different implications for an *interpretation* of social organization" (italics mine.) Among the Piaroa, Kaplan finds all of these interpretations co-existing as mutually compatible representations of a single mode of social organization. First, there is the basic ideal of marrying within one's own local group. If this ideal is put into practice over the generations, the local group will tend to be congruent with one's kindred, and it is obvious that the ideal of local endogamy and the ideal of kindred endogamy are congruent in this context. A marriage rule phrased in terms of kindred endogamy, however, implies a shift from "group" endogamy to "genealogical" endogamy. In conjunction with the classification of parallel cousins as siblings (following the cross/parallel distinction which itself is an aspect of "alliance" endogamy), an ideal of kindred endogamy becomes equivalent to that of bilateral cross-cousin marriage (Lévi-Strauss' "functional" endogamy.) The two-line terminology reproducing this pattern of bilateral cross-cousin marriage expresses the ideal of reaffirming previous alliances. In this way, Kaplan's typology of different rules of endogamy can also be taken to represent a sequence of transformations. The successive codifications of marriage rules do not contradict each other, but represent different *interpretations* of society, each the potential germ of a separate trajectory of ideological elaboration. Here is an excellent example of the co-existence of multiple emic models which are congruent with respect to the underlying structure of social organization (for similar co-occurrences of disparate

models, cf. Kensinger 1984b and Kracke 1984.) J. Shapiro (1984:24, 30, note 28) suggests that "inquiries into intracultural variation should be central to the ethnographic enterprise and are an intrinsic part of the study of social change." The Piaroa appear to be a culture at the very juncture of descent and alliance, with a potential of either continued emphasis on "alliance" endogamy or increasing emphasis on genealogical connection. A crucial factor in deciding which trajectory to follow would probably be the capacity of a society to continue the practice of local "group" endogamy. With a greater number of supra-local alliances, whether the result of segmentation or of linkage with other groups, choice of post-marital residence would entail a unilateral slant in the affiliation of Ego vis-à-vis his parents, and the recognition of kin in neighbouring groups would provide a context for genealogical definitions of kinship. This is probably the kind of explanation which would account for the Sanumá/ Yanomam contrast. While the Sanumá have developed supra-local alliances and a rule of uxorilocal residence, which in turn has been counterbalanced by a strong ideology of patrilineal descent, the Yanomam cling to local village endogamy, ambilocal residence, and a strong emphasis on the solidarity of affines (Ramos & Albert 1977). The Sanumá/ Yanomam contrast illustrates how symmetric alliance can be visualized as both exogamy and endogamy, and that it would be misleading to let the concept of "exchange" exclusively denote the former. A distinction between "exchange" and "endogamy" (Strathern 1984:57), though useful for some purposes, would here mask the invariant metabolic process which both models describe.

Synchrony and Diachrony

We have suggested that natives and anthropologists alike are merely *interpreters* of social behaviour. In analyzing his data from the cross-section of social process represented by his period of fieldwork, it is only to be expected that the ethnographer will tend to de-emphasize the historical dimension. His synchronic analyses of the "ethnographic present," in synthesizing empirical data and their contemporary emic interpretation, will probably fail to take into account the diachronic fluidity both of social organization and of the emic model-building which simultaneously reflects and reproduces it. An obvious conclusion is that where early ethnographic reports diverge from contemporary studies, the former are not necessarily false (cf. Dole 1969:119; 1972:137; Lévi-Strauss 1968b:351-352). Nimuendajú's reports of moiety exogamy among the Gê-speaking Krīkatí, Ramko-kamekra, and Kayapó, refuted 40 years later by Lave (1971) and Turner (1971), may thus represent actual traditions rather than misinterpretation (cf. W. Crocker 1977:268, 273-274, notes 23-25). The problem faced by a culture undergoing rapid change is how to re-interpret, assimilate, or otherwise dispose of elements of classification which are rendered functionally obsolete. Moiety divisions, once outdated in terms of the regulation of marriage, cannot disappear overnight. As such divisions have become increasingly manifest in terms of institutions and real-life organization, they will continue to live a life of their own, fulfilling the role of merely maintaining the cognitive consonance of a culture. It is even possible that an institution such as moieties, on being increasingly threatened with the dissolution of the rationale of its existence, may be even *more* accentuated. Such a cultural defense mechanism may help to explain the intensive emphasis on ceremonial moieties among the Gê, where the principle of direct exchange appears almost obsolete, and the image of reciprocity is so strongly contradicted by social hierarchy. W. Crocker suggests, in a similar vein, that the "ritual lineages" of the Canela may be "vestigial 'time-marks' of

earlier, far more complex structures" (1977: 269). Our argument is not a simple reiteration of classic evolutionism, however. Although sharing the evolutionists' interest in "survivals" of antecedent social structures, our approach differs from evolutionism in attributing to these dormant models the potential of being *reactivated* under certain conditions. Much as Leach (1954) suggested for the Kachin, this potential reversibility at any given time would be inherent in the multiplicity of models maintained by a population about its social structure.

Classification and Organization

> "We seem to be faced with a gulf between culture as an activity of the mind and society as mindless activity."
> – J. Shapiro (1984:24)

The relative autonomy of classification vis-à-vis organization has been recognized by several authors. Even if he expects a certain degree of correspondence between changes in categories and changes in institutions 1972:13), Needham (1963:47) notes that "categories and social action can be treated separately, and . . . both provide criteria for independent analysis." This is amply illustrated elsewhere (1966b, in particular). Maybury-Lewis (1965a:221, 227) similarly observes that rules and "social consequences" are to some extent autonomous. Scheffler (1966:550) notes that "the ideological and transactional domains are in some ways ordered independently of one another," and that "there may be dialectical relationships" between them. Scheffler and Lounsbury (1971:190) conclude that "there is no necessary correlation between type of terminological system . . . and one or another particular aspect of social structure." They distinguish, as we have done, between "the *structure* of certain systems of kin classification" and "the structures of the societies in which they occur" (ibid., 227).

30

Kaplan (1975:6-7), too, distinguishes between her "concern . . . with Piaroa systems of categorizations alone" and her "interest . . . in the way the Piaroa *use* their symbol systems toward particular ends," e.g. in constituting residential units. Similarly, Århem (1981:34) distinguishes between social categories as "elements in the cognitive ordering of the social universe" and social groups as "concrete units of social organization," noting that "categories may or may not correspond to actual social groups." The list, of course, could be extended. The distinction between "ideal" and "real" in social organization is recognized in one way or another in most modern ethnography. Few ethnographers, however, have addressed the dialectical interaction of these two levels over time.

From Code to Behaviour

An analogy between biological and cultural evolution is suggested by the phenomenon of structural congruity itself. While congruity in cultural systems results from independent attempts to codify a particular, shared reality, e.g. different interpretations of a specific structure of exchange, analogous convergences in the evolution of organisms is produced as different genetic stocks encode similar information on the requirements for survival in a given environmental niche. In both instances, congruity derives from parallel sequences of information processing, i.e. from the inclination of separate templates to record the same information.

Much as a genotype is transcribed into a particular phenotype, the rules encoded in a system of classification are transcribed into a particular mode of organization. The relationship between code and behaviour is determined by factors influencing the process of transcription, i.e. by an "epigenetic space" in which different elements of the code interact with each other while being continually modified and "canalized" by current environmental conditions (cf. Waddington 1969:364).

The highly indeterminate relationship between code and behaviour is receiving increasing attention from anthropologists (e.g. Schneider 1965, 1972, 1984; Basso 1970; Kaplan 1972, 1984:134–144; Kensinger 1975, 1980; Kracke 1984:121) disillusioned with those naïve versions of structuralism which have neglected this indeterminacy (cf. next section.) Establishing inconsistencies, contextual variability, and patterns of strategic manipulation in the application of cultural codes is a very important task, which can only be pursued by ethnographers in the field. But it would be wrong altogether to deny the explanatory value of the deductive, cognitive processes which push cultural models, against all odds, towards the semblance of logical consistency. This is the domain of comparative studies, and a justification for structuralism.

Returning to biological analogies, we may note that there are moments when anthropological accounts of the reproduction of social systems indeed recall the replication of biological systems, e.g. mitosis at the cellular level. Barasana *malocas*, for instance, maintain a particular spatial arrangement which appears to be a codification of the structure of social organization which they enclose. *Malocas* split as children "hive off and form new *maloca* communities on their own," and "each new community reproduces the structure of its parent" (S. Hugh-Jones 1977:209). Much as the DNA molecule replicates itself through the attraction of opposites, the application of two-line relationship categories tends automatically to ramify emergent alliance structures, even where they contradict previous alignments (cf. Chagnon 1968:58; Kracke 1984:109, 119). Lounsbury (1964b:1092) speaks of "structural mutations, i.e., changes in underlying principles of classification that affect a whole system." The indeterminate character of the relationship between code and behaviour is well illustrated for the Cashinahua, where a single ideal model of the "proper village" is transcribed into a spectrum of "highly variable" modes of organization (Kensinger 1977:242). Similarly, the two-line relationship terminology to Rivière (1973) represents a "structural definition" of South American Tropical Forest culture, and is treated by Århem (1981) as a "structural code" subject to variable manifestations.

Prescription and Preference

"A man who is tired of issues such as these is tired of social anthropology."
– D. Maybury-Lewis (1965a:228)

Our concern with the transcription of code into behaviour takes us on to the problem of preferential versus prescriptive marriage rules. This has been the topic of considerable debate in anthropology. Needham (1958b: 200–201; 1962:11) distinguishes the two clearly from each other, equating prescriptive systems with Lévi-Strauss' "elementary structures" and preferential systems with "complex structures." Unfortunately, says Needham, Lévi-Strauss himself uses the word "preferential" on occasion "to designate marriages which are in fact prescribed," and conversely, "in certain ethnographic instances he deals with marriage preferences as though they were prescriptions" (1962:10). Nevertheless, Needham assures us, "in 'Les Structures élémentaires de la Parenté,' Lévi-Strauss is concerned to analyze prescriptive rules of marriage, not preferential" (ibid., 11). Although much of what he writes elsewhere (e.g., 1966b) suggests differently, it sometimes appears as if Needham's reason for emphasizing this distinction is that he is concerned with whether an empirical society in actual practice behaves in exact accordance with anthropological models, i.e., with the latitude of "choice" (cf. Schneider 1965). A prescriptive system,

where *all* marriages conform with the ideal, would be expected to generate a real-life structure congruent with the structure generated by the anthropologist at the level of his own model. In other words, the structure of the model would be isomorphic with the structure of real-life social organization. A preferential system, on the other hand, would be the product of contingent circumstances, i.e. more arbitrary and complex, less regular and predictable. However, prescriptive systems in the neat and predictable sense which Needham appears to have in mind are very rare indeed, and anthropological models can generally claim only to hint at the structural *inclination* of a particular society. This autonomy of categories vis-à-vis behaviour has been duly noted by Needham elsewhere (e.g. 1963:47; 1966b: 141–143; 1973). His (1962) interpretation of Lévi-Strauss, however, provoked the protests particularly of Schneider (1965), who has criticized Needham's tendency to confuse models and behaviour in prescriptive systems. Furthermore, Needham's interpretation prompted Lévi-Strauss himself, in his preface to the second edition of "Les Structures élémentaires" (1969), to clarify his own position. He admits having "employed the notions of preference and obligation indifferently" because, in his opinion, they "do not connote different social realities, but rather, correspond to slightly differing ways in which man envisages the same reality" (ibid., xxxi-xxxii). An "elementary structure," he says, can be preferential or prescriptive, because, "preferred or prescribed, the spouse is the spouse solely because she belongs to an alliance category or stands in a certain kinship relationship to Ego," whereas in "complex structures" the "reason for the preference or the prescription hinges on other considerations" (ibid., xxxiii-xxxiv).

The fact that Lévi-Strauss pursues structures which are only imperfectly encoded in the conscious model of marriage preferences is crucial to the debate on prescriptive alliance. A closer look at Lévi-

Strauss' account of structural regularities in preferential marriage systems is quite rewarding. By "preferential," he means "any system in which, in the absence of a clearly formulated prescription, the proportion of marriages between a certain type of real or classificatory relative . . . is higher than were it the result of chance, whether the members of the group are aware of this or not" (1969:xxxiv). "This objective proportion," he continues, "reflects *certain structural properties* of the system" (ibid., italics mine.) He goes on to exemplify by reminding us that matrilateral cross-cousin marriage will generate alliance networks with longer cycles of reciprocity than those which are "observed or imagined" in societies practicing patrilateral cross-cousin marriage. There is "what might be called a matrilateral 'operator' at work in this society and acting as pilot: certain alliances at least follow the path which it charts out for them, and this suffices to imprint a specific curve in the genealogical space" (ibid., xxxiii). Further, "the structural outlines which emerge here and there will be enough for the system to be used in making a probabilistic version of more rigid systems the notion of which is *completely theoretical* and in which marriage would conform rigorously to *any rule the social group pleases to state*" (ibid., italics mine.) This is one of Lévi-Strauss' clearest statements of the dialectical interaction of code and behaviour: a rule (MBD marriage) generates certain structural outlines (cycles of reciprocity) which can be recognized in a more rigid theoretical model, either the anthropologist's (etic) model or a native (emic) model rephrasing the marriage rule in some way (e.g. according to the "method of classes," as in a rule enjoining marriage with a woman of a wife-giving group or category.) Schneider (1965:42) succinctly captures the point: "If a marriage rule is to be treated as an expression of a structural principle, and if a marriage rule such as MoBrDa is taken as one expression of that principle, then it would seem to follow that a preferential rule (as distinct from the prescriptive rule) is equally clearly an expression of that same structural principle."

Maybury-Lewis (1965a), however, finds it useful to maintain Needham's distinction between prescriptive and preferential marriage systems. He articulates this distinction with the question of whether a marriage rule is phrased in terms of relationship categories or in terms of genealogical specification. "*In general*," says Maybury-Lewis (ibid., 208; italics mine), "prescriptive marriage systems are here taken as being those in which there is a rule of marriage with a prescribed *category* of relative." Were it not for the qualification "in general," this would simply amount to a new definition of prescription based on the formulation of the rule rather than on the extent to which it represents an obligation. Lave, in reiterating this position, adds a similar qualification. Marriage, she says (1966:187; italics mine), "*to the best of my knowledge*, is always prescribed in terms of relationship category, never in terms of genealogical ties" (cf. also Lounsbury 1962:1305). Two points should help us understand why this statistical correlation is a fact. First, a relationship category allows a number of genealogical specifications to be subsumed under a single term. In any society where potential spouses include more than one genealogical specification (and to my knowledge this condition is universal), a relationship category is a more economical way of phrasing the marriage rule than to list the different genealogical alternatives. Second, a relationship category has a greater potential for *ex post facto* rationalization of deviant marriages, and is thus less likely to appear incompatible with real behaviour.

The second point above is crucial to the rationale of an analytical distinction between preference and prescription, such as Maybury-Lewis suggests. Maybury-Lewis holds that "the distinction between a prescriptive and preferential marriage system is that in the former all marriages are *treated* as being of the prescribed category whereas in the latter not all marriages are treated as being of the preferred category" (1965a:226, italics mine.) This definition has been reiterated by other authors such as Lave (1966:198) and Thomas (1979:77). Thus defined (i.e. as an *image* of a compliant society), prescription implies regularities in the system of classification which are not to be expected in preferential systems. Maybury-Lewis notes that "a prescriptive marriage rule entails . . . the division of Ego's conceptual universe in a determined fashion, irrespective of the percentage of people who marry" into the prescribed category (1965a:225). In other words, prescription should be seen primarily as a particularly rigid codification at the level of social classification, rather than as a measure of the extent to which behaviour complies with rules and regularities. In a sense, however, the two problems become one. Behaviour *does* accord with the system of classification in prescriptive systems, not so much because rules are followed as because the system of classification bends to accord with behaviour. Of course, such rationalization is likely to appear only in a society where the rules are already perceived as compulsory, i.e. where there is already a strong inclination to behave in compliance with the system of classification. But the use of relationship categories can itself imply a greater latitude of behaviour than that granted by rules based on genealogical specification, both because categories are wider to begin with and because they are more amenable to manipulation. Prescription means greater structural rigidity, but this rigidity does not necessarily extend beyond the level of ideals. It is a feature of the model rather than of reality, and is of slight value for an understanding of behavioural regularities as long as it can be manipulated to legitimate a variety of marriage strategies. The model, in short, may be highly indeterminate with respect to real-life structures of exchange. For this reason, we cannot see the point of Maybury-Lewis' (1965a:225) and Lave's (1966:186) speculation as to whether a prescription is essentially equivalent to a marriage preference followed by 100% of the population. From Maybury-Lewis' definition, we can only conclude that prescription is a phenomenon belonging to the level of classification, and that the extent to which a given preference results in particular behavioural regularities is a separate problem.

Lave (1966:197) claims that preference and prescription simply "tend to fall toward one end or the other of a continuum," where "the more stringent the marriage rules . . . the more closely will formal models be effective in predicting what the anthropologist is likely to find under actual conditions." This is equivalent to saying that a progressively more rigid codification of rules and categories *reinforces* the emergent structure by rendering it more and more compulsory. Such a conception of the spectrum preference/prescription would comply with the perspective of Lévi-Strauss. It does not agree, however, with the definition Maybury-Lewis gives for prescription, which hinges more on the malleability of the system of classification than on the degree to which behaviour is moulded by the model. Maybury-Lewis' definition suggests that it would be possible for a preferential system to be even more faithful to its norms than a prescriptive (cf. Lounsbury 1962:1308), the difference being that in the latter case all behaviour is *represented* as complying with the ideal. If malleability is the diagnostic feature of prescription, as Maybury-Lewis suggests, we must discard Lévi-Strauss' and Lave's concepts of a continuum of increasing obligation. Prescription will not predict so much about what people actually do, as about how their behaviour is perceived.

Lounsbury (1962:1308–1309) shares Needham's and Maybury-Lewis' conviction that there is a valid distinction to be made between prescriptive and non-prescriptive systems, but asserts that it would be a mistake "to let it hinge on the criterion of 'obligation' to marry." A prescriptive terminology is diagnostic of certain aspects of "the legal structure of a society," particularly those that concern "succession and inherited affinity," i.e., not so much obligations as *rights* to marry.

Once again, the issue reduces to whether we consider the locus of social structure to be at the level of mental models or at the level of real-life behaviour. Maybury-Lewis is obviously concerned with regularities at the level of classification. The systems which he calls prescriptive are not necessarily those where behaviour is most uniform, but those where an illusory determinacy between code and behaviour has become an aspect of the code itself. Needham (1973) makes it quite clear that the theory of prescriptive alliance is concerned not with statistical regularities in behaviour, but with systems of social categories. Rivière (1973:5) similarly defines prescription as "a formal feature of a set of social categories." Indeed, if prescriptive marriage systems are tautologically defined as those where Ego must marry someone who can be classified as marriageable (Schneider 1965:66), and this category is stretched to accommodate a very large number of genealogical specifications, it is obvious that the prescription in itself can tell us very little about structures of exchange.

Scheffler (1970) and Korn (1973:36–38) demonstrate that Lévi-Strauss' formulations on "prescription" and "preference" at times seem contradictory, even obscuring his fundamental distinction between "elementary" and "complex" structures. I believe that much of the problem envisaged by Needham, Maybury-Lewis, and Korn derives from the demands on rigid, binary thought posed by the human faculty of classification itself. Rather than recognizing overlapping tendencies and spectra, these authors require discrete, bordered entities: prescription versus preference, symmetric versus asymmetric alliance, and so on (cf. Lounsbury 1962:1304; Schneider 1965:70).

To my mind, the most useful understanding of Lévi-Strauss' and Needham's typologies of kinship systems is as follows. Elementary structures can be recognized wherever there is a significantly systematic, genealogically relevant, positive determination of spouses, whether culturally codified as a genealogically phrased preference or as a prescriptive system of relationship categories. The choice of spouses in complex structures, on the other hand, is only negatively determined by genealogy, but in other respects genealogically irrelevant, and consequently unsystematic, at least from the point of view of kinship. Genealogical regularities are the hallmark of elementary structures, for they represent a record, if you will a ledger, of past exchanges (cf. Scheffler 1974:267, but also Schneider 1972 and 1984:125, for a probably overstated attempt to "nullify a false and misleading mode of comparison.") There should be no doubt that most of the lowland South American cultures discussed in this book exhibit "elementary" features clearly distinguishing them from, for instance, contemporary Western Europe. Not all of them are prescriptive, however, in the sense of having terminologically codified a marriage preference by recognizing relationship categories equating specific affinal and consanguineal positions.

Symmetric and Asymmetric Alliance

Maybury-Lewis and Lévi-Strauss agree on one point, viz. that our focus should be on the structural regularities in exchange reproduced by and reflected in specific marriage rules. The transformation from two- through four- to eight-section systems in Australia, demonstrated by Lévi-Strauss (1969), maintains the fundamental symmetric alliance structure, even though the transition from Kariera- to Aranda-type systems entails the exclusion of the actual bilateral cross-cousin from the category of potential spouses

(Maybury-Lewis 1965a:224). There are really only two fundamental possibilities: (1) a unilateral transfer of spouses (prescriptive MBD marriage), or (2) a bilateral exchange of spouses (prescriptive MBD/FZD marriage) (ibid., 218; cf. Needham 1962:110). This distinction has been phrased in different ways, e.g. asymmetric versus symmetric alliance (Needham), generalized versus restricted exchange (Lévi-Strauss), and so on. As we have shown, however, Lévi-Strauss has treated these alliance structures in a manner different from that of Needham and Maybury-Lewis. To the former, the structures emerge in an objective sense even in non-prescriptive systems, i.e. in terms of real behaviour rather than categories. To the latter, the main point is the existence of the categories, whether or not these correspond to regularities in behaviour. The former emphasizes behavioural structures, the latter structures of classification.

Needham's (1958b, 1962) argument that patrilateral cross-cousin (FZD) marriage belongs with bilateral cross-cousin (MBD/FZD) marriage is correct in terms of the symmetric alliance structure generated by these rules. Maybury-Lewis (1965a:217), however, shows that the "bewilderment" caused by Needham's analysis stems "from the sudden introduction of genealogical terminology into a discussion of categories." Needham argues that a system of consistent patrilateral cross-cousin marriage would equate FZD = MMBDD, rendering FZD marriage equivalent to marriage with a classificatory *matri*lateral cross-cousin, and that the prescribed category would not coincide with any discrete group in an alliance system. However, it is conceivable that a culturally determined genealogical amnesia might ignore the more distant, matrilateral connection, and it is utterly misleading to assume that relationship categories represent actual groups, particularly in non-unilineal systems such as those prevalent in lowland South America. In our South American

sample, we shall encounter several cultures which express an explicit preference for FZD marriage, and it is theoretically possible to envisage the same rule phrased as a "prescription."

The Genealogical Implications of Prescriptive Marriage Rules

"The idea of cross-cousin marriage is, as it were, embedded in the terminology; the kinship terms imply cross-cousin marriage and, what is more, cross-cousin marriage is imperative if the kinship terms are to be kept consistent."
– N. Yalman (1962:556)

To Maybury-Lewis (1965a:208), genealogical specifications are never explicit in emic marriage rules. With Dumont (1953a:35; 1957:24–25), he maintains that "the notion of 'marrying a cross-cousin' is an analytical one, introduced by anthropologists." Whenever a marriage rule is phrased in terms of genealogy, Maybury-Lewis would expect it to be formulated by an anthropologist, as an *etic* model, while *emic* models invariably employ relationship categories (1965a:211). Such categories "may on occasion be genealogically derived, but it has also been shown that frequently they are not" (ibid., 212). If emic models are continually recodified, however, it is difficult to prove that relationship categories are more primary than some genealogically phrased specifications with which they tend to be congruent. Synchronic analyses simply cannot give the final answer. Even if the notion of a genealogically defined cross-cousin appears to be absent in societies with an alliance-organized, Dravidian kin terminology, we know that it represents an explicit concept in others. In some societies (e.g. Barasana, Bará) there are purely descriptive terms for cross-cousins. From the Quechua-speaking natives of Q'ero, Peru, Webster (1977:32) reports a conscious, genealogically phrased distinction between parallel cousins and cross-cousins. The categories *wayqentimpu wawan* ("children of brothers") and *nanantimpu wawan* ("children of sisters") are extended in a classificatory manner, resulting in a "parallel kindred," whereas "conscious consanguinity attenuates rapidly among descendants of *panaturantimpu wawan*" ("children of a sister and brother".)

The distinction between parallel cousins and cross-cousins is based on a consideration of *sex* in reckoning consanguinity (Lévi-Strauss 1969:128). A collateral shift in sex implies genealogical distance, and cross-cousins often become the focus of marriage ideals because they are the only kind of relatives within Ego's kindred which are considered sufficiently distant to be marriageable. As Lévi-Strauss has shown, the cross-cousin marriage rule is the result of a conjunction of kindred endogamy and sibling exogamy, where parallel cousins are classified as siblings. Whether concomitant to sister exchange or to unilateral affiliation (unilocal residence or unilineal descent), parallel cousins are structurally equivalent to siblings, while cross-cousins will be assigned to another group or category. In this respect, sister exchange (symmetric alliance) and unilateral affiliation are congruent principles.

Is it unreasonable to suggest that the significance of collateral shifts in sex is recognized in emic models of marriage ideals? Dumont (1953a:35) certainly found it unreasonable. Kaplan (1973:568) attributes to alliance theorists like Leach, Maybury-Lewis, Dumont, and Needham the conviction that "to phrase kinship categories in genealogical terms is a blatant imposition of analyst's categories upon those of the native." But surely, even if it is rare to find as clear a concept of cross-cousins as that of the natives of Q'ero, the consideration of sex in reckoning collateral consanguinity will be recognized in some form? We have seen that even in the most alliance-organized of societies, where marriage is regulated by

a Dravidian, kin-affine system of relationship categories, Ego is enjoined to marry not simply an "affine," but a child of a parent's *same-sex* affine (cf. Dumont 1953a:35; 1953b:143; Kaplan 1973:562; 1975:130, 132, 137; Trautmann 1981:79, 174). Children of oppositesex affines of parents, on the other hand, will be Ego's kin (siblings and parallel cousins.) In other words, there is no neat separation of "kin" and "affines," where personal, genealogical considerations are superfluous. The Piaroa phrase their marriage rule so as to refer to the first ascending generation, enjoining marriage with "the child of father's *chisapo* ('brother-in-law') or mother's *chóbiya* ('sister-in-law')" (Kaplan 1975:133). This certainly amounts to "reaffirming a former alliance," but it is equally synonymous with marrying a FZC or MBC. In polemizing with descent theorists (e.g. Radcliffe-Brown 1953), Dumont (1953a, 1953b) had every justification for focusing on the emphasis on alliance in Dravidian systems, but a fertile synthesis of the two positions must be that symmetric marriage rules phrased genealogically or in terms of affinal categories are congruent, each emphasizing a different aspect of the same structure. There should be no need to expel entirely any genealogical consciousness attributed to an essentially alliance-organized society. Kaplan (1973:557) criticizes Lévi-Strauss for phrasing "the marriage rule . . . in terms of genealogical connexions, that is as 'cross-cousin marriage.'" She shows (1975: 187, 190), however, that the Piaroa have a second "classificatory scheme," parallel to the kin-affine model, according to which the ideal of "marrying close" does have genealogical denotations, i.e. marrying MBC/FZC. In the case of the Trio, Rivière (1969:64) suggests that "genealogical connexion between parents and child, and between other close kin, is the foremost criterion in the ordering of social relationships." Trio informants unanimously agreed that one should marry the child of either a *nosi* (FZ) or a *ti* (MB), i.e. a bilateral cross-cousin (ibid., 141). There is no reason why a population should not be able to take account of collateral shifts of sex to the same extent that descent-organized societies emphasize *lineal* shifts of sex. The Culina, for instance, offer an explicit, ethnobiological explanation for the cross/parallel distinction (Pollock 1985:11). Scheffler and Lounsbury (1971:37–39) and J. Shapiro (1984:14) call for more "ethnogenealogical" studies, which "show us the meanings attributed to genealogical relationships in particular cultures." Shapiro observes that "if genealogical concepts serve as a necessary but not sufficient bridge to an understanding of what are now being called 'relationship terminologies' . . . , we have to come to terms with why this is so" (ibid.).

The symmetric alliance structure corresponding to the two-line terminology of the Piaroa must be visualized not merely as a feature of classification, but as a regularity at the level of behaviour. In constituting a real-life regularity both at the level of genetics and, more significantly, in terms of the flow of prestations within the endogamous group, this structure carries the potential of being reconceptualized or reinterpreted according to emic models other than the two-line system. An alliance-organized, kin-affine system, in generating genealogical regularities such as the cross/parallel distinction, can stimulate the development of genealogical reckoning as an equally valid way of describing the system. Århem's (1981) analysis of the articulation of symmetric alliance and patrilineal descent among the Makuna suggests that unilineal descent itself may represent the same phenomenon. In analyzing Trio relationship categories, Rivière (1984:39) has traced a semantic shift from co-residential to genealogical aspects. Such shifts in emphasis at the level of classification need imply no change in behaviour, though with time they may liberate new trajectories. Kaplan's material on the Piaroa, and Ramos and Albert's (1977) on the Sanumá/Yanomam contrast, suggest that alliance may be prior to

descent as organizing principle (cf. Lévi-Strauss 1969:323). Endogamous local groups emphasizing the solidarity of co-resident affines may have yielded historically to wider networks of exogamous communities. For these communities, the choice of post-marital residence would have represented a unilateral mode of affiliation easily codified into some principle of "descent," and supra-local consanguineal bonds would have provided an additional impetus to genealogical reckoning.

The Simplest of Social Structures

There are ample reasons, in a comparative analysis of lowland South American social organization, to focus on the structural trajectories of a two-line system of symmetric alliance. If social evolution is seen as the development of increasingly inclusive systems of social reproduction (i.e. of higher levels of integration), a locally endogamous, two-line system would represent a logical starting-point. Speaking of the terminologically bipartitioned, endogamous local groups of the Piaroa, Kaplan (1975:194) notes that, "with regard to types of societal integration, this is the most atomistic of them all." Needham (1967:45) calls a two-section system "what is formally and sociologically speaking an end-point, for it is the simplest of all social structures." Needham suggests that two-section terminologies have developed from exogamous moieties. As Lévi-Strauss (1969:101) points out, however, "it is not the hypothetical succession of the two institutions which should be considered, but rather their structure." For the moment, we are more interested in justifying a unitary treatment of two-line terminologies and dual organization as two different codifications of symmetric alliance. The two features should be distinguished, but definitely not *dissociated*, from each other.

Two-Line Terminologies and Dual Organization

The terminological division of local groups into two opposed but intermarrying categories is sufficiently characteristic of lowland South American culture to have been advanced as its "structural definition" (Rivière 1973). Nevertheless, the structural equifinality of two-line terminologies and systems of exogamous moieties, recognized at the zero generation level by early evolutionists such as Rivers (1968:83, 88), has not sufficed to ensure a unitary treatment of the two phenomena, except by Lévi-Strauss (1969:98–99, 101–102, 123, 141), Needham (1960a:82; 1967:45), and a few others (e.g. Chagnon 1968:57). On the contrary, students of Dravidian systems, finding no concrete dual organization corresponding to the kin-affine dichotomy, have made it a point to disengage two-line terminologies entirely from the issue of corporate groups such as moieties (Dumont 1953a:39; W. Shapiro 1970:386; Scheffler 1971:242, note 11; Kaplan 1973:563; Basso 1973:90; Rivière 1977:39; Schwerin 1982:2, 7; cf. da Matta 1982:161). This is undoubtedly a reaction against the simple developmental schemes of the classical evolutionists, whose "conjectural history" saw no distinction between classification and behaviour, but arranged different aspects of both on top of each other in lineal sequences. To Morgan and Rivers, a bifurcate merging cousin terminology indicated that a population had previously been organized into exogamous moieties, and a system of exogamous moieties was seen as a pattern of behaviour rather than a mode of classification. It is quite another matter to suggest that a two-line terminology and dual organization represent two different *interpretations* of the regularities in social organization generated by symmetric alliance. To mistake, as the evolutionists did, the emic model of exogamous moieties for the actual social structure which it imperfectly reflects, would

be misleading. A model (emic or etic) which represents social structure in terms of morphology (as an arrangement of groups or categories) can only be a static abstraction of a behavioural reality which is dynamic, fluid, and processual. Moiety institutions can only amount to rough *representations* of social structure, the real nature of which consists not of distinct groups or categories but of processes of communication and exchange. Exogamous unilineal moieties require a dichotomy of cousins (cross versus parallel), but the dichotomy of cousins does not require dual organization. This in itself invalidates the sequence postulated by the evolutionists. Recent ethnographers concerned primarily with the participant's own, emic categories, have tended to ignore or even rule out structural connections between two-line terminologies and dual organization. This tendency is understandable insofar as such connections have previously been conceived in terms of historical succession. The correlation or causal connection of relevance, however, is not between these two modes of classification, but between either of them and structures of symmetric alliance. Rivers dealt only with the conjectural succession of congruent systems of classification, failing to see that these could spring independently from an identical, subjacent structure of organization.

Dualism as a Mental Formula

"Societies founded on prescriptive alliance may be interpreted as the most direct forms known of the social expression of a fundamental feature of the human mind."
– R. Needham (1960a:106)

"Whenever a social phenomenon is directly explained by a psychological phenomenon, we may be sure that the explanation is false."
– E. Durkheim (quoted in Needham 1962:126)

"Lévi-Strauss, Needham, and George Homans are all psychological reductionists – each in his own way, of course."
– D. Schneider (1965:29)

Maybury-Lewis found among the Shavante *both* exogamous moieties *and* a terminology with "a strong resemblance to Dumont's Dravidian systems" (1967:75, 216), but rather than view these modes of classification as expressions of the socio-structural polarity inherent in direct exchange, he chose to account for them merely as manifestations of an "antithetical formula" (ibid., 298) of mental origin. The unwillingness of students of Gê-speaking peoples to trace their dual organizations to the duality inherent in direct exchange undoubtedly derives from the fact that most of the contemporary moiety institutions seem altogether disconnected from marriage practices (cf. Kaplan 1981:154). With only a few cases of dual organization emphasizing moiety exogamy, it has probably seemed too much of "conjectural history" to assume that the remaining, agamous moiety divisions all reflect obsolete structures of alliance. Instead, the object of investigation has been a general cosmological dualism, and this mental scheme has been elevated to the status of an explanation (Maybury-Lewis 1979c:312). Such a unilateral account of the relation between classification and behaviour, however, seems but a truncated representation of what we may assume is a process of dialectical causality. The "antithetical formula" of the Gê should probably not be conceived as idiosyncratic and irreducible *à priori,* but as a codification of imperfectly recognized behavioural regularities. This may apply even when the moiety opposition does not coincide with the kin-affine duality generated by actual marriage arrangements. A lower-level, kin-affine polarity, at the level of households, lineages, or clans, can thus be projected onto the entire social universe (cf. Rivière 1973:23; Kaplan 1981:162; 1984: 132). In other words, dual organization need not involve two strictly exogamous moieties in order to qualify as a codification of symmetric alliance. On the other hand, a moiety division may serve as a *template* for alliances, so that if not obstructed by other

factors such as demographic decline (cf. Tapirapé) or factionalism (cf. Kayapó), marriage patterns will tend to align themselves with this division. We expect this tendency to be generated by the behavioural congruity of the moiety division with explicit marriage rules, e.g. a preference for marriage across the village plaza. During periods when marriage practices and moiety divisions for some reason diverge, it would be a mistake to assume that the two are functionally unrelated. Retrospectively, the evolutionist concept of "survivals" may be applicable. Considering the total dynamics of these systems over time, however, it seems as if moiety divisions are just as much a blueprint for future behaviour, capable of being reactivated again and again. The dynamics of moiety formation can be visualized on a spatial-physical level in the growth and regression of corporate groups relating to each other as affines. Seeger (1977) describes the dynamic generation and degeneration of named exogamous "residential clusters" forming arcs in Suyá village circles. The growth of two dominant "residential clusters" to the point where they would each occupy half the village circle would well account for the formation of spatially defined, exogamous moieties.

When confronted with attempts to account for dual organization without any mention of marriage practices, one wonders whether the authors hold the behavioural equifinality of moiety divisions and two-line terminologies to be purely coincidental? If the answer is "yes," are we to think that two-line terminologies are codifications of symmetric alliance, while moieties are merely manifestations of a universal mental dualism? If the answer is "no," do even two-line terminologies derive from the nature of the human mind? Can alliance structures and social organization simply be reduced to properties of the central nervous system? Needham (1960a:102–103, 106; 1966b:156) and Maybury-Lewis, perhaps inspired by certain passages from Lévi-Strauss (e.g.

1969:75), have both inclined towards such unilateral, mental determinism. But there are several objections to this position. First, mental determinism cannot account for variation or change. If dual organization and two-line terminologies are no more than manifestations of a universally human mode of thought, how are we to understand societies organized around three, five, seven, or nine basic categories (cf. Needham 1979)? Second, mental determinism is reductionistic. If social systems are reduced to properties of individual human minds, sociological regularities are not granted an autonomous scientific status. Third, mental determinism does not recognize the receptive aspects of either the human mind or collective systems of classification. By visualizing classification as an essentially autonomous point of departure transcribed in a one-way fashion into organization, anthropologists make the same mistake as would a biologist who refuses to recognize the phylogenetic imprint of the environment on the genetic code. Rather than contenting ourselves with reducing dual organization and two-line terminologies to the antithetical nature of human thought, our task should be to examine why binary thinking has resulted, among different peoples, in two so different interpretations of society.

Transformations of Symmetric Alliance

The ideal of sister or daughter exchange appears to be the simplest way of expressing the pattern of behaviour anthropologists call symmetric alliance (cf. Jackson 1984:163). Continued over the generations, sister exchange tends to generate (1) a high degree of endogamy (i.e. short cycles of reciprocity), (2) a genealogical regularity which can be described as bilateral cross-cousin marriage, and (3) a division of the population into two categories exchanging spouses. In a sense, endogamy and duality are taken for granted in the simple ideal of sister exchange. Two-

line kin terminologies codify both the ideal of endogamy, the genealogical, cross/parallel distinction, and the polarity of affines in symmetric alliance systems. Cross-cousin marriage, implicit in the terminology, can be made more explicit by recodifying the marriage ideal in terms of genealogy, focusing on whether or not there is "a change of sex in passing from the direct line to the collateral line" (Lévi-Strauss 1969:128).

The polarity of affines in Dravidian systems is expressed in terms of the exogamy of egocentric *categories* (kin versus affines) within an endogamous *group*. In order for this polarity to manifest itself sociocentrically, e.g. as corporate moieties, a unilateral mode of recruitment (through post-marital residence or some other mode of affiliation) is required. Only by way of the unilaterally slanted, personal discrimination of relations can the "exogamy" of categories in alliance-organized, Dravidian systems crystallize into the exogamy of *groups*. This transformation appears to involve, besides the shift from categories to groups, a shift from cognatic to unilineal systems and, if you will, a shift from "alliance" to "descent" as organizing principle (cf. Lévi-Strauss 1969:323). The question that preoccupied early evolutionists and occasionally also Lévi-Strauss, the primacy of either cross-cousin marriage or dual organization, may not be of any great importance, but the hypothetical sequence proposed here would support Lévi-Strauss' contention that moiety divisions are more fully "codified," require a more "complete and definitive an awareness," have a more "organized structure," and are "more coherent and rigid" than cross-cousin marriage (1969:101).

The recognition of the structural significance of a collateral shift of sex may develop "epiphenomenally" within the context of a cognatic, alliance-organized, Dravidian system of symmetric alliance such as that of the Piaroa (Kaplan 1984:154, note 18). This genealogical regularity may be a fundamental property both of cognatic, Dravidian

systems and of systems emphasizing unilateral affiliation (unilocal residence or
unilineal descent.) In both cases, parallel
cousins and cross-cousins fall into opposite
categories. We have suggested that local
exogamy would accentuate the dichotomy of
cousins inherent even in locally endogamous,
Dravidian systems. Furthermore, the emic
recognition of this genealogical regularity
may have provided the route of transformation by which an organization in terms of
"alliance" gave way to systems focusing on
"descent."

Methodological Implications

The remainder of this book is offered as an
illustration of the methodological course our
argument compels us to follow. Our
approach to social structure and socio-
structural transformation raises questions
which can only be pursued through
comparative analysis. A primary concern will
be the delineation of structural congruities,
or what Wittgenstein called "family likenesses" (Needham 1971c:30), underlying various
emic representations of social organization.
Our aim is not only to illuminate some social
correlates of various systems of kin classification, but also to suggest some specific ways
in which code and behaviour may interact
over time. It is hoped that this inquiry will
contribute to our understanding of the
trajectories of social transformation
responsible for some of the structural
variation in lowland South America.

Chapter 3
A Note on the Presentation of Ethnographic Data

"In relation to ethnography, ethnology represents a first step toward synthesis... Wherever we meet with the terms *social anthropology* or *cultural anthropology* they are linked to a second and final stage of the synthesis, based upon ethnographical and ethnological conclusions... Ethnography, ethnology, and anthropology do not form three different disciplines, or three different conceptions of the same branch of study. They are in fact three stages, or three moments of time, in the same line of investigation."

   – C. Lévi-Strauss (1963g:355–356)

Sources

The ethnographic data on which this book is based were recorded among some 50 indigenous South American cultures by an even greater number of field-workers. The scope of the ethnographic sample was determined by two factors. First, we sought a balance between depth of analysis, on the one hand, and generality, on the other. Second, the sample inevitably reflects the author's access to relevant literature. Where different linguistic families seem unevenly represented, this does not necessarily reflect the amount or quality of literature which has been published.

For 24 of the cultures in our sample, the author has consulted ethnographical monographs or similar major works (cf. Table 1). Information on the remaining cases has been compiled from published articles summarizing fundamental aspects of social organization. In order to avoid misrepresentation and facilitate extensive cross-checking, our presentation of the ethnographic record is provided with abundant quotations and consistent page references.

Linguistic Classification

"The description and classification of South American Indian languages is one of the biggest pieces of unfinished business in the field of linguistics."

   – J.H. Rowe (1974:43)

The classification of our sample of cultures into linguistic families (Table 1) probably accords with the general consensus as regards Arawak, Carib, Tupí, Pano, Tukano, and Jívaroan (cf. Rodrigues 1974). The classification of Bororo, Karajá, and Nambikwara as "Probable Gê" derives from D.R. Gross (1979:325). The delineation of the Yanoama linguistic family follows E. Migliazza (Ramos & Albert 1977:72; Taylor 1977:92). Whereas Steward (1948c: 750) classifies Bora and Miraña as dialects of Witoto, and Mason (1950:236) identifies them all as Macro-Tupí-Guaraní, we have followed Loukotka, Nimuendajú, and Rowe (Rowe 1974:49) in treating them as independent families.

There have been several attempts at classification of linguistic families into even more inclusive phyla. J.H. Greenberg has suggested that there are links between Gê, Carib, Pano, Witoto, and Guaycurú, and between Arawak, Tupí, Tukano, Jívaroan, Guahibo, Salivan, Trumaí, and Quechua (cf. Steward & Faron 1959:22–23; Sorensen 1973; Rodrigues 1974:55). G.K. Noble has also found affinities between Arawak and

	Page	Culture	Linguistic family	Sources (monographs in italics)
1.	52	Krahó	N. Gê (E. Timbira)	Melatti 1971, 1979
2.	55	Ramkokamekra	N. Gê (E. Timbira)	Nimuendajú *1946*; Nimuendajú & Lowie 1937; Lowie 1946b; Lave 1977; W. Crocker 1977, 1979, 1984
3.	59	Krĩkatĩ	N. Gê (E. Timbira)	Lave 1971, 1973, 1979
4.	62	Apinayé	N. Gê (W. Timbira)	Nimuendajú *1939*; Lowie 1946b; Maybury-Lewis 1960a; da Matta 1973, 1979, *1982*
5.	75	Kayapó	N. Gê	Turner 1971, 1979b; Bamberger 1974, 1979
6.	78	Suyá	N. Gê	Seeger 1977, *1981*
7.	81	Shavante	C. Gê	Maybury-Lewis *1967*, 1971b, 1979b, W. Shapiro 1971
8.	85	Sherente	C. Gê	Nimuendajú *1942*; Lowie 1946b; Maybury-Lewis 1958, 1965b, 1971b, 1979b
9.	98	Caingang	S. Gê	Henry *1941*; Métraux 1946
10.	100	Bororo	Probable Gê	Lévi-Strauss *1936*, 1944, 1963d, 1963e, 1973b; Lowie 1946a; Albisetti 1953; Albisetti & Venturelli 1962; C. Crocker 1969, 1971, 1977, 1979
11.	104	Karajá	Probable Gê	Lipkind 1948; Tavener 1973; Dietschy 1977
12.	106	Nambikwara	Probable Gê	Lévi-Strauss 1948b, *1948c*; Price 1985
13.	122	Machiguenga	Arawak	Farabee 1922; Johnson & Johnson 1975; Casevitz 1977; Camino 1977; Johnson 1979, d'Ans 1974
14.	124	Mehinacu	Arawak	Gregor 1973, 1974, *1977*
15.	128	Trio	Carib	Rivière 1966b, *1969*, 1977; da Matta 1970
16.	130	Kalapalo	Carib	Basso 1970, *1973*, 1975, 1984
17.	133	Kuikuru	Carib	Carneiro 1961; Dole 1969, 1984
18.	134	Karinya	Carib	Schwerin 1982
19.	134	Barama River C.	Carib	Adams 1977, 1979
20.	136	Pemon	Carib	Thomas 1971, 1979
21.	138	Waiwai	Carib	Fock *1963*
22.	141	Txicáo	Carib	Menget 1977
23.	147	Tapirapé	Tupí	Wagley & Galvão 1948; Wagley *1977a*, 1977b
24.	149	Mundurucú	Tupí	Horton 1948; Murphy 1956, *1960*, 1973; Murphy & Murphy 1974
25.	153	Parintintin/ Tupí-Cawahíb	Tupí	Nimuendajú 1948; Lévi-Strauss 1948a; Kracke 1984
26.	155	Tupinambá/ Guaraní	Tupí	Métraux 1948a; 1948b; Clastres 1977
27.	156	Sirionó	Tupí	Holmberg 1948, *1950*
28.	161	Amahuaca	Pano	Farabee 1922; Dole 1979
29.	163	Mayoruna	Pano	Steward & Métraux 1948; Fields & Merrifield 1980
30.	166	Sharanahua	Pano	Siskind *1973*; Torralba 1981
31.	167	Cashinahua	Pano	Girard 1958; d'Ans 1975; Kensinger 1974a, 1974b, 1975, 1977, 1980, 1984b, 1985b
32.	172	Cubeo	Tukano	Goldman *1963*, 1977
33.	175	Barasana	Tukano	S. Hugh-Jones *1974*, 1977; C. Hugh-Jones *1977a*, 1977b
34.	178	Bará	Tukano	Jackson 1975a, 1976, 1977, 1984
35.	180	Makuna	Tukano	Århem *1981*
36.	185	Yanomamö	Yanoama	Chagnon *1968*; Lizot 1971, 1975, 1977; J. Shapiro 1974
37.	187	Yanomam	Yanoama	Ramos & Albert 1977
38.	188	Sanumá	Yanoama	Ramos 1974; Taylor & Ramos 1975; Ramos & Albert 1977; Taylor 1977
39.	193	Jívaro	Jívaroan	Karsten 1920; Farabee 1922; Steward & Métraux 1948; Harner *1972*; Oberem 1974
40.	196	Achuar	Jívaroan	Taylor 1982
41.	198	Aguaruna	Jívaroan	Larson 1977
42.	201	Piaroa	Saliva	Kaplan 1972, 1973, *1975*, 1984
43.	204	Witoto	Witoto	Farabee 1922; Steward 1948c; Gasché 1977
44.	207	Bora/Miraña	Miraña	Steward 1948c; Guyot 1977
45.	210	Trumaí	Trumaí	Murphy & Quain *1955*
46.	213	Warao	Warao	Kirchoff 1948; Steward & Faron 1959; Suárez *1972*
47.	216	Kadiwéu	Guaycurú	Ribeiro 1974
48.	218	Cuiva	Guahibo	Arcand 1972, 1977; Morey 1972

Table 1 The ethnographic sample: linguistic classification and sources

Tupí (cf. Lathrap 1970:78). Rodrigues (1974: 56) instead suggests "a quite close relationship between Tupí and Carib." Yet others have discovered connections between Pano, Guaycurú, Quechua, and Aymará (cf. Lathrap 1970:80; Ribeiro & Wise 1978: 210–211).

Lathrap (1970) and Schwerin (1972) discuss the chronological order in which the different linguistic families reached their present geographical dispersal. Lathrap believes that Arawak was followed by Tupí, Pano/Guaycurú, and Carib, in that order. Schwerin agrees that the dispersal of Arawak is ancient (3 000–2 000 B.C.), but lists Carib, Gê, and Tupí as the order of subsequent "cultural movements."

Distribution

The 48 cultures listed in Table 1 represent the entire extent of tropical lowland South America, from the Orinoco Delta in the North to the Chaco in the South and from the Ecuadorian *montaña* in the West to the steppes of eastern Brazil (Fig. 2). The marginal location of most of the cultures in our sample, far from the main Amazon headwaters, reflects the distribution of more or less intact indigenous groups surviving into the 20th century.

Parameters

" . . . It is evident that in order to make a comparative study in any scholarly sense we have first to make an analysis, in particular terms proper to the problem at issue, of each of the societies to be compared."
– R. Needham (1964a:238)

If our initial question concerns the relationship between the terminological dualism of two-line kin nomenclatures and the corporate dualism of dual organization, our inquiry pertains more generally to the demonstration of ideological or behavioural correlates of specific features of kin classification. We are also interested in establishing significant correlations between various factors relating to ideology or social organization (i.e. group size, post-marital residence, patterns of affiliation, marriage practices, and relations with the outside), so as to hope to be able to delineate the conditions conducive to particular series of transformations (cf. Part III.) Concepts relating to social hierarchy, and particularly to its articulation with dualism (e.g. in diarchy), form a separate inquiry (cf. Chapter 22.)

Kin Terminology

"We shall . . . do well to amend our phraseology and to speak rather of kinship categories, features, or principles of classification than of types of kinship systems."
– Robert Lowie (quoted in Needham 1971c:17).

"The easiest way to handle the discussion is to set out an ideal type against which to assess the variations that occur."
– P.G. Rivière (1984:43)

That systems of kin classification should provide important clues about ideology and social organization is one of anthropology's most cherished tenets. However, recording and analyzing relationship categories is a problematic procedure. It is generally unlikely that the anthropologist's own language (e.g. English) would contain words corresponding to the exact semantic ranges of foreign kin terms. Instead of purporting to "translate" native terms into English, it is more useful to indicate which term would be employed to refer to (or address) a relative of a particular genealogical or affinal position. It is also useful to see such lists not as universally applicable vocabularies, but as ethnographical "snapshots" merely of *tendencies* in kin term usages (cf. Trautmann 1981:215, 231). Such tentative "translation" of relationship categories in terms of genealogy, though perhaps ethnocentric and

Fig. 2. Map showing approximate locations of the 48 cultures in the sample. Note that
dashed lines do not indicate geographical distribution of linguistic families, but serve
only to facilitate location. In reality, different linguistic families overlap. Whereas Gê,
Pano, Jivaroan, Tukano, and Yanoama occupy fairly distinct territories, Arawak,
Tupí, and Carib are more widely dispersed. Thus, for instance, nos. 16, 17 and 22 are
Carib groups living in the linguistically heterogeneous Upper Xingú area.

potentially misleading (Schneider 1984), seems methodologically unavoidable (J. Shapiro 1984:4, 14). Although in covering both consanguineal and affinal terms, "relationship terminology" is a better designation than "kin terminology," I have chosen to retain the latter, less cumbersome expression.

The present author is not qualified to discuss the linguistic or semantic derivations of particular kin terms. When explicitly suggested in the ethnographic sources, such derivations may be quoted in the course of our own argument, but the focus is always on the formal *structure* of kin term usage. The structure of a kin terminology is expressed in the equation of particular genealogical and affinal positions, and in the distinction between others. The structure, it should be remembered, may vary from one social context to another (Basso 1970, 1985:46; da Matta 1970).

The kin terminologies in our sample are presented according to a uniform matrix. We have chosen to superimpose each nomenclature on what appears to be the simplest possible point of departure, a so-called two-section (Needham 1958b:210; 1960b:23; Maybury-Lewis 1967:216) or two-line (Needham 1966b:142, note 2; 1972; Rivière 1973; Kaplan 1975:128) system of kin classification. The justification for this mode of exposition is twofold. First, a number of writers have suggested that two-section systems are logically primordial (Needham 1967:45; Kaplan 1975:194). Second, it has become increasingly apparent that such two-line terminologies are fundamental to the indigenous cultures of lowland South America (Rivière 1973, 1977; Kaplan 1977: 394; Dreyfus 1977; Kensinger 1979a; 1984a; Århem 1981:273–303; Henley 1982:89; Schwerin 1982:6; J.Shapiro 1984:2; Balée 1985).

We generally use the designation "two-line" rather than "two-section," since the latter term tends to connote discrete marriage sections (cf. Needham 1966b:142,

note 2; W. Shapiro 1971:65, note 2) and is sometimes used interchangeably with "exogamous moieties" (Buchler & Selby 1968:244). Alternative designations include a "terminology of symmetric marriage systems" (ibid., 233) and a "kin-affine terminology" (Kaplan 1972:285; 1975:127; Schwerin 1982:8). J. Shapiro (1985) suggests that the fundamental opposition in two-line terminologies is that between consanguineal "siblingship" and affinity.

Dumont's (1953a) classical description of a two-line "Dravidian" kin terminology provides us with a simple matrix for the classification of kin and affines (Fig. 3). Its essence is the merging of cross-collaterals and affines in the three medial generations. This feature is a logical correlate of a continued practice of brother-sister exchange marriage, a symmetric alliance structure which can also be described as bilateral cross-cousin marriage (cf. Trautmann 1981:23–24). The terminologies in our South American sample are all discussed in terms of the ways in which they deviate from this two-line pattern, and some preliminary suggestions are made concerning the ideological or behavioural foundations for these deviations. More conclusive interpretations of this terminological variation are offered throughout Part IV.

Unless otherwise specified, the perspective is that of male Ego, and kin terms are referential. The orthography is that used by the individual ethnographer, but has sometimes been slightly simplified. For obvious reasons, this fidelity to sources obstructs consistency in the representation of specific phonemes.

Local Group Size and Composition

Under this heading are presented historical and contemporary data relating to the average size of local groups and to patterns of post-marital residence (uxori-, viri-, ambi-, or neolocal.)

Gen.	Male		Female	
+ 2	FF MF		FM MM	

| | KIN | | AFFINES | |
Gen.	Male	Female	Male	Female
+ 1	F FB MZH	M MZ FBW	WF MB FZH	WM FZ MBW
0	B FBS MZS WZH	Z FBD MZD WBW	WB MBS FZS ZH	W MBD FZD BW
− 1	S BS ZDH	D BD ZSW	DH ZS WBS	SW ZD WBD

Gen.	Male		Female	
− 2	SS DS		SD DD	

Fig. 3 Alignments of kin and affines in a two-line (Dravidian) system of kin classification.

Patterns of Affiliation Other than Residence

Intentionally avoiding the concept of "descent" (which tends to connote "descent groups"; cf. Schneider 1965:75; Jackson 1975b:320; Murphy 1979), we have used the word "affiliation" for all kinds of socially recognized ties through which individuals are linked to members of previous generations. Scheffler (1966:548) in fact defines descent "in terms of ideological or conceptual phenomena, as a generic label for a variety of forms of genealogical continua." In view of its tenacious, sociological connotations, however, it is advisable to adopt Dumont's (1961:25) definition of "descent" as membership in an exogamous group and of "filiation" as membership in an agamous group. "Affiliation" can be used in the broadest sense possible, encompassing models of inter-generational succession or transmission which need not involve the recognition of any "groups" whatsoever (cf. J. Shapiro's (1984: 20) definition of "filiation.") The mode of affiliation is the key to the reproduction of society over time. Since "society" is very much a matter of exchange, it is obvious that affiliation must constantly be geared to alliance. Succession, in other words, is largely a matter of entering into relationships of inherited affinity (Dumont 1953a; Lounsbury 1962:1308–1309), i.e. into pre-established patterns of exchange. Discussions of such phenomena as name transmission, succession to roles, inheritance, ideologies of procreation, and recruitment to named groups may thus overlap with the subject of alliance.

Hierarchy

Under this topic are discussed various ideological indications of hierarchical classification as well as overt status differences. Relevant phenomena include differentially ranked names and ceremonial roles, an emphasis on relative age or birth-order hierarchies, hereditary succession to chieftainship, diarchy, hierarchies of lesser and greater leaders, permanent class divisions or spouse-giver/spouse-taker relationships, and various strategies to enhance individual prestige (e.g. polygyny, feasting, and trade.)

Alliance

This section presents explicit ideals and preferences relating to the choice of marriage partner as well as statistical information on actual marriage patterns. With J. Shapiro (1984:25), we would let a cross-cultural definition of "marriage" focus on those types of sexual relationship "most concerned with filiation, affinity, and economic ties (that is, with the process of reproducing the social and economic system)." Marriage, from this perspective, involves cohabitation, a sexual relationship, and economic cooperation (Kensinger 1984:240; J. Shapiro 1984:27). Viewed as a process of social reproduction, the marriage alliance involves "a kind of movement . . . of people, goods, and intangible commodities" (Jackson 1984:162; cf. Lévi-Strauss 1969:60–68; Strathern 1984).

External Relations

In conclusion, the relationship of local groups to the outside world is briefly characterized. The features discussed include the degree of isolation or of regional integration, the frequency of warfare, and the extent of inter-village trade. Unfortunately, data pertaining to this parameter are generally difficult to assess in comparative terms.

Part II
The Ethnographic Sample: Classification and Organization in Lowland South America

"The region is an ethnographic swamp where few features rise clearly and vividly above the surface. Whoever undertakes to survey the data confronts a morass of customs dispersed over the vastness of the Amazon Basin with no easily discernible patterns."
– I. Goldman (1963:1)

"It is still difficult to assemble material for any sort of detailed comparative study, since each researcher has emphasized different aspects of the culture he or she was studying."
– P. J. Lyon (1974:xiii)

"In general, lowland ethnography has made significant advances in the past 15 years in many areas of research. The overall picture, however, is a patchwork, with a theoretical contribution here and a methodological advance there. Reviewing the recent literature brings into focus the enormous amount remaining to be done, and shows how rapidly opportunities for future work are being eliminated by the far-reaching effects of 'progress' and 'development' . . . "
– J. Jackson (1975b:330–331)

"It is sure that we will not progress in our systematic understanding of the organization of social time and space in South American societies if we remain isolated, exploring the tautological hermeneutics of one or another of these societies."
– J. C. Crocker (1977:256)

"There is a great deal more to be done in the comparative study of the Central Brazilian societies; although an increasing number of ethnographic studies of individual societies are appearing, comparative treatment has not gone much beyond Lévi-Strauss' suggestions of 1952. . . A more detailed comparative analysis of the Gê, and one that contrasts them with other lowland South American societies, would be extremely rewarding."
– A. Seeger (1981:235–236)

"It is time to take stock of what we have got and where we stand before pushing on."
– P. G. Rivière (1984:1)

Chapter 4
Gê

"The painstaking and minute analysis of one empirical case after another is hard, unglamorous, and modest work."
– R. Needham (1971b:ciii)

1. The Krahó

Kin Terminology (Table 2)

With the exception of *iprõ* for ZSW and *ĩtzũ* for FMB, deviations from the two-line pattern are confined to affines of the three medial generations. An absence of symmetric alliance is suggested by the distinctions between cross-cousins of both sexes and by the distinctions FZ≠MBW, WB≠ZH, DH≠ZS, SW≠ZD. Matrilineal equations include MBC=C=BC, FM=FZ=FZD, MBW=W=BW=ZSW, and FMB=F=FZS. On the other hand, patrilineal principles appear to underlie the equations MF=MB, ZC=DC, and ZH=DH. WM=SW, finally, may reflect some alternation of generations, as WM is in fact SMFW, implying an identification of male Ego with his MF.

Local Group Size and Composition

In 1962–63, 519 individuals were distributed in five Krahó villages (Melatti 1971:347) averaging 104 in each. By 1971, their population had increased to 586 (Melatti 1979:45), with an average of 117 in each village.

Post-marital residence is uxorilocal (ibid., 50).

Patterns of Affiliation Other than Residence

The Krahó maintain several sets of ceremonial moieties. Of these, only the Wakmẽye/Katamye moieties enrol women on the same terms as men. For a woman, membership in other moieties is patrilineal until marriage, at which point she will belong to the moieties of her husband (ibid.,47). Affiliation to the Wakmẽye/Katamye moieties is achieved by the transmission of personal names from *keti/tii* to *itamtxua*, preferably from MB to ZS and from FZ to BD (ibid., 59). As the potential for name transmission is the "only common denominator" of all *keti/tii-itamtxua* relationships (cf. the Apinayé, da Matta 1982:123), it appears that an alternative line of affiliation would be from grandparents to grandchildren, i.e. a system of alternating generations. The MB-ZS and FZ-BD lines are, however, statistically predominant. The MB-ZS line of succession is consistent with the matrilineal equations for male Ego (Melatti 1979:77–78), while the FZ-BD line produces patrilineal features. In the case of the Wakmẽye/Katamye moieties, then, affiliation is matrilateral for men and patrilateral for women. Melatti suggests that the transfer of male names compensates for the transfer of residence implied by uxorilocality. Whereas female names follow men as they move to their uxorilocal residences, male names tend to accumulate in certain domestic groups. The lines of name transmission can be visualized as structural "shadows" of what is essentially a system of parallel lines (cf. Scheffler & Lounsbury 1971:188–189; W.

Table 2
KIN TERMINOLOGY OF THE KRAHÓ
LINGUISTIC FAMILY: Northern Gê (Eastern Timbira)
Male Ego, terms of reference.

GEN.	Male				Female		
+ 2	FF	*keti*	FMB	*ĩtxũ*	FM	*tii*	
	MF	*keti*			MM	*tii*	

	KIN (Lineal kin, parallel collaterals, affines of affines)				*AFFINES* (In-laws, cross collaterals)			
	Male		Female		Male		Female	
+ 1	F	*ĩtxũ*	M	*ĩtxe*	WF	*ipréket*	WM	*hotxwiye*
	FB	*ĩtxũ*	MZ	*ĩtxe*	MB	*keti*	FZ	*tii*
	MZH	*ĩtxũ*	FBW	*ĩtxe*	FZH	*keti*	MBW	*iprõ*
0	B	*ito*	Z	*itoĩ*	WB	*ipré*	W	*iprõ*
	FBS	*ito*	FBD	*itoĩ*	MBS	*ikhra*	MBD	*ikhra*
	MZS	*ito*	MZD	*itoĩ*	FZS	*ĩtxũ*	FZD	*tii*
					ZH	*ipiayõye*	BW	*iprõ*
− 1	S	*ikhra*	D	*ikhra*	DH	*ipiayõye*	SW	*hotxwiye*
	BS	*ikhra*	BD	*ikhra*	ZS	*itamtxua*	ZD	*itamtxua*
			ZSW	*iprõ*				

	Male		Female	
− 2	SS	*itamtxua*	SD	*itamtxua*
	DS	*itamtxua*	DD	*itamtxua*

SOURCES: Melatti 1979:53–56. The term *keti* for FZH derives from ibid., 72.

DEVIATIONS FROM THE TWO-LINE PATTERN	CONCEIVABLE IDEOLOGICAL OR BEHAVIOURAL CORRELATES
FZ≠MBW, MBC≠FZC, WB≠ZH, DH≠ZS, SW≠ZD	Absence of symmetric alliance; kindred exogamy
MBC=C=BC, FM=FZ=FZD, MBW =W=BW= ZSW, FMB=F=FZS	Matrilateral affiliation, uxorilocal residence
MF=MB, ZC=DC, ZH=DH	Patrilateral affiliation
WM=SW	Alternating generations (MF=DS)

Crocker 1984). The MB-ZS line appears to be a recognition, by males, of the fundamental female matriline represented by their sisters. In a less emphasized manner, the FZ-BD line recognizes the ideological continuity of the male patriline, even though it is dispersed.

Personal names among the Krahó are associated with specific social and ceremonial roles (ibid., 67–68). The transmission of names determines recruitment to the Wakmẽye/Katamye moieties and to the ritual plaza group moieties Khoirumpeketxe and Hararumpeketxe (ibid., 47, 59, 67). There are eight plaza groups evenly divided between these latter moieties (cf. the eight plaza groups of the unnamed plaza moieties of the Krĩkatí, and the six plaza groups of the cognate Ko'irumenkača'/Hara'rumenkača' moieties of the Ramkokamekra.) Since male names tend to be associated with both particular plaza groups and particular domestic groups, there should be a certain correspondence between the two kinds of groups. We may infer that plaza groups comprise junior name-holders (ZS) still residing in their natal households, on the one hand, and senior nameholders (MB) residing uxorilocally on the other side of the village, on the other.

A third set of moieties are the age-set moieties Khöikateye and Harākateye, which correspond to the former age moieties Kuigatiye and Harungatiye of the Krĩkati, and the age-class moieties Ko'i-kateye and Harākateye of the Ramkokamekra.

The formal friendship between *hõpin* (female *hopintxwöi*) is transferred along with individual names (ibid., 74). The implication is that the formal friendship bond links specific pairs of MB-ZS lines. Furthermore, there are indications that the two parties belong to opposite moieties (ibid., 75). Melatti notes that the bond between *hõpin* has several "aspects of affinity," and that the term *ikritxua* referring to dead *hõpin* may be cognate to the term *meka?krit*, which means affinal relative. Apparently, "more than one Krahó has transformed his *hõpintxwöi* into his *iprõ*," i.e. wife (ibid., 76).

Hierarchy

The behaviour of affines is asymmetric in the sense that WB should receive presents from ZH, and BW from HZ (ibid., 60). Male wife-givers thus appear to be superior to wife-takers, but female husband-takers to husband-givers. The former relationship is consistent with the senior status of WB suggested by the equation ZH=DH.

Diarchy is evident from Melatti's (ibid., 47) observation that each of the Wakmēye/Katamye moieties "supplies two men to direct the activities of the village." The term *ikhionõ* is used between males who are simultaneously "directors" of the village, leaders of age-sets, or leaders of the boys in initiation rituals (ibid., 74). In addition to signifying a relation of common high status, *ikhionõ* denotes closeness similar to consanguinity. Some of Melatti's informants insisted that in the old days *ikhionõ* used to exchange wives with each other, suggesting a tradition of rank endogamy.

Melatti (ibid., 49) notes that "some people who had occupied important or honorific positions during their lives were buried in the central plaza."

Alliance

Melatti (ibid., 46) claims that the Krahó "have no rule of cross-cousin marriage and none of their various pairs of moieties has the function of regulating marriage." Yet, the Wakmēye/Katamye moiety system is by implication geared to alliance in an indirect sense. As each moiety consists, in fact, of a set of personal names (ibid., 47), and "an individual may not marry somebody because of his name set" (ibid., 68), there are obviously exogamous name-holding groups specific to each moiety. This is also implied by two observations made by Melatti, i.e. that the localized female matrilines tend to accumulate specific male names (ibid., 78), and that matrilineally constituted "residential segments" are strictly exogamous (ibid., 51, 63).

When marrying a consanguine, a Krahó has the terminological means of transforming the consanguineal relationship into an affinal one (ibid., 64). In this context, Melatti focuses on certain similarities between terms used for affines and terms used for dead consanguines. The term *ikrātumye*, for instance, is equivalent to *ipréket* (WF, HF), but derives from *ikrātum*, which is equivalent to *keti* (MB, FZH). This terminological derivation suggests bilateral cross-cousin marriage. In fact, Melatti (ibid., 62, 63) mentions examples of marriage with the FZD, MBD, and even BD.

Two circumstances would be consistent with an inclination towards matrilateral cross-cousin marriage. First, the tendency of male names, transmitted from MB to ZS, to accumulate in particular domestic groups would be particularly emphasized if male Ego upon marriage moved to his MB's group. Secondly, since the generations of a localized female matriline tend to be terminologically equated (e.g. FM=FZ= FZD), the equations MBD=D and MBW= W=ZSW agree with MBD marriage.

External relations

The Krahó have had a peaceful reputation at least since 1809 (ibid., 45).

2. The Ramkokamekra

Kin Terminology (Table 3)

An absence of symmetric alliance is suggested by the distinctions between cross-cousins of both sexes and by the distinctions MB≠ FZH, WB≠ZH, DH≠ZS, SW≠ZD. Matrilineal equations include MBC=C=BC, FM=FZ=FZD, F=FZS, MZC=ZC, MB= MZS. On the other hand, patrilineal principles appear to underlie the equations MF= MB, ZC=DC, FZH=ZH =DH, WB= WBS. Some concept of lineality ought also to be responsible for the distinction FF≠MF, where the suffix *-re* gives the former a diminutive meaning and *-ti* the latter an augmentative (Nimuendajú & Lowie 1937: 573). The equation FZ=FBW, on the other hand, suggests cognatic principles. WM= SW, finally, may reflect some alternation of generations, as has been suggested for the Krahó.

Local Group Size and Composition

The village studied by Nimuendajú had a population of 298 (Nimuendajú & Lowie 1937:566). In 1960, there were two villages numbering 269 and 143 (W. Crocker 1979: 246, note 2). By 1975, the Ramkokamekra population had grown to 514 (ibid., 232).

Post-marital residence is uxorilocal (Nimuendajú 1946:83, 125; Lave 1977:310; W. Crocker 1977:262; 1979:233, 238; 1984: 64, 67).

Patterns of Affiliation Other than Residence

The ideology of affiliation among the Ramkokamekra is fundamentally bilateral (Lave 1977:310; W. Crocker 1977:265; 1979: 234, 238; 1984:64). Nimuendajú, however, perceived the village as divided into two matrilineal, "theoretically exogamous" moieties, although the exogamous rule was rapidly breaking down (Nimuendajú & Lowie 1937:568; Nimuendajú 1946:77, 79, 124).

Besides the matrilineal, exogamous moieties Ko'i-kateye/Harā'kateye, Nimuendajú found two sets of moieties, the Rainy Season moieties (Ka'makra/Atu'kmakra) and the Plaza Group moieties (Ko'irument-kača'/Hara'rumenkača'), in which membership is determined by individual names. Name transmission should ideally be from MB to ZS and from FZ to BD (Nimuendajú & Lowie 1937:569; Nimuendajú 1946:77, 78, 84–85, 87, 88, 110; Lowie 1946b: 490; Lave 1977:311; W. Crocker 1977:260). Affiliation to the Ka'/Atu'k moieties is thus matrilateral for men and patrilateral for women. The six plaza groups (*menkača'*) involve men only. Moreover, there are four male age classes divided equally between two Age-Class moieties denoted by the same names as the exogamous moieties (Ko'i-kateye/Harā'ka-teye) (Nimuendajú 1946:92, 95). Finally, there are at least six men's societies referred

Table 3
KIN TERMINOLOGY OF THE RAMKOKAMEKRA
LINGUISTIC FAMILY: Northern Gê (Eastern Timbira)
Male Ego, terms of reference.

GEN.	Male		Female	
+ 2	FF *ke'de-re* MF *ke'de-ti*		FM *tu'i-re* MM *tu'i-re*	

	KIN (Lineal kin, parallel collaterals, affines of affines)		*AFFINES* (In-laws, cross collaterals)	
	Male	Female	Male	Female
+ 1	F *i-nčū* FB *i-nčū* MZH *i-nčū*	M *i-nčẽ'* MZ *i-nčẽ'* FBW *tu'i-re*	WF *pai-ke't* MB *ke'de-ti* FZH *i-piyõyé*	WM *ha-čwe'i-ye* FZ *tu'i-re*
0	B e *i-tõ, i-ha* y *nyo'he'u-re* FBS e *i-ha* y *nyo'he'u-re* MZS e *ke'de-ti* y *i-tam-čwe'*	Z e *i-tõ, i-ha* y *nyo'he'u-re* FBD e *i-ha* y *nyo'he'u-re* MZD e *tu'i-re* y *i-tam-čwe'-i*	WB *i-mpaye'* MBS *i-kra* FZS *i-nčū* ZH *i-wawé,* *i-piyõye'*	W *i-prõ* MBD *i-kra* FZD *tu'i-re*
– 1	S *i-kra* BS *i-kra*	D *i-kra* BD *i-kra*	DH *i-wawé,* *i-piyõye'* ZS *i-tam-čwe'-i* WBS *i-mpaye'*	SW *ha-čwe'i-ye* ZD *i-tam-čwe'-i* WBD *i-mpaye'*

	Male		Female	
– 2	SS *i-tam-čwe'* DS *i-tam-čwe'*		SD *i-tam-čwe'-i* DD *i-tam-čwe'-i*	

SOURCES: Nimuendajú & Lowie 1937: 574-575; Nimuendajú 1946:105.

DEVIATIONS FROM THE TWO-LINE PATTERN	CONCEIVABLE IDEOLOGICAL OR BEHAVIOURAL CORRELATES
MB≠FZH, MBC≠FZC, WB≠ZH, DH≠ZS, SW≠ZD	Absence of symmetric alliance, kindred exogamy
MBC=C=BC, FM=FZ=FZD, F=FZS, MZC=ZC, MB=MZS	Matrilateral affiliation, uxorilocal residence
MF=MB, ZC=DC, FZH=ZH=DH, WB=WBS	Patrilateral affiliation
FF≠MF WM=SW FZ=FBW	Lineal principles Alternating generations (MF=DS) Cognatic principles

to as *me'kwe'*, a term which is also applied to the age classes. Both the age classes and the men's societies each have two girl associates (ibid., 92, 95).

Nimuendajú notes that the Plaza Group moiety division (ibid., 87) and the Age-Class moiety division (ibid., 92, 95) have nothing to do with the exogamous moieties. He suggests, however, that the plaza groups formerly represented localized clans (ibid.,

90), that the two *mamkye'ti* age-class leaders formerly represented the two exogamous moieties (ibid., 93–94), and that both the Plaza Group moieties and Rainy Season moieties formerly coincided with the exogamous division (ibid., 79, 86). The spatial organization of the moiety systems (Fig. 4) indeed suggests that the exogamous moieties and the Plaza Group moieties were once identical (cf. the Krîkatî). The spatial organization, the recruitment of leaders, and the designations of the Age-Class moieties all indicate that these should also be congruent with the exogamous and Plaza Group moieties. Jointly, these three moiety systems represent the diametric dimension in Ramkokamekra social organization. Perpendicular to this diametric dimension, however, is the division into Rainy Season moieties. The opposition of Ka' and Atu'k signifies a concentric dimension: "plaza" versus "outside", i.e. center versus periphery (cf. the Apinayé moieties Ipog and Kre.) Asymmetry is thus superimposed upon symmetry. Each of the six plaza groups consists of holders of particular masculine names transmitted from MB to ZS. In other words, each plaza group represents a matriline, three in each exogamous moiety. Two of the three plaza group matrilines in each exogamous moiety are represented in both Rainy Season moieties, but the Armadillo group of the Western moiety belongs exclusively to Atu'k, and the Giant Snake group of the Eastern moiety belongs exclusively to Ka'. Whether this would have been correlated with differential degrees of endogamy is impossible to ascertain, but the triadic organization of plaza groups within each exogamous moiety indicates an asymmetrical, hierarchical dimension. In fact, comparative data suggest that the Ka' and Atu'k moieties (like the Ipog and Kre moieties of the Apinayé) may have inclined towards endogamy, which would imply that the Armadillo and Giant Snake groups were particularly privileged.

W. Crocker (1977:267–269) found the

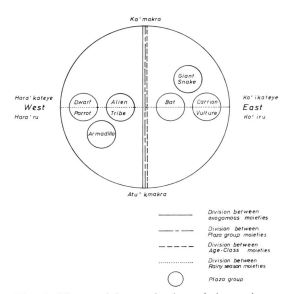

Fig. 4. The spatial organization of the moiety systems and plaza groups of the Ramkokamekra (Nimuendajú 1946)

Ramkokamekra divided into corporate, named, and ideally exogamous, ceremonial matrilineages known as *haakats* (cf. 1979: 235, 239–240, 248, note 13). The *haakats* coincide with lines of male name transmission and the transfer of specific festival rites (1979:242–243). Whether exogamous moieties existed in earlier times, he says, has not yet been definitively determined (1977:268; 1979:234; 1984:77). The two sides of the village are theoretically exogamous, each man ideally marrying "'across the village' (90 to 270 degrees) from his natal house, wherever that was" (1977:273, note 23; 1979:246, note 3). "Everybody is either Ego's *hũũkyê* (consanguineal relative) or *ca'krit* (nonrelated)" (1977:274, note 25). Some of Crocker's informants explained that the uxorilocal houses provide a matrix for matrilineal equations (1977:264).

For both the Ramkokamekra-Canela and the closely related Apaniekra-Canela, tribal membership is reckoned in a parallel manner, i.e. from F to S and from M to D (1977:261; 1979:247, note 9; 1984:94, note 35). Parallel affiliation is also evident at lower levels of integration. Female matri-lines are reinforced by the practice of uxorilo-cal residence, whereas male patrilines, though clearly a part of the "ethnobiological infra-structure", exist "only in a weakly expressed form" (1977:266). The presence of both matrilineal and patrilineal principles of affiliation is evident in the kin terminology (ibid., 266–267, 270–272). W. Crocker suggests that the patterns of name transmis-sion and associated Crow-Omaha termino-logical usages reflect principles of parallel transmission (1977:266–267, 272, note 12; 1979:243, 247, note 5; 1984:80, 82–86, 92–93, notes 30–32).

The maternal uncle plays a very prominent part in the social and ceremonial life of a Ramkokamekra (Nimuendajú 1946:97, 98, 103), not only in that of his ZS, but in that of his ZD, as well (ibid., 96, 124, 126). The ideal of name transmission from MB to ZS and from FZ to BD has been expressed as an ideal of reciprocal exchange of names by brother and sister for their respective child-ren of the appropriate sex (ibid., 78; Lave 1977:311). Under conditions of bilateral cross-cousin marriage, this mode of trans-mission would be congruent with the other possibility granted by the terminology, i.e. from grandparent to grandchild (FF to SS and MM to DD), producing a system of alternating generations.

The term for formal friends (*hupin*) suggests close affinity to the *hõpin* bond of the Krahó (cf. Lave 1979:326, note 6; Melatti 1979:74–76). Nimuendajú (1946:100) writes *hapĩn*.

Hierarchy

Nimuendajú notes that men visiting their maternal homes enjoy greater prestige than the husbands of their kinswomen (Nimuendajú & Lowie 1937:566; Nimuen-dajú 1946:83), indicating that wife-givers rate superior to wife-takers. This may also

be reflected in the augmentative suffix -*ti* in the term for MF, and the diminutive -*re* in FF.

Chiefs were relatively powerful (W. Crocker 1979:235). Nimuendajú (1946:79–82) claims that the two village chiefs are brothers, and mentions moiety-based dual ceremonial offices (ibid., 88, 93, 94, 95) which suggest that the two brothers also would have belonged to separate moieties.

The Ramkokamekra recognize an "honorific order", or "ceremonial aristo-cracy", called *hamrén* (ibid., 77, 93, 97–99; W. Crocker 1984:69). Composed of village chiefs, *mamkye'ti* age-class leaders, and other prominent people, the category of *hamrén* formerly had a distinctive mode of burial, whereby the corpse was interred in front of the house rather than behind it (cf. the plaza burials of the Krahó.)

Members of the village council are "always approached reverentially with a bowlful of food" (Nimuendajú 1946:97).

We have seen, finally, that the spatial alignment of plaza groups (*menkača'*) suggests that these may have been hierarchi-cally arranged within each moiety (Fig. 4). The behaviour of plaza groups at initiation festivals (ibid., 88) also implies such an arrangement.

Alliance

A woman's husband should come from hous-es "on the other side of the village circle" (W. Crocker 1979:233). Name-holding lines, i.e. the localized, female matrilines which serve as matrices for name transmission, are exoga-mous to their male offspring (Nimuendajú 1946:100–101, 124). W. Crocker notes that male Ego should not marry either into his mother's or any of his grandmothers' houses (1977:268). This implies not only that Ego's sister's matriline is excluded, but that women of the matriline into which his FF married (i.e. FM, FZ, FZD = *tu'i-re*) are ineligible as well. Of the two cross-cousins, this excludes the FZD, but not the MBD. Matrilateral cross-cousin marriage would account for two terminological "coincidences" recorded by Crocker (1977:268; 1984:81–82), i.e. the merging of WF and MB in *apreequêt* ("your WF", cf. the Krahó term *ipréket*, Melatti 1979:64), and of female Ego's HZ and FZD. As the generations of each localized matriline tend to be equated (e.g. FM = FZ = FZD), the equation MBD = D also suggests MBD marriage. The prohibition of marriage with any first cousins, reported by Nimuendajú (1946:124), may represent an historically recent trajectory. Finally, there is a convention that "brothers do not marry into the same uxorilocal family" (W. Crocker 1984:64, 89, note 14).

External Relations

Nimuendajú writes that the Krahó, Ramkokamekra, and Krĩkatí "were all living in incessant feuds with both aboriginal and Neobrazilian neighbours" until the early 19th century (ibid., 149). Although originally often at war with each other, since 1814 the three tribes have had less hostile relations (W. Crocker 1979:231, 249, note 18). These Eastern Timbira groups seem to have valued intratribal peace, each group appointing "honorary chiefs" in the others (Nimuendajú 1946:99; W. Crocker 1984:94, note 35). This institution to Nimuendajú (1946:155) "proves that the Timbira attached more importance to permanent peace than to incessant hostility." Their desire for peace may be associated with the wish to trade, e.g. arara feathers from the Apaniekra in exchange for clay tobacco pipes (ibid., 156). When compared with the mainstream of South American peoples, the Timbira probably do not deserve Lowie's (1946b:498) description as "warlike, fighting even against closely related groups."

3. The Krĩkatí

Kin Terminology

Lave (1979:22) presents a relationship terminology based on the system of name transmission. The equations MBD = D and MBW = W recall the matrilineal aspects of Krahó and Ramkokamekra terminologies, and the mirror-image, patrilineal equations are particularly evident for female Ego. Apparently, MBD can also be equated with M. Lave explains that Ego "can emphasize the equation of himself with his name-giver (his mother's brother) and hence refer to his mother's brother's daughter as *ikachui*, 'daughter', or he can take the point of view that his mother's brother's daughter is his mother's name-receiver, socially identified with his mother, and refer to her as *inchigrunto*, 'mother's name-receiver', or just *inchi*, 'mother', for short" (ibid., 22–23).

Local Group Size and Composition

There are six Krĩkatí villages with a total population of about 600 (ibid., 15), which gives an average of 100 people in each. The range of *mekwu* (residents of the local village cluster) includes approximately 200 persons (ibid., 17).

Post-marital residence is uxorilocal (ibid., 42).

Patterns of Affiliation Other than Residence

The rules of Krĩkatí name transmission, encoded in a specific "naming terminology", stipulate that male names should pass from MB to ZS, female names from FZ to BD (Lave 1971:344; 1979:20). Lave (1979:22) reduces these rules of transmission to Crow-Omaha skewing rules. These Crow-Omaha rules, we suggest, indicate the male recognition of a female matriline, and the female recognition of a male patriline. As among the Krahó, names cycle "in space as well as in time," alternating between domestic groups as men transmit their names to their sisters' sons (ibid., 32). Furthermore, name transmission is ideally a reciprocal exchange between cross-sex siblings (ibid., 20, 21, 31).

Precisely as among the Krahó and Ramkokamekra, name transmission among the Krĩkatĩ seems to be an expression of parallel affiliation. Other indications of this type of ideology include the parallel inheritance of male versus female property (Lave 1971:342) and of the ceremonial trading relationship, *kuwuure,* from F to S and from M to D (ibid., 345, note 4; Lave 1979: 18; but cf. Lave 1973 for a rejection of the equation of cross and parallel transmission proposed by Scheffler and Lounsbury 1971: 188–189).

Lines of MB-ZS name transmission integrate corporate name-holding groups (Lave 1979:29). The transmission of names is associated with succession to specific ceremonial roles (ibid., 25, 31, 37) and the inheritance of formal friendship relationships (ibid., 18). Members of a name-holding group thus share moiety affiliations, formal friendship bonds, and ceremonial roles (ibid., 24, 30). Even if all the members of a name-holding group have the same affiliations in all three moiety systems, the groups belonging to a particular moiety in one system do not all belong to the same moiety in another. In other words, the three systems are not congruent. Two of them, however, almost coincide. All but one of the 11 name-holding groups belonging to Plaza moiety 1 also belong to the Kuigatiye moiety, and all but one of the 10 groups belonging to the Harungatiye moiety also belong to Plaza moiety 2 (ibid., 27). This alignment supports Nimuendaju's hypotheses concerning the former equivalence of exogamous and Plaza Group moieties among the Ramkokamekra.

Of the three major moiety systems of the Krĩkatĩ, the Kuigatiye/Harungatiye moieties correspond to the Ko'i-kateye/Harã'kateye moieties of the Ramkokamekra and the Khöikateye/Harãkateye moieties of the Krahó. Accordingly, Lave describes these as "former age moieties, no longer differentiated into age sets" (ibid., 26). The Kapi/Kaikula moieties are "associated with rainy season and dry season activities, respectively," and with the concentric opposition plaza/house circle (ibid., 27–28), both attributes of which recall the Rainy Season moieties Ka'makra and Atu'kmakra of the Ramkokamekra (cf. also the Ipog and Kre moieties of the Apinayé.) As we have seen, the unnamed Plaza moieties of the Krĩkatĩ are almost congruent with the Kuigatiye/Harungatiye moiety system. Each Plaza moiety consists of four named plaza groups, each of which in turn consists of name-holding groups. Plaza groups are paired two by two across the moieties for log-racing ceremonies. In a similar, perhaps associated sense, name-holding groups are also paired, if not overtly. As formal friend relationships are inherited with individual names from MB, "it would be equally accurate to talk about a tie of formal friendship linking two name-holding groups" (ibid., 30).

Finally, name-holding groups are divided into older and younger halves (ibid., 25). The distinction is between those who have not yet transmitted names, and those who have. The name-holding groups "might be characterized as individualized versions of the age-set organization," preserving the principle that a man changes status with age (i.e. from the status of name-receiver to that of name-giver) (ibid., 37). As we have suggested for the Krahó, senior name-holders would reside uxorilocally on the side of the village opposite to that of the unmarried junior name-holders still residing in their natal house-holds. Name-holding groups and plaza groups would thus link unmarried males from a household on one side of the village and married males from a household on the opposite side (cf. Lave 1977:318). If there should be more or less permanent bonds of alliance between two such households, it is not unreasonable to speculate that the diametrically opposite plaza group or line of formal friends would correspond to the inverse line of males, i.e. married males from the former household and unmarried males from the latter.

Hierarchy

The relationship between male name-givers and name-receivers is "severely asymmetrical" (Lave 1979:20–21). This asymmetry, however, fades as the name-receiver grows older. Prestige not bound to age occurs in the form of "honorary positions" based on the performance of specific ceremonial roles which adhere to the possession of particular name-sets (ibid., 37). Since male name-sets are generally transmitted matrilineally, this indicates status discrepancies between matrilines.

The pairing of opposite plaza groups and name-holding groups in formal friendship suggests affinal relationships (cf. Melatti 1979:75–76 on Krahó *hōpin*.) But even if these bonds ideally unite groups from opposite exogamous moieties (i.e. counterparts to the Ko'i-kateye/Harã'kateye moieties of the Ramkokamekra), they may be internal to Kapi or Kaikula (ibid., 27). This conclusion is consistent with our suggestion that the corresponding, asymmetric Ka'/Atu'k division among the Ramkokamekra runs perpendicular to the exogamous moieties. The implication is that the Kapi and Kaikula moieties may have inclined towards endogamy. Within these strata, further endogamous subdivisions may have linked differentially ranked pairs of matrilines

from the two exogamous moieties Kuigatiye and Harungatiye. An asymmetric dimension of ranked, endogamous strata may thus have been superimposed on the diametric, exogamous division.

Cross-sex siblings are paired for name exchange in accordance with their birth order, i.e. firstborn son and firstborn daughter, second son and second daughter, and so on (ibid., 20). Furthermore, there is an explicit ideal that each set of same-sex siblings should reproduce the order of names in the name-giving sibling set of the preceding generation (ibid., 21), much like the birth-order hierarchies of the Tukano-speakers. This suggests that name-holding groups may have been regarded as ordered hierarchically according to seniority.

Diarchy is evident from Lave's observation that the Kuigatiye and Harungatiye moieties each have chiefs (ibid., 26). These "serve as a pair, and when one of the two quits or dies, a new pair is chosen." The Kapi/Kaikula moieties also each have their own chiefs (ibid., 28).

Alliance

Lave writes that sexual ties should not be formed with any people referred to by kin terms or naming terms (ibid., 24), which implies that name-holding lines are ideally exogamous.

As among the Krahó and Ramkokamekra, the equation MBD = D would be consistent with matrilateral cross-cousin marriage.

External Relations

Warfare and raids have not occurred for several decades (ibid., 34, 36).

4. The Apinayé

"We should probably be more cautious when tempted to dismiss the work of our great predecessors in the light of new outlooks or recent observations. What they have seen and recorded is gone and we cannot be sure that we are actually observing the same kind of evidence."

   – C. Lévi-Strauss (1968b: 351–352)

"I see no justification . . . for assuming without supporting evidence that early data are erroneous merely because they differ from current forms."

   – G. E. Dole (1972:137)

Kin Terminology (Tables 4 and 5)

In Nimuendajú's terminology (Table 4), the distinctions WB≠ZH, DH≠ZS, and SW≠ ZD appear to contradict symmetric alliance. On the other hand, the equations MB=FZH and FZ=MBW strongly suggest it. The distinction FF≠MF, employing the diminutive suffix -re and the augmentative -ti, is identical to that suggested by Nimuendajú for the Ramkokamekra. It is, however, challenged by Maybury-Lewis (1960a:204) and da Matta (1979:93). A patrilineal mode of classification can be recognized in the equations MB=MBS and FZH=FZS (id-krã-tum + diminutive -re), and in FZC=ZC (id-krã-duw). On the other hand, the equations FZ=FZD and MBW= MBD (túi + -re) are matrilineal. The co-existence of these equations suggests parallel affiliation.

Nimuendajú's cousin terminology is particularly problematic. The complexity is reduced, however, when we consider that the terms ged-re/géde-ti and tam-cwu are equivalent to the vocative id-krã-tum and id-krã-duw, respectively, i.e. as senior and junior ends of a relationship of name transmission (da Matta 1979:109). Indeed, except for i-tõ for MZS, all cousin terms appear to convey a meaning denoting relative age. Túi(-re) (female name-giver) refers to the first ascending generation, and id-pigukwá, for a female Ego, is reported to mean elder brother. The different possibilities for male Ego can be illustrated thus:

	MZS	MZD	MBS	MBD	FBS	FBD	FZS	FZD
Terms denoting elder	–	+	+	+	+	+	+	+
Terms denoting younger	–	–	–	–	+	+	+	+

Apparently, matrilateral cousins other than MZS are always senior, whereas patrilateral cousins can be either senior or junior. A possible interpretation is that there is a permanent rank discrepancy between the matrilateral and patrilateral sides of Ego's kindred, i.e. between wife-givers and wife-takers. In da Matta's terminology, however, both matrilateral and patrilateral cross-cousins can be equated with either senior or junior generations.

The distinction between female cross-cousins suggests an absence of symmetric alliance. On the other hand, according to Nimuendajú both female cross-cousins are classified with parallel cousins (MBD= MZD, FZD=FBD), so that instead of cross versus parallel there is a division of matrilateral versus patrilateral cousins. By equating MZS with B, however, Nimuendajú's terminology suggests closer consanguinity with the matrilateral side. The disregard for the sex of linking relatives (i.e. for cross/parallel distinctions) evident in Nimuendajú's cousin terms suggests cognatic principles of affiliation. Although da Matta's terminology (Table 5) extends sibling terms to parallel cousins, distinguishing these from cross-cousins in the two-line manner, his equation SW=ZSW also suggests cognatic principles. With Maybury-Lewis (1960a), we are prepared to accept that Nimuendajú's terminology may have been erroneous, but we are first and foremost compelled to

Table 4
KIN TERMINOLOGY OF THE APINAYÉ (1930)
LINGUISTIC FAMILY: Northern Gê (Western Timbira)
Male Ego, terms of reference.

GEN.	Male		Female	
+ 2	FF *ged-re* *(id-krā-tum)*		FM *túi*	
	MF *géde-ti* *(id-krā-tum)*		MM *túi*	

	KIN (Lineal kin, parallel collaterals, affines of affines)		*AFFINES* (In-laws, cross collaterals)	
	Male	Female	Male	Female
+ 1	F *cū-re*	M *id-nõ*	WF *tu'kayá*	WM *papa-géty*
	FB *cū-re*	MZ *id-nõ*	MB *id-krā'tum*	FZ *túi*
	MZH *čū-ti*	FBW *dyili-re*	FZH *id-krā'tum*	MBW *túi*
0	B *id-tõ*	Z *id-tõty*	WB *id-bái*	W *id-prõ*
	FBS *id-krā'tum-re*	FBD *túi-re*	MBS *id-krā'tum-re*	MBD *id-pigukwá*
	id-tam-cwu	*id-tam-cwu*		*(túi-re)*
	MZS *i-tõ*	MZD *id-pigukwá*	FZS *id-krā'tum-re*	FZD *túi-re*
			id-krā-duw	*id-krā-duw*
		WBW *(túi-re)*	ZH *id-piedyó*	BW *papa-dĩ*
− 1	S *id-kra*	D *id-kra*	DH *tu'ká*	SW *cwai-ti*
	BS *id-kra*	BD *id-kra*	ZS *id-krā-duw*	ZD *id-krā-duw*

	Male	Female
− 2	SS *id-krā-duw*	SD *id-krā-duw*
	DS *tam-cwu*	DD *tam-cwu*

SOURCES: Nimuendajú 1939:111–112. Terms in brackets are alternative usages listed by Nimuendajú in his revised Brazilian version from 1956 (da Matta 1979:121–122). Not indicated above is the alternative *tam-cwu* for FZC. *Id-pigukwá, tukayá, id-krā-tum/-duw* may be vocative (ibid., 117, 123; Seeger 1981:141).

DEVIATIONS FROM THE TWO-LINE PATTERN	CONCEIVABLE IDEOLOGICAL OR BEHAVIOURAL CORRELATES
WB≠ZH, DH≠ZS, SW≠ZD FF≠MF	Absence of symmetric alliance Lineal principles
MB=MBS, FZH=FZS, FZC=ZC FZ=FZD, MBW=MBD	Patrilateral affiliation Matrilateral affiliation, uxorilocal residence
MZD=MBD, FBC=FZC	Cognatic principles

explore any structural solutions which might account for the anomalies. The significance of equations disregarding cross/parallel distinctions will be discussed in Chapter 20.

Nimuendajú's use of *id-krā-duw* (name-receiver) for SC but *tam-cwu* for DC may indicate that FF was preferred to MF as name-giver. In a matrilineal moiety context, FF would be structurally equivalent to MB, the focus of the *geti/id-krā'tum* category. Possibly, the diminutive suffix *-re* in Nimuendajú's *ged-re* serves to merge FF with

63

Table 5
KIN TERMINOLOGY OF THE APINAYÉ (1965)
LINGUISTIC FAMILY: Northern Gê (Western Timbira)
Male Ego, terms of reference.

GEN.	Male		Female	
+ 2	FF	*geti*	FM	*tui*
	MF	*geti*	MM	*tui*

	KIN (Lineal kin, parallel collaterals, affines of affines)		*AFFINES* (In-laws, cross collaterals)	
	Male	Female	Male	Female
+ 1	F *pam* / *tõ-re* FB *pam* MZH *pam*	M *nã* MZ *nã* FBW *nã*	WF *imbré-geti* (*tukóyá*) MB *geti* FZH *geti*	WM *papam-geti* / *papan-geti* FZ *tui* MBW *tui*
0	B *tõ* FBS *tõ* MZS *tõ*	Z *tõdy* (*pigkwá*) FBD *tõdy* (*pigkwá*) MZD *tõdy* (*pigkwá*)	WB *imbré* MBS *geti/pam* / *krà* FZS *pam/geti* / *tamtxúa* ZH *idpienhon, -ti* / *ponmre*	W *improm* / *iprom, iprõ* MBD *nã/tui* / *krà* FZD *tui/nã* / *tamtxúa* BW *papany*
− 1	S *krà* BS *krà*	D *krà* BD *krà* ZSW *txóiti*	DH *tukó-ti* ZS *tamtxúa* WBS *tamtxúa*	SW *txóiti* ZD *tamtxúa* WBD *tamtxúa*

	Male	Female
− 2	SS *tamtxúa*	SD *tamtxúa*
	DS *tamtxúa*	DD *tamtxúa*

SOURCES: Da Matta 1979: 91–95; 1982:116–118. Terms in brackets are vocative forms (1982:117, 123). Terms for cross-cousins derive from 1979:120–122; *tõ-re* from 1982:116, 120; *papangeti* from ibid., 123; *iprom* or *iprõ* from ibid., 89, 117, 123; and the suffix *-ti* in *idpienhon-ti* from ibid., 118.

DEVIATIONS FROM THE TWO-LINE PATTERN	CONCEIVABLE IDEOLOGICAL OR BEHAVIOURAL CORRELATES
WB≠ZH, DH≠ZS, SW≠ZD	Absence of symmetric alliance
MB=MBS, FZH=FZS, FZC=ZC	Patrilateral affiliation
FZ=FZD, MBW=MBD, MBC=C	Matrilateral affiliation, uxori-local residence
SW=ZSW	Cognatic principles

his lower-generation equivalent, MB, or to denote affection (Nimuendajú 1939:iv).

The affinity of the terms *tu'ká* (*tukó-ti*) for DH and *tu'kayá* (*tukóyá*) for WF (i.e. daughter's MMH) suggests alternating generations of a female matriline (i.e. WM–D) reminiscent of the equation SW= WM (son's MFW) of the Krahó and Ramkokamekra. DH and WF, in fact, would represent alternate, co-resident generations of the patriline opposite to Ego's, if two uxorilocal households were consistently to exchange men in a symmetric alliance arrangement.

Da Matta explains his multiple terms for cross-cousins by suggesting that male Ego can identify himself either with his F, producing the equation FZC=ZC, or with his MB, yielding MBC=C (1973:291; 1982:126–127, 129). The former equation is Omaha, the latter Crow. Da Matta (1979:123; 1982:127) suggests that Crow equations are used when an Apinayé emphasizes the relationship between himself and his name-giver (MB), while Omaha equations are used when he stresses the adoptive parent (FB). Name-giving, then, would correspond to the matrilineal aspects of the system, while adoptive parenthood would account for the patrilineal aspects. Da Matta (1982:127) notes that this is an example of how relationship terminologies acknowledge institutional arrangements.

However, this does not exhaust the question of which factors decide whether a cross-cousin is referred to by parallel or cross-collateral terms (pam/nã or geti/tui). Where MBS/MBD are referred to as geti/nã, or FZS/FZD as pam/tui, this fits the Crow-Omaha pattern, but where the terms are reversed, other considerations may be involved. The equation MBS=F (pam) makes sense in relation to the matrilineal equation MBW=MBD (tui), since F and MBW are structural siblings. The equation FZD=M (nã) similarly accords with the patrilineal equation FZH=FZS (geti), since M and FZH are equivalent to siblings, but is also congruent with ZD marriage.

Local Group Size and Composition

Reports from 1824 speak of four Apinayé settlements ranging in size from 500 to 1,400

inhabitants with a total population of 4,200 (Nimuendajú 1939:7; Lowie 1946b:480), i.e. an average of 1,050 per settlement. In 1859, three villages remained, each with an average population of 600–667. In 1897, the three villages were down to a total of about 400, i.e. an average of 133. In 1926, the total population was estimated at 150, a figure verified by Nimuendajú himself in 1928 (1939:8). At this time, there were once again four villages, which gives an average of 37 inhabitants each.

Post-marital residence is uxorilocal (ibid., 21, 72; da Matta 1979:106, 117; 1982:40).

Patterns of Affiliation Other than Residence

Nimuendajú (1939:21–22) found the Apinayé divided into matrilineal moieties (Kolti and Kolre), membership of which was effected through name transmission from MB to ZS and from MZ to ZD. Marriage, however, was regulated by the four exogamous kiyé. Each such unit supposedly consisted of male patrilines and female matrilines wholly unrelated to each other. Males of kiyé A always married females of kiyé B, males of kiyé B females of kiyé C, and so on. Recruitment was parallel, so that S followed F and D followed M (ibid., 29–31). The result of such an arrangement, as noted by Lévi-Strauss (1969:49, 228–229; 1963d:129), would be the reproduction of four endogamous units composed of men from one kiyé and women from another. In fact, Fox (1967:144–145) suggests bilateral cross-cousin marriage and a two-section structure within each such group. Fox's diagram, however, does not take into account the prohibition, reported by Nimuendajú (1939:73), against marriage with a MBD, or even with any first cousin.

Maybury-Lewis (1960a:199) believes that "in all probability marriage was not in fact regulated by the kiyé nor determined by the parallel descent system." We shall briefly consider each of his arguments for this position.

Statistically, Maybury-Lewis notes that the Apinayé population at the time of Nimuendajú's field-work would have been too small to support an alliance system such as that of the *kiyé*. This is probably true, but as we are primarily interested in discovering whether or not a system such as that described by Nimuendajú is at all feasible, we might point to the possibility that the *kiyé* framework of the 1930's represented an institutional survival from periods when villages averaged over 1000 people.

Furthermore, Maybury-Lewis notes that the *kiyé* system should group all of Ego's male kin and affines into one category, and all his female kin and affines into another, but that this does not at all agree with the actual kin terminology provided by Nimuendajú. Several aspects of the terminology certainly seem to contradict the structure of the *kiyé* system. On the other hand, we would expect the terminology to set up classificatory subdivisions within each *kiyé*, in accordance with supplementary distinctions, e.g. between marriageables and non-marriageables. Obviously, as male Ego's Z belongs to the *kiyé* into which he is to marry, the *kiyé* system would not imply that all opposite-sex members of the appropriate *kiyé* are eligible. Cross-*kiyé* equations are more difficult to explain. Maybury-Lewis himself, however, emphasizes that parallel descent is not the only principle of affiliation in Apinayé society (ibid., 198). For instance, we may expect the two moiety systems to be responsible for some of those aspects of the terminology which are incomprehensible in the context of the *kiyé* system.

Maybury-Lewis addresses Nimuendajú's zero generation terminology as the only locus of "structural differences" vis-à-vis the Eastern Timbira. Arguing from comparative data on Eastern Timbira terminologies, he suggests that several Apinayé terms have been erroneously recorded by Nimuendajú.

Among these are *id-pigukwá* for MZD, *id-krã'tum-re* and *túi-re* for FBC, and *id-tam-cwu* for FBD. In the case of *id-pigukwá*, Maybury-Lewis considers it "clear that the categories to which these terms refer have been erroneously listed, for they cut across the possible categories of any known kinship system and do not seem to be susceptible to any formalization such as has hitherto been reported" (ibid., 208). By reducing Nimuendajú's Apinayé terminology to that of the Eastern Timbira, Maybury-Lewis certainly disposes of some cumbersome problems. On the other hand, to do so is to deny the possibility that the Apinayé may have undergone a very specific development within the Gê context. Two circumstances that strengthen this possibility are, on the one hand, a meticulous ethnographer's unique description of the *kiyé* system, and on the other, the exceptionally high population estimates of the early reports.

To justify his doubts about Nimuendajú's cousin terms, Maybury-Lewis (ibid., 203) suggests that his predecessor never really understood "the connection between a two-section system and cross-cousin marriage." Had he understood this connection, Maybury-Lewis argues, Nimuendajú would have shown some surprise at finding, among the Sherente, a system of exogamous moieties in conjunction with patrilateral cross-cousin marriage, and, among the Eastern Timbira, exogamous moieties in conjunction with a prohibition against both kinds of cross-cousin marriage. Narrowly defining dual organization as a system of exogamous moieties and bilateral cross-cousin marriage reproduced by a two-section kin terminology, Lévi-Strauss (1963d:123, 124) also found dual organization "incompatible" with the consecutive kin terminology and marriage rules of the Sherente, and with the triadic structure implicit in the ambiguous role they assign to the bride's maternal uncle. In response to Lévi-Strauss, Maybury-Lewis (1958:127) himself argued that "there are no grounds for postulating the existence of matrilateral cross-cousin marriage wherever consecutive kinship terms are found." As to Maybury-Lewis' evaluation of Nimuendajú, we should point out that a faulty understanding of kinship theory need not cast a shadow over the care with which kinship terms are recorded. But there is another objection to Maybury-Lewis' argument. In his monograph on the Akwẽ-Shavante, he himself comes to the conclusion that exogamous moieties need not involve a perfectly symmetrical two-section terminology. The Shavante distinguish ZH from WB, MB from FZH, and FZ from MBW, even though they have exogamous moieties. Maybury-Lewis notes that, from the existence of exogamous moieties, we cannot with certainty infer cross-cousin marriage (1958:126). That is, "it does not follow that there can be no further modification of the rule that the moieties exchange women" (1967:238). Using the same insight, Nimuendajú's data on the Sherente and Eastern Timbira are not as anomalous as Maybury-Lewis first assumed. The Sherente cross-cousin distinction may simply reflect one such "further modification" of moiety reciprocity, and an Eastern Timbira prohibition of first cross-cousin marriage may have amounted to no more. Such modifications, of course, are extremely interesting in terms of the long-range trajectories of structural transformation they may initiate.

Maybury-Lewis concludes his 1960 article by suggesting that "marriage among the Apinayé was regulated by a system of matrilineal exogamous moieties" and that the formal *kramgéd* friendship bonds united individuals belonging to opposite moieties (1960a:211–212).

Da Matta (1973, 1979, 1982) provides a thorough analysis of Apinayé modes of affiliation, based on his own fieldwork carried out three decades after that of Nimuendajú. His informants could not account for the word "*kiyé*", but the cognate *pikiyê-re* means "part" or "division" (da

Matta 1982:61). It is interesting to note that the Eastern Timbira employ the term *kyé* for exogamous moiety (Nimuendajú 1946:93). Da Matta agrees with Maybury-Lewis that the so-called *kiyé* could not have regulated marriage, but finds that nor do the moieties. In fact, by reducing two of Nimuendajú's four *kiyé* to decorations associated with the other two (da Matta 1973:286; 1982:84, 87), he proposes that these remaining two *kiyé* are equivalent to the ceremonial moieties Ipognotxóine and Krenotxóine. From a comparative outlook, this exercise is validated by Nimuendajú's observation among the Sherente, that "preparing festive adornment was the most essential task of the clans, as indicated by the almost exclusive reference to distinctive clan decoration in the clan names and their numerous synonyms" (Nimuendajú 1942:21).

Recruitment of males to the Kolti/Kolre moieties is by name transmission from *geti* to *tamtxua*, i.e. from GF to GS or (ideally) from MB to ZS (da Matta 1973:284; 1979: 109; 1982:70, 112). For female Ego, transmission is from *tui* to *tamtxua*, i.e. from GM to GD or from FZ to BD. This pattern is identical to that for the Wakmẽye/Katamye moieties of the Krahó, the Ka'/Atu'k moieties of the Ramkokamekra, and all the three moiety systems of the Krĩkatĩ. Underneath this mode of transmission, we have suggested, lies a fundamental ideology of parallel affiliation. In the Apinayé case, this suggestion is validated by da Matta's (1982:120, 125) recognition of a sociological identification, reflected in the kin terminology, "between genitor and son and between genetrix and daughter."

We shall mention two points on which da Matta's data differ from those of Nimuendajú. First, da Matta denies any distinction between FF and MF (Nimuendajú's *ged-re* and *géde-ti*). Maybury-Lewis (1960a: 204) found that the Krahó equivalents of these terms were used interchangeably (cf. Melatti 1979:54). Lowie suggests that the suffix *-re* in higher generations "presumably denotes affection" (Nimuendajú 1939:iv). A system of exogamous matrilineal moieties would place FF with MB in Ego's moiety, as the most suitable, second ascending generation name-giver. In fact, Nimuendajú (1939:22) gives the MMB as an alternative name-giver, i.e. the equivalent of FF in a moiety system. To the extent that Apinayé name transmission reproduced a system of unilineal moieties, there would have been a structural rationale for the distinction between paternal and maternal grandfathers recorded by Nimuendajú. A tentative explanation of Nimuendajú's *ged-re*/*géde-ti* distinction assumes that FF, by means of the affectionate suffix *-re*, is in a sense lowered to the generation of his matrilineal equivalent, MB.

The second point on which da Matta and Nimuendajú differ concerns female name transmission. While da Matta offers the FZ-BD link so well known from the Eastern Timbira, Nimuendajú claims that transmission was from MZ to ZD. In fact, he explicitly contrasts the Apinayé and Ramkokamekra in this respect (Nimuendajú 1939:22, note 28; 1946:78). Da Matta (1982:70) suggests that the MZ-ZD line may be an error deriving from the role of adoptive parents in Apinayé naming. The *geti* or *tui* chosen as name-giver to Ego is, in fact, approached by Ego's adoptive parent (*pam kaág* = adoptive father, *na kaág* = adoptive mother). The adoptive parent must be an actual, classificatory, or fictive same-sex sibling of the child's same-sex genitor (da Matta 1973:284; 1979:108; 1982:73, 114). It is through the adoptive parent that Ego's *geti* or *tui* is traced, which "leads to much wider possibilities for choice and variation" (da Matta 1973:284). It may be argued that if Ego's *pam kaág* or *na kaág* is indeed structurally equivalent to a same-sex sibling of a parent (and therefore also to that parent), the name-giver traced through him or her is likely to be someone already addressed by Ego as *geti* or *tui*, and the "possibilities for choice and variation" not much greater. The

significance of the adoptive parent may be of a different nature, as will become evident as we consider his or her crucial role as mediator between Ego and his or her affinal category. Inasmuch as same-sex siblings of parents are *not* altogether equivalent to parents, this may explain the anomalous terms for parallel cousins reported by Nimuendajú.

Turning now to da Matta's version of the *kiyé*, the Ipog/Kre moieties, we note that transmission of membership also involves adoptive parents (*pam kaág* and *na kaág*). Moreover, it is effected by means of a formal friendship bond (*krã-geti* = male formal friend; reciprocal *pá-krã*), the *kramgéd* relationship which Maybury-Lewis (1960a:211) suggests united individuals belonging to *opposite* moieties. We may summarize transmission of Ipog/Kre membership (symbolized by body paint designs, a pervasive sign of affiliation among the Gê) as follows. Ego is asked to become *krã-geti* to his *krã-geti*'s adoptive son. In the next generation, Ego asks his *krã-geti*'s adoptive son (now *pá-krã* to Ego) to be *krã-geti* to Ego's own adoptive son. In other words, the line of transmission alternates between the consecutive generations of two lines of adoptive parenthood (Fig. 5). Assuming, as an ideal model, that adoptive parents are same-sex siblings of the child's same-sex genitor (da Matta 1973:284), and that the *kramgéd* relationship is established between individuals of the same sex (ibid., 287), the two lines of adoptive parenthood thus united are structurally equivalent to male patrilines or, for female Ego, to female matrilines. Although his analyses are ambiguous (cf. da Matta 1982:88–89), da Matta's (1979:110–111) information suggests that all individuals of both lines belong to the same moiety, Ipog or Kre (cf. Dietschy 1977:302, 303). In other words, FB, male Ego, and BS belong to the same moiety as their corresponding *kramgéd* line, and MZ, female Ego, and ZD to that of their *kramgéd* line.

On the other hand, there are several

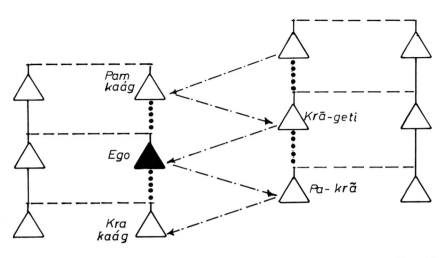

Fig. 5. Ideal model of the transmission of membership in the Ipognotxóine/Krenotxóine moieties by means of the *kramgéd* relationship (cf. da Matta 1979:111; Dietschy 1977:302).

---- Classificatory siblings

⋮ adoptive parenthood

—·—·—▸ *kramgéd*

reasons to assume that *krã-geti* is a classificatory WF. Not only is this suggested by the cognate terms *geti* for MB/FZH and *imbregeti* for WF, but da Matta actually points to a number of circumstances which are consistent with the identification of *krã-geti* as an affine. *Krã-geti* and *pá-krã* are "non-kin" always situated on opposite sides of the village; their relationship is marked by asymmetry, avoidance, extreme formalism, and a mystical component "from which we can infer an aspect of 'affinity'"; finally, the *krã-geti*, compensated with meat pies just like the bride's father (cf. Nimuendajú 1939: 33; da Matta 1982:124), is responsible for the incorporation of his *pá-krã* into the social and ritual structure (da Matta 1973:288; 1979:111–112; 1982:35, 38, 90, 94–97, 102, 109). Moreover, a man speaking with the daughter of his *krã-geti* addresses her as *improm-ti*, an augmentative form of *improm* (W) (da Matta 1979:94–95; 1982:89).

If we go back to Nimuendajú (1939), his data on the *kramgéd* bond are even more suggestive of affinity. An informant explained that *kramgéd* should ideally be selected among distant members of Ego's *kiyé*, but that demographic decline had restricted the choice to rather close kin (ibid., 32–33). According to a diagram (ibid., 31) illustrating the genealogical context of several *kramgéd* relationships, a male Ego's *krã-geti* (*kramgéd-ti*) can be an actual WF or a FBS (cf. Nimuendajú's equation of FBS with male cross-cousins, i.e. prototypical affines). Apparently, the wife of a male Ego's *pam kaág* (i.e. FBW) may serve as Ego's *kramgédy* (female *kramgéd.*) Since two brothers in this particular case had married two sisters, the same *kramgédy* was simultaneously related to Ego as FBWZ through another FB. From the point of view of a female Ego, the male *krã-geti* may be a ZH. In short, out of five *kramgéd* bonds, four clearly involve affines, and the fifth (FBS) a category which for some reason has been classified with affines. A tentative explanation for the affinal status of FBS assumes that this kinsman, if sufficiently older than Ego, may already have established himself as household head in the affinal half of the village circle, by the time Ego is to be

69

introduced to his potential affines. It may be argued that this would also apply to MZS, but as MZS will have been a member of Ego's natal household, just like MB, he is too much of a consanguine (*i-tõ*=B) to be classified as an affine.

The implication of our argument thus far is that the adoptive father (*pam kaág*), in mediating between his adoptive son (BS) and the latter's relatives on the opposite side of the village, is expected to reinforce both consanguineal and affinal ties, the former by means of name transmission from the boy's *geti* (MB), the latter through the *kramgéd* bond, whereby the boy establishes contact with his potential affines.

In constructing an ideal model of the articulation of affiliation and alliance among the aboriginal Apinayé, we were not content with observing contemporary analogies, "on a theoretical formal level" (da Matta 1973: 288), between relations of alliance and affiliation, but sought to suggest the historical foundations for such analogies. This means that the model will not attempt to show how the Apinayé system actually "functioned" at the time of da Matta's or even Nimuendajú's fieldwork, only the principles of which the ethnographic present may represent a poorly integrated transformation. Such speculation may be justified in the light of the disastrous demographic decline which apparently struck the Apinayé during the latter half of the 19th century.

From the point of view of male Ego, the fundamental mode of Apinayé moiety affiliation is matrilateral. The Kolti/Kolre moieties emphasize the continuity of matrilineal consanguinity from MB to ZS. The position of Ego's senior matrilateral kinsmen is ambivalent, however. Owing to the practice of uxorilocal residence, Ego's mother's brothers will be household heads in the opposite, affinal half of the village circle. In other words, Ego's MB is structurally equivalent to his WF, even if MBD marriage is explicitly prohibited. The elaborate contrast between Ego's *geti* and *krã-geti*

produces the necessary distinction among men of the opposite half of the village circle, between kin and affines. The *kramgéd* relationship, transmitting membership in the Ipog/Kre moieties, underscores the social distance associated with affinity. Its affinal nature is particularly evident from the fact that male Ego calls his *krã-geti*'s daughter *improm*, i.e. W. The *kiyé* moieties Ipog and Kre, then, should not be conceived as lines of consanguineal continuity, but as alliance-organized units restricting marriage to within themselves. The two parties of the inherited affinal bond are lines of parallel kin, e.g. FB – male Ego – BS (Fig. 5).

By distinguishing between same-sex siblings as substitutes and mediators in the interaction with affines, the intertwined, individual lines on both sides of each *kramgéd*-organized group are able to "dodge" their affinal counterparts and mystify their endogamous marriage practices. As in Australian eight-section systems, this indirectness of alliance reciprocity is consistent with a prohibition on first-cousin marriage (cf. Oberg 1973:205). Maybury-Lewis perceived the affinal nature of the *kramgéd* bond, suggesting that it united individuals of opposite exogamous moieties. Nimuendajú's mistake was to visualize what he calls the *kiyé* as corporate, parallel descent lines, instead of as alliance-organized, endogamous categories integrated by a much less tangible ideology of parallel affiliation.

The two lines of adoptive kinship united in a *kramgéd* relationship are classificatory affines to each other. Yet, all males in both lines belong to the same *kiyé* (Ipog or Kre, or further endogamous subdivisions thereof.) Together, they constitute what may be described as an endogamous kindred with exogamy extending to the first cousin. The cognatic aspects of the system are entirely consistent with the disregard for the sex of linking relatives which makes Nimuendajú's terminology seem so anomalous. The equations MBD=MZD and FZD=FBD, which apparently occurred in some contexts, suggest the foundations of an Eskimo cousin terminology. The *kiyé* system is mainly concerned with delineating the outer boundaries of the endogamous categories, rather than with maintaining an internal dichotomy of kin and affines, such as is produced with a bifurcate merging nomenclature. As there is no consistent separation of parallel- and cross-sex collaterals, we have no reason to dismiss the possibility that distant parallel cousins (e.g. FFBDD) may have been as eligible as distant cross-cousins. In fact, marriages with parallel kin have actually been reported by da Matta (1982: 108, 175, note 5). Instead of a parallel- versus cross-cousin dichotomy, the spatial separation of kin and affines in the diametrical village layout appears to have served as a matrix for alliance (cf. the Ramkokamekra; W. Crocker 1977:274, note 25). Opposite-side households headed by men born to Ego's natal household (e.g. MB, MZS, B) would have been excluded from the affinal category, either through the application of the kin terminology or through name-giving ceremonies establishing the consanguineal nature of the matrilineal ties. Owing to uxorilocal residence, different parallel cousins are raised on opposite sides of the village. The MMZDD belongs to Ego's side, but the FFBDD to that of his affines. Similarly, the MZD belongs to Ego's natal household, whereas the FBD is much less likely to do so. It is not unreasonable to suggest that the anomalous cousin terminology, by which matrilateral cousins *(id-pigukwá)* are less marriageable than patrilateral ones, may be related to these facts. Similar considerations may have been operative among the Sherente and Txicáo. By the time da Matta carried out his fieldwork in the 1960:s, Apinayé relationship terminology had apparently reverted to a more conventional, kin/affine dichotomy. The equation SW=ZSW, however, distinctly recalls the cognatic features of Nimuendajú's cousin terms.

Hierarchy

In an article suggesting fundamental similarities between the kinship system of the Apinayé and that of the Inca, Zuidema (1969:138) proposes that the "endogamic 'castes'" produced by the marriage system were hierarchically ranked. This hierarchy, furthermore, would have corresponded to different degrees of endogamy practiced by Apinayé chiefs. The most endogamous marriages would have yielded the highest ranking offspring, while secondary, less endogamous marriages produced children of lower rank. Not only were the different wives of a chief differentially ranked, but also, according to seniority, the children of a particular mother (ibid., 135). Though speculative, this interpretation accords well with the pervasive birth-order hierarchies evident from different peoples of the South American lowlands. The terminological distinction between elder and younger siblings is widespread, while the explicit, birth-order ranking of siblings and their descendent lineages is particularly emphasized among Tukano-speakers and the Gê-affiliated Bororo. Zuidema's approach, moreover, provides an ideological rationale for the crucial distinction between same-sex siblings, a feature we have already suggested is fundamental to the logic of Apinayé alliance. The rules of marriage and affiliation attributed to the *kiyé* jointly suggest that these groups, and their constituent lines, were formed by a process of segmentation based on the distinction of siblings. Such a segmentary model of Apinayé kinship brings to mind not only the ranked patrilines of the Tukano-speakers, but also the *panacas* of Inca Peru, where the descendent *panaca* of each king maintained a specific position in a social hierarchy defined by the royal genealogy.

Zuidema (1969:138), Dietschy (1977:302), and da Matta (1979:110; 1982: 162) note that the *kiyé*, whether four or two in number, are hierarchically conceived. Ipognotxóine signifies "person of the center", while Krenotxóine means "person of the periphery". Such concentric representations of asymmetry are widespread in the South American lowlands. Da Matta (1982:38) remarks that village expansion requires another circle of houses outside the first, and that "it is said that people do not like living in the outer circle," implying once again that the periphery is associated with social inferiority. The asymmetrical, concentric dimension would have been particularly emphasized in the huge villages of the early 19th century.

According to Nimuendajú (1939:19–21; Lowie 1946b:489), the village chief invariably belongs to the Kolti (Kólo-*ti*, augmentative/Kólo-*re*, diminutive) moiety, and succession is primarily from MB to ZS. Nevertheless, the office of "'counselor' and master of ceremonies," whose share in the distribution of food "at least equals the chief's," suggests an element of diarchy, as does the occurrence of separate moiety leaders at certain festivals. In addition to chieftainship, other high-status positions also matrilineally transmitted are the ceremonial roles associated with the "great names" owned by each moiety (Nimuendajú 1939: 22–24; Lowie 1946b:493; da Matta 1979:108; 1982:67). Reminiscent of the "honorary positions" of the Krîkatí, these indicate status discrepancies between matrilines. The Kolti and Kolre moieties each has its own hierarchy of corresponding ceremonial roles (da Matta 1982:67).

Alliance

In addition to the *kiyé* marriage rules, Nimuendajú (1939:73) claims that marriage is prohibited with women of the *id-pigukwá* category. From this explicit rule, he concludes that "an Apinayé must not wed his parents' sibling's daughter." According to Nimuendajú, the *id-pigukwá* category includes the MBD and MZD, but not the

FZD and FBD. Taken in conjunction with the equation $MZS=B\neq FBS$, this marriage rule seems to be based on a concept of exogamy defined by the mother's kindred. Moreover, Nimuendajú says that the Apinayé "avoid all unions between kin of the first and second degree in the ascending and descending line." The impression is that *all* primary cross-cousins are banned, i.e. even patrilateral ones. This is the impression on which Oberg (1973:205), Maybury-Lewis (1960a:194), and Lévi-Strauss (1963d:129–130) base their analyses. Maybury-Lewis (1960a:208) suggests that *id-pigukwá* actually designates cross-cousins. If this were the case, the rule prohibiting marriage with an *id-pigukwá* would serve to maintain first-cousin exogamy, and Nimuendajú's conclusion would be relevant. Da Matta (1982:117), however, lists *pigkwá* as vocative for *tõdy*, i.e. Z and female parallel cousin. From da Matta's definition, the *id-pigukwá* prohibition would fit Maybury-Lewis' simple, two-section model, but Nimuendajú's definition, and his conclusion concerning "parents' sibling's daughter," would be inexplicable. The explicit prohibition of the MBD suggests a system tending toward FZD marriage (Fig. 6). Zuidema (1969:137) proposes that the distinction $WF\neq MB$ may indicate that first cross-cousin marriage was generally not permitted, but that endogamous marriages (to FZD, ZD, and even yMZD) may have been a privilege of chiefs.

In the 1960:s, da Matta (1979:83, 112) found no indications of either exogamous categories or cross-cousin marriage preferences. In fact, he claims that it is possible for a man and a woman designated by any relationship terms to marry, provided they are distant relatives (da Matta 1982: 109). When asked where his affines (*iprom kwóyá*=wife's relatives) are, an Apinayé "will do no more than indicate the houses on the other side of the village that are opposite his own and where, ideally, his sons should find their wives." Consanguinity is mapped onto the village layout, so that "adjacent groups have more blood (or stronger blood) in common than groups that are separated from one another." An apparent contradiction, in this model, is the position of the married MB vis-à-vis his unmarried ZS. Spatially, the MB is a classificatory WF, a condition which is congruent with the apparent inclination toward matrilateral marriage among the Eastern Timbira. Among the Apinayé, it seems that the consanguineal aspect of the MB (*geti*, i.e. prototypical name-giver) has been sufficiently pronounced to ban the actual MBD (*id-pigukwá*) from marriage.

The formal similarities between affinal relations and the *kramgéd* relationship is, according to da Matta (1973:289), merely a metaphor. He explicitly asserts, however, that "there can be marriage with the children of a *krã-geti*," although he found no instances of it (da Matta 1979:112). Even if the *krã-geti* is not the actual WF himself (but note that Nimuendajú (1939:31, 33) provides an example), several circumstances indicate that he is recognized as an affine (perhaps a classificatory B of WF), particularly the term *improm-ti* for his daughter. It thus appears that the intra-*kiyé kramgéd* bonds between males represent endogamous categories superimposed on the spatial exogamy of the two village sides (cf. Dietschy 1977:303).

As Maybury-Lewis (1960a:196) points out, "provided that there are always sufficient numbers of males and females in each *kiyé*, there is no limit to the number of distinct and unrelated descent lines which each may contain." Maybury-Lewis estimates that at least four "descent lines" for each sex are required in every *kiyé*, if the exogamic rule includes first cross-cousins. The closest marriage possible to Ego, given the prohibition of primary cross-cousins, is with second cousins such as MMBDD or FFZSD. In view of the more explicit character of the MBD prohibition (Nimuendajú 1939:73), however, we may speculate that the expansion of exogamy to embrace all primary cousins is a subsequent modification of a system tending toward FZD marriage (Fig. 6). Structurally, consistent FZD marriage is equivalent to distant matrilateral cross-cousin marriage, as Ego's FZD will simultaneously be his MMBDD (cf. Needham 1962:109–110). Thus, the trajectory represented by the Apinayé system does not necessarily imply a departure from the general Timbira ideal of matrilateral marriage, only that the matrilateral first cousin (the actual MBD) is avoided. The male heads of affinal households (potential fathers-in-law) are classificatory maternal uncles. Even if they are married to paternal aunts, Ego marries the daughter of his father-in-law rather than that of his mother-in-law. To the extent that there has been a tendency toward FZD marriage, we suggest that it was originally concomitant to marriage practices perceived as essentially matrilateral, although in reality bilateral. This is corroborated by the ideal that a man should find his wife in the houses of his father's *iprom kwóyá* (affines). In a system described by the anthropologist as approximating patrilateral cross-cousin (FZD) marriage, the emic rule may well be that a man should marry the daughter of one of his father's wife's (i.e. his mother's) male kinsmen, e.g. his MFZS (the ZS of his father's father-in-law), whose simultaneous status as FZH is ignored in this particular context (cf. Fig. 6). Such unilateral considerations imply that certain genealogical relationships are emphasized or neglected in some contexts, others in others. This is consistent with the latitude of choice and variation in the cross-cousin terminology provided by da Matta.

It will be seen (Fig. 6) that a model of FZD marriage requires only three lines of each sex in every *kiyé*. As affinal relationships for male Ego are primarily reckoned between men, and those of female Ego between women, it is not incorrect to say that the *kiyé*, from the point of view of each sex, are endogamous. It will be seen, finally, that the anomalous category *id-pigukwá* (MBD= MZD) in this ideal model would correspond

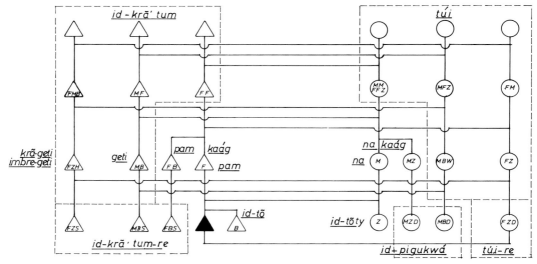

Fig. 6. Hypothetical reconstruction of endogamous Apinayé alliance structure prior to the prohibition of marriage to any primary cross-cousin.

to zero generation females of those matrilines of Ego's endogamous group which are prohibited to him, and that the wide categories *id-krã-tum(-re)* and *tui(-re)* are also provided with a logical foundation.

If patterns of alliance among the Apinayé may once have approximated patrilateral cross-cousin marriage, expressed and perceived as matrilateral marriage, by Nimuendajú's time exogamy had extended to embrace all first cousins. We may note that a suggestion by Oberg (1973:205), that the expanded exogamy responsible for the "second-cousin marriage rule" should be associated with demographic concentration, appears valid if we trace it back to the huge villages of the early 19th century.

External Relations

Towards the end of the 18th century, the Apinayé repeatedly raided settlers for iron tools (Nimuendajú 1939:3). Though generally perceived as peaceable (cf. Nimuendajú 1946:149; Lowie 1946b:498), their "martial spirit" was apparently strong enough to have made the tribe a desirable ally for Brazilians fighting for independence from Portugal in the 1820:s (Nimuendajú 1939:6, 120–121). A century later, the Apinayé were on uneasy terms with their neighbours, the Krahó (ibid., 12–13). Relations with other tribes, such as the Shavante, the Krîkatî, and the Karajá, alternated between periods of peace and of warfare (ibid., 121; Dietschy 1977: 301). Lowie (1946b:488) writes that "autonomous Apinayé villages continue to display mutual repugnance."

Of all the Timbira tribes, the Apinayé appear to have been the most accomplished in river navigation (Nimuendajú 1939:4), suggesting an interest in trade. The demand for beads is offered as the motive for attacks on the Kupã-rob on Lago Vermelho (ibid., 120). The exceptionally large settlements, and the demands on surplus production presumably posed by trade and manufacture, explain why the Apinayé maintained impressively large manioc plantations (ibid., 3).

5. The Kayapó

Kin Terminology (Table 6)

An absence of symmetric alliance is suggested by the distinctions between cross-cousins of both sexes and by the distinctions WB≠ ZH, DH≠ZS, SW≠ZD, S≠ZDH, and D≠ZSW. On the other hand, the equations MB=FZH and FZ=MBW suggest symmetry. Patrilineal equations can be recognized in M=MBD, MF=MB=MBS, FZC=ZC=DC, ZH=DH, and BW=SW, while matrilineal principles appear to underlie the equations ZH=ZDH and BW=ZSW. The affinity of the terms for WF and WB suggest a patrilineal link, while that of the terms for SW and WM (i.e. SMFW) may reflect some alternation of generations. Bamberger (1974:369) notes that the equations constituting *ngêt* and *kwatuy* vis-à-vis *tabdjuó* reflect categories of potential name-givers and name-receivers.

Local Group Size and Composition

The population of the Kayapó village of Gorotire in 1897 was estimated at 1,500 (Bamberger 1979:142). Now this number approximates the entire Kayapó people, distributed in seven or eight communities (ibid., 129), which gives an average between 187 and 214 per village. For 1966, Bamberger (ibid., 131) lists eight villages ranging from 80 to 280 inhabitants and averaging 171.

Post-marital residence is uxorilocal (Turner 1971:367; 1979b: 179; Bamberger 1979:138).

Patterns of Affiliation Other than Residence

The category *ombikwa* ("my own people") refers to Ego's kindred, a cognatic kin group which functions as a corporate entity almost exclusively in ceremonial contexts (Bamberger 1979:135). *Ombikwa* are distinguished from non-kin, who are called *mēbaitebm* ("people to one side (or outside) of my own people") (ibid., 135, 138).

Recruitment to moieties is by induction into a men's house or a women's society by a same-sex adoptive parent (*bam ka'ak*= adoptive father). The adoptive parent should be a non-relative. Moiety membership for men is thus based on symbolic patrifiliation, while for women it is based on symbolic matrifiliation. A woman's moiety affiliation should preferably accord with that of her husband, and may be thus adjusted, if necessary. This combination of parallel affiliation and moiety endogamy recalls the situation among the Apinayé.

Turner (1971:366) notes that the Kayapó lack descent rules of any kind, with the exception that the formal friend (*kràb-djuò*) relationship can be patrilineally inherited. Bamberger (1974:373) calls the *kràb-djuò* "godparents" by virtue of their parental role in initiation ceremonies. The *kràb-djuò*, like the *bam ka'ak*, should be a non-relative, but since the relationship is patrilineally inheritable, it too is linked to patrifiliation. The roles of *bam ka'ak* and *kràb-djuò* correspond closely to the *pam kaág* and *krã-geti* of the Apinayé. The major structural difference is that the *bam ka'ak* should be a non-relative, whereas the *pam kaág* should be a close patrilateral kinsman.

The preferred lines of name transmission are those typical of the Northern Gê: from FZ to BD and from MB to ZS (Turner 1979b: 183; Bamberger 1974:368, 369, 371). Bamberger (1974:369, 371, 373, 376) interprets the ideal of name exchange as an aspect of "cross-sex sibling reciprocity." The FZ and MB "play the leading ritual roles in the drama of young Kayapó lives" (Bamberger 1979:136). Yet, an underlying ideology of patrilateral affiliation is evident in the emphasis on close ties between FZ and BC, which is not equalled by the relation of MB to ZS (Turner 1971:369–370). The "skewed

Table 6
KIN TERMINOLOGY OF THE KAYAPÓ
LINGUISTIC FAMILY: Northern Gê
Male Ego, terms of reference.

GEN.	Male		Female	
+ 2	FF *ngêt*		FM *kwatuy*	
	MF *ngêt*		MM *kwatuy*	

	KIN (Lineal kin, parallel collaterals, affines of affines)		*AFFINES* (In-laws, cross collaterals)	
	Male	Female	Male	Female
+ 1	F *bam*	M *nã*	WF *'umrêngêt*	WM *'ùpayndjuò*
	FB *bam*	MZ *nã*	MB *ngêt*	FZ *kwatuy*
	MZH *bam*	FBW *nã*	FZH *ngêt*	MBW *kwatuy*
0	B *kamu*	Z *kanikwoy*	WB *'umrê*	W *prõn*
	FBS *kamu*	FBD *kanikwoy*	MBS *ngêt*	MBD *nã*
	MZS *kamu*	MZD *kanikwoy*	FZS *tabdjuò*	FZD *tabdjuò*
			ZH *'ùdjuò*	BW *'ùpayn*
− 1	S *kra*	D *kra*	DH *'ùdjuò*	SW *'ùpayn*
	BS *kra*	BD *kra*	ZS *tabdjuò*	ZD *tabdjuò*
	ZDH *'ùdjuò*	ZSW *'ùpayn*		

	Male		Female	
− 2	SS *tabdjuò*		SD *tabdjuò*	
	DS *tabdjuò*		DD *tabdjuò*	

SOURCES: T.S. Turner (Bamberger 1979:136)

DEVIATIONS FROM THE TWO-LINE PATTERN	CONCEIVABLE IDEOLOGICAL OR BEHAVIOURAL CORRELATES
MBC≠FZC, WB≠ZH, DH≠ZS, SW≠ZD, S≠ZDH, D≠ZSW	Absence of symmetric alliance
M=MBD, MF=MB=MBS, FZC=ZC=DC, ZH=DH, BW=SW	Patrilateral affiliation
ZH=ZDH, BW=ZSW	Matrilateral affiliation, uxori-local residence

pattern of emphasis on the sister's relationship to her brother's children" is an attempt to counterbalance the separation of the brother from the sister's household (Turner 1979b:183). This conclusion recalls W. Crocker's (1977) interpretation of patrifiliation among the Ramkokamekra, although the Kayapó apparently represent an accentuation of the feeble patrilineal inclinations of the former.

The lines of name transmission do not result in corporate, name-holding groups, as among the Krahó (Bamberger 1974:375–376). In this respect, the Kayapó resemble the Krîkatí, whose disinterest in the corporate properties of name-holding categories puzzled Lave (1979:30).

Turner (1979b:209, 211) notes that all Kayapó villages have for several decades been one-moiety villages (i.e., villages have split along moiety lines), but that junior and senior age-sets within each moiety have adopted some aspects of the symmetrical relationship between the two divisions of a conventional moiety structure. The capacity of moieties to become autonomous is obviously related to the ideal of moiety endogamy.

It is noteworthy that the Kayapó cross-cousin distinction, contrary to that of the Eastern Timbira, ascribes to the matrilateral cross-cousins a senior status (by equating them with M and MB), and the patrilateral cross-cousins a junior (by equating them with ZC). This difference is consistent with the correlated difference in emphasis on matrilineal affiliation among the Eastern Timbira, and on patrilineal affiliation among the Kayapó. The Apinayé, who allow both for Crow- and Omaha-type cousin terms, occupy a position intermediate to these.

Hierarchy

As among the Apinayé, traditional Kayapó villages may have had more than one ring of uxorilocal houses (Turner 1971:367), suggesting that a concentric representation of hierarchy was reflected in the village layout.

Village leadership primarily consists of ceremonial privileges (Bamberger 1979: 138). Diarchy was practiced in the large Kayapó villages of Gorotire and Kuben-kranken. Ceremonial privileges also adhere to a limited set of "great names" (*idji mêtch*) which distinguish "good", "great", or "beautiful" (*me mêtch*) from "common" or "little" people (*me kakrit*) (Bamberger 1974: 365–367, 368, 371; da Matta 1982:68). The holders of "great names" are readily distinguished in the different styles of ceremonial ornaments (earspools, neck ornaments, bracelets) which they wear. Since male names are inherited matrilineally, these privileges would distinguish between matrilines of different rank.

Alliance

Kayapó moieties at the time of Turner's (1971:367) fieldwork were not exogamous. On the contrary, they are "*ex post facto* endogamous," since women join the society on the same side of the plaza as the men's house to which their husbands belong. This inclination towards moiety autonomy is consistent with the shift to one-moiety villages, and relates to the fact that rules of moiety recruitment seem altogether disconnected from genealogical considerations. The liberal mode of recruitment to Kayapó moieties appears to be a transformation of the rules employed by the Apinayé, where the adoptive parent is still genealogically more or less equivalent to the same-sex parent.

Bamberger (1974:376) emphasizes that "the Kayapó system of naming is predicated on a brother-sister exchange," i.e. a man transmits his name to his sister's son in exchange for the transmission of his sister's name to his own daughter. This reciprocity between cross-sex siblings is formally congruent with cross-cousin marriage. Formally, Northern Gê name transmission could be argued to agree both with MBD marriage, in which case the MB-ZS line would represent succession in the uxorilocal household, and with FZD marriage, in which case the MB-ZS and FZ-BD lines complement alliance, linking each individual with those of his or her cross-sex sibling's children with whom he or she is not already linked through marriage.

Turner (1979b:182) isolates a "normative proscription" prohibiting brothers or male parallel cousins from marrying into the same uxorilocal household. This rule accentuates a man's subordination in relation to his wife-givers, as Turner points out. It is equally interesting in that it involves an ideological distinction between same-sex siblings. This again recalls the Apinayé, where we have suggested that the distinction of same-sex siblings in the context of marital alliance may have been related to an ideology of age-rank. To the extent that sets of same-sex siblings are regarded as ranked according to birth order, their different marriages would be expected to accord with an hierarchical arrangement of uxorilocal households, or matrilines. This, of course, recalls the birth-order ranking of names (i.e. name-holding MB-ZS lines) among the Krĩkatí.

External Relations

Bamberger (1974:375) writes that "as Kayapó villages are neither on good terms nor within walking distance of each other visiting is only an occasional occurrence" (cf. Lowie 1946b:488–489). The Kayapó have a long-standing record of factionalism and feuding, encouraged by the traditional opposition of two men's houses, one for each moiety (Bamberger 1979:133). This "poten-tially explosive political situation . . . may account for the fact that there have been no reports of villages containing two men's houses since 1936."

The warlike reputation of the Kayapó spread fear among neighbouring tribes such as the Tapirapé (ibid., 129). A report from 1806, however, mentions Kayapó paddlers in a flotilla of canoes making a "commercial descent of the Araguaia-Tocantins to Pará" (Maybury-Lewis 1965b:350).

6. The Suyá

Kin Terminology (Table 7)

An absence of symmetric alliance is suggest-ed by the distinctions MB≠FZH, FZ≠MBW, MBC≠FZC, WB≠ZH, DH≠ZS, and SW≠ZD. Patrilineal equations can be recognized in M=MBD, MB=MBS, C=FZC, FZH=ZH=DH, and WB=WBS. The equation ZC=SC is congruent with a context of preferential matrilateral cross-cousin

marriage combined with an Omaha-type cousin terminology, by which ZC would tend also to be the children of FZS, who is equated with S. The same combination explains the inclusion of WBD in the marriageable category *hron*, since the implied equation of MBD and WBD follows logically from the Omaha equation MB=MBS. The equation WM=WBW may also derive from the preference that a man (here: WB) should marry his MBD, to whom he applies the same term as he uses for his M (here: WM). The equation C=FZC, finally, would be consis-tent either with FZ marriage, or with FZD marriage in conjunction with matrilateral affiliation (which would be congruent with lines of succession linking F-FZS-S), or with a system of MBD marriage in which the wife-taker (FZS) is ranked junior to the wife-giver (MBS) (cf. the Sherente).

Local Group Size and Composition

Suyá population today totals about 140 individuals (Seeger 1977:342; 1981:236). Of these, two-thirds derive from the Eastern Suyá of the Xingú and Suyá-missu Rivers, and one-third from the greatly diminished Western Suyá (also known as Tapayuna or Beicos de Pau), who were transferred to the Xingú in 1970 (Seeger 1977:342; 1981:9). A report from 1884 describes a village of nine houses and about 150 inhabitants (Seeger 1981:50). A village destroyed by Juruna Indians in 1915 is said to have numbered 15 houses (ibid., 52). A census of the Eastern Suyá in 1960 gives the probably too conserva-tive figure of 65 (ibid., 54). The Western Suyá were estimated by the National Indian Agency to number 1,200 in the 1960:s, but Seeger (ibid., 55) believes that an estimate of about 400 would be closer to the truth. Only 41 Western Suyá survived to arrive at Xingú.

Post-marital residence is generally uxorilocal (Seeger 1977:345, 351; 1981: 29, 49, 68), but virilocal exceptions derive from

Table 7
KIN TERMINOLOGY OF THE SUYÁ
LINGUISTIC FAMILY: Northern Gê
Male Ego, terms of reference.

GEN.	Male		Female	
+ 2	FF *gitumu*		FM *tuwuyi*	
	MF *gitumu*		MM *tuwuyi*	

	KIN (Lineal kin, parallel collaterals, affines of affines)		*AFFINES* (In-laws, cross collaterals)	
	Male	Female	Male	Female
+ 1	F *ture*	M *tire*	WF *tumbre-ngedi*	WM *tumē-ngedi* *twoi-ngedi*
	FB *ture*	MZ *tire*	MB *ngedi*	FZ *tuwuyi*
			FZH *wiyaiyō tukà*	MBW *ngit-ta-teng-nā*
0	B *kambü*	Z *kandikwoiyi*	WB *tumbre*	W *hron*
	FBS *kambü*	FBD *kandikwoiyi*	MBS *ngedi*	MBD *tire*
	MZS *kambü*	MZD *kandikwoiyi*	FZS *kra*	FZD *kra-ndiyi*
		WBW *tynē-ngedi twoi-ngedi*	ZH *wiyaiyō tukà*	BW *hron*
− 1	S *kra*	D *kra-ndiyi*	DH *wiyaiyō*	SW *twoiyi*
	BS *kra*	BD *kra-ndiyi*	ZS *taumtwü*	ZD *taumtwü*
			WBS *tumbre*	WBD *hron*

	Male		Female	
− 2	SS *taumtwü*		SD *taumtwü*	
	DS *taumtwü*		DD *taumtwü*	

SOURCES: Seeger 1981:130–133. *Gitumu* means "old *ngedi*" (ibid., 129), but the terms are
said definitely to signify different kinds of relatives.

DEVIATIONS FROM THE TWO-LINE PATTERN	CONCEIVABLE IDEOLOGICAL OR BEHAVIOURAL CORRELATES
MB≠FZH, FZ≠MBW, MBC≠FZC, WB≠ZH, DH≠ZS, SW≠ZD	Absence of symmetric alliance
M=MBD, MB=MBS, C=FZC, FZH=ZH=DH, WB=WBS	Patrilateral affiliation
ZC=SC, W=WBD, WM=WBW C=BC=FZC	Matrilateral cross-cousin marriage 1. FZ marriage, or 2. FZD marriage in conjunction with matrilateral affiliation (would be congruent with succession F-FZS-S), or 3. MBD marriage, with wife-taker (FZS) ranked junior to wife-giver (MBS)

"complications arising from the widespread
marriage of captives" (ibid., 73). Virilocality
is also practiced by political leaders, who
maximize their kinship ties by remaining in
the proximity of their fathers and emphasizing patrilateral affiliation (ibid., 202).

Patterns of Affiliation Other than Residence

Suyá men are divided into two ceremonial moieties, Ambànyi and Krenyi (Seeger 1977: 348; 1981:71). Recruitment to the moieties is effected by name transmission shortly after birth. Pairs of brothers usually belong to opposite moieties (1981:72, 138, 141). The ideal name-giver for a boy is a *ngedi* (MB), while female names pass from FZ (*tuwuyi*) to BD (ibid., 136, 138, 261). Seeger's genealogies indicate that "a given name is used in alternate generations" (ibid., 137). Name-receivers and name-givers (ZS and MB) share the same social identity, and "in some senses they are one being" (ibid., 141). Their respective terms of address, *krã-tumu* and *krã-ndu*, which are also found among the Apinayé and the Kayapó, can be literally translated as "old head" and "new head". House names, too, are matrilineal (ibid., 73; 1977:351). Two or more houses may form a residential cluster sharing the same name (1981:74) and a rule of exogamy (ibid., 73, 123). Yet, such groups are neither lineages nor clans, as genealogy is not emphasized and there is no context in which they are corporate (ibid., 74, 145). Political leadership is inherited patrilineally (ibid., 203). The formation of political factions tends to involve some virilocality (ibid., 202), and "the core of most factions is, depending on the age of the leader, either a group of brothers or a father and his sons" (ibid., 74).

Hierarchy

A differentiation of siblings according to birth order appears to underlie the convention that "often the firstborn is given an Ambàn name set and the second-born a Kren name set" (Seeger 1981:138). Seeger (ibid., 141) notes that "siblings should never have the same name set; thus a different *ngedi* is

needed for each one." Each name set carries specific rights and obligations (ibid., 137). Chieftainship is inherited patrilineally (ibid., 203). Chiefs, their wives, and their children of both sexes may be buried in the village plaza (Seeger 1977:346).

Alliance

Named houses or residential clusters are exogamous (Seeger 1977:351; 1981:73, 123). From the point of view of a particular male Ego, the rule is that sexual relations are prohibited with any person from his own natal house, while a WZ, BW, or WBD (any of whom may share his post-marital residence) is sexually accessible (*hron*) (Seeger 1981:126, 132). Ideal marriages include matrilateral cross-cousin marriage, sets of siblings marrying each other, and sister exchange (ibid., 129). Seeger claims that FZD marriage "is supposed to be prohibited," but notes that the ideal of sister exchange (symmetric alliance) would contradict such a rule, and that FZD marriages do in fact occur. The "most frequently stated marriage norm" is that a man should marry a real or classificatory D of a real or classificatory MB (*ngedi*) (ibid., 129, 132, 261; 1977:351). To marry the daughter of a MB apparently means avoiding the relation of extreme "shame" (*whiasàm*) otherwise obtaining between affines (Seeger 1981:125). It would also mean marrying into a residential cluster from which one has already received one's social identity, or affiliation, i.e. by name transmission from a *ngedi*, unless the differentiation of name-givers to a set of brothers is supplemented with an hypothetical rule banning marriage with the daughter of a name-giver. Similarly, there is a connection between affinity and patrilineally inherited, ceremonial *ñumbre-krà-chi* relations, in that the same degree of *whiasàm* is exhibited toward WF and a *ñumbre-krà-chi* (ibid., 143). This parallel recalls the formal friendships of the Apinayé, and Seeger in fact equates the two (ibid., 145). He concludes that there are "no clearly defined intermarrying groups," even if kin terminology, naming, and ceremonial relationships are all interrelated in a complicated pattern.

External Relations

The Suyá villages, each "the center of its own universe" (Seeger 1977:342), have been in constant conflict with other tribes, including the Mundurucú, the Trumai, the Juruna, the Kayapó, and the Waura (Seeger 1981:50–53).

7. The Shavante

Kin Terminology (Table 8)

An absence of symmetric alliance is suggested by the distinctions MB≠FZH, FZ≠MBW, WB≠ZH, DH≠ZS, and SW≠ZD. Patriliny is evident in the equations FZH=ZH=DH and FBW=BW=SW. Cognatic principles underlie the affinity of the terms for C and young ZC (*ĩ-ra-wapté*), and for F and MB (*ĩ-mãwapté*). The bracketed term *ĩ-za'mũ* for FZH is structurally correct insofar as it applies to men who have married women of Ego's lineage, but as it has derogatory connotations not applicable to the relation between Ego and his FZH, *simenẽ* is used instead (Maybury-Lewis 1967:220). This appears to be simply "a courtesy out of deference to his seniority" (ibid., 228). The word *'rebzu'wa* for MBW is apparently an extension of the term for MB (ibid., 226). The terms *simenẽ* and *'rebzú*, which recur on all three medial generations of the affinal side, are appropriately glossed as "any person who is *wasi're'wa*" ("people separated from me") to Ego (ibid., 217). The distinctions M≠MZ and C≠BC (*ĩ-'ra≠*

aibi/otĩ), finally, do not contradict the kin-affine dichotomy.

Whereas Maybury-Lewis (1967:216; 1971b:382) calls the kin terminology of the Shavante "a simple two-section system," Scheffler (1971:247, note 16) remarks that it "has the Dravidian-Iroquois base," but that it appears to be "incompatible with 'dual organization'." This conclusion is based on the presence of a distinct set of affinal terms, which suggests that the system is more Iroquois than Dravidian. The presence of distinct affinal terms, however, does not contradict dual organization. On the contrary, unlike a Dravidian system, it allows first ascending generation cross-collaterals to be classified as kin or affines, depending on the rule of moiety affiliation (cf. Chapter 21). Thus W. Shapiro (1971:66) finds that the terminology disqualifies as "sib- or moiety-based" because of the presence, rather than absence, of Dravidian features.

Local Group Size and Composition

For 1962, Maybury-Lewis (1967:333) lists population estimates for eight Shavante villages, ranging between 80 and 300 and averaging 183.

Post-marital residence is generally uxorilocal (Maybury-Lewis 1967:86, 308; 1968b; 1979b:233), but males born in the household of the chief tend to reside virilocally (Maybury-Lewis 1967:317).

Patterns of Affiliation Other than Residence

The Western Shavante have patrilineal exogamous moieties, with two exogamous patriclans in one moiety, and a third clan in the other (Maybury-Lewis 1967:75; 1971b: 381; 1979b:233). Though uxorilocality ought in theory to result in the residential dispersal of patrilines, the strategy of a number of

Table 8
KIN TERMINOLOGY OF THE SHAVANTE
LINGUISTIC FAMILY: Central Gê
Male Ego, terms of reference.

GEN.	Male	Female
+ 2	FF î-rdá MF î-rdá	FM î-rdá MM î-rdá

	KIN (Lineal kin, parallel collaterals, affines of affines)		*AFFINES* (In-laws, cross collaterals)	
	Male	Female	Male	Female

+ 1	F î-māmā
	FB î-māmā
	
	MZH î-namté
		M î-datie
		MZ î-nā
		
		FBW asimhî
			WF î-māpari'wa
			MB 'rebzu'wa
			       î-māwapté
			FZH simenē
			       (î-za'mū)
				WM î-māpari'wa
				FZ î-tebe
				
				MBW 'rebzu'wa

0	B e î-dúmrada
	     y î-nō
	FBS e î-dúmrada
	       y î-nō
	MZS e î-dúmrada
	       y î-nō
		Z e î-dúmrada
		    y î-nō
		FBD e î-dúmrada
		       y î-nō
		MZD e î-dúmrada
		       y î-nō
			WB î-āri
			
			MBS simenē
			        'rebzú
			FZS simenē
			       'rebzú
			ZH î-za'mū
				W î-mrō
				
				MBD simenē
				        'rebzú
				FZD simenē
				        'rebzú
				BW asimhî

− 1	S î-'ra
	BS î-'ra
	     aibi
		D î-'ra
		BD î-'ra
		     otî
			DH î-za'mū
			ZS simenē
			      'rebzú
				SW asimhî
				ZD simenē
				      'rebzú

GEN.	Male		Female	
− 2	SS DS	î-nihúdu î-nihúdu	SD DD	î-nihúdu î-nihúdu

SOURCES: Maybury-Lewis 1967:216–217. ZC, when small, is addressed as î-ra-wapté ("a sort of î-'ra (C)"), the reciprocal of î-mawapté ("a sort of î-māmā (F)") for MB (ibid., 227, 229).

DEVIATIONS FROM THE TWO-LINE PATTERN	CONCEIVABLE IDEOLOGICAL OR BEHAVIOURAL CORRELATES
MB≠FZH, FZ≠MBW, MB≠ZH, DH≠ZS, SW≠ZD	Absence of symmetric alliance
FZH=ZH=DH, FBW=BW=SW	Patrilateral affiliation
C=ZC, F=MB (î-ra-wapté/ î-māwapté)	Cognatic principles

brothers to marry a number of sisters serves to maintain lineage cohesion, even to the point where uxorilocal household clusters (segments of the village arc) come to be identified with specific patrilines (Maybury-Lewis 1967:88; 1968b; 1979b:233). Lineages, in fact, are the corporate groups on which the political system is based (1967:169; but cf. W. Shapiro 1971:65 and Murphy 1979:221–222, for a critique of the notion of lineage in this context.) In the village of Areões, factions representing the three clans occupied discrete segments of the village arc, two of which were opposed to the third, according to a dyadic model "complete with twin chiefs" (1967:195). Ego's fellow clansmen are called *waniwihã* ("people of my side"), and distinguished from nonclansmen, *wasi're'wa* ("people separated from me") (ibid.,167). This dichotomy, however, is not completely congruent with the lineality of clans and moieties. While there is a marked antithesis between brothers-in-law, it does not persist through the generations, as F and MB (father's brother-in-law) are not opposed to each other. The term *ĩ-mãwapté* for MB, in fact, means "a sort of F", and Ego's relationship to both categories is characterized by respect reciprocated with affection (ibid.,227–228). The closeness of the MB-ZC bond undoubtedly derives from the practice of uxorilocality, and is formally recognized in a number of ways: the MB introduces his ZS into his first ceremonies, supplies him with *sõ'rebzu* neck-cords, bestows a name on him, and is recognized as his "friend" (*zawi-di*) (ibid., 226, 232–233). The *zawi-di* bond is also said to apply to members of the same age-set (ibid., 164), a relationship which also intersects the patrilineal moieties. Ideally, all age-mates classed as affines are formal friends (*ĩ-amõ*) (ibid., 108).

Maybury-Lewis (ibid., 235) rules out the possibility that name transmission among the Shavante implies succession, as "there is no way in which (ZS) could be said to succeed to the status of the (MB)." Yet, he suspects that "originally a boy was expected to succeed to his maternal uncle's name" (ibid., 233), and notes that some names are connected with particular offices, or roles (ibid., 74, note 1). We have suggested that uxorilocality itself provides a context for MB-ZS succession, in the sense that ZS succeeds his MB as male sibling to the very tangible female matriline of each household. This appears to be the fundamental rationale of male matriliny wherever it occurs among the Gê, and is elsewhere (ibid., 302–303) recognized by Maybury-Lewis in the suggestion that "matrilocality is really a more meaningful concept for (the Apinayé and Timbira peoples) than matrilineality."

Despite the formalized MB-ZS ties among the Shavante, Maybury-Lewis maintains that they are "staunchly" patrilineal, admitting an aspect of matriliny only to women. This latter phenomenon, in fact, reminds him of the parallel affiliation of the Apinayé.

The conjunction of uxorilocal residence and the marriage strategy by which patrilineal groups are kept together, results in the phenomenon that "a lineage which occupies one segment of the village will in the next generation move to another" (Maybury-Lewis 1971b:384). Assuming the dyadic structure reported from Areões, this should amount to an alternation of lineage residence with each generation. Any model of the spatial distribution of lineages, then, is but a momentary representation (Maybury-Lewis 1979b:233). A similar alternation occurs within each household, where WF and DH shift sides with the passing of each generation (Maybury-Lewis 1967:96–97). This continuous spatial alternation of generations has been recognized by the Shavante themselves, and is probably the structural principle on which much of the ceremonial alternation has been modeled. Thus, "alternate age-sets are linked by an especially close tie" (ibid., 112), and both the position of the young men's council relative to that of the mature men, and the position of the bachelor's hut, "alternates with each successive initiation" (ibid., 162).

Hierarchy

The Shavante chief is referred to by the honorific title *he'a*, and the more influential members of his faction are known as *ĩdzu* (ibid., 190–191). Specific Shavante names tend to belong to given patrilines and are sometimes associated with particular ceremonial roles, such as leading the singing and dancing at ceremonies (ibid., 192–193, 235). The name Páhiri'wa, for instance, is generally bestowed on sons of the chief or of his brother, and each of these sons tend to assume ceremonial leadership of an age-set. Two leaders are appointed for each age-set (ibid., 191).

As appears to be universal with uxorilocality, ZH is inferior to the WB, into whose natal household he moves upon marriage (ibid., 85–86, 220, 223, 228). Males of a chief's household avoid such subordination by residing virilocally (ibid., 317). In the fixed order of households around the village arc, the two chiefs tend to occupy the two end houses (aamrã), as it is thought that these "should be occupied by men of some prestige" (ibid., 172, 195, 244, 329). The order of households remains constant "even if the semi-circle is turned 'inside out'." Even though households are uxorilocal, the conscious strategy of groups of brothers to marry groups of sisters results in "a tendency for lineages to be localized in segments of the village semi-circle." This would be consistent with a practice of continued intermarriage between households opposite each other on the village crescent (cf. the Sherente and Dietschy 1977:303). In the case of the two aamrã, the implication would be an ideal of rank endogamy superimposed on the exogamous moieties.

Alliance

In addition to the exogamy of clans and moieties, and the strategy of a group of brothers to marry a group of sisters, there are yet other considerations. As the DH-WF and ZH-WB relationships are clearly asymmetrical, the Shavante avoid direct sister exchange, which would lead to a confusion of statuses and "muddle up a relationship which is of great institutional significance" (Maybury-Lewis 1967:223). The terminological distinctions WB≠ZH and MB≠FZH are

supported by the explicit opinion that these positions cannot simultaneously be occupied by the same man, from the viewpoint of Ego (ibid., 223, 225–226). Since sister exchange is excluded, MBD cannot be FZD (ibid., 228). Yet, the cross-cousins are not terminologically distinguished, but both fall into the category of simenē/'rebzú, which is the category from which a Shavante takes his wife. Within this category of potential spouses, however, the actual MBD is "rarely, if ever, married," since MB is assimilated with the category ĩ-mamã (thus waniwihã) instead of ĩ-mãpari'wa (wasi're'wa). Of FZD marriage, Maybury-Lewis writes that the "Shavante certainly do not forbid such a marriage," but he inclines "to think that they prefer to avoid a situation where Ego would become ĩ-za'mũ (DH) to someone (FZH) who could be his ĩ-za'mũ." The assimilation of FZH with the category of ĩ-za'mũ is based on the definition of this term as "men who have married women of Ego's lineage" (ibid., 220), whereby Ego would inherit the affinal relationship to his father's ZH. It is unlikely, however, that the superiority of WB over ZH could persist as a permanent status discrepancy between patrilineages, since households are alternately dominated by fathers-in-law from opposite clans. The neutralization, or even reversal, of status discrepancies in succeeding generations is consistent with the use of the term simenē for FZH, instead of the derogatory ĩ-za'mũ. Perhaps a more precise glossing of ĩ-za'mũ would be "men who have married zero or descending generation women of Ego's lineage." The fact that actual patrilateral cross-cousin marriage is rare may simply derive from the same kind of exogamic considerations (i.e. a reluctance to marry first cousins) that exclude the MBD, if less emphatically. Maybury-Lewis (ibid., 228–229) admits that his argument is "not wholly satisfactory." An alternation of status in succeeding generations of two patrilines should not pose any difficulties for the Shavante, whose entire society (household structure, distribution of clans, ceremonial life) is based on alternation. Even where status discrepancies between wife-givers and wife-takers are contradicted in the *same* generation, i.e. in the rare cases approaching direct exchange, the ambiguity is resolved by "ignoring the relationship on one side, and proceeding as if there had only been one set of marriages, establishing an asymmetrical relationship rather than some sort of exchange" (ibid., 225).

External Relations

The Shavante have had an aggressive reputation since the late 18th century, and it was not until the 1950:s that the Indian Protection Service established continuous and peaceful contact (ibid., 5). Though there may once have been conflicts with the Tapirapé, the Shavante particularly recognize the Karajá and the Bororo as neighbours and traditional enemies (ibid., 11). Nevertheless, a few trade beads possessed by the Eastern Shavante were obtained by barter from the Karajá (ibid., 12), and there have been reports of military alliances with this tribe (Maybury-Lewis 1965b:350).

8. The Sherente

Kin Terminology (Tables 9 and 10)

In Nimuendajú's (1942) terminology for the Sherente, Lévi-Strauss (1963d:123) notes that FZS=ZS, WB=WBS and FZH=ZH=DH, all of which suggest patrilineal principles. The equations MB=MBS and M=MBD are of the Omaha type (Maybury-Lewis 1965a:222; 1971b:385) and also point to patriliny. On the other hand, Lévi-Strauss observes that Nimuendajú reports several terminological identifications of individuals who would belong to different patrimoieties.

Of these, the equation M=MZ=MZD indicates female matriliny. The equation B=Z=MBC implies either that F and MB are considered more or less equivalent, as among the Shavante, or that the mother's kindred serve as point of departure for some classification.

An absence of symmetric alliance is suggested by the distinction between cross-cousins and by the distinctions MB≠FZH, FZ≠MBW, WB≠ZH, DH≠ZS, and SW≠ZD. The distinction between Z/FBD, on the one hand, and MZD, on the other, suggests that matrilateral parallel cousins are classified as "affines of affines" from the point of view of Ego's patrilineal group (cf. the Tukano-speakers.) The equation MZD=MBD recalls the same ethnographer's version of Apinayé kin terminology, and its anomalous *id-pigukwá* category (cf. Fig. 6). The equation C=BC=FZC, finally, duplicates that of the Suyá and suggests either FZ marriage or, if combined with matrilateral affiliation, FZD marriage. The latter solution would be consistent with a MB-ZS line of succession and a cycle of alternating generations linking F, FZS, and S (cf. Fig. 8). The equation FZS=S would also be compatible with MBD marriage and a unidirectional status discrepancy between wife-givers and lower-ranking wife-takers (FZS="son"). Combined with uxorilocality, the term *i-krã-wapte'* ("a sort of son") could imply that the FZS is regarded as a "substitute" for the sons lost to other households.

Maybury-Lewis (1979b:224–225) found that the Sherente relationship terminology so closely resembles that of the Shavante, that it too is best set out according to a two-line matrix. The Sherente distinguish between *wanõrĩ* and *wasimpkoze*, "a we/they distinction exactly analogous to the Shavante distinction between *waniwihã* and *wasi're'wa*."

The disagreement between Nimuendajú and Maybury-Lewis is slight. The latter denies the use of *ĩ-natké*(-ri'e) for MZD (1958:125) and of *baknõ* for FZD. FZC and

Table 9
ḰIN TERMINOLOGY OF THE SHERENTE (1937)
LINGUISTIC FAMILY: Central Gê
Male Ego, terms of reference.

GEN.	Male		Female	
+ 2	FF *i-krda* MF *i-krda*		FM *i-krda* MM *i-krda*	

	KIN (Lineal kin, parallel collaterals, affines of affines)		*AFFINES* (In-laws, cross collaterals)	
	Male	Female	Male	Female
+ 1	F *i-mumā'* FB *i-mumā'* MZH *i-mumā'*	M *i-natki'* MZ *i-natki'* FBW *i-natki'*	WF *aimāpli'* MB *nōkliekwa'* FZH *i-zakmū'*	WM *aimāpli'* FZ *ī-tbe* MBW *nōkliekwa'*
0	B e *i-kumre'* y *i-nō-ri'e* FBS e *i-kumre'* y *i-nō-ri'e* MZS y *i-nō-ri'e*	Z e *i-kumre'* y *i-nō-ri'e* FBD e *i-kumre'* y *i-nō-ri'e* MZD *i-natki'-ri'e* y *i-nō-ri'e*	WB *aīkā-ri'e* MBS e *i-kumre'* *nōkliekwá-rĭe* FZS *kremzu'* *i-krā-wapte'* ZH *i-zakmū'*	W *i-mrō* MBD e *i-kumre'* *i-natki'-ri'e* FZD *baknō'* *i-krā-wapte'* BW *mizai'* *asimhĭ*
− 1	S *i-krā* BS *i-krā-wapte'* *bremĭ'*	D *i-krā* BD *i-krā-wapte'* *baknō'*	DH *i-zakmū'* ZS *kremzu'* WBS *aīkā-ri'e*	SW *asai'* ZD *kremzu'* WBD *aīkā-ri'e*

	Male		*Female*	
− 2	SS *i-nirdu'* DS *i-nirdu'*		SD *i-nirdu'* DD *i-nirdu'*	

SOURCES: Nimuendajú 1942:23–25. *I-krā-wapte'* means "a sort of *i-krā*"
(cf. Maybury-Lewis 1967:227).

DEVIATIONS FROM THE TWO-LINE PATTERN	CONCEIVABLE IDEOLOGICAL OR BEHAVIOURAL CORRELATES
MB≠FZH, FZ≠MBW, MBC≠FZC, WB≠ZH, DH≠ZS, SW≠ZD	Absence of symmetric alliance
M=MZ=MBD, MB=MBS, FZH=ZH=DH, WB=WBS, FZS=ZS	Patrilateral affiliation
MZ=MZD	Matrilateral affiliation, uxorilocal residence
B=Z=MBC	Cognatic principles, equation F=MB (cf. Maybury-Lewis 1979b:244)
eZ=eFBD≠MZD	Matrilateral parallel cousins classified as "affines of affines" (cf. Tukano-speakers)
C=BC=FZC	FZ, FZD, or MBD marriage (cf. Suyá).

86

ZC are all children of women of Ego's lineage (*kremzú*) (ibid., 126). Instead of classifying all WBC as *aikãrĩ*, Maybury-Lewis gives *asimhĩ* for WBD, which contradicts his (1979b:227) definition of *asimhĩ* as women who have married men of Ego's lineage. The same applies, of course, to the use of *asimhĩ* for WBW. Other cross-moiety identifications include ZH=ZDH (*ĩ-zakmũ*) and SW=ZSW (*asaĩ*). The former of these could possibly be explained as the result of an equation of Z and ZD deriving from uxorilocality, but the latter is as incongruous with exogamous moieties here as it is among the Apinayé, where we have suggested that it may reflect cognatic principles associated with kindred endogamy. Finally, Maybury-Lewis apparently found no evidence for an equation of siblings and MBC, nor for the identification of BC and FZC as "a sort of C".

Maybury-Lewis glosses *asimhĩ* among the Sherente as "any woman who has married a man of Ego's lineage," with the exception of those belonging to Ego's mother's lineage, and of SW (*asaĩ*) (ibid., 227). Among the Shavante, *asimhĩ* includes both BW and SW, but BW is sometimes mentioned by the separate term *saihĩ*, glossed as WZ (Maybury-Lewis 1967:221; 1979b:231). The assimilation of BW and WZ accords well with the strategy of a group of brothers to marry a group of sisters. Among the Sherente, this assimilation has proceeded to the point where they are denoted by the common term *asimhĩ* (Nimuendajú 1942:25). As we have seen, however, the latter distinguish between the BW/WZ, on the one hand, and the SW (*asaĩ*), on the other. If Sherente zero generation terminology appears better adapted to the practice of plural marriage, Maybury-Lewis finds no explanation for why there is a special term for SW, "distinguishing the daughter-in-law from the other women who have married into Ego's lineage" (1979b: 231). This distinction, however, also appears well suited to reflect actual social organization among the Central Gê. As each generation of a patriline shift residence,

asimhĩ (BW/WZ) and *asaĩ* (SW) should belong to separate uxorilocal house-holds. The same interpretation may be offered for the distinction between *kremzú* and *awasnĩ*, i.e. *wasimpkoze* of different generations (Maybury-Lewis 1979b:225, 227).

As in his analysis (1960a) of Apinayé kin terms, Maybury-Lewis' (1958:124; 1979b: 225) aim appears to be to reduce the terminology of the Sherente to as simple a two-line structure as possible. Certainly, a kin-affine dichotomy can be discerned among all the Gê tribes. Once this has been established, however, it is even more rewarding to concentrate on studying *deviations* from the two-line structure. It is from careful analysis of terminological variation that the subtle nuances of Gê classification will be allowed to protrude. By being sensitive to the possible significance of such variation, instead of dismissing the "anomalies" as ethnographical errors, we should attain a fuller foundation for suggesting which variables are relevant to transformation. In defense of the terminologies provided by Nimuendajú, we suggest that it is important not to underestimate the changes which may have taken place since the time of his fieldwork. A vast amount of other, highly detailed data, which have since largely been verified, testifies to the meticulousness with which he recorded his information. Finally, data from other lowland South American tribes sometimes make Nimuendajú's equations seem less anomalous (e.g. the FBC≠MZC distinction of the Tukano-speakers, the FBS=MBS≠MZS equation of the Txicáo, and the equation Z=MZD=MBD/FZD of the Nambikwara dialect C.)

Local Group Size and Composition

In the 1960:s, there were four Sherente villages with a total population of 330 (Maybury-Lewis 1979a:215), i.e. an average of 83 in each. Early reports suggest considerably larger villages (Nimuendajú 1942:7, 11).

Table 10
KIN TERMINOLOGY OF THE SHERENTE (1956)
LINGUISTIC FAMILY: Central Gê
Male Ego, terms of reference.

GEN.	Male		Female	
+ 2	FF *ĩ-krdá*		FM *ĩ-krdá*	
	MF *ĩ-krdá*		MM *ĩ-krdá*	

	KIN (Lineal kin, parallel collaterals, affines of affines)		*AFFINES* (In-laws, cross collaterals)	
	Male	Female	Male	Female
+ 1	F *ĩ-mumã*	M *ĩ-natké*	WF *aimãplĩ*	WM *aimãplĩ*
	FB *ĩ-mumã*	MZ *ĩ-natké*	MB *nõkliekwá*	FZ *ĩ-tbe*
	MZH *ĩ-mumã*	FBW *ĩ-natké*	FZH *ĩ-zakmũ*	MBW *nõkliekwá*
0	B e *ĩ-kumrẽ*	Z e *ĩ-kumrẽ*	WB *aikãrĩ*	W *ĩ-mrõ*
	y *ĩ-nõrĩ*	y *ĩ-nõrĩ*		
	FBS e *ĩ-kumrẽ*	FBD e *ĩ-kumrẽ*	MBS *nõkliekwá*	MBD *ĩ-natké*
	y *ĩ-nõrĩ*	y *ĩ-nõrĩ*		
	MZS e *ĩ-kumrẽ*	MZD e *ĩ-kumrẽ*	FZS *kremzú*	FZD *kremzú*
	y *ĩ-nõrĩ*	y *ĩ-nõrĩ*		
		WBW *asimhĩ*	ZH *ĩ-zakmũ*	BW *asimhĩ*
– 1	S *ĩ-kra*	D *ĩ-kra*	DH *ĩ-zakmũ*	SW *asaĩ*
	BS *bremĩ*	BD *baknõ*	ZS *kremzú*	ZD *kremzú*
	ZDH *ĩ-zakmũ*	ZSW *asaĩ*	WBS *aikãrĩ*	WBD *asimhĩ*

	Male		*Female*	
– 2	SS *ĩ-nihrdú*		SD *ĩ-nihrdú*	
	DS *ĩ-nihrdú*		DD *ĩ-nihrdú*	

SOURCES: Maybury-Lewis 1958:132–134; 1979b:225.

DEVIATIONS FROM THE TWO-LINE PATTERN	CONCEIVABLE IDEOLOGICAL OR BEHAVIOURAL CORRELATES
MB≠FZH, FZ≠MBW, MBC≠FZC, WB≠ZH, DH≠ZS, SW≠ZD	Absence of symmetric alliance
M=MZ=MBD, MB=MBS, FZH=ZH=DH, WB=WBS, FZS=ZS	Patrilateral affiliation
WBW=WBD, ZH=ZDH	Matrilateral affiliation, uxorilocal residence
BW=WBW, SW=ZSW	Cognatic principles

After a mid-20th century nadir, the population had increased to approximately 800 in 1979 (Maybury-Lewis 1979a:215).

Post-marital residence is uxorilocal (Maybury-Lewis 1967:303, 308; 1971b:384; 1979b:232), but, by marrying groups of sisters, groups of brothers tend to stick together as among the Shavante (Maybury-Lewis 1979b:228, 233). This explains why Nimuendajú (1942:16, 23, 31, 32), and initially even Maybury-Lewis (1958:131; 1979b:232–233), perceived the Sherente as "patrilocal".

Patterns of Affiliation Other than Residence

Closely related to the Shavante (cf. Maybury-Lewis 1965b), the Sherente duplicate their system of exogamous patrilineal clans and moieties (Nimuendajú 1942:9, 16; Maybury-Lewis 1967:301–303, 308). Chieftainship is transmitted patrilineally (Nimuendajú 1942:16; Lowie 1946b:489). There are four men's associations cross-cutting the two moieties *šiptato'* (South) and *sdakrã* (North) (Nimuendajú 1942:50, 59–64). Recruitment to these is such that a boy is "kept from joining his father's organization" (ibid., 43). Male names are transmitted within each moiety "patrilineally to grandsons and great-nephews" (Nimuendajú 1942:17, 44; Lowie 1946b:493), female names "from the moiety of their maternal uncle" (Nimuendajú 1942: 22), according to "some rule, the father's association being the decisive factor" (ibid., 54).

Nimuendajú failed to obtain the details of female name transmission. This is unfortunate, as there are reasons to believe that rules relating to female name transmission would have provided a key to understanding how Sherente affiliation and alliance may have interlocked. Whereas male names are the property of the moieties, female names are the property of particular associations (ibid., 43, 52, 63). Discussing extramarital intercourse, Nimuendajú (ibid., 63–64) reports that the association which had conferred a name on a wanton "*ipso facto* laid claims to her." It is reasonable to assume that the same would have applied to marriage. This would be consistent with Nimuendajú's assertion that "at all events it is never the society of the girl's father that confers the name on her" (ibid., 54). Furthermore, "an adulteress divorced by her husband was taken by her maternal uncle to the place of assembly of some society not her father's and there surrendered for sexual intercourse" (ibid., 64). It is highly significant that female names among the closely related Shavante are transferred by representatives of the age-sets (which, as we shall see, may have been the original foundation for Sherente associations) who hold the office of "baby makers" (*aiuté'mañãrĩ'wa*) (Maybury-Lewis 1958:130; 1967:151–152). The "baby makers" danced with the named girls, pursued them to their huts, and pounded on the thatch. Since Maybury-Lewis writes that "the prerogative of officiating as 'baby makers' is held by one lineage at a time," it is difficult to see whether these acted as representatives of their age-set or of their lineage. Possibly, the age-sets acted *on behalf* of particular constituent lineages, the latter of which were the rightful entities to lay claims to a particular category of girls. The fact that contemporary Shavante girls are often married by the time they receive their names is undoubtedly a recent disruption brought about by demographic decline.

Nimuendajú conjectures that the transfer of female names by the members of one association to the daughters of those of another follows a specific sequence: *ake'mha – annõrowa' – krara' – krieri'ekmũ – ake'mha* (1942:54, 61). He found, however, instances where this order was reversed (from *krara'* to *annõrowa*, and from *krieri'ekmũ* to *krara'*). Nimuendajú (ibid., 64) explicitly denies that the associations figure in connection with marriage. Lévi-Strauss (1963d:125, 126) nevertheless interprets the various permutations of the circuit of men's associations as if "each moiety were composed of two marriage classes in a system of generalized exchange." His illustrations of this structure, however, are selected from among a number of ceremonial constellations reported by Nimuendajú, some of which contradict Lévi-Strauss' model. The organization of mask-making does accord with his model (but cf. Maybury-Lewis 1958:127–128), but the age sequence of the associations deriving from the origin myth (*ake'mha – krara' – annõrowa' – krieri'ekmũ*), and formerly recognized on the warpath, is *not* congruent with the sequence relevant to female name transmission, to transfer from one association to another, or, in reverse order, to the transfer of the Padi rite (Nimuendajú 1942:59–60, 61; cf. W. Crocker 1979 for an account of the transmission of festival rites among the Ramkokamekra.) Furthermore, the marriage-class interpretation of the men's associations is contradicted by Nimuendajú's assertion that each association has two leaders, one from each moiety (ibid., 12, 60), by the fact that the stock of female names belonging to each association is transmitted to girls of both moieties (ibid., 54–55), and by the diagram of the bachelors' hut, showing how the four associations cut across the two moieties (ibid., 50). Although it is conceivable that the several alignments suggestive of a four-section system represent vestiges of a yet earlier arrangement (cf. Fig. 10), the four men's associations encountered by Nimuendajú were *not* grouped two by two into exogamous moieties, but were all intersected by them. The exogamic *šiptato'/sdakrã* dichotomy necessitates a distinction of eight, rather than four, categories of men.

If, as in the case of wantons, an association could claim for marriage the women upon whom it had conferred names, it can be seen that the rules of female name transmission are of vital significance. It will be recalled that the association of the girl's father is excluded, yet that this very association is the "decisive factor" determining name transmission. As we have been told that female names are transmitted from the moiety of the girl's maternal uncle, a reasonable conjecture is that the association from which she derives her name (and spouse) represents affines of her father (either his WB or ZH, i.e. the girl's MB or FZH). Since each association has members from both moieties, it is conceivable that the moiety division within each association (as evident, for instance, in the spatial organization of the bachelors' hut) is recognized in this context. In fact, if Nimuendajú had not explicitly excluded the association of the girl's father as name-giver, and denied patrilineal

recruitment to the associations, we would have suggested that the men's associations were endogamous groups superimposed on the exogamous moieties, and that the double transfers of girl's names (ibid., 43, 54–55) represented the claims of each half of an association on the daughters of the other half. Indeed, as will be demonstrated, there are reasons to believe that the chief's marriage was endogamous to his own association, the *krara'*. Given the exclusion of the father's association as name-giver and the dispersal of patrilines through the associations, we must assume that this was a privileged exception, and consider a circuit such as that thought by Nimuendajú to determine the transfer of female names. It should be remembered, however, that such a circuit resembles Lévi-Strauss' model of generalized exchange in a formal sense only: in each case of name transmission or intermarriage, the exogamic moiety division cross-cutting the associations would have to be taken into consideration.

Given four associations and the rule that a son does not succeed his father, there are three possible alternatives for recruitment to the associations. Assuming that female name transmission and marriage connects the four associations unilaterally according to a fixed sequence, only one of these alternatives locates the two kinds of cross-cousins in different associations, complying with the terminological distinction between cross-cousins and with the unilateral marriage ideals. If male Ego consistently joins the association opposite to that of his F in the quadripartite circuit, there is a structural separation of the two cross-cousins (Fig. 7). Ego replicates the position of his FF, which is consistent with male name transmission. Moreover, the maternal uncle of Ego's potential spouse belongs to Ego's own association, which is consistent with the focal role of the girl's MB in female name transmission. These congruities support Lévi-Strauss' (1963d:126) hypothesis of MBD marriage among the ancestors of the Sherente, and his model of a circuit of generalized exchange cycling back and forth betwen the two patrimoieties. On the other hand, Nimuendajú's (1942:25) claim that male Ego may marry his FZD, but *not* his MBD, would be equally consistent with the principle of alternating generations determining male name transmission, and also with the observation that the order of the four men's associations in female name transmission can be reversed (as would be the case in alternate generations of a system of patrilateral cross-cousin marriage.) Furthermore, the exclusion of the MBD follows logically from the assimilation of the MB with the category of "father" (Maybury-Lewis 1979b:242–244). The role of the MB as Ego's "father" in the opposite moiety is evident in a number of contexts (Nimuendajú 1942:28, 29, 37, 58–59, 63, 64, 65; Lowie 1946b:493; Lévi-Strauss 1963d:124). (On Ego's own side of the village, same-sex parallel aunts and uncles (i.e. a girl's MZ and a boy's FB) serve as substitute parents in ceremonial contexts (Nimuendajú 1942:46, 49, 54, 55, 58), as among the Apinayé and Kayapó.)

Even if succession to the men's associations at the time of Nimuendajú's fieldwork was from FF to SS, or had deteriorated to following no "fixed rule" at all (Nimuendajú 1942:43) , several circumstances suggest that these, like the plaza groups of the Eastern Timbira, previously had a matrilineal aspect. We know that the men's associations, the essence of which is their stock of feminine names, cut across the patrilineal moieties. The MB is Ego's "father" in the opposite moiety, and his daughter is excluded from marriage. If the associations represented double lines of MB-ZS succession crossing back and forth between the moieties, and there was an inclination toward FZD marriage, membership would be transmitted from Ego's F *via* his FZS (WB) to his S (Fig. 8; cf. equation FZS=S). From the point of view of Ego's patrilineal moiety, this would be congruent with male name transmission

from FF to SS. In other words, the matrilineal lines of men constituting the men's associations, cycling between the two patrilineal moieties, would produce the system of alternating generations codified in male name transmission. It is conceivable that the quadripartition reported by Nimuendajú, which in any case places Ego and his MB in separate associations, was the result of a subdivision of matrilineal moieties (cf. Lévi-Strauss 1963d:126) in connection with a shift to unilateral marriage. The possibility that the Sherente pattern of FF-SS succession represents a permutation of a MB-ZS line would be consistent with the almost universal occurrence of MB-ZS name transmission among the Gê (cf. the Krahó, Ramkokamekra, Krîkatî, Apinayé, Kayapó, Suyá, Bororo, and even the closely related Shavante.) In most of these tribes, in fact, a transfer between alternate generations is explicitly and terminologically an alternative to MB-ZS transmission.

We have been told that the FZD is an acceptable spouse, but not the MBD. We also have reason to believe that male Ego can claim for marriage a girl upon whom his own association has conferred a name. From Nimuendajú's (1942:43) description of Bruẽ's initiation into the *krara'*, we would infer that the *sdakrā* girl's MB, to whom Bruẽ handed the decorative outfit which would be transferred to the girl together with her name, was a classificatory FB of Bruẽ (Fig. 9). The girl's MB, as her protector in the opposite moiety, served as mediator between her (Bruẽ's "FZD") and her potential spouse, who, by having conferred her name, could later claim her for marriage. The role of the FB as mediator between male Ego and his affines again recalls the Apinayé and Kayapó. Bruẽ, the girl's MB (Bruẽ's "FB"), and the girl's F exemplify the triad which Lévi-Strauss (1963d:124) found "incompatible" with dual organization. By inference from the clues provided by Nimuendajú, the girl's F would have belonged to the *krieri'ekmũ* association and

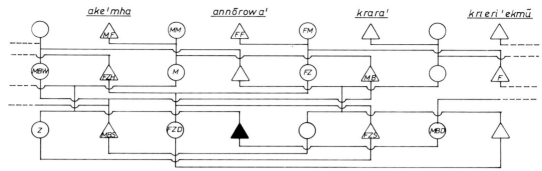

Fig. 7. Hypothetical alliance structure of the Sherente, assuming that male Ego marries a daughter of a member of the association subsequent to his own, and is recruited to the association opposite to that of his father in the quadripartite circuit.

the *sdakrã* moiety, Bruĕ's classificatory FB (the girl's MB), like Bruĕ himself, to the *krara'* association and the *šiptato'* moiety, and Bruĕ's F to the *šiptato'* moiety but not to the *krara'* association. (The structural distinction between classificatory brothers (Bruĕ's F and "FB"), reminiscent of the Apinayé, is a matter to which we shall shortly return.) In accordance with the ideal of symmetrical name transfers (Nimuendajú 1942:54–55), we may assume that a *krara'* of the *sdakrã* moiety (a classificatory MB of Bruĕ) simultaneously mediated a name transfer from a classificatory MBS to one of Bruĕ's classificatory sisters (a daughter of a *krieri'ekmŭ* in the *šiptato'* moiety.)

Actually, Nimuendajú informs us that Bruĕ upon marriage did not choose a daughter of a *krieri'ekmŭ*, nor even of a *sdakrã*. In view of a factional dispute between the *šiptato'* and *sdakrã* moieties (cf. the Kayapó), Bruĕ chose to marry not his FZD Krĕdi, which would have been natural, but a girl of his own moiety, his MBDD Waktidi' (ibid., 26). From Nimuendajú's conviction that feminine names are bestowed between the associations according to a specific sequence, and from his report that the name Waktidi' is conferred by the *annõrowa'* (ibid., 55), we must conclude that Bruĕ married not only within his own moiety but even within his own association,

the *krara'*. Chief Bruĕ's marriage is an obvious case of privileged endogamy, parallel to instances attributed to the Cera moiety of the Bororo, and must be comprehended in its uxorilocal context.

Nimuendajú's account of traditional Sherente culture often amounts to a reconstruction of what he assumed it to have been, prior to the dissolution he felt he was witnessing in the 1930:s (Nimuendajú 1942:8; Maybury-Lewis 1979b:219). This reconstruction assumed two exogamous patrilineal moieties, each containing four localized patriclans. Each clan maintained a special bond, the *narkwá* relationship, with the one located directly opposite to it on the traditional, horseshoe-shaped village arc (Nimuendajú 1942:9, 23). The last major village with such a horseshoe design disappeared shortly after the turn of the century (ibid., 11). Since each clan had its assigned place on the village arc (ibid., 16–17; Lowie 1946b:491), postmarital residence was assumed to be "patrilocal" (Nimuendajú 1942:23). Maybury-Lewis (1979b:232), however, has shown that residence is uxorilocal. As each generation of a patriline must shift household, the spatial distribution of clans recognized by Nimuendajú can only have represented a temporary state of affairs. Should there have been specific bonds of alliance uniting

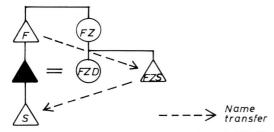

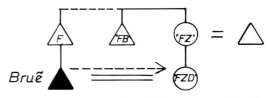

Fig. 8. The congruity of MB-ZS and FF-SS transmission in a system of patrilateral or bilateral cross-cousin marriage.

Fig. 9. An interpretation of the context of Bruĕ's initiation (Nimuendajú 1942:43).

pairs of clans from opposite moieties, it is conceivable that the spatial arrangement of clans along the village arc simply was inverted with every new generation, while the underlying order was preserved (Fig. 10). Each pair of clans would have formed an endogamous group, much as has been suggested for the Apinayé and the Bororo (cf. Lévi-Strauss 1963d:129). Nimuendajú (1942:21) also remarks that such *narkwá* pairs occupy different status positions, which suggests a rationale for endogamy. It is interesting to note Nimuendajú's claim that one clan in each moiety (the Prase' and Krozake' clans) was regarded as an alien tribe incorporated into the Sherente (Nimuendajú 1942:19, 20, 22; Maybury-Lewis 1979b:224). Such ethnic representations of specific, more or less endogamous social enclaves are widespread among stratified societies, and call to mind the low-ranking Makú of the north-west Amazon. Precisely as have the Makú, the Prase'/Krozake' stratum distinguished itself for not observing the ideals of exogamy (Nimuendajú 1942:25).

We regret that Nimuendajú does not provide us with any information on the extent to which the *narkwá* pairs and the men's associations were congruent. Both kinds of division, we observe, cut across the two moieties and are four in number. Moreover, both are represented as having originally been three, the fourth element being a subsequent addition.

When Maybury-Lewis worked among the Sherente in the 1950:s, he too had the impression that their social organization had grown "hazy" and was an "organizational shambles" (1979b:223; cf. 1958:130). The exogamy of moieties, clans, and lineages was ideal rather than real (1979b:223–224). Yet, the two-section relationship terminology, with its *waňorĩ/wasimpkoze* dichotomy distinguishing kin from potential spouses, was "perfectly adapted" to, and ideally congruent with, the obsolescent Wairĩ'/Doĩ moiety system (ibid., 224, 228; 1965a:222–223). Maybury-Lewis therefore set out to discover how the Sherente used the relationship terminology "at a time when they no longer knew people's moiety affiliations." He found that people knew which lineage, and therefore which clan, other members of the community belonged to, and that clan membership determined whether a person was referred to as *waňorĩ* or *wasimpkoze* (1979b:229). In other words, even if the moieties had been lost, they were implicitly remembered through the survival of their constituent clans and the continued application of the two-line terminology.

Hierarchy

Chieftainship, associated with specific emblems, is inherited patrilineally (Nimuendajú 1942:13, 16; Lowie 1946b:489). Diarchy is strongly developed, as "virtually all offices are dual, i.e. held by one representative of each moiety" (Nimuendajú 1942:12, 18, 60, 62, 65, 76). The office of village chief

93

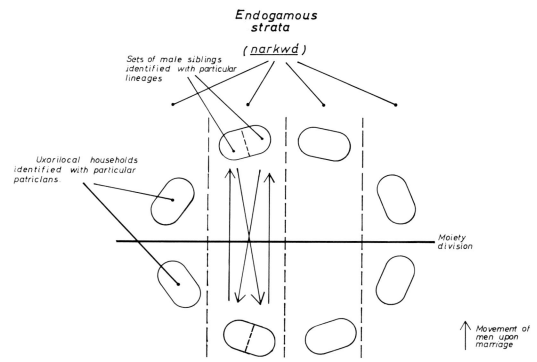

Fig. 10. Schematic reconstruction of the spatial manifestation of Sherente alliance structure, prior to the dissolution of village layouts *c*. 1900. (Should unilateral FZD marriage have been general, the alliance circuit and the positions of allied lineages and clans would have been reversed in each generation.)

is an exception. Although Nimuendajú claims that the chief is "selected irrespective of his moiety," Bruë's successor would have been the seventh in a dynasty of patrilineal kin, which must all have been *šiptato'* (ibid., 16, 18). The only other exception is "the allotment of the name Waktidi', invariably borne by a single girl of the *šiptato'* moiety." It can scarcely be a coincidence that this was the name of the chief's (Bruë's) wife (ibid., 26). Bruë's marriage, as we have seen, appears to be a case of privileged endogamy.

In addition to chieftainship, there are indications of other hereditary status positions. The patrilineal clans appear to be associated with different ceremonial privileges (ibid., 21–23; Lévi-Strauss 1963d:121). The two innermost clans of the village horse-shoe, the Kuze' and Krẽprehi' clans

respectively to the south and north of the village axis (the "path of the Sun" separating the two moieties), "occupy a preferential status." This status is apparently connected with specific masculine names, such as the "greatest" of names, Sliemtõi, which is reserved for members of the Kuze' clan (Nimuendajú 1942:45). Considering our earlier suggestion that there may have been a correspondence between the four men's associations and the four pairs of *narkwá* clans, it is interesting to note that the spatial organization of the men's associations in the bachelors' hut reproduces the dimension of rank evident in the village layout. Precisely as the Kuze'/Krẽprehi' clans are located in the easternmost apex of the village horseshoe, the "oldest" of the men's associations (the *krieri'ekmũ*) occupies the easternmost part of the bachelors' hut (Nimuendajú 1942:50, 59–61). Significantly, the "next oldest" association (the *annōrowa'*) occupies the westernmost part, by the door, a position formally analogous to that of the prestigious *aamrã* (the two end households of the horseshoe) of the closely related Shavante. Although the "incorporated tribes", the Prase' and Krozake', are received with a derogatory attitude (ibid., 20), suggesting that their positions in the horseshoe (corresponding to the *aamrã* of the Shavante) are low in prestige, this is contradicted by Bruẽ's (i.e. the village chief's) marriage to the daughter of a Prase' man (ibid., 26). The girl, moreover, bore the ceremonially distinguished name Waktidi' (ibid., 18, 55–56). Apparently, positions at the extreme eastern or extreme western end of the horseshoe are both connected with prestige among the Central Gê, although it seems that the Sherente and Shavante have assigned absolute pre-eminence to opposite directions. As both positions have in common the proximity to the central axis, it is interesting to recall Lévi-Strauss' (1963e:145) suggestion that privileged clans among the Bororo should be contiguous with one of the two axes. Although this hypothesis is classed by Maybury-Lewis (1960b:26) as "fragile", Lave (1979:42–43), in a similar vein, notes that older Krĩkatĩ males derive political advantage from locating their households so as to keep in touch with both their consanguineal and affinal domestic clusters.

The hierarchical representation of the four men's associations in terms of relative age, with "older" groups addressing "younger" groups as "sons" (Nimuendajú 1942:59–60), would be consistent with a system of generalized exchange, in which each wife-giving uxorilocal group, being the post-marital residence of its wife-taking group's "sons", is referred to as "sons" by this latter group. We have noted, however, that the age sequence of the four associations recognized, for instance, on the warpath, is not identical to the circuit by which feminine names are transferred. Considering the likelihood that name transmission implies a right to claim the girl in marriage, this incongruity remains an unsolved problem. Also contradicting such an interpretation of the age hierarchy, the unidirectional status discrepancy between *i-zakmũ* (ZH) and *aikãri* (WB), which again duplicates Shavante conditions (Maybury-Lewis 1967:220; 1979b:228), implies that wife-givers are ranked higher than wife-takers. In fact, this is fundamental to uxorilocality. Lévi-Strauss (1963d:123) took the unidimensional relationship between brothers-in-law as an indication of matrilateral cross-cousin marriage (on Lévi-Strauss' apparent confusion of *aikãri* and *aimãplĩ*, cf. Maybury-Lewis 1958:127). An interpretation of the hierarchy of groups addressing each other as *wa-kra* ("sons") that would be consistent with Lévi-Strauss' interpretation of the *i-zakmũ/aikãri* relationship would connect the *wa-kra* usage with the terminological equation of FZS and S (*i-krã-wapte'* = "a sort of son"). Among the Shavante, the *i-krã-wapte'* category classifies the ZS, rather than FZS, as "a sort of son" (cf. Maybury-Lewis 1967:227, 229). In both cases, the "sons" would be wife-takers in a context of MBD marriage, the difference being whether the perspective of the WF (Shavante) or WB (Sherente) is applied. If the group which Ego calls *wa-kra* contains his sister's sons or father's sister's sons, and these may claim their matrilateral cross-cousin (Ego's D or Z, respectively) for marriage, the age hierarchy of the four associations would be consistent with the higher rank of wife-givers evident in the relationship between brothers-in-law. The implication of *wa-kra* and *i-krã-wapte'* would be "sons-in-law" or "substitute sons", rather than "sons' group".

The Shavante distinction between FZH and ZH/DH, implying differences of age and status, does not appear to have been employed by the Sherente. On the other hand, a similar principle may be responsible for the distinction between *kremzú* and *awasnĩ*, i.e. between *wasimpkoze* ("other side people") younger/equal and older respectively in relation to Ego (Maybury-Lewis 1979b:225, 227). Both distinctions may reflect the residential alternation of consecutive generations of male *wasimpkoze*.

Apparently cross-cutting all the clans and associations, a class of prestigious and eminent dignitaries (including the village chiefs, leaders of men's associations, etc.) is distinguished by the celebration of a special funeral rite, the *aikmã*, in their honour (Nimuendajú 1942:10, 12, 35, 100).

Alliance

According to Nimuendajú, a Sherente may marry his FZD but not his MBD (Nimuendajú 1942:25; Lowie 1946b:492; Lévi-Strauss 1963d:123; Needham 1958b:212; 1962:102; Maybury-Lewis 1979b:218). On the other hand, there is a tendency to marry close matrilateral kin, as long as the actual MBD is avoided (Nimuendajú 1942:26; Lowie 1946b: 492; Needham 1962:102). These data comply with Needham's (1962:109–110) observation that consistent FZD marriage will yield an identification of FZD and MMBDD. Just as we have suggested for the Apinayé, the Sherente tendency to marry close matrilateral kin indicates that FZD marriage may simply have been the unintentional result of an ideal of matrilateral marriage in conjunction with the MBD prohibition. The MBD prohibition, of course, follows from the special position of the MB as a close kinsman in the affinal moiety (Maybury-Lewis 1979b: 243). The implied unilateral (matrilateral) slant in genealogical reckoning is well illustrated in the marriage of Shernã', son of Bruẽ. His marriage to Sibedi', who is his MMFZDD but simultaneously (and at closer range) his FMZDD, is described by Nimuendajú (1942:26), and probably perceived by the Sherente, as a union with "the granddaughter of his matrilineal great-aunt."

The ideal of matrilateral marriage is also illustrated in the endogamous marriage of Bruẽ himself, to his MBDD. For male Ego, matrilateral marriage is equivalent to replicating the marriage of one's father.

Maybury-Lewis (1979b:227–228) writes that Ego cannot marry his *ĩ-natke*, "that is, any woman in his mother's clan." In his list of kinship terms, however, he defines *ĩ-natke* as "any female in Ego's mother's lineage." As a clan may be represented by more than one lineage, this latter definition would not exclude repeated intermarriage between a pair of clans. Theoretically, it would amount to patrilateral cross-cousin marriage, requiring at least two lineages in each of the participant clans. As "it was regarded as a good thing for a group of brothers to marry a group of sisters" (ibid.), and sororal polygyny was "regarded as proper" (Nimuendajú 1942:26; Lowie 1946b:492), the implication is that alliances between lineages were expected to follow a predetermined pattern. The model (Fig. 10) corresponds to Lévi-Strauss' (1963d:125) diagram of generalized exchange within a system of exogamous moieties. Lévi-Strauss discovered that this structure, with its inherent alternation, permeated Sherente ceremonial life, e.g. the order of the four men's associations, which may have been modeled after circuits of alliance. This hypothesis appears more feasible when we consider that post-marital residence is uxorilocal, rather than virilocal. Exactly as we have suggested for the Shavante, the residential alternation of patrilines would present a very tangible manifestation of the alliance cycle. Once perceived in some form by the actors themselves, the model may have been transcribed onto the ceremonial ideology. Lévi-Strauss' suggestion that the associations were equivalent to marriage classes, two in each moiety and linked by MBD marriage, needs significant modification in order to be applicable to the Sherente of Nimuendajú's time. The facts that the associations, like the moieties, had rights to specific wantons (Nimuendajú 1942:16–17, 63–64; cf. the Eastern Timbira, Nimuendajú 1946:96), and that an adulterous relationship of Ego's wife with a fellow-member legitimizes his transference to another association (Nimuendajú 1942:60), suggest that they were relevant to alliance. Even if joined in an alliance circuit, however, we know that no association was assigned in its entirety to one or the other of the moieties. Even if Ego married into a predetermined association, he would have to take the exogamous moieties into consideration. As we have already suggested, the effect is a distinction of eight, rather than four, categories of men. The structure explored in Fig. 7 would be congruent with Lévi-Strauss' model of a two-by-two grouping of the associations, i.e. it does not require that the associations enrol men of both moieties. This may, as we have indicated, represent an earlier state of affairs. When the associations are intersected by the moieties, however, the formation of two endogamous circuits is inevitable.

Another modification required in Lévi-Strauss' model is the MBD prohibition. The facts that the FZD is eligible, and that there is a tendency to marry close matrilateral kin, would be consistent with an alliance structure in which a large proportion of marriages approximated the FZD/MMBDD category (Fig. 11). Formally, FZD marriage would be compatible with the quadripartite alliance circuit only if the sequence were reversed in each generation. This is consistent with Nimuendajú's report that the sequence of female name transmission can be reversed, although apparently maintaining the same order.

As has been shown to be the case also with MBD marriage, the only possible way in which FZD marriage can be reconciled with the quadripartite circuit, and the rule that a man does not join the association of his F, is if Ego consistently joins the association of his FF, whose name he also shares. This is consistent with a two-by-two moiety alignment of the four associations. Male

Ego's WB and ZH would represent the two associations of the opposite moiety, and F the other association of Ego's own moiety. Although consistent with such a moiety alignment, the FF-SS succession does not necessarily imply that an entire association can be assigned to one or the other moiety. Precisely as would be the case with MBD marriage, the fact that each association enrols men of both moieties indicates that there must be more than one alliance circuit.

In response to Lévi-Strauss, Maybury-Lewis (1958:132) suggested that the endogamous subgroups of the Bororo and Apinayé "cannot be likened to the Sherente associations or the Canella age-classes, simply because these latter institutions involve a cyclical rotation." The point we have been making here, however, is that each such rotation (and there should be at least two) would formally constitute an endogamous subgroup. If this conclusion is legitimate, Lèvi-Strauss' (1963d:130) "underlying structure" has been expressed among the Sherente, as well.

External Relations

Prior to *c.* 1850, the Sherente had hostile relations with the Shavante, the Krahó, the Karajá, and the Neobrazilians (Nimuendajú 1942:6–7,74–75; but cf. report on Sherente-Shavante-Karajá alliance in Maybury-Lewis 1965b:350). The Sherente "lived in amity," however, with the Kayapó, whom they joined in a commercial descent of the Araguaia-Tocantins River in 1806 (Maybury-Lewis 1965b:350).

Nimuendajú notes that "vestiges" of co-operation and a "sense of racial solidarity" united the several Sherente settlements, and that tribal integration was politically manifest in the council of village chiefs (Nimuendajú 1942:9–10; Lowie 1946b:489). Maybury-Lewis (1979b:221–222), however, reports that factionalism, hostility, and feuding characterize relationships between con-

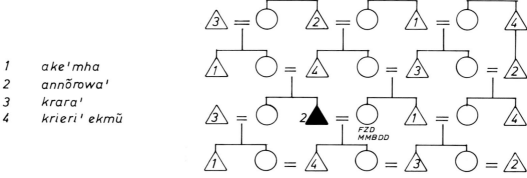

1   a ke' mha
2   annõrowa'
3   krara'
4   krieri' ekmũ

Fig. 11. Implications of consistent marriage with a FZD/MMBDD in the context of the quadripartite circuit of Sherente men's associations. (Note that the presence of men of both moieties in each association, reported by Nimuendajú, implies that there must have been at least two endogamous categories.)

temporary Sherente communities, resulting in their comparative isolation.

9. The Caingang

Kin Terminology

The list of kin terms provided by Henry (1941:177–178) is highly classificatory. Siblings and first cousins are all classified as *nyungnyên*. There are categories denoting all males considerably older than Ego (*yûgn*), all females considerably older than Ego (*nyô*), all people somewhat younger than Ego (*yavi*), all people much younger than Ego (*yi* = child), sexually accessible females (*plu* = wife), and kin of sexually accessible females, i.e. "affines" (*yômblâ*).

Local Group Size and Composition

The Caingang live in small nomadic bands made up of men related as brothers, as fathers and children, or as affines (ibid., 9, 97). Henry (ibid., xxi) estimates that the total population at Duque de Caxias in 1914 may have been between 300 and 400, but by the early 1930:s epidemics had reduced it to 106.

Métraux (1946:447) mentions a census from 1827 listing five groups in the Guarapuava region with a total population of 972 and an average of 194. Apparently, some of these groups "are simply appellations of moiety or class subdivisions" (ibid., 446), while some are true subgroups.

Post-marital residence was formerly uxorilocal, but neolocality has become increasingly frequent (ibid., 464).

Patterns of Affiliation Other than Residence

Métraux (ibid., 461–462) notes that Baldus found exogamous patrilineal moieties among the Caingang of Palmas. The Aweikoma-Caingang studied by Henry had no moieties (Henry 1941:36), but a division into five theoretically exogamous groups (*kôika he*), each associated with a particular body-paint design and a set of personal names (ibid., 175–176). Henry (ibid., 59, 88) suggests that Caingang society "shows traces of what may once have been a more complex social system," and Métraux (1946:462), concludes that "a former patrilineal clan system is indicated" (cf. Nimuendajú 1946:82–93). In fact, some of the body-paint designs are identical to those distinguishing the patrilineal clans of the Shavante (cf. Maybury-Lewis 1967:166). The significance of patrilateral affiliation is evident from patrilineal succession to chieftainship (Métraux 1946:463), the inheritance of "paternal loyalties" (Henry 1941:97; cf. the patrilineal inheritance of formal friendships among the Apinayé, Kayapó, and Suyá), and the recruitment of ceremonial parents (kôkla and mbe) from among the affinal relatives of the child's father (ibid., 104).

Hierarchy

According to Baldus, the two moieties at Palmas were each split into two groups, and the four resultant subgroups were ordered "according to their prestige as follows: Votóro, Kadnyerú (Kañerú), Aniky, and Kamé" (Métraux 1946:461). Among these Caingang of Palmas, the father decided to which of the two subgroups of his moiety the child would belong. Although Métraux notes that "the reason for this preferential ranking could not be ascertained," the rank order is consistent with Nimuendajú's earlier report from the Caingang between the Tieté and Ijuhí Rivers (ibid., 462). Nimuendajú observes that their two moieties are associated with the ancestral twins Kañerú and Kamé, the former of whom was "fiery and resolute," the latter "mentally and physically slow." Each of these two moieties was divided into three (formerly four) ranked classes (cf. Nimuendajú 1946:98), one of which was called Votóro, superimposed on the Kañerú/Kamé dichotomy. In battle, members of the Kadnyerú moiety always form the first line, whereas the Kamé function as a reserve (Métraux 1946:467; cf. the order of the four Sherente subgroups formerly recognized on the warpath, and W. Crocker 1979:248, note 17, on "warrior" troops in Ramkokamekra festival rites.)

The fact that the subgroups reported by Baldus were distinguished by their facial painting suggests that the five body-paint groups listed by Henry may have had a similar origin. Much as the body-paint designs theoretically determine marriage patterns among the Aweikoma-Caingang (Henry 1941:88, 176), Horta Barboza reports that the subgroups of the exogamous Kadnyerú/Kamé moieties are juxtaposed so that individuals of a certain Kadnyerú subgroup can only marry individuals of a particular Kamé subgroup, and vice versa (Métraux 1946:462). The articulation of a quadripartite hierarchy and prescribed alliances between subgroups of the exogamous moieties suggests either rank endogamy or Lévi-Strauss' model of generalized exchange. Recruitment to the subgroups, however, is indeterminate (Henry 1941:176; Métraux 1946:461–462).

Chieftainship is patrilineally inherited (Métraux 1946:463), and there are indications that polygyny may have been a chiefly privilege (ibid., 464).

Alliance

Henry (1941:19, 33) reports that sexual relations among the Aweikoma-Caingang exclude only parents and blood siblings, "admitting every kind of marriage known to anthropology." Specifically, a man's marriage to his three sister's daughters is mentioned (ibid., 37). Métraux (1946:464) also notes that a girl often marries her MB. Sororal polygyny and polyandrous "joint marriages" are a major factor of social cohesion. One report suggests that a man may not marry his cousin, but that he may take her as a concubine until her own marriage. Other indications of exogamy include the obsolete rule that a man cannot marry a woman sharing the same body-paint design (Henry 1941:59, 88, 176), and Horta Barboza's report on prescribed alliances between subgroups of the exogamous Kadnyerú/Kamé moieties (Métraux 1946: 462).

Henry (1941:51–63, 108–111) emphasizes the Caingang "obsession" with feuding and murder, and Métraux (1946:467) writes that such feuds may develop into regular warfare.

10. The Bororo

Kin Terminology (Table 11)

An absence of symmetric alliance is suggested by the distinctions WB≠ZH and MBD≠FZD. As noted by Lévi-Strauss (1936:282), the equation FF=WF is congruent with FZ marriage, as are the equations FM=WM, FZ=BW, and DH= SS. Patrilateral cross-cousin marriage is suggested by the equations WF=FZH, FZD =BW, and SW=ZD, and in a different way by the equation Z=MBD. Avuncular (ZD) marriage is suggested by the equations WBS=DS, MBD=ZD, and BW=ZD. Matrilineal equations include MF=F, FM= FZ=FZD, MM=M, MZ=Z, Z=ZD, D= DD, and ZH=ZDH. Patrilineal principles appear to underlie the equations B=S, WB=WBS, Z=D, and BW=SW. Lineal principles are also apparent in the distinctions FF≠MF, FM≠MM, SS≠DS, and SD≠DD.

In two cases, Albisetti and Venturelli (1962) contradict themselves when listing reciprocals. Thus, WBD is listed as íno arédu r. (ibid., 475), but the reciprocal for female Ego's FZH is listed as i-rágo p. or íno arédu p. (ibid., 463). Similarly, ZDH (the reciprocal of WMB) is listed as in-odówu (p.) in one context (ibid., 475) but as i-wagédu p. or íno imédu r. in another (ibid., 459).

C. Crocker suggests (1971:390) that the Bororo relationship terminology forms, "as we might expect," a two-section system, but that it is unusual in applying to "the other section" certain lineal equations "associated with the importance given to patrifiliation."

Local Group Size and Composition

When visited by Lévi-Strauss in 1936, the village of Kejara numbered approximately 140 individuals (Lévi-Strauss 1936:270). In 1967, the three village clusters of the Eastern Bororo totalled slightly more than 500 (C. Crocker 1979:247), averaging about 167 per cluster. In earlier times, there were villages of 500 and more (ibid.,264). A report from 1888 mentions a village of 350 that had originally had 1,000 inhabitants (Lowie 1946a:419).

Post-marital residence is uxorilocal (Lévi-Strauss 1936:272; C. Crocker 1977:245; 1979:267, 281, 299).

Patterns of Affiliation Other than Residence

Lévi-Strauss (1936:270) originally described the divisions Tugare and Cera as two exogamous, matrilineal phratries divided into four and six clans, respectively. A second bipartition, cutting across the phratry division, defined the two moieties Câboge-woge (Upper) and Cebegewoge (Lower) (ibid., 271–272; Lowie 1946a:421, 427). Some clans apparently belonged entirely to one or the other moiety, while others were internally subdivided into Upper and Lower sections. Moreover, different houses belonging to the same clan had different names relating to their respective kinship statuses (e.g. the Older Brothers, the Younger Brothers). Matrilineal affiliation is evident in both the inheritance of valuable female ornaments (Lévi-Strauss 1936:277), and the succession to chieftainship, thought by Lévi-Strauss to pass from MB to ZS (ibid., 285). In a later context (Lévi-Strauss 1963e:142), he calls the Tugare and Cera divisions moieties instead of phratries, and reduces their number of constituent clans to four each. Although the existence of two perpendicular bipartitions was challenged by Maybury-Lewis (1960b:23), Lévi-Strauss at a yet later

Table 11
KIN TERMINOLOGY OF THE BORORO
LINGUISTIC FAMILY: Probable Gê
Male Ego, terms of address.

GEN.	Male		Female	
+ 2	FF	*i-edógwa*	FM	*im-arúgo*
	MF	*i-ógwa*	MM	*i-múga*

	KIN (Lineal kin, parallel collaterals, affines of affines)				*AFFINES* (In-laws, cross collaterals)			
	Male		Female		Male		Female	
+ 1	F	*i-ógwa*	M	*i-múga*	WF	*i-edógwa*	WM	*im-arúgo*
			MZ	*i-túie (r.)*			FZ	*im-arúgo p.*
					FZH	*i-edógwa*	MBW	*im-arúgo*
0	B	*i-mána*	Z	*i-túie*	WB	*íno imédu p.*	W	*it-oredúje*
		íno imédu r.		*íno arédu r.*				
							MBD	*íno arédu p.*
							FZD	*im-arúgo p.*
	WZH	*i-mána p.*	WBW	*i-túie (p.)*	ZH	*in-odówu*	BW	*i-rágo*
		íno imédu p.		*íno arédu p.*				*im-arúgo*
− 1	S	*íno imédu r.*	D	*íno arédu r.*	DH	*i-wagédu*	SW	*i-rágo*
							ZD	*i-rágo p.*
								íno arédu r.
	ZDH	*in-odówu (p.)*	ZSW	*i-rágo p.*	WBS	*íno imédu r.*	WBD	*íno arédu r.*
				im-arúgo p.				

	Male		Female	
− 2	SS	*i-wagédu*	SD	*i-rágo*
	DS	*íno imédu r.*	DD	*íno arédu r.*

SOURCES: Albisetti & Venturelli 1962:452–475. Abbreviations
r. and p. signify *rógu* and *péga*, respectively.

DEVIATIONS FROM THE TWO-LINE PATTERN	CONCEIVABLE IDEOLOGICAL OR BEHAVIOURAL CORRELATES
MBD≠FZD, WB≠ZH	Absence of symmetric alliance
WF=FZH, BW=FZD≠MBD, SW=ZD≠WBD, Z=MBD	Patrilateral cross-cousin marriage
FF=WF, FM=WM, FZ=BW, DH=SS	FZ marriage
WBS=DS, MBD=ZD, BW=ZD	ZD marriage
MF=F, FM=FZ=FZD, MM=M, MZ=Z, Z=ZD, D=DD, ZH=ZDH	Matrilateral affiliation, uxori-local residence
B=S, WB=WBS, Z=D, BW=SW	Patrilateral affiliation
FF≠MF, FM≠MM, SS≠DS, SD≠DD	Lineal principles

date (1973b:74–75, 81) was able to refer to the information collected in 1965 by C. Crocker, whose "informants corroborated those of Lévi-Strauss in saying that for some purpose the village was formerly divided into 'upper' and 'lower' halves on a north-south axis running through the middle of the village" (C. Crocker 1969:57–58).

C. Crocker (1971) confirms that there are four named clans in each moiety, each subdivided into Upper and Lower (sometimes also Middle) sections. Furthermore, each clan is composed of between six and 10 named lineages. Recruitment to lineage, clan, and moiety is by matrilineal name, transmission. However, through bonds of ceremonial kinship, "the Bororo seem to accomplish the paradoxical feat of being both matrilineal and patrilineal at once." Thus, almost all mature men have several ceremonial fathers in their own moiety, and a similar number of ceremonial mothers in opposite moiety. Crocker notes that "relations based on patrifiliation are exceedingly important in the non-ritual affairs of daily life", and suggests that the lineal equations within the opposite section of the kin terminology are "associated with the importance given to patrifiliation" (ibid.).

Although recruitment to clans is matrilineal, Crocker (1969:47) points out that the ideology of common descent within clans refers to a shared relationship with their "totems" (ibid., 46; 1977:247; but cf. Lévi-Strauss 1936:298), rather than to genealogical relations. In fact, Bororo corporate groups are "not founded upon an idiom of genealogical unilineality," and the characterization of these groups as "matrilineal" is completely false" (C. Crocker 1977:245). Households and clans are name-holding groups, and the "matrilateral bias" in conventional name transmission simply derives from the fact that households are uxorilocal (ibid., 246). The "patrilateral cast" characteristic of prestations *between* groups is also a logical consequence of uxorilocality, as lines of males are the bonds linking the localized lines of females. Crocker is "tempted to speak of 'double descent' or 'complementary (patri-)filiation'" (ibid., 256). He concludes that "the Bororo are uxorilocal residentially, matrilineal corporately, and patrilateral ceremonially, because it is logical." Patrilateral, cross-moiety bonds are of crucial

significance to alliance. A man's ceremonial friend, *i-orubadari*, should ideally be a yFB, and it is considered correct that the two exchange sisters (C. Crocker 1979:285).

As among the Northern Gê, Bororo name transmission prototypically involves Ego's MB and FZ (actually, FFZ or FFM), i.e. mother's senior male relatives and father's senior female relatives. However, among the Bororo the MB is name-giver to both boys and girls, and the agnatic women merely assist in the ceremony (ibid., 258–259).

A clan's rights to represent a totemic *aroe* spirit can be transferred to a clan in the opposite moiety, always from F to S (ibid., 265). Apparently, then, a defining feature of the matrilineal clans can also be transmitted patrilineally. Considering the trans-generational bonds of alliance and patrifiliation between clans of opposite moieties, it seems reasonable to assume that such totemic rights alternate between moieties, much as the spatial distribution of Shavante lineages (cf. Maybury-Lewis 1979b:233). Such periodic inversion, or alternation, would be logically congruent with the significance of second ascending generation kin such as FFZ (C. Crocker 1979:258) and MMB (ibid., 277). If transmission within clans was fundamentally from MMB to ZDS, it would coincide with the patrilineal cycles. Transmission from F to S, then, would achieve the same result as intra-moiety, matrilineal transmission from MMB to ZDS. The motives for patrilateral cross-cousin marriage presented to Crocker emphasize that this type of marriage results in an equation of MMB and FF. "There is, then," Crocker concludes, "some feeling that generative male sexuality should oscillate every generation between two categories of women" (ibid., 281).

Hierarchy

Three or four of the lineages in each clan are hierarchically ranked, and the clan head should come from the lineage which is ranked highest (C. Crocker 1971:387). Hierarchy, including jural authority, is based on the relative age of individuals and lineages, but as "one cannot compare Tapirs and Crows," ranking ideally occurs *within* clans only. Yet, the two ritual chiefs of the village derive from specific clans (Bado Jebage = "Planners of the Village") (Albisetti 1953:625; C. Crocker 1969:46), and precisely these clans are allotted the privilege of marrying within their own moiety (Albisetti & Venturelli 1962:450; Maybury-Lewis 1960b:25). Furthermore, Bororo "privately and as individuals" often contrast clans of the same moiety "in terms of the prestige and general behaviour of their members and by the amounts and values of their traditional rights" (C. Crocker 1969:56). Lévi-Strauss (1936: 278; cf. Lowie 1946a:427, 428) clearly perceived "une hiérarchie économique des clans riches, modestes et pauvres." Within a clan, the inequality of name-sets, in terms of the amounts of ritual items and ceremonies associated with them, is the basis for "the formal order of relative prestige, ceremonial precedence, and, in a loose sense, legitimate power among the units of a clan" (C. Crocker 1979:263). Crocker suspects that, in earlier times, competition for prestige was a dominating feature of Bororo political life (ibid., 264).

With larger populations and deeper genealogies, Bororo villages in the past expanded by establishing junior households directly behind those of greater seniority, thereby expressing dimensions of rank spatially in a series of concentric residential rings (ibid., 267–268; Lévi-Strauss 1936:271; Lowie 1946a: 421; cf. the Apinayé and Kayapó.)

According to Lévi-Strauss (1936:285), chieftainship is probably inherited matrilineally from MB to ZS (cf. Albisetti 1953:625; Lowie 1946a:427), and can extend over the entire tribe, as in the case of Tušawa of Kejara, respected chief of all the Bororo along the Vermelho and upper Sao Lourenco

(Lévi-Strauss 1936:283). Contrary to what is usually the case with diarchy in moiety systems, both the two ritual chiefs of the Bororo village belong to the same moiety (Cera) (Lévi-Strauss 1944:267; Lowie 1946a: 427; cf. the Ramkokamekra.) Lévi-Strauss (1936:302) suggests as an hypothesis that the clan from which the Upper moiety traditionally derived its chiefs has become extinct. The two chiefs represent the mythical twins Bakororo and Itubori, "of whom the former takes precedence" (Lowie 1946a:427; cf. the Caingang.)

Alliance

On the basis of Father Albisetti's information on marriage preferences, Lévi-Strauss (1963d:128; 1963e:143) suggested that Bororo society was in fact composed of three endogamous strata corresponding to the divisions Upper, Middle, and Lower. Maybury-Lewis (1958:132) regarded Lèvi-Strauss' demonstration of the existence of such endogamous groups as quite clear, but C. Crocker considers Albisetti's information on this point "completely unfounded," and rejects Lévi-Strauss' interpretation as false (C. Crocker 1971:388). In the light of similar conclusions drawn for the aboriginal Apinayé, Sherente, and Karajá, however, the possibility should not be dismissed that the Upper, Middle, and Lower divisions may at one time have been geared to endogamous marriage preferences.

Lévi-Strauss (1936:279) writes that each clan contracts alliances with a limited number of clans in the opposite phratry (moiety). Furthermore, marriage preferences distinguish between different divisions within each clan. These distinctions are maintained by means of the name-sets. In other words, the name-sets, with their age-based, ranking implications, determine the preferential unions within each clan (ibid., 283; Lowie 1946a:427). Albisetti and Venturelli (1962: 450) provide a diagram over preferred and tolerated alliances between Bororo clans. According to this diagram, the Tugare clans always marry outside the moiety, while two pairs of clans in the Cera moiety are allowed to intermarry. C. Crocker (1971:387) writes that approximately 85% of all recorded marriages are moiety exogamous, and that there are "preferential marital and ritual bonds between lineages of different moieties."

Crocker (1977:250) notes that WB may well be ZH, indicating the occurrence of sister exchange. He has also encountered a preference for patrilateral cross-cousin marriage (C. Crocker 1979:281). Another ideal is sister exchange between male Ego and his ceremonial friend (*i-orubadari*), who should preferably be a yFB. This would imply FZ (and BD) marriage, as Lévi-Strauss predicted, but Crocker (ibid., 285) interprets the ideal as "a formal preference for marriage with either type of cross-cousin, with a certain emphasis on the patrilateral side." The preference for the FZD, he says (ibid., 286), should be understood as "a partly metaphorical statement of the ideal intimacy between a man and his father's group." As potential wives to male Ego, Crocker (ibid., 292) lists FZ, FZD, BD, and MBD.

External Relations

The Bororo are apparently remarkable for their "traditional lack of blood feuds, intervillage warfare, and social disharmony" (C. Crocker 1969:45; 1979:249).

11. The Karajá

Kin Terminology

Dietschy (1977:299) notes that Karajá kin terms form a system classified by Dole (1969) as "bifurcate generation". All opposite-sex kin of Ego's own generation whether siblings, parallel cousins, or cross-cousins, are called *lerã*. The equation DH=ZS (*waralabi*) may explain why Lipkind (1948:186) attributed to the Karajá a preference for marriage with "a cousin on the mother's side" (Dietschy 1977:299). Terms for grandparents and grandchildren are reciprocal (*ulahi* between grandson and grandmother, *ulabié* between grandson and grandfather), suggesting a principle of alternating generations.

Local Group Size and Composition

Reports from 1845 speak of 2,000 inhabitants merely in the four villages of the Shambioá branch (Lipkind 1948:180), implying an average of 500 per village. In 1939, Lipkind counted a total of 1,510 Karajá divided among 30 villages (ibid., 179–180) with an average of 50 in each. In the late 1960:s, there were slightly more than 1,000 Karajá, almost all concentrated in eight villages (Tavener 1973:434), which gives an average of roughly 125 per village.

Post-marital residence is uxorilocal (Lipkind 1948:186; Dietschy 1977:298, 300).

Patterns of Affiliation Other than Residence

Lipkind (1948:186) describes Karajá kinship structure as one of "double descent". Affiliation is traced on both sides, "the greater emphasis falling on the mother's line." Yet, moiety membership, ceremonial roles, and chieftainship are patrilineally inherited. Dietschy (1977:297–298) claims that the Karajá moieties ("Upriver" and "Downriver"; cf. the Bororo) reported by Lipkind are merely two of three patrilineal, ritual men's societies. The third group, which may now be extinct, would have derived from three classes of "prestigious families" corresponding to the three hereditary "offices" or ceremonial roles listed by Lipkind: those of chief, priest, and food-divider. The articulation of male patrilines associated with particular meeting-places in the plaza, on the one hand, and female matrilines localized each in its own uxorilocal household, on the other, to Dietschy (1977:300) suggests parallel or "sex affiliation". A principle of alternating generations is evident in the terms for grand-parents and grandchildren, in name trans-mission, and in succession to the roles of "favourite children" (*deridu*) or "beautiful children" (*iolo*) within the lines of prestige (ibid.,299).

Formal friends (*wali-na*) consider each other "younger brothers" and are con-sequently not supposed to marry each other's sister.

Hierarchy

The "prestigious families" which hold the roles of chief, priest, and food-divider, and whose "favourite" and "beautiful children" are given "preferential treatment" (Lipkind 1948:186; Dietschy 1977:298–299), indicate permanent status differences between patrilines. Dietschy (1977:297, 299) reports an explicit rule enjoining marriage with the daughter of a member of one's own ritual men's association, suggesting three ranked, endogamous strata (cf. the Bororo.)

In villages where diarchy occurs, the two chiefs occupy the households at each end of the village house row (ibid.,298), positions formally reminiscent of the Shavante *aamrã*.

Alliance

Lipkind's (1948:186) assertion that the preferred spouse is a matrilateral cousin (presumably a cross-cousin) may have been inspired by the equation DH=ZS (Dietschy 1977:299), but as Dietschy points out, this equation would be equally consistent with bilateral cross-cousin marriage. The Karajá rule is that Ego should marry a *lerã*, a

category including his sisters but also his cousins, both cross and parallel. Dietschy adds that "les soeurs propres sont naturelle-ment exclues." Following the rule of endogamy, each association would be composed of a restricted number of F–S lines exchanging daughters or sisters. Dietschy predicts that "ils sont donc amenés à se marier, à la limite, à une cousine croisée bilatérale, en même temps fille du frère de la mère et de la soeur du père, ou à une cousine parallèle." His statistics from 1955 show that 35% of the marriages were with a FZD and 22% with a FBD. These numbers, he suggests, reflect the rule of patrilateral endogamy. Another 14% were with a MBD, 8% with a ZD, 6% with a MZD, 6% with a BD, 1% with a FZD/MBD, and 8% with unrelated women. The rarity of bilateral cross-cousin marriage may reflect either a hesitation to practice sister exchange (cf. the Shavante), or a disinterest in tracing consanguinity bilaterally.

Dietschy suggests "en passant que le mariage avec la cousine croisée patrilatérale mène automatiquement à une affiliation par sexe de père en fils et de mère en fille." It is true that the recognition of FZD as a distinct type of relative implies a reckoning of both F–S and M–D consanguinity (cf. the Apinayé, Fig. 6), whereas the MBD category is commonly delineated simply with referen-ce to previous alliances, i.e. as "the daughter of father's brother–in–law". Parallel affilia-tion, however, reduces FZD to Z, which should make it inconsistent with patrilateral cross-cousin marriage, precisely as Scheffler and Lounsbury (1971:175) suggest for the Sirionó (cf. also the Txicáo.) On the other hand, the Karajá differ from the Sirionó and Txicáo in that the former equate sisters and cross-cousins, whereas the latter two groups do not. Significantly, three other Gê tribes for which we have suggested preferential FZD marriage, i.e. the Apinayé, Sherente, and Bororo, all also appear to have inclined toward a generational cousin terminology (Apinayé: FBD=FZD=MBD, MZD=

MBD; Sherente: Z=FBD=MBD, MZD= MBD; Bororo: Z=MBD). A preliminary hypothesis, then, is that parallel affiliation (or "transmission", in Scheffler's and Lounsbury's words) may be compatible with FZD marriage where the two-line distinction of siblings and cross-cousins is dissolving. This would be consistent with our suggestion that generational cousin terms may serve to delineate an endogamous, rather than an exogamous, category of "sisters". This suggestion, verified among the Karajá, is especially appropriate for the Apinayé, Sherente, Bororo, and Karajá, where ranked, endogamous subgroups are particularly evident. The distinction between true sisters and marriageable "sisters" is no problem to the Karajá (Dietschy 1977:299), whereas the Apinayé, Sherente, and Bororo have tended to equate MBD with sisters or parallel cousins, as distinct from the marriageable FZD. Whereas parallel affiliation in conjunction with a two-line dichotomy of zero generation kin terms would generate a preference for the MBD by reducing FZD to Z (Sirionó, Txicáo), the introduction of rank endogamy and generational cousin terms appears instead to have been conducive to patrilateral preferences (Apinayé, Sherente, Bororo, Karajá).

External Relations

The Karajá have traditionally been at war with their neighbours, Gê and Tupí alike (Lipkind 1948:180). With the Tapirapé, however, they have periodically maintained close and friendly relations (ibid.;Dietschy 1977:300). There is also mention of an alliance with the Sherente and Shavante (Maybury–Lewis 1965b:350). Their skill at manufacturing dugouts (Lipkind 1948:184), and their interest in trade with the Brazilians (ibid., 180), suggest a tradition of commerce. Three or four neighbouring villages maintain ceremonial ties, and beyond this there are ties of alliance and formal friendship (ibid.,

186–187). Nevertheless, inter-village feuds are common.

12. The Nambikwara

Kin Terminology
(Tables 12, 13, and 14)

Lévi-Strauss (1948c) presents kin terminologies from three different Nambikwara dialects. Among the equations and distinctions listed for dialect A 1/2 are none that deviate from the two-line pattern. Elsewhere (Lévi-Strauss 1969:102), he mentions the Nambikwara as "faultlessly built up about the dichotomy of cousins and the intermarriage of two classes." In dialect A 1/2, the second ascending generation is equated with first ascending generation affines.

In dialect B 1/2, the second ascending generation is *not* equated with first ascending generation affines, except occasionally the MF. There are no equations or distinctions contradicting the two-line pattern.

Dialect C, on the other hand, presents several deviations. The second ascending generation is equated with first ascending generation affines, as in dialect A 1/2, but FZ≠MBW=WM, which suggests matrilateral cross-cousin marriage. Completely contradictory is the equation W=FZD=MZD, suggesting not only patrilateral cross-cousin marriage, but also that the matrilateral parallel cousin would be eligible. The distinction DH≠ZS suggests an absence of symmetric alliance. When ZD is also SW or yBW, the term *sinaíso* is used. To a degree, then, SW= ZD, which accords with patrilateral cross-cousin marriage.

The practice of ZD marriage generates specific usages. Thus, when Z is married to MB, ZC is called *zóa*. Since these children also must be MBC to Ego, the term should also be applicable to MBC. Similarly, when Ego's D is married to her MB (i.e. Ego's

106

WB), her children (Ego's DC) are equated with SC (*ŝoéso*). By implication *ŝoéso* would also be applicable to WBC.

The distinction SC≠DC implies a principle of lineality (cf. the Bororo.) The distinction F≠FB appears to be unique to dialect C of the Nambikwara, occurring in no other Gê-affiliated group. We have seen, however, that distinctions between same-sex siblings are implicit in other Gê groups, e.g. the Apinayé.

Local Group Size and Composition

Lévi-Strauss (1948c:35) lists four relatively well-defined groups ranging in size from 12 to 34 (average 22), and smaller units ranging between 6 and 12. Temporarily, smaller bands can unite into groups of up to 75 individuals.

Apparently, there are no rules or practices which suggest preferences for a specific mode of post-marital residence (ibid., 49).

Patterns of Affiliation Other than Residence

Children are named after their parents, generally their mother, suggesting matrilateral affiliation (ibid., 39, 79). C. Cooke found that names were transmitted from father to son and from mother to daughter, which implies that affiliation is parallel (Scheffler & Lounsbury 1971:189).

Whether or not a result of demographic decline, two bands (B1 composed of 18 individuals, C of 34) lived side by side in moiety fashion, each affines to the other and both carefully maintaining the distinction (Lévi-Strauss 1948c:77). Each side preserved its own campfire positions, chief, and dialect, and the terminological kin-affine dichotomy distinguishing the two bands from each other. The group as a whole was clearly alliance-organized, rather than built up

around some ideology of unilateral affiliation. It would suffice, writes Lévi-Strauss (ibid., 79), to satisfy the requirements of dual organization, if this newly formed group preserved the memory of its dual origin by continuing to avoid mixing the two groups of campfires. This, however, would require a unilocal rule of residence, so that all fires are clearly associated with the group to which belong resident spouses of one sex only. With the ambilocal residence reported by Lévi-Strauss (ibid., 49), intermarriage would muddle the spatial representation of the two-section division.

Hierarchy

Polygyny is a privilege of the chief (Lévi-Strauss 1943, 1948b:366). Chieftainship is not hereditary, and the chief's authority is slight (Lévi-Strauss 1948b:367). He is prominent, however, in ceremony and warfare (Lévi-Strauss 1948c:94).

Alliance

Lévi-Strauss (1948c:19, 25) writes that the kin terminology offers possibilities of oblique marriage, i.e. marriage between persons belonging to adjacent generations. Since grandparents are equated with parents-in-law, for instance, Ego can marry uncles and aunts with a minimum of terminological confusion. To alleviate the contradictions which do arise, there are alternative series of descriptive terms which complement or replace the classificatory terminology (ibid., 23–24, 26). In dialect C, the terms *ŝoéso* and *zóa* are applied specifically when the child's mother has married an uncle (ibid., 31). Of eight marriages listed for this group, three are oblique. All three involve the marriage of a MB to his ZD (ibid., 32). Lévi-Strauss (ibid., 34, 80) speaks of "preferential marriage" between MB and ZD, and notes that such unions introduce an asymmetry between the brother's and the sister's

Table 12
KIN TERMINOLOGY OF THE NAMBIKWARA (Dialect A 1/2)
LINGUISTIC FAMILY: Probable Gê
Male Ego, terms of reference.

GEN.	Male		Female	
+ 2	FF asoúnosu		FM a?éinosu	
	MF asoúnosu		MM a?éinosu	

	KIN (Lineal kin, parallel collaterals, affines of affines)		*AFFINES* (In-laws, cross collaterals)	
	Male	Female	Male	Female
+ 1	F ahuínosu	M a?kénosu	WF asoúnosu	WM a?éinosu
	FB ahuínosu	MZ a?kénosu	MB asoúnosu	FZ a?éinosu
	MZH ahuínosu	FBW a?kénosu		
0	B e akenánosu	Z e toánuso	WB asúkosu	W asiésu
	y alónsu	y aríndesu	MBS asúkosu	MBD asiésu
	FBS alónsu	FBD aríndesu	FZS asúkosu	FZD asiésu
	MZS alónsu	MZD aríndesu	ZH asúkosu	
− 1	S a?kíraru	D a?kíneru	DH asineéru	SW asíntu
			ZS asineéru	ZD asíntu

	Male		Female	
− 2	SS	asuíttu	SD	asuíttu
	DS	asuíttu	DD	asuíttu

SOURCES: Lévi-Strauss 1948c:19–21

DEVIATIONS FROM THE TWO-LINE PATTERN	CONCEIVABLE IDEOLOGICAL OR BEHAVIOURAL CORRELATES
None	

children. The sister's children will belong to a generation above that of the brother's. Similarly, a woman who has married her uncle will belong to a generation above that of her parallel cousins. Lévi-Strauss suggests that the equation of parallel cousins with younger siblings, emphasizing a difference in seniority, indicates that oblique marriage was once as important among the groups speaking dialects A and B, as it still is for group C.

Oblique marriage may also explain why MZD is equated with the category of spouses and cross-cousins (*iátta*) in dialect C. With an inclination towards matriliny, Ego will identify himself with his MB, for whom ZD marriage implies marrying Ego's Z or MZD.

In spite of the obvious inclination towards ZD marriage, the "fundamental principle" underlying Nambikwara alliance is the marriage of cross-cousins (Lévi-Strauss 1948c:32, 79). ZD marriage, in fact, may merely represent a continued exchange between male cross-cousins, in the sense that each reclaims his ZD in exchange for his Z (Lévi-Strauss 1968a:180).

Table 13
KIN TERMINOLOGY OF THE NAMBIKWARA (Dialect B 1/2)
LINGUISTIC FAMILY: Probable Gê
Male Ego, terms of reference.

GEN.	Male		Female	
+ 2	FF *ŝónde* MF *ŝónde* *kúnde*		FM *ŝirúnde* MM *ŝirúnde*	

	KIN (Lineal kin, parallel collaterals, affines of affines)		*AFFINES* (In-laws, cross collaterals)	
	Male	Female	Male	Female
+ 1	F *mínde* FB *mínde*	M *nāde* MZ *nāde* FBW *denaúdnere*	WF *kúnde*	WM *hi?índe*
0	B e *ōutāde* y *akenaāde* FBS *akenaāde* MZS *akenaāde*	Z e *tōaāde* y *ōaniuinikere* FBD *ōaniuinikere* MZD *ōaniuinikere*	MBS *árute* FZS *árute* ZH *árute*	W *rére*
– 1	S *nkíraende*	D *ínkeninde*	DH *asirare* ZS *asirare*	SW *siídare* ZD *siídare*

	Male		Female	
– 2	SS *asuíte* DS *asuíte*		SD *asuíte* DD *asuíte*	

SOURCES: Lévi-Strauss 1948c:29–30. Terms for parallel cousins derive from discussion in text (ibid., 34).

DEVIATIONS FROM THE TWO-LINE PATTERN	CONCEIVABLE IDEOLOGICAL OR BEHAVIOURAL CORRELATES
None	

External Relations

In the 19th century, the Nambikwara were greatly feared by Brazilians (Price 1985:18). Unrelated bands of Nambikwara meet only to exchange items in limited supply, such as women, seeds (e.g. beans), and ceramics (Lévi-Strauss 1948c:91). Lévi-Strauss (ibid., 93) also describes the formalized exchange of valuables such as thread, wax, *urucu*, shells, earrings, bracelets, necklaces, tobacco, feathers, and porcupine quills. Discontentment with the outcome of barter may itself be an incentive to warfare (ibid., 94; 1948b: 367). Relations between groups hover between fear and hostility, on the one hand, and the desire to exchange goods, on the other.

Table 14
KIN TERMINOLOGY OF THE NAMBIKWARA (Dialect C)
LINGUISTIC FAMILY: Probable Gê
Male Ego, terms of reference.

GEN.	Male		Female	
+ 2	FF	*koóka*	FM	*šiíko*
	MF	*koóka*	MM	*šiíko*

	KIN (Lineal kin, parallel collaterals, affines of affines)			*AFFINES* (In-laws, cross collaterals)			
	Male		Female		Male		Female	
+ 1	F	*uáinko*	M	*náuko*	WF	*koóka*	WM	*šiíko*
	FB	*hími*	MZ	*náuko*	MB	*koóka*	FZ	*asiátaba*
							MBW	*šiíko*
0	B	e *iáia*	Z	e *iáia*	WB	*iópa*	W	*iátta*
		y *sabáni*		y *sabáni*				
					MBS	*tiímo*	MBD	*iátta (?)*
						(zóa)		*(zóa)*
			MZD	*iátta*	FZS	*tiímo*	FZD	*iátta*
					ZH	*iópa*		
– 1	S	*taáta*	D	*taátero*	DH	*šiauítte*	SW	*(šinaíso)*
					ZS	*áišinu*	ZD	*áišinu, iátta (?)*
						(zóa)		*(šinaíso, zóa)*
					WBS	*(šoéso)*	WBD	*(šoéso)*

	Male		Female	
– 2	SS	*šoéso*	SD	*šoéso*
	DS	*šiúsi (šoéso)*	DD	*šiúsi (šoéso)*

SOURCES: Lévi-Strauss 1948c:31. Terms in brackets are employed only with specific marriage arrangements. Apparently, *iátta* can denote any cross-cousin, MZD, or ZD (ibid., 34).

DEVIATIONS FROM THE TWO-LINE PATTERN	CONCEIVABLE IDEOLOGICAL OR BEHAVIOURAL CORRELATES
DH≠ZS	Absence of symmetric alliance
FZ≠MBW=WM	Matrilateral cross-cousin marriage
W=MZD	Eligibility of matrilateral parallel cousins
MBC=ZC, WBC=DC	Avuncular marriage
SC≠DC	Lineal principles
F≠FB	Distinction of same-sex siblings

Conclusions: Gê

"The various types of groupings found in these societies . . . are . . . a series of expressions, each partial and incomplete, of the same underlying structure, which they reproduce in several copies without ever completely exhausting its reality."
– C. Lévi-Strauss (1963d:130)
"The entire Gê area is a gold mine for studies of variability in native classificatory and behavioral models."
– J. Jackson (1975b:321)
"Nous avons parlé . . . à plusieurs reprises, de tendances, d'états latents, parce que non reconnus ou mal reconnus par les sujets, mais accessibles à une analyse des conséquences virtuelles . . . Si on concevait les états latents, non comme des données insignifiantes, mais comme des virtualités qui peuvent – ou n'arrivent pas à – se réaliser, on serait peut-être plus proche d'un esprit de finesse que d'un esprit de géométrie."
– H. Dietschy (1977:306)

Male-Female Dualism and Parallel Affiliation

It is appropriate to begin our concluding discussion of the Gê-speaking peoples by establishing that they tend to organize their societies in terms of two fundamental dichotomies. One of these distinguishes between the domains of the two sexes, the other between kin and affines. The former dichotomy is evident in the spatial separation of a male-oriented center (the village plaza and men's house) from a female-oriented periphery (the circle of uxorilocal houses). It is also evident in the pervasive principles of parallel affiliation which appear to underlie the "double descent" aspects of the Bororo and Karajá, and the "cross transmission" of names from MB to ZS and from FZ to BD among all the Northern Gê. The Bororo and most of the Northern Gê have kin equations suggesting both patrilineal and matrilineal principles recognized, if sometimes indirectly, by both sexes. The Suyá and Central Gê, however, have no equations suggesting male matriliny, and the Nambikwara have none indicative of female patriliny. These terminological slants in affiliation correlate well with what has been reported on other aspects of social classification. In several respects, the Suyá and Central Gê particularly emphasize patrilateral affiliation, whereas the Nambikwara stress matrilateral ties. Perhaps the strongest indications of lineality can be recognized in the terminological distinction of different kinds of grandparents and grandchildren, which occurs among the Timbira tribes, the Bororo, and dialect B of the Nambikwara.

In addition to the cross transmission of names among the Northern Gê, parallel affiliation is apparent in tribal recruitment among the Ramkokamekra and Apaniekra; the transmission of property and *kuwuure* relationships among the Krĩkatí; name transmission among the Nambikwara; the identification of F=S and M=D among the Apinayé; the same-sex adoptive parents of the Apinayé and Kayapó; and the conspicuous opposition of ceremonial male patriliny and female matriliny (uxorilocality) among the Central Gê, Bororo, and Karajá.

Dual Organization

"One would expect alliance to be in some way critical to an understanding of the elaborate moiety systems of the Gê, and it is of course ironic that in the very societies where one would also expect to find a prescriptive marriage rule it is by no means always present."
– J. Kaplan (1981:154)

The dichotomy of kin and affines is expressed in different ways among the Gê. Among the Nambikwara (dialects A and B), it is implicit in the perfectly symmetrical two-line terminology. Among most of the other Gê-affiliated tribes, the exogamic dichotomy is expressed spatially in the ideal exogamy of opposite village "sides". In some of these cases (the

Central Gê, Bororo, and Ramkokamekra), the exogamous village sides have been demarcated in the form of named, exogamous moieties. The Nambikwara are the only Gê-affiliated people lacking moiety institutions of any kind (exogamous or agamous), though they alone may apply a perfectly consistent two-line terminology. The complementary distribution of moiety institutions and two-line terminologies among the Gê suggests that the former represents a structural alternative to the latter, a reification of the reciprocal exchange relationship encoded in the terminology (cf. Lévi-Strauss 1969:103). The striking correlation with local group size suggests that moiety formation is encouraged when the terminology is no longer capable of dividing the entire society effectively into kin and affines. While the Nambikwara local group is generally composed of less than 50 people, most of the other Gê tribes have lived in villages of over 150, and none (except the Aweikoma-Caingang, who appear to have lost a former moiety system) in groups averaging less than 50.

Residence

The physical demarcation of two exogamous categories presupposes a rule of unilocal post-marital residence. Whereas the Nambikwara and the Aweikoma-Caingang have no such rule, all the tribes recognizing moiety divisions are emphatically uxorilocal. The Aweikoma-Caingang, who may previously have had moieties such as those of the Caingang of Palmas, were formerly uxorilocal. Although generally uxorilocal, the Suyá and Shavante recognize virilocality as a chiefly prerogative. This is consistent with their greater emphasis on patrilateral affiliation.

The development of conventions relating to choice of residence would be meaningful primarily where extended exogamy precludes the automatism of continued reciprocity

associated with close, direct marriage exchange. The local endogamy of the small, ambilocal bands of Nambikwara is reflected in the consistent, Dravidian equation of cross-cousins and spouses. All the other Gê have separate categories for these relations, suggesting that primary cross-cousins are not the ideal spouses. In fact, the exclusion of all first cousins appears to have been explicit among the Ramkokamekra and the Apinayé.

Unilateral Affiliation and Alternating Generations

Rules of unilocal residence are associated with ideologies of unilateral affiliation, whether "harmonic" or "disharmonic" vis-à-vis residence. The matrilineal, male name-holding groups of the Bororo and Northern Gê reflect and reinforce the pattern of residence. Among the Eastern Timbira and the Bororo, the name-holding groups tend to be named, localized, and corporate. In the sense that women of the uxorilocal households to which they correspond are excluded from marriage, they are also exogamous. Succession to these groups is expressed in terms of the transmission of personal names, to which adhere specific ceremonial roles including that of the chief. Among the Sherente and Karajá, the male name-holding groups are patrilineal, i.e. disharmonic with respect to the rule of residence. Rather than reinforcing uxorilocality, male affiliation in these tribes complements and balances it. The Kayapó, Apinayé, and Suyá are intermediate cases, where the tension between matrilateral and patrilateral affiliation is particularly evident. Among the Kayapó, the MB-ZS lines of name transmission are less emphasized than the patrilineal FZ-BD lines. Among the Suyá, chieftainship is inherited patrilineally. Whereas formal friendship among the Eastern Timbira unites pairs of matrilines, it joins pairs of patrilines (real, adoptive, or symbolic) among the Suyá, Apinayé, and Kayapó.

Among all the Northern Gê, an alternative line of name transmission is from grandparent to grandchild, for male Ego specifically from FF to SS. The implicit structural equivalence of MB and FF is codified in all the Gê terminologies in our sample except those of the Central Gê and the Suyá (where, after all, *gitumu* is a form of *ngedi*), and is consistent with a system of bilateral cross-cousin marriage in combination with matrilateral affiliation. Uxorilocal residence, in fact, suffices to account for the equation of FF, MB and Ego, as they are all related as brothers to the successive generations of a single, localized line of females, and as they should all ideally marry successive generations of another, affinal matriline. Thus, the kin-affine dichotomy may be applied to allied pairs of uxorilocal households as well as to exogamous moieties. Among the Eastern Timbira and the Bororo, both the matrilineal name-holding groups and moieties, and the terminological identification of FF and MB, recognize the structural regularities generated by the articulation of uxorilocality and symmetric alliance.

Taking both sexes into account, the cross transmission of names among the Northern Gê is structurally congruent with both parallel transmission (Scheffler & Lounsbury 1971:188–189; Lévi-Strauss 1973c:110; W. Crocker 1984) and a system of alternating generations. Among the Sherente and Karajá, however, the identification of MB and FF disappears. Names are instead transmitted directly and exclusively from FF to SS or FFB to BSS. Whereas uxorilocality and symmetric alliance remain fundamental, the emphasis on the patrilateral affiliation of males precludes identification with MB, producing instead a pure system of alternating generations. Precisely as Lévi-Strauss has predicted, these alternating generations are the result of a disharmonic system of uxorilocal residence and patrilateral affiliation. The identification of Ego with his FF is

consistent with the two-generation cycle whereby patrilines alternate between two exogamous uxorilocal households. The close ties with the MB, and his assimilation to the category of Ego's "own people", however, indicates that the patrilateral inclination of the Central Gê is far from unambiguous. It is obvious that the distinction between "matrilineal" Timbira and "patrilineal" Sherente (Maybury-Lewis 1958:132) cannot be very sharp (cf. Maybury-Lewis 1967: 302-303). Significantly, among the Shavante the MB bestows a name on Ego, even though clans (which among the closely related Sherente are name-holding groups) are patrilineal. Maybury-Lewis believes that a Shavante boy may originally have been expected to succeed to the name of his maternal uncle. Some Shavante names are associated with specific ceremonial roles, suggesting a situation more or less identical to that of the Northern Gê. It is possible that the MB is simply expected to bestow the name on a young Shavante, whereas the name itself derives from a patrilateral relative such as the FF. The inverse situation has been reported from the Apinayé, where a FB mediates in the name transmission from MB to ZS.

A crucial determinant of variation in patterns of affiliation among the Gê is the extent to which males have succeeded in creating male loyalties to counteract and balance the female loyalties implicit in uxorilocal residence. Among the Eastern Timbira and the Bororo, these male loyalties are predominantly matrilineal, i.e. they are modelled after patterns of residence. Among the Central Gê and the Suyá, however, strategic marriages and occasional virilocality tend to keep patrilateral kin together. In these tribes, as among the Kayapó and Karajá, patrilateral affiliation is ideologically more pronounced (cf. W. Crocker 1984:83). Among the Kayapó, the build-up of patrilateral loyalties takes place in the men's house, and among the Karajá, in patrilineally inherited ceremonial men's societies. In all these cases, keeping agnates together appears to be associated with factionalism and the struggle for leadership. Succession to chieftainship is patrilineal among the Suyá, Central Gê, Caingang, and Karajá, and data from the Suyá and Shavante suggest that chiefly authority was generally associated with expansive, virilocal households. Not surprisingly, it is precisely these patrilineally inclined groups which have gained a special notoriety for continuous feuding and warfare, contrasting with the decidedly more peaceful Bororo and Timbira tribes.

Recruitment to Moieties

Patterns of affiliation to lower-level units such as name-holding groups, or clans, are reflected in the constitution of moieties. Among the Northern Gê, moiety recruitment is generally effected by cross transmission of names from MB to ZS and from FZ to BD. The Kayapó, however, recruit new moiety members by means of induction by a symbolic, same-sex parent. Nimuendajú reported moieties matrilineal for both sexes among the Ramkokamekra and Apinayé. The Bororo also have matrilineal moieties, whereas those of the Central Gê, Caingang, and Karajá have been patrilineal.

There are several indications that some moiety divisions among the Gê, rather than simply opposing affinally related sets of siblings, may have been aligned with an ideologically emphasized distinction between elder and younger brothers. Firstborn boys among the Suyá are generally recruited to the Ambànyi moiety, second sons to the Krenyi. Among the Caingang, the moieties are represented as an asymmetrical pair of twins. Relationships which generally involve opposite moieties in some cases oppose two real or classificatory brothers. This is the case with diarchy among the Ramkokamekra and Bororo, and with formal friendship among the Karajá. Inversely, adoptive parents are recruited

from Ego's affines among the Bororo and Caingang. Even where they incline toward exogamy, Gê moieties seem to elude the diagrammatic regularity of unilineal kin groups by allowing latitude in the rules of recruitment.

Instances of cross-cutting pairs of moieties indicate that dual divisions may be applied to distinctions other than that between exogamic village "sides". In such contexts, recruitment of siblings to alternate moieties need not contradict the genealogical implications of a kin-affine dichotomy. Instead, the distinction may signify that brothers of different status are expected to enter separate spheres of social interaction, which may or may not involve different endogamous enclaves superimposed on the exogamic dichotomy. Such asymmetric divisions may have been the original foundation for any ideals suggesting recruitment of two same-sex siblings to opposite moieties.

Birth-Order Hierarchy

The distinction between same-sex siblings of different age has been codified in the terminologies of the Ramkokamekra, Nambikwara, and Central Gê. It appears also to have been fundamental to the system of adoptive parents among the Apinayé, the birth-order ranking of names among the Kríkatí and Suyá, the assignment of Caingang children to different moiety subgroups, and the rule prohibiting Kayapó and Ramkokamekra siblings from marrying into the same household. Relative seniority, in fact, appears to be the idiom in terms of which the Gê-speaking peoples express their ideas of social hierarchy. Reports from the Eastern Timbira (Ramkokamekra, Kríkatí), Kayapó, and Central Gê suggest that age-class systems have tended to congeal into more permanent hierarchies.

All the Gê tribes except the Nambikwara recognize specific social categories of high status. These prestigious categories are composed of people possessing specific names to which adhere honorary ceremonial roles. To this pervasive complex belong the "great names" of the Apinayé, Kayapó, and Sherente; the *ikhionõ* of the Krahó and *hamrén* of the Ramkokamekra; the ranked name sets of the Krĩkatí, Suyá, and Bororo; the "prestigious families" and "beautiful" or "favourite children" of the Karajá; and the prestigious Votóro subgroup of the Caingang. Among the Shavante, Sherente, Bororo, and Karajá, prestigious households are assigned specific positions in the spatial layout of the village. In all but the last of these instances, these positions tend to be located next to points where the moiety axis intersects the village circle. If their houses were arranged in a circle, even the Karajá would reproduce this spatial order. Since it agrees with the ideals that closeness of consanguinity should correlate with spatial propinquity (cf. C. Crocker 1969:46; da Matta 1982:109), and that households should be located so as to keep in touch with both consanguineal and affinal groups (cf. Lave 1979:42–43), the location of prestigious households next to each other but on opposite sides of the moiety axis would be consistent with a situation where two brothers were chiefs of opposite moieties.

People of high prestige also qualify for special burial ceremonies among the Sherente, Suyá, Krahó, and Ramkokamekra. Among the latter three groups, this involves interment in the plaza, yet another spatial representation of hierarchy.

Rank Endogamy

"If hierarchy tends to exclude symmetry and the two maintain a precarious balance, it is precisely this balance that creates the dynamism of the Apinayé and Timbira social world."
– R.A. da Matta (1982:162)

The logical outcome of the articulation of hierarchy with a fundamental kin-affine dichotomy is the differentiation of endogamous strata, or "castes", superimposed on the exogamic division. Each moiety would maintain its own hierarchy, as illustrated in the pervasive practice of diarchy among the Gê, and particularly in the parallel hierarchies of ceremonial roles among the Apinayé. The cross-cutting moiety systems of the Ramkokamekra, Krĩkatí, Apinayé, and Bororo suggest that the asymmetric division in these tribes is conceived as essentially dual, contrasting center versus periphery or upper versus lower.

If endogamous strata did intersect the exogamic moieties or village "sides", we would expect to find institutions regulating or providing a matrix for the continuity of such endogamous alliances. We have found several indications that the pervasive institution of "formal friendship" may indeed have had such a function. In several tribes, formal friends are explicitly identified with affines. Among the Eastern Timbira and Bororo, formal friend relationships articulate matrilineal lines of men from either moiety, whereas among the Suyá, Apinayé, Kayapó, and Central Gê, the units thus linked are patrilines. The Sherente and Bororo recognize close bonds between specific clans in opposite moieties. We have suggested that the cross-moiety *narkwá* bonds of the Sherente may at one time have corresponded to the four men's associations, which also bring together men from both moieties in ranked categories relevant to name transmission. Moreover, affinal members of Shavante age-sets (of which the associations of the Sherente appear to be a permutation) are all considered as formal friends. The patrilineally inherited "loyalties" of the Caingang may represent another instance of the same phenomenon.

The delineation of endogamous subgroups may underlie the appearance of generational cousin terms among the Apinayé, Sherente, Bororo, and Karajá. Among the Karajá, marriage is explicitly enjoined within such an expanded "sibling" category.

Rank endogamy appears to be the structural expression of an articulation of hierarchy and symmetric alliance (cf. Dumont 1957). Whereas matrilateral cross-cousin marriage establishes and maintains the hierarchical dimension, symmetric alliance on a society-wide basis would exclude the emergence of rank discrepancies. However, by establishing endogamous enclaves, hierarchy can be maintained even where exchange is immediately reciprocal. While in asymmetric alliance systems dimensions of rank are aligned with relations of alliance, in symmetric systems the two dimensions are perpendicular.

The conclusion that unilateral marriage among the Sherente would result in endogamous subgroups needs a qualification, one which may be applicable to other Gê as well. It is probable that the "endogamy" attributed to the two inverse circuits is only formal and relative, and that their distinctness is repeatedly bridged by pairs of same-sex siblings. The equivalence and exchangeability of same-sex siblings may among the Gê be less of a sociological reality than a formal property of anthropological kinship diagrams. The most tangible evidence in this direction is the observation that Suyá brothers are alternately recruited to the Ambànyi and Krenyi moieties. Similarly, the importance of adoptive parents (parent's same-sex siblings) among the Apinayé and, in attenuated form, among the Kayapó and Sherente, indicate that the distinction between F and FB or M and MZ may be of considerable structural significance. Terminological features agreeing with this conclusion include the distinction M≠MZ among the Shavante and F≠FB among the Nambikwara (dialect C), and the distinctions between elder and younger siblings among the Ramkokamekra, Nambikwara, and Central Gê. We have suggested that the so-called kiyé of the Apinayé may have been formed by segmentation based on the distinction of same-sex siblings. The correspondence between levels of relative endogamy, on the one hand, and a birth-order hierarchy, on the other, is consistent with Zuidema's

interpretation of the Apinayé. If same-sex siblings are assigned to different moieties according to birth order, this would be consistent with the asymmetrical representation of the moieties. Among the Suyá, the Ambànyi is the moiety of firstborns, the Krenyi that of second sons. Caingang moieties were associated with a pair of asymmetrically conceived twins. Diarchy, which generally involves one leader from each moiety, among the Ramkokamekra devolves upon two brothers.

Considering that the quadripartite sequence of men's associations among the Sherente also determined the order according to which Ego's membership might be altered, it is possible that the associations were once age-grades. The birth order of a set of brothers would thus have accorded with the age hierarchy of the associations. If the associations were once divided two by two between the moieties, this would have implied that brothers belonged alternately to one or the other moiety, as among the Suyá. Moreover, such a differentiation of brothers could account for the kind of rule which among the Kayapó and Ramkokamekra prohibits brothers from marrying into the same household. It would also be consistent with the birth-order ranking of names among the Krĩkatí. In fact, Nimuendajú (1942:64) suggests that the associations of the Sherente represent a "petrified" version of an age-class system such as that of the Ramkokamekra. Parallels even include the localization of the four places of assembly. Lévi-Strauss (1963d:125) also offers an age-grade interpretation of the myth describing the origin of the four associations. Among the closely related Shavante, references to the still functioning age-sets are used to distinguish between siblings (Maybury-Lewis 1967:155). Significantly, names of Sherente men's associations recur as designations of Shavante age-sets (ibid., 161; cf. Maybury-Lewis 1958:130). Among the Shavante, alternate age-sets are linked by an especially close tie, suggesting a two-by-two alignment

116

with the moieties, such as has been inferred for the quadripartite circuits of the Sherente. The "petrification" of age-class hierarchies into circuits of groups recruiting life-long members may have occurred in other tribes as well. In the one-moiety villages of the Kayapó, age-sets have assumed some of the functions of moieties. For the Krîkatí, finally, Lave (1979:33, 34, 36, 37) suggests that the name-based Kuigatiye/Harungatiye moieties are former age-set moieties which have ceased to function.

Marriage Preferences

Symmetric alliance rarely takes the form of direct sister exchange among the Gê. An exception may be the Nambikwara, who are unique in equating WB=ZH. Among the remainder of Gê-affiliated tribes, bilateral cross-cousin marriage is subject to various modifications and consequently much more attenuated. Among the Eastern Timbira, the co-existence of the equations FM=FZ= FZD and MBD=D suggests that the matrilateral cross-cousin would have been the ideal spouse. This interpretation rests on the observation, explicit among the Ramkokamekra, that uxorilocal households provide the matrix for lineal equations. Among the Ramkokamekra, rules stipulating into which households male Ego may marry exclude the FZD, but not the MBD. W. Crocker also notes some additional terminological indications of MBD marriage in this tribe. Another Northern Gê group, the Suyá, explicitly favour MBD marriage. The Apinayé appear also to have preferred matrilateral marriage, but the exclusion of the actual MBD may have resulted in a statistical predominance of FZD/MMBDD marriage. Among the Central Gê, as among the Apinayé, there is a preference for matrilateral marriage but a prohibition on actual MBD marriage. The expectable inclination towards FZD/MMBDD marriage

is consistent with Nimuendajú's observation that a Sherente may marry his FZD but not his MBD. Some structural features relating to the role of the men's associations nevertheless suggest that MBD marriage may previously have been the rule. Both the Bororo and the Karajá prefer patrilateral marriage, and the FZD is frequently chosen in both tribes. It appears that FZD marriage may be accompanied by two different constellations of rules and preferences: either an ideal of matrilateral marriage in conjunction with a prohibition of the actual MBD (Apinayé, Central Gê), or the desire to reinforce patrilateral bonds in a society emphasizing uxorilocal residence and/or matrilineal name transmission (Bororo, Karajá; note that among the Northern Gê this is accomplished in female name transmission from FZ to BD). It seems probable that the ideal of matrilateral marriage is the most fundamental of these rules. The norm that male Ego should marry the daughter of his MB (i.e. his father's brother-in-law) is implicit in the parallel transmission of "inherited affinity" in simple two-line kin terminologies. The rule of matrilateral marriage among the Northern and Central Gê may thus represent a recodification of regularities previously encoded in kin terminologies, emphasizing the WF-DH relationship and ignoring possible patrilateral connections with the WM.

As long as sister exchange is a common form of marriage, the rule enjoining matrilateral marriage would not generate any unilateral slants in alliance structures. Where sister exchange for some reason (e.g. expansion of local group size) is no longer common, the matrilateral preference may initiate a trajectory in the direction of asymmetric alliance systems. This trajectory was apparently obstructed by the MBD prohibition among the Apinayé and Central Gê. The resultant inclination towards FZD/ MMBDD marriage retained the symmetric alliance structure of bilateral cross-cousin marriage. The same applies to preferential

| | Eastern Timbira | | | W. Timbira | | |
	Krahó	Ramkokamekra	Krîkatí	Apinayé	Kayapó	Suyá
Cross-cousin equations	MBD=D FZD=FZ	MBD=D FZD=FZ	MBD=D/M FZD=FZ	MBD=D/M/FZ FZD=FZ/ZD/M	MBD=M FZD=ZD	MBD=M FZD=ZD
Moiety recruitment	Naming	Naming	Naming	Naming	Abduction	Naming
Name transmission	MB to ZS FZ to BD GP to GC	MB to ZS FZ to BD GP to GC	MB to ZS FZ to BD GP to GC	MB to ZS FZ to BD GP to GC	MB to ZS FZ to BD GP to GC	MB to ZS FZ to BD GP to GC
Adoptive parent				Same-sex sibling of parent	Non-relative	
Distinction of same-sex siblings		Relative age; diarchy of brothers	Birth-order ranking of names	Adoptive parent	Marriages into same household prohibited	Alternate r ment to Am and Krenyi
Parallel affiliation		Tribal membership	Inheritance; *kuwuure*	Identification F=S, M=D; *pam/nã kaág*	Symbolic patri-/matrifiliation: *bam/nã ka'ak*	
Post-marital residence	Uxorilocal	Uxorilocal	Uxorilocal	Uxorilocal	Uxorilocal	Uxorilocal; chiefs virilo
Moiety subgroups (here: nameholding MB–ZS lines corresponding to localized female matrilines)	Exogamous; tend to be localized	Exogamous; corporate, named *haakats;* plaza groups	Exogamous; corporate	Exogamous; ceremonial roles	Exogamous; less emphasized than FZ–BD lines	Exogamous localized (n houses); na set rights an obligations
Unilateral affiliation		Matrilineal moieties Ko'i-kateye/Harã'kateye		Matrilineal moieties Kolti/Kolre	Patrifiliation emphasized	Patrilineal succession
Exogamous dichotomy		Ko'i-kateye/Harã kateye; village sides; *hũũkyê/ca'krit*		Village sides	*ombikwa/mẽbaitebm*	
Diarchy	Applicable	Applicable	Applicable	Applicable	Applicable	
Endogamous divisions superimposed on exogamous dichotomy	Formal friendship (*hõpin*) between nameholding matrilines; *ikhionõ*	Formal friendship (*hupin*)?; Ka'makra/Atu'kmakra	Formal friendship between nameholding matrilines; pairs of plaza groups: Kapi/Kaikula	Formal friendship (*kramgéd*) between adoptive patrilines; Ipog/Kre	Formal friendship (*kràb-djuò*) between patrilines	Formal frie (*ñumbre-kr* between pa Ambàn/Kr
High-status groups	*ikhionõ;* plaza burials	*hamrén;* high-status plaza groups; plaza burials	Honorary positions adhering to specific name-sets	"Great names"	"Great names"	Rights and obligations adhering to specific nam plaza buria
Probable marriage preferences	MBD marriage	Matrilateral marriage, but first cousins prohibited	MBD marriage	FZD/MMBDD (matrilateral marriage, but first cousins prohibited)	Diversified	MBD marr

Table 15 Comparative data on the Gê

118

	CENTRAL GÊ		SOUTHERN GÊ	PROBABLE GÊ		
	Shavante	*Sherente*	*Caingang*	*Bororo*	*Karajá*	*Nambikwara C*
...oss-cousin ...ations	MBD=ZD FZD=FZ	MBD=Z/M FZD=D/ZD	MBD=Z FZD=Z	MBD=Z/ZD FZD=FZ	MBD=Z FZD=Z	MBD=ZD/MZD FZD=ZD/MZD
...iety recruitment	Birth (patri-lineal)	Birth/naming (patrilineal)	Birth (patri-lineal)	Naming	Birth (patri-lineal)	
...me transmission	MB to ZS	FF to SS FFB to BSS	Patrilineal?	MB to ZS	FF to SS	Matrilineal/parallel
...optive parent		Same-sex sibling of parent	Affine of F	Classificatory MB, FZ		
...stinction of ...ne-sex siblings	Age-sets; relative age	Recruitment to associations?; relative age	Recruitment to moiety subgroups; moieties represent mythical twins	Diarchy of clan brothers representing mythical twins	Formal friends (equivalent to affines) called "brothers"	Relative age
...rallel ...liation	Ceremonial male patriliny and domestic female matriliny			Ceremonial male patriliny and domestic female matriliny	Ceremonial male patriliny and domestic female matriliny	
...st-marital ...idence	Uxorilocal; chiefs virilocal	Uxorilocal	Uxorilocal	Uxorilocal	Uxorilocal	Ambilocal
...iety subgroups	Patrilineal clans	Patrilineal clans	Patrilineal (?) body-paint groups (*kôika he*)	Matrilineal clans	P..trilineally inherited ceremonial roles; men's societies	
...ilateral ...liation	Patrilineal lineages, clans and moieties	Patrilineal lineages, clans and moieties; patrilineal succession	Patrilineal moieties and succession	Matrilineal lineages, clans and moieties; matrilineal succession	Patrilineal moieties and succession	
...ogamous ...hotomy	*waniwihā/wasi're'wa*	*wanōrī/wasimpkoze; šiptató/sdakrā;* Wairí/Doí	Kañerú/Kamé	Tugare/Cera		Two-line terminology
...archy	Applicable	Applicable		Applicable	Applicable	
...dogamous divi-...ns superimposed ...exogamous ...hotomy	Formal friend-ship (*zawi-di*)?; affinal age-mates (*ī-amō*)	*narkwá* bonds; men's associations?	Patrilineally inherited loyalties	Formal friendship (*i-orubadari*); Cábogewoge/Cebegewoge cross-moiety bonds of alliance and patri-filiation between clans	Formal friend-ship (*wali-na*)?	
...gh-status groups	*aamrā* house-holds; *īdzu*	"Great names" reserved for specific clans; innermost *narkwá* pair; eldest or youngest association; those qualifying for *aikmā*	Votóro	High-status name-sets, lineages, and clans (e.g. Bado Jebage)	"Prestigious families"; *deridu, iolo*	
...obable marriage ...eferences	FZD/MMBDD (matrilateral marriage, but MBD prohibited)	FZD/MMBDD (matrilateral marriage, but MBD prohibited)	ZD, etc.	FZD marriage	FZD marriage	Bilateral cross-cousin marriage; ZD

...ble 15 Comparative data on the Gê (cont'd)

FZD marriage among the Bororo and Karajá.

A conclusion which emerges from the Gê data is that whereas the equation WB=ZH indicates the permissibility of symmetric alliance, a terminological distinction between the two positions is not directly indicative of *asymmetric* alliance, as many alliance theorists have assumed (cf. Lévi-Strauss 1963d:122–123). The most that can be said of the WB≠ZH distinction, and others which contradict symmetric alliance, is that it suggests a relative rarity of sister exchange.

Avuncular (ZD) marriage appears to have been frequent among the small, endogamous bands of the Caingang and Nambikwara, whereas the ideal of patrilateral marriage among the Bororo has apparently resulted in some FZ marriages.

Cousin Terms

Terms for cross-cousins vary significantly among the Gê. We have suggested that the equations FM=FZ=FZD and MBD=D among the Eastern Timbira reflect the localized lines of females reproduced through the practice of uxorilocal residence. The Apinayé admit these same equations, but alternatively identify MBD with M. The M=MBD equation is applicable also to the Kayapó, Suyá, and Sherente, and occasionally to the Krĩkatí. It is obvious that this equation represents a codification of the FZ–BD lines of female name transmission and the relatively greater emphasis on patrilateral affiliation among the Apinayé, Kayapó, Suyá, and Sherente.

FZD is equated with ZD among the Kayapó, the Central Gê, dialect C of the Nambikwara, and occasionally the Apinayé, but with D among the Suyá and, according to Nimuendajú, the Sherente. Except for the Nambikwara, where both cross-cousins are equated with ZD, the FZC=ZC equation appears also to reflect patrilateral affiliation.

The equation FZC=C, on the other hand, would be consistent with either FZ or FZD marriage (the latter in conjunction with an equation of M and D) or with MBD marriage (where the wife-taking FZS is accorded junior status.)

The equation MBD=ZD among the Shavante, Bororo, and Nambikwara (dialect C) probably represents two different trajectories. Among the Nambikwara, it undoubtedly reflects the practice of ZD marriage. Among the Shavante, all cross-cousins and ZC are classed together as opposite-side people, i.e. classificatory affines. Among the Bororo, on the other hand, a likely solution is that the MBD=ZD equation is the result of an articulation of the matrilineal equation Z=ZD and the generational equation Z=MBD (*íno arédu*). The Bororo equate FZD with FM and FZ, precisely as do the Eastern Timbira.

Tendencies to equate parallel- and cross-sex, zero generation kin are characteristic of the Apinayé, Sherente, Caingang, Bororo, Karajá, and Nambikwara C. Generational cousin terms may reflect the emergence of ranked, endogamous subgroups among several Gê-speaking peoples. This interpretation accords well with other data on the Apinayé, Sherente, Bororo, and Karajá.

A set of distinct affinal terms distinguishes the terminologies of most Gê-affiliated people from the Dravidian systems prevalent throughout the remainder of lowland South America. By not automatically equating first ascending generation cross-collaterals of both sexes with affines, this feature is consistent with their unilineal tendencies and with an extended exogamy no doubt related to the considerable size of their villages. Once sister exchange is more or less abandoned and distinct affinal terms are introduced, the two types of cross-cousins are less likely to continue to be equated. Iroquois, in other words, may be conducive to Crow-Omaha.

The only instances of simple bifurcate merging cousin terms (i.e. where MBD and

FZD are equated but as a class distinguished from siblings and parallel cousins) are dialects A and B of the Nambikwara, and the Shavante. The Nambikwara, finally, are the only Gê-affiliated tribe to equate cross-cousins and spouses in the prescriptive, Dravidian manner. We have seen that the presence of Dravidian cousin terms corre-lates with small local groups. As village size increases, and cross-collaterals are no longer automatically equated with affines, the various other possibilities of classification are activated. Our review of the distribution of cousin terms illustrates some of the emergent principles which may have generated this variation.

Chapter 5
Arawak

13. The Machiguenga

Kin Terminology (Table 16)

Casevitz' terminology is a perfect example of the two-line pattern. Noteworthy is the reciprocity of terms for grandparents and grandchildren, which suggests alternating generations. Farabee's list, collected half a century earlier, suggests equations such as FF=MB, FM=FZ, and ZS=ZD. His *notirili* (MB) may be derived from the vocative *notineri* (DH/ZS), in which case it recalls the equation MB=ZS among the nearby Mayoruna.

For positions M, S, and D, Casevitz' and Farabee's lists agree. For positions F, Z, W, GS, and GD, Farabee has apparently listed terms of address (cf. Casevitz 1977:137–138). *Pikonkiri* (FF/MF) may be derived from *pigokini* (WF/MB/FZH), *payiro* (FM/MM) from the vocative *paguiro* (WM/FZ/MBW). *Naniro* (ZS) is the dislocated vocative for *paniro* (SW/ZD).

The anomalous *nutcaringi* (FZ), *iña* (B), *numatcienga* (MBS/FZS), and *itcaria* (ZD) remain to be explained.

Local Group Size and Composition

Machiguenga residence is characterized by "small mobile settlements of two to three households averaging twenty to thirty people or single household units of four to nine occupants" (Johnson & Johnson 1975:636). Johnson (1979:54) writes that the Machiguenga "typically live in widely scattered clusters of nuclear families numbering from 9–30 individuals."

Although there is no explicit rule of unilocal post-marital residence, uxorilocality is statistically predominant (Johnson & Johnson 1975:638). Casevitz (1977:124, 129), in fact, refers to "la règle de résidence matrilocale." Johnson (1979:54) writes that marriages are preferably endogamous, and that residence rules simply state that "both a bride and a groom should remain near their relatives after marriage."

Patterns of Affiliation Other than Residence

Johnson (1979:54) writes that kinship is reckoned bilaterally. An inclination towards parallel affiliation may underlie the observation that "women emphasize close female relatives and men emphasize close male relatives" (Johnson & Johnson 1975:638). Casevitz (1977:124, 129) deduces "filiation indifférenciée" among the Machiguenga, but concludes that a minimum of four interchanging (matrilocal) local groups is implied by the system of marriage alliance (ibid., 130).

The proposition (ibid., 134) that female Ego reproduces the marriage of her MM and male Ego that of his FF is consistent with the alternation of generations implicit in the equation of grandparents and grandchildren. It follows that great-grandparents occupy the same position as parents (ibid., 135), and so on.

Hierarchy

In the past, influential shamans known as *itinkame* could muster hundreds of people for house-building projects (Johnson & Johnson 1975:637). In classical "big man" style,

Table 16
KIN TERMINOLOGY OF THE MACHIGUENGA
LINGUISTIC FAMILY: Arawak
Male Ego, terms of reference.

GEN.	Male	Female
+ 2	FF *pibisarite* (*pikonkiri*) MF *pibisarite* (*pikonkiri*)	FM *pibisarote* (*payiro*) MM *pibisarote* (*payiro*)

	KIN (Lineal kin, parallel collaterals, affines of affines)		*AFFINES* (In-laws, cross collaterals)	
	Male	Female	Male	Female
+ 1	F *piri* (*apa*) FB *piri* MZH *piri*	M *piniro* (*pinero*) MZ *piniro* FBW *piniro*	WF *pigokini* MB *pigokini* (*notirili*) FZH *pigokini*	WM *pibaguirote* FZ *pibaguirote* (*nutcaringì*) MBW *pibaguirote*
0	B *pirenti* (*iña*) FBS *pirenti* MZS *pirenti*	Z *pitsiro* (*intco*) FBD *pitsiro* MZD *pitsiro*	WB *pibanirite* MBS *pibanirite* (*numatcienga*) FZS *pibanirite* (*numatcienga*) ZH *pibanirite*	W *pitsinanete* (*nueña*) MBD *pimenguegare* FZD *pimenguegare*
− 1	S *pitomi* (*pitomi*) BS *pitomi*	D *pishinto* (*pisinto*) BD *pishinto*	DH *pitineri* ZS *pitineri* (*naniro*)	SW *paniro* ZD *paniro* (*itcaria*)

	Male		Female	
− 2	SS	*pibisarite* (*tcaunka*)	SD	*pibisarote* (*tcainka*)
	DS	*pibisarite* (*tcaunka*)	DD	*pibisarote* (*tcainka*)

SOURCES: Casevitz 1977:122–123,137–138. The term *pimenguegare* (MBD/FZD) is also used for "fiancée" (ibid., 123). Terms in brackets derive from Farabee (1922:38). Cf. also d'Ans 1974.

DEVIATIONS FROM THE TWO-LINE PATTERN	CONCEIVABLE IDEOLOGICAL OR BEHAVIOURAL CORRELATES
Casevitz: None Farabee: MB=ZS ? (See text.)	 Matrilateral affiliation, uxorilocal residence

itinkame attracted labour by hosting major beer parties. In accordance with what is probably a very general mechanism for expanding individual prestige (cf. the Barasana), polygyny would have been a crucial asset in the hosting of feasts and ceremonies (Camino 1977:134). Farabee (1922:16) notes that headmen usually had three or four wives.

Apparently, a Machiguenga chief could be sufficiently influential to ask a village of Piro to settle close to his own territory, in order to facilitate alliances (Casevitz 1977: 137). Traditions from the beginning of this century mention the exchange of daughters between two major chiefs from opposite extremes of Machiguenga territory (ibid., 140), which suggests an ideal of rank endogamy.

Alliance

The kin terminology of the Machiguenga prescribes bilateral cross-cousin marriage and sister exchange (Johnson & Johnson 1975:637, 638; Johnson 1979:54, 57). Whereas Johnson (1979:54) writes that marriage is preferably endogamous, Casevitz (1977:124, 129) emphasizes the importance of local exogamy. The short-cycle exchange implied by a preference for FZD marriage (ibid., 129, 133, 134) is consistent with Casevitz' conclusion that bonds of alliance between two local groups are perpetuated in each generation. Thus, even though local groups are exogamous, constellations of such groups would tend toward endogamy (ibid., 130).

A system of alternating generations, in itself consistent with FZD marriage, is suggested by the occurrence of marriages between grandparents and grandchildren (ibid., 126–127), and by the observation that grandchildren "reproduce" the marriages of their grandparents (ibid., 134).

In a sample of 20 Machiguenga marriages, nine (45%) complied with the preference for actual or distant patrilateral cross-cousin marriage, three were matrilateral cross-cousin marriages, three involved direct exchange, four were oblique (two with ZD, two with FZ), and one was external to genealogical considerations (ibid., 138–139).

External Relations

Nineteenth-century reports describe the Machiguenga as a peaceful people, and contemporary institutions "show no signs of recent warfare or extensive feuding" (Johnson & Johnson 1975:637). Casevitz (1977: 134, 136, 137) observes that the Machiguenga system of marriage alliances has an inherent capacity for integration of distant groups. Ever since the days of the Inca, the Machiguenga have been involved in extensive exchange networks linking the tropical forest with the Andean highlands (Gade 1972; Camino 1977). The most active "middlemen" of this trade were apparently the Piro, probably the "Anti" of Inca tradition. Until the beginning of this century, Piro expeditions on their way to markets upstreams along the Urubamba annually pillaged Machiguenga villages in search of slaves, canoes, and garden produce (Camino 1977: 132–133). Camino (ibid., 133–135) suggests that the *itinkame* "big men" of the Machiguenga may have emerged as a response to these Piro intrusions. Posted at the mouths of tributaries inhabited by Machiguenga, *itinkame* tactics to avoid Piro attacks included planting gardens for the exclusive purpose of "serving" the Piro and diverting their interest from settlements along the tributaries. Machiguenga "big men" also developed some peaceful trade with the intruders.

15. The Mehinacu

Kin Terminology (Table 17)

The only feature which contradicts the two-line pattern is the generational equation of vocative terms for siblings and cross-cousins. The referential nomenclature, however, maintains the distinction.

Table 17
KIN TERMINOLOGY OF THE MEHINACU
LINGUISTIC FAMILY: Arawak
Male Ego, terms of address.

GEN.	Male		Female	
+ 2	FF *atu*		FM *atsi*	
	MF *atu*		MM *atsi*	

	KIN (Lineal kin, parallel collaterals, affines of affines)		*AFFINES* (In-laws, cross collaterals)	
	Male	Female	Male	Female
+ 1	F *papa*	M *mama*		
	FB *papa*	MZ *mama*	MB *ua*	FZ *aki*
0	B *nuje*	Z *nujeju*		W *ninyu*
	FBS *nuje*	FBD *nujeju*	MBS *nuje*	MBD *nujeju*
			(*nutanuléi*)	(*nutanuleju*)
	MZS *nuje*	MZD *nujeju*	FZS *nuje*	FZD *nujeju*
			(*nutanuléi*)	(*nutanuleju*)
− 1	S *nutāi*	D *nitsupalu*	DH (*inyerí*)	SW (*inswí*)
	BS *nutāi*	BD *nitsupalu*	ZS *nuwā*	ZD *nutamitswī*

	Male		Female	
− 2	SS *weku*		SD *weku*	
	DS *weku*		DD *weku*	

SOURCES: Gregor 1977:277. All terms are vocative except the bracketed, referential *nutanuléi/ nutanuleju* for cross-cousins and, apparently, the bracketed *inyerí* (DH) and *inswí* (SW) (ibid., 283). The vocative *ninyu* for W derives from another context (Gregor 1974:336).

DEVIATIONS FROM THE TWO-LINE PATTERN	CONCEIVABLE IDEOLOGICAL OR BEHAVIOURAL CORRELATES
B=MBS=FZS, Z=MBD=FZD Terms of address only)	Cognatic principles

Local Group Size and Composition

The Mehinacu village had 57 inhabitants at the time of Gregor's fieldwork (Gregor 1973:242). Ideally, a man resides uxorilocally "for a period of several months to several years" (Gregor 1974:343), or "until he has had several children" (Gregor 1977:266), at which time he returns permanently to his natal household. Gregor (1974:336) writes that a man *"usually* returns to his natal household" (italics mine), suggesting that a period of bride-service followed by virilocal residence is statistically the rule, as well. Elsewhere, however, Gregor (1977:267) asserts that "there is no regularly followed rule of post-marital residence." The actual pattern, then, is best described as ambilocal (Gregor 1973:242, 1974:333).

Patterns of Affiliation Other than Residence

Mehinacu kinship is reckoned bilaterally (Gregor 1973:242; 1974:333, 336; 1977:261,

289, 297, 299). Parents expect their same-sex children to embody their own virtues, duplicating their "former selves" (nuwēi) along lines of parallel succession (Gregor 1977:270).

The combination of bifurcating terms for the first ascending generation and Hawaiian cousin terms tends to generate "double relationships", e.g. when children are taught to address a father's brother both as FB (papa) by their father, and as MB (ua) by their mother (ibid., 290). This clearly illustrates how anomalous Hawaiian cousin terms are in a two-line context (cf. Dole 1969). Although Gregor (1977:289, 299) explains "double relationships" as an inevitable result of the articulation of bilateral kinship reckoning and endogamy, the example he mentions suggests that such ambiguity would be eliminated if the terminology was consistently bifurcated. Bilateral affiliation and endogamy is a widespread combination in the Amazon lowlands, but is generally accompanied by bifurcate merging cousin terms, which consistently distinguish kin from affines. In the Mehinacu case, it is obvious that the Hawaiian cousin terms are the source of the confusion.

Another peculiarity of Mehinacu kinship is that children produced by a man in his marriage and in his extra-marital affairs are recognized as being of the "same foot" (ikitsapa pinyerí), implying that "the children are 'real kin' who are prohibited from having sexual relations or marrying and who will one day have important in-law relationships with one another's spouses" (ibid., 293). The Mehinacu theory of multiple paternity thus widens Ego's set of kinsmen.

The system of name transmission from grandparents to grandchildren (Gregor 1974: 336; 1977:256–257) suggests a principle of alternating generations. Each Mehinacu child receives the names of both its paternal and maternal grandparents of the same sex. Since a person may never mention the name of an in-law, however, a mother must call her children by her own parents' names, an a

father must call his children by those of his. A girl is thus recognized by her mother as a successor to her MM, while a boy is recognized by his father as a successor to his FF. In the context of stringent male-female dualism, the interrelatedness of parallel affiliation and alternating generations is once again apparent. The mediation of an official name-giver, finally, recalls name transmission among the Gê-speaking Timbira.

Hierarchy

Although not apparent from the vocative terminology, there is a distinction between elder and younger siblings (tapuri/jeri) within the nuclear family (Gregor 1977:278). Older siblings are more likely to be initiated as chiefs.

There is a tendency for chiefly roles and offices to be transmitted from father to son (ibid., 270). Whereas most Mehinacu recall only very shallow genealogies, the chief maintains a deep genealogical memory (ibid., 263).

Ideally, only chiefs practice polygyny (Gregor 1974:341). As can be expected where males reside uxorilocally in order to conduct their bride-service, the son-in-law is in a "highly subordinate position" in relation to his wife's household (Gregor 1974:343; 1977:283, 285).

Alliance

The Mehinacu village is endogamous (Gregor 1973:242; 1977:297), but households are exogamous (Gregor 1974:343). Suitable spouses are classificatory, bilateral cross-cousins (Gregor 1973:242; 1977:280, 288). Approximately 65% of all Mehinacu marriages conform to this rule (Gregor 1974:333). The contention that first cousins are unmarriageable is undoubtedly related to the Hawaiian cousin terminology (Gregor 1977:288). Some Mehinacu informants,

126

however, maintain that first cross-cousins are "a little bit" marriageable (ibid., 278), i.e. presumably more so than siblings or parallel cousins. Because of the Hawaiian equation of siblings and cross-cousins, the latter category is defined by reference to the first ascending generation (ibid., 290). In other respects, too, the logic of the two-line structure survives. Thus, it is considered wrong to have sexual relations with an in-law's spouse (ibid., 295). Such affairs are regarded as sufficiently disruptive to justify the termination of affinal relationships (ibid., 296). Finally, sister exchange remains an explicit ideal (ibid., 285).

External Relations

Although involved in the Upper Xingú exchange network as specialists in zoomorphic vessels and cotton (Basso 1973: 56), the Mehinacu prefer to marry within their own village (Gregor 1973:242; 1974: 333; 1977:297).

Conclusions: Arawak

Owing to the very modest size of our Arawak sample, our conclusions can only be tentative. Lévi-Strauss (1945:41–42) finds it significant that the Palikur had dual organization, "since as members of the Arawak stock they belong to the higher cultural level of the tropical area." Indeed, the impressive chiefdoms of the Mojo, Bauré, and Paressí in eastern Bolivia were all Arawak-speakers (Métraux 1948c; 1948d:408–424; Steward & Faron 1959: 252–259). We have seen that the Machiguenga previously maintained authority structures capable of integrating impressive numbers. The Machiguenga and Mehinacu both retain polygyny as the prerogative of chiefs, and both may previously have had an ideal of rank endogamy. Significantly, Hill (1985:29, 31–32, notes 5, 8) reports strong tendencies toward hierarchy and rank endogamy among Arawakan groups in Venezuela.

The two kin terminologies in our sample maintain the fundamental two-line pattern, although it is contradicted by the generational, vocative cousin nomenclature of the Mehinacu. Farabee's early kin terms from the Machiguenga suggest equations of grand-kin with cross-collaterals (FF=MB, FM= FZ).

Both groups live in small communities of less than, or just above, 50 people. Although post-marital residence is *de facto* ambilocal, both cultures appear to maintain an ideal of uxorilocality, even if only as an initial period of bride-service among the Mehinacu.

Both the Machiguenga and the Mehinacu reckon bilateral affiliation, and both have elements of an ideology of parallel transmission. Both, too, recognize principles of alternating generations, so that a boy succeeds his FF and a girl her MM.

Both groups, finally, prescribe bilateral cross-cousin marriage and sister exchange, and have a generally peaceful reputation. The Machiguenga express a preference for FZD marriage, and there are occasional marriages to a ZD or FZ.

Chapter 6

Carib

15. The Trio

Kin Terminology (Table 18)

An equation which contradicts the two-line pattern is ZSW=SW=MBW. The implied identification S=ZS suggests cognatic principles, while that of MB=ZS points to matrilineal continuity for males. Matrilineal principles are also suggested by the Crow-type equation MBC=C. On the other hand, several equations indicate patrilineal principles. These include FZH=FZS, FZH=ZH, FZC=ZC, ZH=DH, and ZH=ZS. Indications of avuncular marriage include FZ=MM, M=FZD, MB=FZS, MBW=Z, MBC=ZC, WB=ZS, WF=ZH, and when Ego has married his MBD, MBS=DH.

Local Group Size and Composition

The average Trio village numbers about 30 individuals (Rivière 1969:74). The rule of post-marital residence is normally uxorilocal (Rivière 1966b:551; 1969:270, 275; 1977:41). However, Rivière (1977:41) writes of Carib societies in general that the occurrence of patrilocal residence among sons of strong chiefs is in need of further investigation.

Patterns of Affiliation Other than Residence

The Trio lack unilineal descent rules of any kind (Rivière 1966b:551; 1969:62; 1977:41). F and MB are both respected in a similar sense. It is only when MB and ZS come to be related as affines that this particular relation

"hardens slightly" (1966b:553). Rivière's informants differed on the subject of biological parent-child relationships. One gave a decidedly patrilineal theory of procreation, others a bilateral, and yet others an account suggesting parallel affiliation (Rivière 1969:62–63). Rivière discovered "a conceptual vertical cohesion" between husbands of Ego's female patrilateral kin and between Ego's mother's patrilateral kin (cf. terms *ti*, *pito*, and *imuku*) (ibid., 79). In fact, P. Frikel maintains that the Trio are patrilineal (ibid., 65).

Rivière (1966a:738; 1966b:554–555; 1969:278–279) points out that consistent MBD/ZD marriage would tend to produce an alternation of generations similar to that generated by FZD marriage. Moreover, in terms of the genealogically skewed representation of wife-givers and wife-takers (e.g. FZS=MB, MBS=ZS), Ego's affines as a category occupy alternate generations (i.e. first ascending and first descending) of the kin terminology (Rivière 1966b:550; 1969:276).

Hierarchy

Rivière (1966b:550) writes that status differences expressed in terms of relative age are reflected in the kin terminology by removing cross-kin to adjacent genealogical levels (FZC to +1, MBC to −1). These differences, however, do not coincide with a dimension of respect between wife-takers and wife-givers, for the obvious reason that both kinds of cross-cousin can be married (ibid., 550–551; 1969:276). The term *pito* occurs in many Carib languages, everywhere implying inferiority (e.g. slave, servant, ZS,

Table 18
KIN TERMINOLOGY OF THE TRIO
LINGUISTIC FAMILY: Carib
Male Ego, terms of reference.

GEN.	Male	Female
+ 2	FF *tamu* MF *tamu*	FM *nosi* *kuku* MM *nosi* *kuku*

	KIN (Lineal kin, parallel collaterals, affines of affines)		*AFFINES* (In-laws, cross collaterals)	
	Male	Female	Male	Female
+ 1	F *ipapa* FB *ipapa* MZH *ipapa*	M *imama* MZ *imama* FBW *imama*	WF *tamu* *ti* MB *ti* FZH *ti* *konoka*	WM *nosi* *kuku* FZ *nosi* *kuku* MBW *nosi, kuku,* *wai, akami,* *ipaeye*
0	B e *ipipi* y *akami* FBS e *ipipi* y *akami* MZS e *ipipi* y *akami* WZH e *ipipi*	Z e *wai* y *wari* FBD e *wai* y *wari* MZD e *wai* y *wari*	WB *pito* *konoka* MBS *pito* *imuku* FZS *pito* *ti* ZH *pito, ti, imu-* *ku, konoka*	W *ipi* MBD *emerimpa* *emi* FZD *emerimpa* *imama* BW *emi*
− 1	S *imuku* BS *imuku* ZDH *ipamĭ*	D *emi* BD *emi* ZSW *ipaeye*	DH *pito* *imuku* ZS *pito* *imuku*	SW *akami, emi* *ipaeye* ZD *emerimpa* *emi*

	Male		Female	
− 2	SS	*ipa*	SD	*ipa*
	DS	*ipa*	DD	*ipa*

SOURCES: Rivière 1969:284

DEVIATIONS FROM THE TWO-LINE PATTERN	CONCEIVABLE IDEOLOGICAL OR BEHAVIOURAL CORRELATES
SW=ZSW	Cognatic principles
MBW=ZSW, MBC=C	Matrilateral affiliation, uxori-local residence
FZH=FZS, FZH=ZH, FZC=ZC, ZH=DH, ZH=ZS	Patrilateral affiliation
FZ=MM, M=FZD, MB=FZS, MBW=Z, MBC=ZC, WB=ZS, WF=ZH, MBS=DH	Avuncular marriage

DH), except among the Trio, where it is reciprocal (Rivière 1969:81; 1977:40). Basically, the *pito* relationship implies exchange, a meaning which it maintains in all the Carib societies where it occurs. Whether this exchange relationship should have implications of rank or inequality of status depends on other features subject to cultural variation. The reciprocal nature of the term *pito* among the Trio is consistent with Rivière's observation that "it would be wrong to describe the son-in-law as living in a state of submission to his father-in-law."

Alliance

Rivière (1966a:739) writes that "there is no doubt that the present marriage practices of the Trio are a development (or degeneration) of bilateral cross-cousin marriage." He (1969:88, 273) demonstrates how the kin terminology of the Trio can reveal the probably fairly recent imposition of ZD marriage on a pre-existing system of pure bilateral cross-cousin marriage. The prescribed category (*emerimpa*="potential spouse") includes female cross-cousins of both kinds and also the ZD (Rivière 1966b: 551). The rule is that a man should marry the daughter of a *nosi* or *ti*, "with perhaps the slightly greater emphasis being placed on the *nosi*" (Rivière 1969:141). This rule would, in fact, accommodate marriages with FZ, MZ, FZD, and MBD (who are all daughters of *nosi*), and with ZD and FZD (daughters of *ti*). The primary meanings of *nosi* and *ti* in this context, however, are FZ and MB, respectively, whereby the emphasis on *nosi* implies a slight preference for FZD over MBD.

The frequency of ZD marriage is considerable, as is evidenced by Rivière's remark that, in one-third of all Trio marriages, the Z can be expected to be the WM (ibid., 270). In contrast to Lévi-Strauss' account of the Nambikwara, ZD marriage among the Trio is "neither secondary nor privileged, but

primary and fundamental" (ibid., 273). Rivière (ibid., 271, 275, 279) suggests that this marriage practice among the Trio was a strategy of introversion following European contact, and that a common element of all systems of ZD marriage may be the shortage of women, so that "it is necessary in order to obtain a wife to take a woman from the next generation". Whether designed to maintain the purity or cohesion of social subgroups, or for the survival of populations suffering from demographic decline, avuncular marriage is a strategy to guard, through endogamy, the boundaries of society (ibid., 281–282). Consistent with this conclusion is the observation that the Trio village or village cluster is predominantly endogamous (1966b:551, 556; 1969:143, 154, 270).

External Relations

Endogamous marriage strategies, yielding only local, tightly closed cycles of reciprocity (Rivière 1969:277), produce a "picture of Trio society as consisting of a series of introverted and isolated village communities" (ibid., 271).

16. The Kalapalo

Kin Terminology (Table 19)

Judging from Basso's (1973:78–80) exposition of Kalapalo kin categories, the terminology is faultlessly faithful to the two-line pattern.

Local Group Size and Composition

The Kalapalo village visited by Basso numbered about 110 inhabitants in 1968 (Basso 1970:414; 1973:4). Apparently, there is no rule of unilocal post-marital residence, as households can be composed of "almost

130

Table 19
KIN TERMINOLOGY OF THE KALAPALO
LINGUISTIC FAMILY: Carib
Male Ego, terms of reference.

GEN.	Male		Female	
+ 2	FF *isawpigi* MF *isawpigi*		FM *initsu* MM *initsu*	

	KIN (Lineal kin, parallel collaterals, affines of affines)		*AFFINES* (In-laws, cross collaterals)	
	Male	Female	Male	Female
+ 1	F *isuwi* FB *isuwi* MZH *(isuwi)*	M *isi* MZ *isi* FBW *(isi)*	WF *ijogu* MB *ijogu* FZH *(ijogu)*	WM *itsigi* FZ *itsigi* MBW *(itsigi)*

0	B e *efiñano*
	      y *efisu*
	FBS e *efiñano*
	      y *efisu*
	MZS e *efiñano*
	      y *efisu*
		Z e *ifasu*
		      y *ikene*
		FBD e *ifasu*
		      y *ikene*
		MZD e *ifasu*
		      y *ikene*
			WB *(ifandaw)*
			
			MBS *ifandaw*
			
			FZS *ifandaw*
			
			ZH *(ifandaw)*
				W *ifandaw*
				
				MBD *ifandaw*
				
				FZD *ifandaw*
				
				BW *(ifandaw)*

– 1	S *mukugu* BS *mukugu*	D *ndisi* BD *ndisi*	DH *ifatuwi* ZS *ifatuwi*	SW *ifati* ZD *ifati*

	Male		Female	
– 2	SS DS	*ifijaw* *ifijaw*	SD DD	*ifijaw* *ifijaw*

SOURCES: Basso 1973:78–80. Terms in brackets are assumptions based on Basso's structural definitions.

DEVIATIONS FROM THE TWO-LINE PATTERN	CONCEIVABLE IDEOLOGICAL OR BEHAVIOURAL CORRELATES
None	

any combination of kinsmen and affines" (Basso 1973:52). For a man, the choice of residence hinges on the strength of his own kinsmen in his natal village, so that uxorilocality generally occurs among "men who have few kinsmen or none who control a household group in the village they are affiliated with" (ibid., 93).

Patterns of Affiliation Other than Residence

Ego reckons affiliation to his kindred, or *otómo*, a "series of linked sibling sets" defined in terms of common, patrilateral and/or matrilateral filiation (Basso 1970:406; 1973: 52, 78). There are no units delineated accord-

131

ing to any principle of descent (Basso 1973:74), and the categories of kin and affines are conceptual rather than discrete entities (Basso 1970:411).

Name-giving, however, ideally exhibits some regularity, as "each parent gives to the child the names belonging to his own parent, according to the appropriate sex" (Basso 1973:85). Thus, a boy receives names from FF and MF, a girl from FM and MM. Where repeated intermarriage has occurred between two terminologically defined categories of kinsmen, each child will thus be affiliated with both sides. When it comes to marriage, however, the cross-sex definition of the prescribed *ifandaw* category effectively reconstructs the two categories. In terms of relations between males, Ego sides with his F and becomes opposed as affine to his MB, while female Ego sides with her M as opposed to FZ. Thus, it can be seen that parallel affiliation is a logical concomitant of Dravidian, two-line systems. Consistent with this conclusion is the fact that inheritance of the special *anetu* status ("village representative") follows a rule of parallel transmission, male *anetu* being succeeded by their eldest sons and female *anetu* by their eldest daughters (ibid., 133).

Hierarchy

Newly married spouses who have moved into the households of their affines have to obey a number of restrictions and obligations which give them a somewhat subordinate status (Basso 1973:92–93). A co-resident DH or SW is expected to be subservient in the presence of his or her affines (ibid., 108). One of the determinants of village leadership is the possession of many subservient relatives who can lend both material and verbal support. Another determinant is the leader's ability to accumulate several of the four ceremonial roles (*ifi*="ceremonial specialist", *oto*="ceremonial sponsor", *fuati*="shaman", *anetu*="village represen-

tative"), all of which bring rewards for services. By actively performing several of these roles, an individual can secure a steady flow of wealth, which is invested in the loyalty of kin and affines or, through the acquisition of new wives, scarce trade commodities, or esoteric skills, in new social ties (ibid., 107, 124). The acquisition of these special statuses is often interrelated, e.g. *oto* deriving their position from an inherited *anetu* status (ibid., 111), or *fuati* qualifying as such by virtue of their capacity as *oto* (ibid., 113). By means of the *anetu* status, an impetus toward leadership is thus inherited from F to S. It is also interesting to note that this inherited position is especially associated with inter- and intra-village trading, as in the *uluki* ceremony, when trading begins in the *anetu's* house and continues clockwise around the village circle (ibid., 135–136).

Alliance

Within the cognatic *otómo* category, only *ifandaw* (cross-cousins) can be married (Basso 1970:410; 1973:87; 1975:209; 1984:33). Sibling exchange between *ifandaw* is considered "highly desirable" (Basso 1970:410, 413; 1973:88). Marriages which are formally "arranged" are most often between persons already classified as *ifandaw* to each other (Basso 1973:88). The exchange of spouses between two groups of kinsmen can continue for several generations, though Basso points out that such temporary alliances differ from those prescribed between corporate, exogamous groups such as moieties (ibid.,89–90). Polygyny is usually the result of such "formal alliances between two groups of kinsmen" (ibid., 101).

External Relations

The villages of the Upper Xingú have specialized in the production, for trade, of different commodities, such as ornaments,

132

ceramics, bows, gourds, cotton, *urucú*, and salt (Basso 1973:55–56). Kinship ties similarly unite all the Upper Xingú villages (ibid., 74, 86). There are no established preferences relating to endogamy or exogamy, as one person may have reasons for preferring marriage within his own village group, while another chooses to marry out (ibid., 87). Basso (1970:414–415; 1973:102) notes that depopulation has stimulated local exogamy among the Kalapalo. External alliances are intimately tied to the career of particular men as village leaders (Basso 1973:107). The *anetu* institution, which emphasizes the political importance of external relations by making the role of "village representative" inheritable, is specifically associated with inter-village trading (ibid., 132, 135–136).

17. The Kuikuru

Kin Terminology

The Kuikuru have an Hawaiian (generation) cousin terminology, which equates cross-cousins with siblings and parallel cousins. Dole (1969:111) found that a few older informants, however, employed a special term (*ufau*) for cross-cousins, suggesting that the generation terminology represents a transformation of what was originally a bifurcate merging nomenclature. Basso (1970:411–412) explains the rarity of the *ufau* category by reference to the different speech contexts of generational and bifurcating terms, noting that the cognate Kalapalo term *ifaú* (plur. *ifandaw*) has impolite connotations. Whereas Dole simply classifies Kalapalo zero generation terminology as generational, Basso (ibid., 407–409) shows how the *ifisúandaw* category can be defined in several different ways, depending on context. Thus, although *ifisúandaw* in one context may refer to all kin of Ego's generation, in another it may be restricted to those kin whose parents are same-sex *ifisúandaw*,

a definition whereby it is contrasted with *ifandaw* (i.e. cross-cousins, potential spouses.)

Local Group Size and Composition

In the early 1950:s, the Kuikuru village on the Upper Xingú numbered 145 individuals (Carneiro 1973:98; Dole 1969:107). Postmarital residence is ambilocal, but with a statistical predominance of virilocality (Dole 1969:108). Virilocality is apparently also, after a period of residence with the bride's parents, the explicitly stated ideal (ibid.,107, 109; 1984:46).

Patterns of Affiliation Other than Residence

Kinship is reckoned bilaterally, but kindred are neither named nor corporate (Dole 1969:109). Headmanship, however, may be inherited patrilineally. Dole (ibid., 109–110) suggests that the Kuikuru may formerly have practiced unilocal residence, local exogamy, and cross-cousin marriage. These are explicit ideals, nowadays generally contradicted in practice.

Hierarchy

Political status is patrilineally inheritable (ibid., 109). Formerly, polygyny was the privilege of headmen or champion wrestlers (Dole 1984:50).

Alliance

The Kuikuru state a preference for bilateral cross-cousin marriage (1969:108). There is also a preference for local exogamy, but Dole's statistics show that more than 75% of all marriages are locally endogamous. Dole (ibid., 110) suggests that the present inclination towards endogamy is a fairly recent response to demographic instability.

A man and his sister ideally try to arrange the marriage of their children (Dole 1984: 50). Cross aunts (FZ) and uncles (MB) are thus *kitofo* ("speakers") for the prospective mates. Dole's informants specifically mentioned FZD and ZD as legitimate spouses (ibid., 58–59).

External Relations

The high measure of endogamy suggests village introversion, but Basso (1973:56) lists the Kuikuru among those Upper Xingú villages involved in specialized production for exchange. The Kuikuru and Kalapalo both specialize in the production of gourds and necklaces of *iño* shell.

18. The Karinya

Kin Terminology (Table 20)

Traditional Karinya kin terminology is flawlessly bifurcated according to the two-line pattern. Notable, however, are the lineal equations WF=WB and W=BW=SW= MBD=FZD=ZD, which suggest some principle of continuity among agnates. In the Cachama dialect, moreover, *káxtopo* is extended to second ascending generation males, and yZ is equated with D in the category *mwiyi* (Schwerin 1982:19).

Local Group Size and Composition

Local groups "definitely average more than 100", some containing up to 700 inhabitants, although the latter type of settlement may be a recent phenomenon (ibid., 17). Post-marital residence is "preferentially uxori-local, but statistically virilocality occurs almost as frequently" (ibid., 21). In practice, then, residence is ambilocal.

Patterns of Affiliation Other than Residence

Although there is "no clear principle of descent," Schwerin (ibid., 17) notes a "matrilateral bias" in Karinya social organization.

Alliance

The Karinya incline strongly toward village endogamy (ibid., 18). Cachama is 72% endogamous, but the community is large, and only one-third of all marriages are endogamous to the local neighbourhood (ibid., 21). The *tákano* category, which equates W=MBD=FZD=ZD, suggests bilateral cross-cousin and ZD marriage.

External Relations

Generalizing for most Carib tribes, Schwerin (ibid., 38) suggests that the abandonment of local group endogamy is a fairly recent result of increased external contact, acculturation, and population growth. He characterizes Carib societies as "atomistic", but local endogamy is a statistical fact rather than a rule (ibid., 39, 40). Finally, he postulates that the application of a "kin-affine" (i.e. two-line) system of social classification, or as Schwerin prefers to call it, ^ "kin integration system," works effectively only in small groups, whereas in groups of more than 100 members, "the system begins to break down" (ibid., 43).

19. The Barama River Caribs

Kin Terminology

The kin terminology of the Barama River Caribs is very similar to that of the Karinya (Schwerin 1982:24). Among the several

Table 20
KIN TERMINOLOGY OF THE KARINYA
LINGUISTIC FAMILY: Carib
Male Ego, terms of reference.

GEN.	Male		Female	
+ 2	FF *támuru* MF *támuru*		FM *anotik* MM *anotik*	

	KIN (Lineal kin, parallel collaterals, affines of affines)		*AFFINES* (In-laws, cross collaterals)	
	Male	Female	Male	Female
+ 1	F *dümwü* FB *dümwü* MZH *dümwü*	M *asano* MZ *asano* FBW *asano*	WF *káxtopo* *te?wü* MB *káxtopo* FZH *káxtopo*	WM *boxpwü* FZ *bowpwü* MBW*boxpwü*

0	B e *še?wo*
	   y *piri*
	FBS e *še?wo*
	   y *piri*
	MZS e *še?wo*
	   y *piri*
		Z e *ba?wa*
		   y *ka?mi*
		FBD e *ba?wa*
		   y *ka?mi*
		MZD e *ba?wa*
		   y *ka?mi*
			WB *te?wü*
			
			MBS *te?wü*
			
			FZS *te?wü*
			
			ZH *te?wü*
				W *tákano*
				
				MBD *tákano*
				
				FZD *tákano*
				
				BW *tákano*

− 1	S *úmulu*
	
	BS *úmulu*
		D *demwidi*
		
		BD *demwidi*
			DH *pwátimwi*
			    pwarimwi
			ZS *pwátimwi*
			    pwarimwi
				SW *tákano*
				
				ZD *tákano*

	Male		Female	
− 2	SS *pwari* DS *pwari*		SD *pwari* DD *pwari*	

SOURCES: Schwerin 1982:18–22.

DEVIATIONS FROM THE TWO-LINE PATTERN	CONCEIVABLE IDEOLOGICAL OR BEHAVIOURAL CORRELATES
None	

cognate terms, there is the equation of MBD=FZD=ZD in the *takano* category, suggesting continuity in affinal relationships and possibilities of ZD marriage.

Local Group Size and Composition

In the 1930:s, the Barama River Caribs lived in small, seminomadic groups constituting a largely endogamous population of about 200 (Adams 1977:11). Forty years later, the population was still predominantly endogamous but numbered about 550.

Marriage involved an initial period of uxorilocal residence, but local groups were usually composed of brothers or parallel cousins with wives and children (ibid., 12, 13). Instead of succeeding their fathers-in-law, mature sons-in-law at some point "moved away, regrouped with their male collateral group, and recreated society" (Adams 1979: 6–7).

Patterns of Affiliation Other than Residence

Adams (1979:9–10) writes that "a matri-centered trans-generational continuity provided a social backbone to which separate male generations attached." Among males, there was no corresponding principle of linear succession, but the group of male siblings or parallel cousins was "a fundamental reference for social organization" (ibid., 5, 10).

In the 1930:s, the population was divided into two largely endogamous groups of about 100 individuals each (ibid., 5). These groups were referred to as "Top Side" and "Bottom Side", and each maintained its own two-line system of internal kin-affine differentiation.

Hierarchy

Barama River Carib society was "highly egalitarian" (Adams 1979:5). The inequality between "vulnerable individualized wife-takers" and their superior wife-givers, whose households they served for a number of years, was only temporary (ibid., 6, 9).

Alliance

Among the Barama River Caribs, oblique marriages such as ZD marriage and even grandfather–granddaughter marriage are treated by Adams (1977:11) as variations on a fundamental structure of bilateral cross-cousin marriage (symmetric alliance.) In terms of explicit rules, the marriageable category for male Ego consisted of female cross relatives in Ego's own and first descending generations (Adams 1979:4). At least one-third of the marriages recorded by Gillin were between primary cross-cousins (ibid., 5). A typical marriage is arranged by a mother between her D and her B or BS, which amounts respectively to ZD and FZD marriage.

External Relations

The Barama River Caribs were a small, isolated population without either friendly or hostile neighbours (Adams 1977:15; 1979:5, 9).

20. The Pemon

Kin Terminology (Table 21)

Except for the Hawaiian equation of zero generation females, Pemon kin terminology accords perfectly with the two-line pattern. Precisely as Basso (1970:407–409) demonstrated for the Kalapalo, the Hawaiian equation of female siblings and parallel cousins with female cross-cousins is context specific, i.e. applied whenever consanguineal proximity is stressed, while the alternative term for cross-cousins (wa?ni mure=child of uwa?nin, i.e. FZ or MBW) is used only when the kin-affine distinction is emphasized (Thomas 1979:76–77).

Local Group Size and Composition

Pemon settlements range from one to seven households, each composed of one or more nuclear or extended families (ibid., 65). The size of local groups, then, appears to vary between 10 and 70 people.

Post-marital residence is predominantly uxorilocal (ibid., 78), but men often try to return to their parents' group after a period with that of their affines (Schwerin 1982:30).

Patterns of Affiliation Other than Residence

Affiliation is bilateral, and the kindred category encompasses affines of all the three medial generations (Thomas 1979:66).

136

Table 21
KIN TERMINOLOGY OF THE PEMON
LINGUISTIC FAMILY: Carib
Male Ego, terms of reference.

GEN.	Male		Female	
+ 2	FF *utamo* MF *utamo*		FM *unok* MM *unok*	

GEN.	*KIN* (Lineal kin, parallel collaterals, affines of affines)		*AFFINES* (In-laws, cross collaterals)	
	Male	Female	Male	Female
+ 1	F *papai* FB *papai* MZH *papai*	M *amai* MZ *amai* FBW *amai*	WF *umui* MB *umui* FZH *umui*	WM *uwa?nin* FZ *uwa?nin* MBW *uwa?nin*
0	B *urui* FBS *urui* MZS *urui*	Z *na?nai* FBD *na?nai* MZD *na?nai*	WB *uyese* MBS *uyese* FZS *uyese* ZH *uyese*	W *unopi* MBD *na?nai wa?ni mure* FZD *na?nai wa?ni mure* BW *na?nai*
− 1	S *umuku* BS *umuku*	D *uyensi* BD *uyensi*	DH *upoitori* ZS *upoitori* WBS *upoitori*	SW *upase* ZD *upase* WBD *upase*

	Male		Female	
− 2	SS *upayan* DS *upayan*		SD *upayan* DD *upayan*	

SOURCES: Thomas 1971:10–15. The term *wa?ni mure* for MBD and FZD derives from Thomas 1979:76.

DEVIATIONS FROM THE TWO-LINE PATTERN	CONCEIVABLE IDEOLOGICAL OR BEHAVIOURAL CORRELATES
Z=MBD=FZD=BW	Cognatic principles

Hierarchy

The Pemon recognize leaders (*tyeburu*) who counsel in disputes between families throughout the tribal territory. As is generally the case with uxorilocality, wife-givers (WF, WB) are superior to wife-takers (DH, ZH) (ibid., 78).

Alliance

Thomas (1971:7) writes that "the Pemon terminology is linked to a now much debilitated but still functioning system of bilateral cross-cousin marriage." The generational equation of female siblings and cross-cousins, which appears to contradict this

137

marriage practice, is assumed by Thomas (ibid., 9) to be of fairly recent origin. The term for "sweetheart" (*uyawasiri*) may at one time have designated the category of opposite-sex cross-cousins and potential spouses (ibid., 8). Marriage is enjoined with a category including opposite-sex cross-cousins, but this class can be determined only by reference to the first ascending generation (Thomas 1979:63, 76–77). Thus, the ideal of symmetric alliance (sister exchange) is preserved, even though the social distance implied by the relationship between opposite-sex affines is suppressed. Thomas believes that this circumlocution of affinality should be related to the Pemon preference for close marriage, both genealogically and spatially. Of the 35% of all marriages which are contracted with kin, the two basic categories are (1) marriages with cross-cousins (*wa?ni mure*), and (2) marriages with *upase* (including the ZD) (ibid., 78).

External Relations

Much as Dole (1969) suggests for the Kuikuru, Thomas (1971:9) assumes that the equation of all zero generation females, which contradicts the ideal of cross-cousin marriage, derives from disturbances associated with the "extremely strong external influences on the Pemon during the last one hundred years (by diamond miners, merchants, missions, civil authorities, etc)." The strong preference for local endogamy, then, may be of recent origin.

21. The Waiwai

Kin Terminology (Table 22)

Stripped of some of the alternative usages, the Waiwai terminology shows clear two-line characteristics. Fock (1963:189, 191) warns that "all terms cannot with complete

certainty be regarded as having been correctly given," but it is important to examine the possible implications of anomalous equations.

The equation yB=BS implies patrilineal principles, while the inclusion of ZS in the same category (*piti*) suggests cognatic principles, as does BD=ZD. The term *wachi* for yFBD appears to have no equivalent in the case of MZD, suggesting that distinctions of relative age are a concern primarily among patrilateral kin.

An absence of symmetric alliance is suggested by the distinctions MB≠FZH, FZ≠MBW, DH≠ZS, and SW≠ZD. The referential term *wayamnu* ("potential spouse") for WBW also contradicts symmetric alliance while the term *okopurwa* for the same position indicates that Ego's WB may claim his own ZD in marriage. The term *apa* for WF and eFZH seems inexplicable, while the word *ñoño* for WF, WB, and ZH suggests that marriage may be possible with both ZD and BD (i.e. the category *pali*, always children of *ñoño*). This would account for the distinction C≠BC. The equations eFZH= MF and DH=MBS are also consistent with ZD marriage, while yFZH=FZS again may indicate patrilineal principles. W. Shapiro (1966:87) lists the Waiwai as an example of societies in which avuncular marriage is practiced without any repercussions on kinship terminology. On the contrary, we have just indicated four equations suggesting ZD marriage.

Turning now to female affines, the referential term *wayamnu* for "possible spouses" (Fock 1963:190) equates MBW= MBD=FZD=BW=SW. All positions but MBW support an interpretation of *wayamnu* as "women married into Ego's patriline." The inclusion of MBW appears to reflect matrilineal principles, through either the succession MBW–MBD (female matriliny) or the succession MB–Ego (male matriliny). The equation MBW=M seems impossible to explain, as does the term *achi* for BW. *Achi* for yFZ, on the other hand, suggests patriliny. The term *okopurwa* for yFZD and yZH would be consistent with FZ marriage, while *okopurwa* for SW can be best explained as an extension of its application to S. The significance of the term *wahrei* for yFZD is obscure.

Local Group Size and Composition

The total population of Waiwai in 1955 was 170 (Fock 1963:189), but villages comprised no more than 30 or 40 individuals (ibid., 195, 205). Reports from 1837 suggest an average village size of 50 (ibid., 5). Estimates from 1884, which mention a village of nine houses and some 200 inhabitants, may have been exaggerated (ibid., 6).

Fock writes that the Waiwai practice "an unqualified form of matrilocal residence" (ibid., 134), but that this ideal is only occasionally and temporarily fulfilled, primarily during the first year after marriage (ibid., 200).

Patterns of Affiliation Other than Residence

Fock (ibid., 192) suggests that kinship is reckoned bilaterally. The group designation *yanan*, however, is applied to a category of relatives including M but excluding F and C, which leads Fock to deduce "a rudimentary system of exogamous, matrilineal clans" (ibid., 194). From the "traces of matri-lineage" occasionally encountered among the Waiwai, he concludes that the ideal of matrilocality was formerly a general rule (ibid., 203). A child of a Waiwai father and a Mouyenna mother is recognized as a Mouyenna, even when uxorilocality is not practiced, suggesting matrilateral affiliation irrespective of residence. Personal property is inherited in a parallel manner, from F to S and from M to D. To a certain extent, chief-tainship is patrilineally inheritable (ibid., 203–205).

Hierarchy

The distinction between elder and younger siblings of the same sex as Ego is "very pronounced" (ibid., 190).

The *wåshma* obligation compels male Ego to serve his WB and WF as long as uxorilocal residence persists (ibid., 135, 201). The subordination of the ZH is reflected in a complaint recorded by Fock: "You are my sister's husband (*poimo*), but you don't obey me." (Note, however, that *poimo* is used reciprocally between brothers-in-law). A man can evade his *wåshma* obligations by letting his Z marry his WB, whereby the demands of the two brothers-in-law cancel out.

The most important families place them-selves furthest from the doors of the communal house, as these locations are considered the best (ibid., 198, 205). The *yayalitomo* (chief) of a village is customarily called *apa*, i.e. "father", to convey respect, yet his status corresponds to that of the dominant person (WF or WB) in a *wåshma* relationship (ibid., 190, 203). The equation F=WF, then, appears to be the result of a conjunction of patrilineal age-rank and temporary uxorilocality. A village head will be surrounded by married sons who have returned from uxorilocal residence, by un-married sons who have yet to leave, and by daughters' husbands in the midst of bride-service, all similarly subordinate to the chief. Chieftainship is patrilineally inheritable.

Invitations to common meals and dance festivals are transmitted between individuals according to a specific order, which to Fock suggests "a developed system of rank" for which the Waiwai have no "social basis", but which may be "a matter of a rudiment or of loan from cultures more stamped by rank" (ibid., 208).

Alliance

The term *wayamnu* includes cross-cousins in the category of potential spouses, and

Table 22

KIN TERMINOLOGY OF THE WAIWAI
LINGUISTIC FAMILY: Carib
Male Ego, terms of address.

GEN.	Male		Female	
+ 2	FF *pácho*		FM *chacha*	
	MF *pácho*		MM *chacha*	

	KIN (Lineal kin, parallel collaterals, affines of affines)		*AFFINES* (In-laws, cross collaterals)	
	Male	Female	Male	Female
+ 1	F *apa*	M *yeme*	WF *tamchi ñoño, apa*	WM *chacha*
	FB *apa*	MZ *yeme*	MB *tamchi*	FZ *chacha y achi*
	MZH *pácho apa*	FBW *yeme*	FZH *e apa, pácho y poimo*	MBW *yeme (wayamnu)*
0	B *e ñoño y piti*	Z *e achi*	WB *poimo y ñoño*	W *chuwya*
	FBS *ñoño*	FBD *e achi y wachi*	MBS *poimo*	MBD *poimo (wayamnu)*
	MZS *ñoño*	MZD *achi*	FZS *poimo*	FZD *poimo (wayamnu) y okopurwa, wahrei*
	WZH *poimo piti*	WBW *achi, okopurwa (wayamnu)*	ZH *poimo, ñoño y okopurwa*	BW *achi (wayamnu)*
– 1	S *okopurwa*	D *okopurwa*	DH *poimo*	SW *okopurwa (wayamnu)*
	BS *piti*	BD *pali*	ZS *piti pali*	ZD *pali*

	Male		Female	
– 2	SS	*pali*	SD	*pali*
	DS	*pali*	DD	*pali*

SOURCES: Fock 1963:185–189. All terms but *wayamnu* (in brackets) are vocative. Alternative usages considered questionable by Fock have been omitted.

DEVIATIONS FROM THE TWO-LINE PATTERN	CONCEIVABLE IDEOLOGICAL OR BEHAVIOURAL CORRELATES
yB=BS, yFZH=FZS, Z=yFZ	Patrilateral affiliation
BS=ZS, BD=ZD, MZH=FZH, WZH=WB=ZH	Cognatic principles
MB≠FZH, FZ≠MBW, DH≠ZS, SW≠ZD	Absence of symmetric alliance
WBW=D, WF=ZH, eFZH=MF, DH≠MBS	Avuncular marriage
MBW=BW, MBW=MBD	Matrilateral affiliation
D=yFZD, S=yZH	FZ marriage

140

cross-cousin marriage is both permitted and frequent (ibid., 190). Fock writes that "only a *wayamnu* can be married", and as cross-cousins are the only consanguines belonging to this category, the most frequent marriages are those between cross-cousins (ibid., 134, 202). Marriages also occur with both ZD (ibid., 191, 202) and FZ (ibid., 201). Sister exchange is practiced in order to neutralize the asymmetrical *wåshma* relationship between WB and ZH (ibid., 135, 201).

External Relations

Fock (ibid., 135) assumes that the local group was formerly identical with the uxorilocal extended family, and that consequently it was exogamous, as several Waiwai villages still are. The Waiwai have been on peaceful terms with tribes such as the Parukoto, Mouyenna, Taruma, and Pianokoto. Around the 1890:s, however, the Waiwai were almost exterminated by aggressive tribes such as the Cara and Paricote (ibid., 6–9).

22. The Txicáo

Kin Terminology (Table 23)

The Txicáo, who represent an isolated, almost extinct branch of the Carib family (Menget 1977:324, 338, note 1), have a complex kin terminology which deviates from the usual Carib two-line pattern in a number of ways.

The equation W=BW=MBD≠FZD (*emuye*) strongly suggests matrilateral cross-cousin marriage, and the distinctions MB≠FZH, FZ≠MBW, WB≠ZH, DH≠ZS, and SW≠ZD are all consistent with asymmetric alliance.

The equation FBS=MBS (*imun*), recorded also by Nimuendajú among the Apinayé and Sherente, suggests a rudiment of genera-

tional cousin terms. Among the Apinayé and Sherente, this equation may indicate that a married FBS may be classified with other males of affinal households, whereas neither B nor MZS, both of whom are raised in Ego's natal household, could possibly be equated with affines. Among the Txicáo, the same equation represents an articulation of the matrilineal MBC=C and the patrilineal FBS=S.

There are a number of lineal equations, most of which imply matrilineal continuities. These include FM=FZ=FZD, F=FZS, MB=B, B=ZS, Z=ZD, MBC=C, WBD=SD, ZH=ZDH, MBW=MBD, and W=ZSW. On the other hand, the equations FZH=ZH, WB=WBS, and FBS=S are patrilineal. This articulation of matrilineal and patrilineal principles, strikingly reminiscent of the Northern Gê, suggests parallel affiliation.

Local Group Size and Composition

The Txicáo numbered 75 individuals in 1975 (Menget 1977:324). Menget (ibid., 338, note 3) believes that when the Txicáo were more numerous (150 to 200 people), there may have been two villages. This suggests an average village size of 75 to 100 people. However, the Arara of the lower Xingú, with whom the Txicáo are closely related (ibid., 338, note 1; Durbin 1977:35), in 1862 numbered 343 adults (Nimuendajú 1948: 223).

Post-marital residence among the Txicáo is uxorilocal (Menget 1977:325, 332).

Patterns of Affiliation Other than Residence

Menget (1977:324) notes that the Txicáo lack any "groupes de filiation" or social divisions. Affiliation is fundamentally bilateral, the maximal kindred coinciding with the local community (ibid., 324, 326). As among the

Table 23
KIN TERMINOLOGY OF THE TXICÁO
LINGUISTIC FAMILY: Carib
Male Ego, terms of reference.

GEN.	Male		Female	
+ 2	FF	*iramlu*	FM	*inut*
	MF	*iramlu*	MM	*inut*

	KIN (Lineal kin, parallel collaterals, affines of affines)		*AFFINES* (In-laws, cross collaterals)	
	Male	Female	Male	Female
+ 1	F *imu* (*pupa*)	M *ye*	WF *ahutpun*	WM *ahutpun*
	FB *imu*	MZ *ye*	MB *awon ilu*	FZ *inut*
	MZH *imu*	FBW *ye*	FZH *ibam*	MBW *emuye*
0	B *e ilu* / *y imana*	Z *inarut*	WB *ebaymun* (*taumpe*)	W *emuye*
	FBS *e ilu, imun* / *y imana*	FBD *inarut*	MBS *imun*	MBD *emčin emuye*
	MZS *e ilu* / *y imana*	MZD *inarut*	FZS *imu* (*pupa*)	FZD *inut*
			ZH *ibam* (*pupa*)	BW *emuye*
− 1	S *imun* (*taumpe*)	D *emčin*	DH *ibarum*	SW *ebae*
	BS *imun*	BD *emčin*	ZS *imana* (*yaramlu*)	ZD *inarut* (*ebečan*)
	ZDH *ibam*	ZSW *emuye*	WBS *ebaymun*	WBD *iben*

	Male		Female	
− 2	SS	*iben*	SD	*iben*
	DS	*iben*	DD	*iben*

SOURCES: Menget 1977:330. The terms in brackets for ZS and ZD are archaic forms, encountered only in mythical discourse (ibid., 331), while those for F, WB, FZS, ZH and S are terms of address (ibid., 334–335).

DEVIATIONS FROM THE TWO-LINE PATTERN	CONCEIVABLE IDEOLOGICAL OR BEHAVIOURAL CORRELATES
W=BW=MBD≠FZD	Matrilateral cross-cousin marriage
MB≠FZH, FZ≠MBW, WB≠ZH, DH≠ZS, SW≠ZD	Absence of symmetric alliance
FBS=MBS	Cognatic principles (articulation of matrilineal equation MBC=C and patrilineal equation FBS=S)
FM=FZ=FZD, F=FZS, MB=B, B=ZS, Z=ZD, MBC=C, WBD=SD, ZH=ZDH, MBW=MBD, W=ZSW	Matrilateral affiliation, uxorilocal residence
FZH=ZH, WB=WBS, FBS=S	Patrilateral affiliation

Gê, the continuity of local female matrilines is a product of uxorilocality rather than of a principle of unilateral affiliation (ibid., 325). Yet, the relationship between MB and ZS suggests a measure of succession, or identity transmission. Whereas F and S are ideologically opposed as wife-takers (ZH) and wife-givers (WB), unable to share a common name, a MB may transmit his name to his ZS (ibid., 336, 337). Moreover, a man frequently uses the same nickname for his MB and his ZS, which also implies a certain matrilineal continuity among males. Menget equates the equivalence of MB and ZS with that of brothers (cf. the term *ilu* for B and MB), among whom name transmission may also occur. Contrary to the affinal opposition of F and S, MB and ZS are thus classified as "co-époux" (cf. the equation MBW=W= BW=ZSW). This can best be understood in a context of preferential matrilateral cross-cousin marriage and uxorilocal residence, where a man succeeds his MB in moving to, and ultimately assuming leadership of, the same affinal household. The category of potential spouses (*emuye*) would thus be congruent with the category of women born in a particular household. The remaining matrilineal equations can all be seen to reflect household continuities produced in the articulation of matrilateral marriage and uxorilocal residence (Fig. 12). Menget's analysis of the vocative terminology (ibid., 334–336) provides additional equations supporting this interpretation: Ego addresses his ZH by the same term (*pupa*) as he uses for his F and FZS, and his WB by the word (*taumpe*) he uses for his S.

Patrilineal equations, on the other hand, indicate that there is some recognition of the dispersed patrilines. In fact, patrilineal ties provide the idiom in which distinctions between affines are expressed: men of previously unrelated wife-taking groups are generally called "father", and wife-givers are called "son" (ibid., 337–338), wholly in accordance with the dispersion of a patriline in a context of uxorilocal residence and MBD

marriage. Since a man inhabits the same household as his F until marriage, the patrilineal equations may also be based on identification with particular households.

It is interesting to note the parallels, in terms of terminological equations and inferences drawn from these, between the Txicáo and the Sirionó. In both cases, there are a number of equations of the Crow-Omaha type (ibid., 331–332) and a MBD–FZS spouse equation rule (ibid., 332–333; Scheffler & Lounsbury 1971:35). Scheffler & Lounsbury (1971:108–112) conclude that the Crow-Omaha equations of the Sirionó actually reflect a rule of parallel transmission. Similarly, the majority of lineal equations listed by Menget (1977:330–331) for the Txicáo are reducible to the implicit equivalence of a M and her D or a F and his S (Table 24).

Menget (ibid., 332) writes of "une dominance très nette, vu l'isolement relatif de l'équation de forme Omaha, des catégories qui assimilent entre elles des générations de femmes, qu'il est difficile de ne pas mettre en rapport avec le seul élément de permanence qui nous est donné dans la structure du groupe, l'unité résidentielle mère-fille." It is certainly reasonable to attribute the massive evidence of matrilateral affiliation to the rule of uxorilocality, but the several patrilineal equations suggest an interpretation similar to that of Scheffler and Lounsbury for the Sirionó, i.e. parallel affiliation. This interpretation is particularly attractive for the Txicáo, as it has been used by its authors to explain the MBD–FZS-spouse equation rule: from the point of view of male Ego, FZD is a less suitable mate since the parallel-transmission rule makes her "covertly equivalent" to his Z (Scheffler & Lounsbury 1971:175).

Hierarchy

Menget (1977:334) notes that an important dimension of the kin terminology is the

143

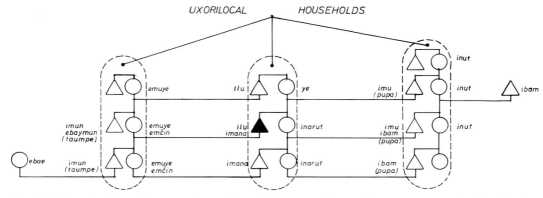

Fig. 12. Uxorilocal residence and matrilateral cross-cousin marriage as a matrix for lineal equations among the Txicáo. (Terms in brackets are vocative.)

opposition between "un aspect Senior et un aspect Junior," as between grandparents and grandchildren, parents and children, elder brothers and younger brothers, parents-in-law and children-in-law, FZH and WBS, and significantly, between ZH and WB. The asymmetrical relation between brothers-in-law (*ibam* and *ebaymun*) is consistent with an inclination towards matrilateral cross-cousin marriage, and the equations FZH=ZH and WB=WBS suggest temporary patrifilial categories based on the common household affiliation of F and S prior to the latter's marriage. For any male Ego, ZH derives from the household in which FZH has been living most of his adult life. In fact, there is a good chance that ZH is FZS, i.e. the son of FZH, with whom he is terminologically equated. Similarly, WB and WBS will be residing in the same household for a major part of Ego's adult life, assuming that WB is roughly coeval with Ego. Over time, however, each patriline will be dispersed among several households, providing an idiom of seniority in which to express their interrelations. According to this patrilineal idiom, wife-takers (ZH) are senior to wife-givers (WB), and addressed as "fathers" vis-à-vis "sons" (ibid., 336). Both FZH and ZH are associated with the natal household of Ego's father, whereas WB and WBS are identified with the household into which Ego's sons

will marry. The relation between ZH and WB (wife-taker and wife-giver) is homologous to that between F and S (ibid., 337). This "inégalité terminologique" is consistent

Kin term	Equations suggesting female matriliny	Equations suggesting male patriliny
inut	FM=FZ=FZD	
awon	MB=MMB	
iben		BS=BSS (f.s.)
		BD=BSD (f.s.)
	MBD=MMBD (f.s.)	
ahutpun	WF=WMF (m.s.)	
	WM=WMM (m.s.)	
	HM=HMM (f.s.)	
		HFZ=HZ (f.s.)
	HZ=HZD (f.s.)	
ebae	BW=MBW (f.s.)	
ilu	MB=MMB (m.s.)	
imana	ZS=ZDS (m.s.)	
inarut	Z=ZD=ZDD (m.s.)	
imun		BS=FBS (m.s.)
	MZSS=ZSS (m.s.)	
	MBS=MMBS (m.s.)	
emčin	MZSD=ZSD (m.s.)	
emuye	MBW=MMBW (m.s.)	
	ZSW=ZDSW (m.s.)	
ibam		ZH=FZH (m.s.)
	ZH=ZDH (m.s.)	
ebaymun		WB=WBS (m.s.)
	WB=WMB (m.s.)	
yaramlu (archaic)	ZS=ZDS (m.s.)	
ebečan (archaic)	ZD=ZDD (m.s.)	
ebin	B=MB (f.s.)	
	MB=MMB (f.s.)	
imlen	ZD=MZDD (f.s.)	
emleyum	HZS=HZDS (f.s.)	
	HMB=HMMB (f.s.)	

Table 24 Txicáo lineal equations suggesting parallel affiliation (Menget 1977:330–331)

144

with the flow of goods and services between brothers-in-law, which is in part modelled on the economic relationship between F and S (ibid., 338). On the other hand, the relation between MB and ZS, who both marry into the same household, is homologous to that between elder and younger brother, or co-spouses. In fact, polyandrous marriages involving MB and ZS apparently do occur among the Txicáo (ibid., 333).

Alliance

Menget (ibid., 332–333) notes that the terms *emuye* (W=MBW=MBD≠ FZD . . . , m. s.) and *emleyum* (H=FZS=HZS . . . , f.s.) "paraissent indiquer clairement une prescription matrimoniale au niveau purement terminologique." The terms can be etymologically reduced to "mother of my son" and "father of my son," respectively.

Menget suggests that the alternative terms *awon* and *ilu* (eB) for Ego's MB represent options relating to two different forms of marriage: *awon* is employed when there is question of MBD marriage, whereas *ilu* is used when Ego wants to emphasize their equivalence as polyandrous co-spouses (ibid., 331).

Distant *inarut* (ideally non-marriageable sisters and parallel cousins), such as MZDDD, can be transformed into marriageable *emuye* (ibid., 333). Menget notes that such possibilities for oblique marriages recur among other Carib groups, such as the Trio. He also reports temporary or secondary marriages with captives (ibid., 325).

External Relations

After a tradition of hostility and raiding, the Txicáo were pacified and integrated into the Upper Xingú community in 1965–67 (ibid., 324).

Conclusions: Carib

As has been suggested by Needham (1972: 23) and Rivière (1977:39), two-line kin terminologies are characteristic of most Carib cultures. Out of 16 Carib societies for which she had adequate information, Dole (1969:112) lists 14 as bifurcate merging, one as bifurcate generation (cf. the Kuikuru), and one as isolating (Eskimo). Of the six terminologies in our sample, only those of the Waiwai and Txicáo include equations and distinctions which contradict symmetric alliance, and in the case of the Waiwai, even this may be erroneous (Fock 1963:189,191).

Temporary uxorilocality (i.e. bride-service) is reported from the Waiwai, Kuikuru, Barama River Caribs, and Pemon. Uxorilocal residence is an explicit ideal among the Waiwai, Trio, Karinya, and Txicáo, while virilocality is more strongly preferred among the Kuikuru and Pemon. In practice, most groups are ambilocal.

Affiliation is generally bilateral. Nevertheless, the Waiwai, Karinya, and Barama River Caribs exhibit certain matrilateral inclinations, while the Trio have an implicitly patrilateral cast. Patrilineal succession to chieftainship is reported from the Waiwai, Kalapalo, and Kuikuru. The patrilineal implications of certain kin equations among the Waiwai, Trio, Karinya, and Txicáo may reflect patrilineal succession or other elements of patrilateral affiliation for males. Matrilineal equations among the Waiwai, Trio, and Txicáo appear to derive from uxorilocal residence. Parallel transmission is evident in the ideology of the Waiwai, Trio, and Kalapalo, and implicit in the terminology of the Txicáo. The Trio and Kalapalo, furthermore, show signs of alternating generations.

There is a correlation between local group size and the nature of external relations. The Xingú Caribs and the Karinya have larger settlements and frequent external contact, whereas the Trio, Barama River Caribs, and Pemon all live in small, very isolated groups.

There is also a correlation between group size/degree of isolation and the occurrence of avuncular marriage. The four tribes with an average group size of less than 50, i.e. the Waiwai, Trio, Barama River Caribs, and Pemon, all practice ZD marriage, whereas no such marriages are reported from the remaining four. FZ marriage, similarly indicative of close endogamy, is reported from the Waiwai. In several equations, the kin terminologies of the Waiwai and Trio have codified ZD marriage. The Waiwai terminology, furthermore, includes equations consistent with FZ marriage. The Txicáo appear to be unique in prescribing MBD marriage.

Most of the Carib peoples distinguish between siblings according to relative age. Distinctions of relative age are integral to Dravidian, two-line kin terminologies (Dumont 1953a:36). Lave (1966:194) also notes a correlation between "age-based differences in status" and avuncular marriage. Rivière (1977:40), on the other hand, emphasizes the affinal term *pito* (variously translated as slave, servant, client, brother-in-law, son-in-law, and ZS) as "the right idiom for expressing an asymmetrical relationship" in Carib societies.

Chapter 7
Tupí

23. The Tapirapé

Kin Terminology (Table 25)

Since Wagley (1977a) does not list any affinal terms, few terminological indications pertaining to alliance can be ascertained. The generational equations B=FBS=MZS= MBS=FZS and Z=FBD=MZD=MBD =FZD suggest cognatic principles. J. Shapiro (1984:9), however, reports that "comparison with the kin classifications of linguistically related groups provides persuasive evidence for the former existence of a bifurcate-merging, and hence probably Dravidian, relationship system."

Local Group Size and Composition

Before 1900, there were five villages with at least 200 individuals in each (Wagley & Galvão 1948:167). In 1939, there remained only one village with a population of 147 (ibid., Wagley 1977a:95). From accounts of the ideal Tapirapé village, with ceremonial organization intact, Wagley (1977a:124) estimates that "any Tapirapé village would have to have at least two hundred people."

Ideally, post-marital residence is uxorilocal (Wagley & Galvão 1948:169; Wagley 1977a:93). The several deviations from this rule derive from the severe depopulation suffered by the Tapirapé during the first decades of this century (Wagley 1977a:95).

Patterns of Affiliation Other than Residence

According to Wagley (1977a:102–103; 1977b:373), Tapirapé men are divided into unnamed ceremonial moieties, each of which consists of three age grades named after species of bird. Recruitment to the moieties is patrilineal (Wagley & Galvão 1948:171; Wagley 1977a:101, 104). Each individual of both sexes also belongs to one of eight Feast Groups (tãtáupawã, or tantanopao), to which recruitment is parallel, so that men belong to their father's group and women to their mother's. Wagley (1977a:116) suggests that the tantanopao may have had more important functions in the past. Today, however, they have no connecton with the regulation of marriage other than the preference that a man and wife should belong to the same group (ibid., 115; cf. Kracke 1984:123, note 2). Wagley claims that the Tapirapé, to accord with this rule, frequently change their affiliation upon marriage, as do the Kayapó and Krahó. Dietschy (1977:300) denies such modifications, claiming instead that membership is life-long for both sexes, but that endogamous marriages do occur. Wagley (1977a:115) mentions the possibility that the rule of tantanopao endogamy may have been "more strongly enforced sometime in the past." If the tantanopao represent vestiges of groups which traditionally inclined towards endogamy, some interesting suggestions emerge. In a 1937 letter to Baldus, Nimuendajú himself compared the tantanopao with the kiyé of the Apinayé, both of which combined parallel affiliation and endogamy (Dietschy 1977:301). As among the Apinayé and Karajá, the conjunction of parallel affiliation and the endogamous marriage prescription implies that a male Ego's spouse ideally should belong to the same category as his Z. This may explain why their "bifurcate generation" kin terminologies equate cross-cousins with siblings (cf. Dietschy 1977:299, 301). As a sub-

Table 25
KIN TERMINOLOGY OF THE TAPIRAPÉ
LINGUISTIC FAMILY: Tupí
Male Ego, terms of reference.

GEN.	Male		Female	
+ 2	FF *cheramuya* MF *cheramuya*		FM *chanuya* MM *chanuya*	

	KIN (Lineal kin, parallel collaterals, affines of affines)		*AFFINES* (In-laws, cross collaterals)	
	Male	Female	Male	Female
+ 1	F *cheropu* FB *cherowurani*	M *ampí cheu* MZ *ampí cheu urani*	MB *chetoturangi*	FZ *chanche*
0	B e *cherikeurangi* y *cheriwurangi* FBS e *cherikeurangi* y *cheriwurangi* MZS e *cherikeurangi* y *cheriwurangi*	Z e *cheranura* y *kocha* FBD e *cheranura* y *kocha* MZD e *cheranura* y *kocha*	MBS e *cherikeurangi* y *cheriwurangi* FZS e *cherikeurangi cheriwurangi*	MBD e *cheranura* y *kocha* FZD e *cheranura* y *kocha*
− 1	S *charanúra* BS *charanúra*	D *cheranchura* BD *cheranchura*	ZS *cherekawiana*	ZD *chekochamemura*

	Male		Female	
− 2	SS *cheremamino* DS *cheremamino*		SD *cheremamino* DD *cheremamino*	

SOURCES: Wagley 1977a:314.

DEVIATIONS FROM THE TWO-LINE PATTERN	CONCEIVABLE IDEOLOGICAL OR BEHAVIOURAL CORRELATES
B=FBS=MZS=MBS=FZS, Z=FBD=MZD=MBD=FZD	Cognatic principles

sequent trajectory, the generational cousin terminology may in itself serve to extend exogamy to include all first cousins (cf. Dole 1969:114). In other words, terminological modifications associated with kindred endogamy may generate inconsistencies resolved only by an expansion of exogamy.

Aside from the patrilineal moieties, Wagley and Galvão (1948:172) observe that "Tapirapé kinship is bilateral." Wagley (1977a:99) appears to accept the suggestion, based on comparative Tupí ethnography, that the generational cousin terminology may be a modification of an earlier, bifurcating system with preferential cross-cousin marriage between matrilocal extended families.

Hierarchy

A man of prestige strengthens his position by attracting as many young men to his household as possible. To do so, he adopts a number of classificatory "daughters," whose marriages continually add new men to the uxorilocal household (Wagley & Galvão 1948:172).

As among the Karajá, high-status ceremonial roles are inherited. Here, also, the inheritors are known as "beautiful children" (*anchirikakantu*) and given special treatment during their early years (Wagley 1977a:121). The so-called "big names" (cf. the "great names" of the Apinayé, Kayapó, and Sherente) generally pass from F to eldest S and from M to eldest D, i.e. according to a rule of parallel transmission. The inheritance of *anchirikakantu* status suggests permanent rank discrepancies between different lines.

Baldus' description of Tapirapé ceremonial organization differs slightly from that of Wagley (Dietschy 1977:300). The former reports that the *wirã*, named after birds, are not moieties divided into age-grades, but three patrilineal groups of mature men, one of which is composed of "men of prestige." Each *wirã* has two leaders deriving from separate houses, suggesting that the three *wirã* intersect the diametric moiety division. The ambiguity concerning the *wirã*, i.e. whether they represent age-grades or more permanent status distinctions, recalls hierarchical divisions among the Ramkokamekra, Krĩkatí, and Sherente. Although we cannot dismiss the possibility that there may have been changes in function, it is possible that the age-grade model is merely an emic representation of a more permanent hierarchy.

Alliance

Formerly there was a preference for village endogamy (Wagley & Galvão 1948:173).

Cousins called "brother" and "sister" of close connection (first degree?) are not married, but "marriage with those of distant relationship is not infrequent." Dietschy (1977:301) compares this marriage with distant "sisters", in conjunction with a "bifurcate generation" kin terminology, with similar conditions among the neighbouring Karajá. We have suggested that the generational cousin terminology, although initially an adjustment to kindred endogamy, may in itself be responsible for the subsequent prohibition of marriage to actual cross-cousins, i.e. for the expansion of exogamy. The generational cousin terms erase the crucial cross-versus-parallel dichotomy of two-line systems, which serves to neutralize consanguinity between cross-cousins in order to facilitate close marriage.

External Relations

The Tapirapé have been at war both with the Kayapó and the Karajá (Wagley & Galvão 1948:167; Dietschy 1977:300; Wagley 1977b: 374–375). When there were several Tapirapé villages, there was also some inter-village antagonism *within* the tribe (Wagley & Galvão 1948:173). Wagley (1977a:83), however, writes that relations between Tapirapé villages were always "essentially peaceful." Because of the considerable distances between villages, visiting was nevertheless infrequent (ibid., 85).

23. The Mundurucú

Kin Terminology (Table 26)

An absence of symmetric alliance is suggested by the distinction MBC≠FZC. The equation MBD=BW suggests matrilateral cross-cousin marriage. As noted by Murphy (1956:421; 1960:93–94) and W. Shapiro (1968:50–52), several equations are congruent with avuncular marriage, including ZD=BW, ZD=MBD, ZS=MBS, MB=FZS, and MM=FZ. Horton (1948:277) observes that female Ego equates B=DH, which is also indicative of ZD marriage. Dietschy (1977:305), too, remarks that "le mariage 'oblique' est conservé dans la terminologie de la parenté."

The vocative terminology, by equating siblings and parallel cousins with cross-cousins, fits into a pattern widespread among Tupí-speaking peoples (Murphy 1956:421).

The distinction FM≠MM implies lineality, and the equation MM=FZ≠FM suggests patrilineal principles.

Local Group Size and Composition

In the middle of the 19th century, there were at least 20 Mundurucú villages with a total population of about 5,000 (Murphy 1956: 416), which gives an average village size of about 250. From 1877, there is a list of 21 villages with populations ranging from 100 to 2,600 and a total population of 18,910 (Horton 1948:272), implying an average of 900 per village. At the turn of the century, another estimate suggests 1,400 individuals in 37 communities (ibid.), i.e. an average of 38. In this count, the largest village had 700 inhabitants, the smallest less than a dozen. In 1931, there is a report of 19 settlements with a total of between 1,200 and 1,400 inhabitants, i.e. an average between 63 and 74. The seven "traditional-style" savannah communities visited by Murphy and Murphy (1974:26) totalled 350 people, which gives an average village size of 50. Impressive concentrations of people are suggested by late 18th century accounts of Mundurucú armies mustering some 2,000 warriors (Horton 1948:273).

A report from 1867 (cf. Dietschy 1977:304) suggests virilocal residence (Horton 1948:277; Murphy 1956:428). More recent ethnographers conclude that residence is uxorilocal, but that chiefly households are often

virilocal (Murphy 1956:414, 425, 426, 429; 1960:74, 100, 102–103; 1973:215; Murphy & Murphy 1974:76). Murphy suggests that the Mundurucú were predominantly virilocal and their patrilineal clans localized, prior to a shift to uxorilocality in the early 19th century (1956:428, 430, 432; 1960:74, 76, 79, 81–82). This shift would have been due to "economic pressures which increased the importance of maintaining the integrity and continuity of the female, household work-group," specifically the growing trade in manioc flour. It would have involved progressively prolonging the period of bride-service until eventually uxorilocal residence became permanent (cf. the Sanumá). Murphy's historical reconstruction is challenged by Dietschy (1977:303–306), who points out that the combination of patrilateral affiliation and uxorilocal residence is not as anomalous as has been thought (cf. the Central Gê). Dietschy suggests that the Mundurucú are yet another instance of parallel or sex affiliation, a feature which they share with the nearby Tapirapé, Karajá, and Apinayé. Murphy's argument that historical accounts of ZD marriage imply virilocality is not valid, says Dietschy, as "le mariage 'oblique' s'accorde bien avec la résidence matrilocale dans un système de descendance patrilinéaire." Marriage with a ZD would always comply with the exogamy of the patrilineal moieties, and provide a means of remaining in one's natal house-hold instead of being compelled to serve a father-in-law elsewhere. Avuncular marriage is a convenient way to legitimize privileged patrilocality in a uxorilocal society.

Patterns of Affiliation Other than Residence

Horton (1948:276–277) found the Mundurucú grouped into 34 patrilineal sibs divided among two exogamous moieties, a Red moiety of 15 sibs and a White moiety of 19 sibs. Murphy (1956:418; 1960:72) reports

150

Table 26
KIN TERMINOLOGY OF THE MUNDURUCÚ
LINGUISTIC FAMILY: Tupí
Male Ego, terms of reference.

GEN.	Male	Female
+ 2	FF *adjutdjut* MF *adjutdjut*	FM *awahwah* MM *adjungdjung*

	KIN (Lineal kin, parallel collaterals, affines of affines)		*AFFINES* (In-laws, cross collaterals)	
	Male	Female	Male	Female

+ 1	F *webai*
	     baibai
	FB *baibai*
		M *usi*
		     aiī
		MZ *aiī*
			WF *(wanyū)*
			
			MB *odjorit*
			     (wanyū)
				
				FZ *adjungdjung*

0	B e *wanyūyū*
	     y *okitpit*
	     (oköt)
	FBS e *wanyūyū*
	     y *okötköt*
	MZS e *wanyūyū*
	     y *okötköt*
		Z *wešit*
		     (daū)
		
		FBD *wěsit*
		     (daū)
		MZD *wešit*
		     (daū)
			WB *(usum)*
			
			MBS *wešī*
			     (wanyū, oköt)
			FZS *odjorit*
			     (wanyū, oköt)
			ZH *(usum)*
				
				MBD *wešī*
				     (daū)
				FZD *daūū*
				     (daū)
				BW *wešī*

– 1	S *opöt*
	
	BS *opöt*
		D *orašit*
		     (daū)
		BD *orašit*
		     (daū)
			DH *(oköt)*
			
			ZS *wešī*
			     (oköt)
				
				ZD *wešī*
				     (daū)

	Male	Female

– 2	SS *rašenyebit*
	
	DS *rašenyebit*
		SD *rašenyebit*
		     (daū)
		DD *rašenyebit*
		     (daū)

SOURCES: Murphy 1956:420; 1960:92–93. The term for BW is given in the text (Murphy 1960: 94). Terms in brackets are vocative.

DEVIATIONS FROM THE TWO-LINE PATTERN	CONCEIVABLE IDEOLOGICAL OR BEHAVIOURAL CORRELATES
MBC≠FZC	Absence of symmetric alliance
MBD=BW	Matrilateral cross-cousin marriage
ZD=BW, ZC=MBC, MB=FZS, MM=FZ	Avuncular marriage
B=FBS=MZS=MBS=FZS, Z=FBD=MZD=MBD=FZD (voc.)	Cognatic principles
FM≠MM MM=FZ≠FM	Lineal principles Patrilateral affiliation

that the Mundurucú can list 38 clans, but that only 30 survived at the time of his fieldwork. Of the 38 clans, 16 belonged to the Red moiety and 22 to the White. Whereas the first name of a Mundurucú is that of his clan, the second name is transmitted according to a three-generation cycle, so that male Ego receives the name of his FFF, and female Ego that of her FMM (Murphy and Murphy 1974: 75). Since lines of females alternate between the two patrilineal moieties, FMM will have belonged to the same moiety as female Ego (Murphy 1960:83). A set of brothers will tend to reproduce the set of names borne by the set of brothers to which their FFF belonged (cf. the Krĩkatí). In addition to clan membership and names, the roles of chief and shaman are patrilineally inherited (Murphy 1956: 417). Ceremonial roles, in fact, were the main "manifest function" of the clans in the 19th century (ibid., 419).

Murphy and Murphy write that although there are patrilineal clans, the rule of uxorilocality precludes the formation of true patrilineages, except in the case of chiefly families, who seem to be exempt from this rule (1974:76–77; Murphy 1956:417; 1960:84, 88, 121, 122). Inversely, patrilateral affiliation has inhibited the development of true matrilineages (Murphy 1960:87, 111).

Hierarchy

Polygyny is a privilege of men of rank (Horton 1948:277; Murphy 1956:426, 431; 1960:88). The observation that sons and daughters of war chiefs intermarry suggests rank endogamy. Early reports describe a hierarchy of chiefs. The report that military expeditions were led by two village chiefs (Murphy 1956:417) suggests diarchy.

Since virilocality is the continued privilege of chiefly families, who often develop households comprising three generations of men related in the male line (Murphy & Murphy 1974:76–77), the implication is that chiefly status is patrilineally inheritable. This is

verified by the report that the village chief is ideally the oldest son of the previous chief (ibid., 78; Murphy 1956:417; 1960:84, 121). We may conclude that there are permanent status differences between patrilines.

During the 19th century, the chief's status was enhanced by his role as middleman in the trade with Brazilians (Murphy 1956:431; 1960:39, 42, 49, 121, 125).

Alliance

The system of exogamous moieties, and the associated practice of classificatory bilateral cross-cousin marriage, is the "primary regulator of marriage and definer of the incest taboo" (Murphy & Murphy 1974:72, 145, 147; Murphy 1956:418, 423, 424, 430; 1960:88, 89). Avuncular marriage appears to have occurred frequently enough among the Mundurucú to be amply reflected in the kin terminology, particularly in the equation, for female Ego, of B and DH (Horton 1948:277; Murphy 1956:421; 1960:90, 93–94). Early reports do mention women's marriage with their MB (ibid.; Murphy 1956:428; 1960:90), but the feasibility of such marriages is "vigorously denied" by contemporary Mundurucú (Murphy 1956:418, 421, 428, 432; 1960:90). Whereas Murphy speculates that ZD marriage may have been associated with a former practice of virilocal residence, Dietschy (1977:303–306) objects that this type of marriage is compatible with uxorilocal residence as long as patrilateral affiliation is emphasized. Avuncular marriage, by legitimizing patrilocality, would be a particularly attractive strategy in a society torn between a patrilineal ideology and a convention of uxorilocality. Murphy (1960:94) notes that the equation BW= MBD≠FZD suggests matrilateral cross-cousin marriage, which is congruent with consistent ZD marriage (cf. W. Shapiro 1968). Contemporary informants claim that either cross-cousin is a suitable spouse.

External Relations

In the late 18th century, the Mundurucú were aggressively expanding their territory (Horton 1948:271; Murphy 1956:415; 1960: 30–31,48). Among their many enemies were close neighbours such as the Parintintin, and possibly as distant ones as the Apinayé (Horton 1948:273). Warfare and the taking of trophy heads was a central element of Mundurucú culture, and an elaborate organization had been developed for its execution (ibid., 277–278). Murphy & Murphy (1974:29) write that the Mundurucú had "a reputation for tremendous prowess in warfare," and that they were "the fiercest of all the tribes in the central Amazon" (ibid., 79–80). Yet, the patrilineal organization cross-cutting local groups keeps inter-village relationships *within* the tribe remarkably peaceful (ibid., 77–78; Murphy 1956:416).

Mundurucú villages are "neither endogamous nor exogamous, and marriage within or outside of the village was permissible" (Murphy 1956:418). Although a man "might be expected to mate with an eligible girl of his own village," it is the custom of young men to visit a number of villages in search of a spouse (ibid., 424). Most married Mundurucú men, in fact, were born in other villages (ibid.; Murphy 1960:102). Dietschy (1977:306), however, suggests that the problem of the articulation of patriliny and uxorilocality in societies such as that of the Mundurucú can be resolved by presupposing a former inclination toward village endogamy.

Their demand for White people's trade goods prompted the Mundurucú to serve as mercenary warriors against still hostile tribes (Murphy 1956:415). This "symbiosis with the Whites" lasted throughout the 19th century. As early as 1819, the Mundurucú had also become deeply involved in the sale of manioc flour to the Brazilian settlers, a principal trade commodity until it was eclipsed by wild rubber in the late 19th century (ibid., 415,

430, 431; Murphy 1960:38–39, 48–49). In such trade, the chief served as middleman between his village and the Whites, thereby gaining in prestige.

25. The Parintintin and Tupí-Cawahíb

Kin Terminology (Table 27)

Kracke (1984:101) characterizes the kin terminology of the Parintintin (or Kagwahiv) as "two-line in nature" and as "in perfect accord with a system of exogamous moieties."

Local Group Size and Composition

Lévi-Strauss (1948a:299) cites Nimuendajú's (1948:283) suggestion that the Parintintin and the Tupí-Cawahíb are two remnants of a single Tupí tribe, the Cabahiba (Cawahiwa; cf. Kracke 1984:99), which was destroyed by the Mundurucú. In 1915 the Takwatip group of the Tupí-Cawahíb numbered 300 people (Lévi-Strauss 1948a:299, 301).

Post-marital residence appears to have been predominantly virilocal in both cases, but "contrary practices" have been recorded for the Tupí-Cawahíb, and the aversion of the Parintintin for labour obligations in connection with marriage suggests uxorilocal bride-service (ibid., 303; Nimuendajú 1948: 292). Kracke (1984:105, 113, 115–116) confirms that Parintintin (or Kagwahiv) bride-service is expected to last several years. In fact, permanent uxorilocal residence is frequent (ibid., 116). Avunculocality results when a man adopts his ZS in order to teach him "the duties of a son-in-law" (ibid., 113).

Table 27

KIN TERMINOLOGY OF THE PARINTINTIN (KAGWAHIV)
LINGUISTIC FAMILY: Tupí
Male Ego, terms of reference.

GEN.	Male		Female	
+ 2	FF	*amonh ji ramonha'ga*	FM	*jaryj*
	MF	*amonh ji ramonha'ga*	MM	*jaryj*

	KIN (Lineal kin, parallel collaterals, affines of affines)			*AFFINES* (In-laws, cross collaterals)			
	Male		Female		Male		Female	

GEN.	Male		Female		Male		Female	
+ 1	F	*ruv apĩ*	M	*hy yhẽ*	WF	*tutyr*	WM	*jaji*
	FB	*ruvy*	MZ	*hy'y*	MB	*tutyr*	FZ	*jaji*
	MZH	*ruvy*	FBW	*hy'y*	FZH	*tutyr*	MBW	*jaji*
0	B	*irũ'ga reki'yr*	Z	*rendyr kújahẽ*	WB	*rayro'yr nhanhi-membyra'ga*	W	*rembirekohẽ nhanhi-membyrahẽ*
	FBS	*irũ'ga reki'yr*	FBD	*rendyr kújahẽ*	MBS	*rayro'yr*	MBD	*amotehe nhanhi-membyr*
	MZS	*irũ'ga reki'yr*	MZD	*rendyr kújahẽ*	FZS	*amotehe nhanhi-membyr*	FZD	*nhanhi-membyrahẽ*
					ZH	*rayro'yr*	BW	*nhanhi-membyrahẽ*
– 1	S	*ra'yra'ga*	D	*ra'yrahẽ*	DH	*ti'ga*	SW	*kunhamem-byrahẽ*
	BS	*ra'yra'ga*	BD	*ra'yrahẽ*	ZS	*ti'i ti'ga*	ZD	*kunhamem-byrahẽ*

GEN.	Male		Female	
– 2	SS	*rymymomíno*	SD	*rymymomíno*
	DS	*rymymomíno*	DD	*rymymomíno*

SOURCES: Kracke 1984:102. Kracke (ibid., 101) glosses *nhanhimembyr* as "child of my *jaji*" and *amotehe* as "lover".

DEVIATIONS FROM THE TWO-LINE PATTERN	CONCEIVABLE IDEOLOGICAL OR BEHAVIOURAL CORRELATES
None	

Patterns of Affiliation Other than Residence

The Tupí-Cawahíb were divided into several patrilineal sibs (Lévi-Strauss 1948a:303). The Parintintin (or Kagwahiv) recognize patrilineal, exogamous moieties (Nimuendajú 1948:290; Kracke 1984:99–100). Kracke suggests that these are an "innovation" or "somewhat recent acquisition" grafted onto the more general Tupí-Guaraní feature of exogamous clans: "The moieties could be the Kagwahiv variant of the patriclans that appear in other Tupí-Guaraní-speaking tribes, including other branches of the old 'Cawahib'" (1984:104, 120, 122). Kracke's genealogical data suggest that there are in fact three exogamous clans (ibid., 99, 104–106), producing "a precise inversion" of the situation reported from the Western Shavante: "Where the Kagwahiv . . . have a dualistic ideology covering a triadic system of exogamous clans, the Western Shavante have a triadic ideology covering a real system of exogamous moieties" (ibid., 118).

Each patrilineal moiety is said to have a fund of names for each stage of the life cycle, but a child's first name is bestowed by one of his mother's brothers, "who thus places his claim on the infant as a spouse for his own recently born child when they should reach maturity" (ibid., 104, 107–108).

Hierarchy

Among the Tupí-Cawahíb, chieftaincy was inherited from father to son, and a hierarchy of officials served beneath the chief (Lévi-Strauss 1948a:304). Chiefs apparently struggled to extend their domination over ever greater numbers of sibs. Polygyny appears to have been rare (Kracke 1984:116), perhaps privileged.

Kracke (ibid., 121) compares the model of "ostensibly endogamous units apparently formed by exchanging pairs of 'patrilines'" with Lévi-Strauss' analysis of the Bororo. Parintintin endogamy, however, is only a "formal property of the ideal system," and there is presently no hint of an hierarchical ordering of the patrilines.

Alliance

The Tupí-Cawahíb practiced bilateral cross-cousin marriage and avuncular marriage (Lévi-Strauss 1948a:304). The Parintintin norm of moiety exogamy is strong but seems poorly integrated with other aspects of their life and culture (Kracke 1984:103–104). Of the three models of Parintintin marriage determination, the claims on each other's children represented by the reciprocal exchange of infants' names between "genealogically defined but not natively recognized 'patrilines'" tends to "carry the most weight" (ibid., 100, 108–109, 118). This system of betrothal through name transmission results in bilateral cross-cousin marriage. Comparative data suggest that infantile betrothal is common among other Tupí-Guaraní peoples, and the principle underlying the Kagwahiv marriage cycle, that of "a child being given in return for a wife," is widely expressed in preferences for marriage with a ZD or FZD (ibid., 120).

Considering the connection between name-giving and marriage arrangements, Kracke's (ibid., 112) observation that it is proper to ask the girl's FB to act as an intermediary is reminiscent of the adoptive parents of the Apinayé.

External Relations

The Parintintin were as intensely warlike as the Mundurucú (Nimuendajú 1948:285, 290), and as passionate head-hunters (ibid., 291). The Tupí-Cawahíb also decapitated enemies killed in battle (Lévi-Strauss 1948a:304).

26. The Tupinambá and Guaraní

Settlements of the coastal Tupí-speakers were large, and agriculture well developed. From figures given by Métraux (1948b:95), we may conclude that Tupinambá villages averaged between 444 and 771 people. Clastres (1977:71) estimates that "the population of the simplest Tupinambá villages (four *maloca*) must have included around four hundred persons, whereas that of the most substantial (seven or eight *maloca*) reached, or exceeded, three thousand persons." The archaeological record suggests a considerable population density in prehistoric times (Morey & Marwitt 1978:254).

Both tribes appear to have been founded on patrilineal extended families or sibs, and the aim of each male was virilocal residence (Métraux 1948a:85, 87; 1948b:111–112). Métraux suggests that the Guaraní "probably" practiced uxorilocal residence in ancient times. Uxorilocality was the explicit rule among the Tupinambá, but by marrying his ZD a man could avoid having to adopt the subordinate role of son-in-law in the household of his WF. Since ZD marriage is endogamous to the uxorilocal household, its major rationale may have been to legitimize virilocal residence in a strongly patrilineal society. The Tupinambá equation ZC=MBC is undoubtedly a codification of avuncular marriage (W. Shapiro 1966:83). Métraux also reports that a man could free himself from his duties towards his affines by marrying his D to his WB, neutralizing the asymmetric in-law relationship by putting the latter in the subordinate position of DH. As among the Mundurucú, chiefs appear to have been exempt from the rule of uxorilocality. In a uxorilocal society, the strategy to maintain strong, cohesive patrilocal households coincides with the privileged endogamy of avuncular marriage. Cross-cousin and ZD marriage were the preferred unions among both the Tupinambá and Guaraní (Métraux 1948a:87; 1948b:111–112).

Polygyny was a sign of rank, and there are instances of men having as many as 30 wives. The virilocality of chiefs is consistent with the fact that chieftainship is inherited patrilineally, from F to eldest S (Métraux 1948a: 85; 1948b:113–114). Some chiefs extended their power over a great many villages.

Both the Tupinambá and the Guaraní were excessively devoted to warfare and cannibalism, and built well fortified villages (Métraux 1948a:82, 88; 1948b:103, 119). There are several historical accounts of military expeditions mustering several thousand warriors (Clastres 1977:72–74). The Guaraní ventured across the Chaco, raiding even tribes under Inca rule (Nordenskiöld 1917; Métraux 1948:75–76), their demand for precious metals probably having originated in the extensive trade networks linking the Andes with the Atlantic coast. In the 1540:s, several thousand Tupinambá similarly left the coast of Brazil in a mass emigration to Peru (Métraux 1948b:98).

27. The Sirionó

Kin Terminology (Table 28)

The distinctions MBC≠FZC and WB≠ZH suggest an absence of symmetric alliance. The equations W=MBD and WB=MBS point to matrilateral cross-cousin marriage. On the other hand, the equation SW=ZD implies that patrilateral cross-cousin marriage would be equally feasible.

Equations consistent with avuncular marriage include FZ=MM and FZH=MF. Both these equations would correspond to actual genealogy if F married his ZD, i.e. if M was FZD. The lineal equations of male affines follow a pattern which seems to underscore the potential for ZD marriage. If F married his ZD, MB would be FZS. If MB married his ZD, MB would be ZH and MBS would be ZS. If Ego married his ZD, WF would be ZH and WB would be ZS. Provided FZS was married to Z, he would be WF. Finally, if MBS was WB and married his ZD, he would be DH. W. Shapiro (1968: 42) presents what he believes is "the full list" of terminological indications of avuncular marriage among the Sirionó: MM=FZ, MB=FZS, MBS=DH, WF=ZH, and MBS=ZS. To this list, then, we would add MF=FZH, MB=ZH, WB=ZS, and WF= ZS.

Equations suggesting matrilateral affiliation include FZ=FZD and WBW=SW, the

Table 28
KIN TERMINOLOGY OF THE SIRIONÓ
LINGUISTIC FAMILY: Tupí
Male Ego, terms of reference.

GEN.	Male		Female	
+ 2	FF *ámi* MF *ámi*		FM *ári* MM *ári*	

	KIN (Lineal kin, parallel collaterals, affines of affines)		*AFFINES* (In-laws, cross collaterals)	
	Male	Female	Male	Female
+ 1	F *éru* FB *éru* MZH *éru*	M *ézi* MZ *ézi* FBW *ézi*	WF *ámi* MB *ámi* FZH *ámi*	WM *ári* FZ *ári* MBW *ári*
0	B *anónge* FBS *anónge* MZS *anónge* WZH *yánde*	Z *anónge* FBD *anónge* MZD *anónge* WBW *akwáni*	WB *akwaníndu* MBS *akwaníndu* FZS *ámi* ZH *ámi*	W *yánde* WZ *yánde* MBD *yánde* FZD *ári*
– 1	S *edídi* BS *edídi*	D *edídi* BD *edídi*	DH *akwaníndu* ZS *akwaníndu*	SW *akwáni* ZD *akwáni*

	Male		Female	
– 2	SS *áke* DS *áke*		SD *áke* DD *áke*	

SOURCES: Holmberg 1950:52–54.

DEVIATIONS FROM THE TWO-LINE PATTERN	CONCEIVABLE IDEOLOGICAL OR BEHAVIOURAL CORRELATES
MBC≠FZC, WB≠ZH	Absence of symmetric alliance
W=MBD≠FZD, WB=MBS≠FZS	Matrilateral cross-cousin marriage
MM=FZ, MF=FZH, MB=FZS, MBS=DH, WF=ZH, MBS=ZS, MB=ZH, WB=ZS, WF=FZS	Avuncular marriage
FZ=FZD, WBW=SW	Matrilateral affiliation, uxorilocal residence
FZH=FZS	Patrilateral affiliation
WZH=WZ	Extension from WZ

latter of which equates Ego's son with his MB. On the other hand, the equation FZH= FZS suggests patrilineal principles. Jointly, the equations FZ=FZD and FZH=FZS strongly imply parallel affiliation.

Holmberg (1950:54) concludes that the Sirionó kinship system is of the Crow type. Needham (1961:250) points out that the terminology is not "strictly" Crow, *inter alia* because FZS is equated with FZH instead of F, but in a later context (1964a:233) submits that "it makes certain so-called 'Crow' equations." W. Shapiro (1968:41–43) shows that Crow terminology is not characteristic of any of the Tupí peoples, and asserts that a close examination of Holmberg's terminology reveals that "the Sirionó system is not really of this type." Instead, Shapiro

157

discovers several lineal equations indicative of an Omaha system. His account of the logic of the Sirionó kinship system is based on an ideal model of reciprocal, avuncular marriage between two patrilines (ibid., 45–47). Finally, Scheffler and Lounsbury (1971:108–112) argue that the Sirionó system is neither truly Crow nor truly Omaha, since "the identifiable uterine equivalences concern only females," and "the identifiable agnatic continuities concern only males." From this they formulate their "parallel-transmission rule," and suggest that "certain female kin-class statuses . . . are transmitted from mother to daughter, and the corresponding male kin-class statuses are transmitted from father to son."

Local Group Size and Composition

Sirionó bands may consist of only 30 or 40 people, while larger ones have as many as 120 (Holmberg 1948:458). The bands of Acíba-eoko and Eantándu, studied by Holmberg (1950:51), numbered 94 and 58 respectively.

Post-marital residence is reported to be uxorilocal (Holmberg 1948:461; 1950:50), but W. Shapiro (1968:45) suspects "that it is in fact patrilocal."

Patterns of Affiliation Other than Residence

Because of uxorilocal residence, "groups of matrilineal relatives tend to cluster together in the house and to form extended families" (Holmberg 1950:50). Polemizing with Postal and Eyde (1963), Needham (1964:233) contends that Holmberg's ethnography "shows that Sirionó society is not cognatic but is ordered by a matrilineal rule of descent." This conclusion is based on the occurrence of Crow-type kin equations, on the observation that orphans may be raised by matrilineally related women (Holmberg 1950:49), and on the report that a man may inherit a wife from his MB (ibid., 83). Need-

ham emphasizes the distinction between positing matrilineal "principles of social classification," and claiming that there are "corporate matrilineal descent groups" (1964:237). Yet, he is not content with establishing the existence of matrilineal categories, but also suggests that the Sirionó have "matrilineal descent groups," i.e. "matrilineages," albeit without implying "any corporate activities other than those which Holmberg ascribes to the extended families" (ibid., 234).

Brothers frequently marry groups of sisters, so that patrilineal kin can keep together in spite of uxorilocality (cf. the Shavante.) Chieftainship is inherited patrilineally (Holmberg 1950:60).

Hierarchy

Polygyny is a mark of chiefly status (ibid., 59). Chieftainship is inherited patrilineally by the eldest son (Holmberg 1948:459; 1950: 60).

Alliance

Holmberg claims that the Sirionó practice matrilateral cross-cousin marriage, and that "marriages do not occur outside of this type of relationship" (1948:461). Elsewhere (1950:81), he says that although MBD marriage is the "preferred form," and FZD marriage is forbidden, a classificatory cross-cousin or a non-relative may be substituted. There is a strong tendency for groups of brothers to marry groups of sisters (ibid., 81–82). Bands are largely endogamous (ibid., 50, 81).

Needham (1961:246) concludes that it is "perfectly clear" that marriage in Sirionó society is "explicitly and exclusively prescribed" with the matrilateral cross-cousin. In other words, the Sirionó qualify as "a clear instance of asymmetric alliance." W. Shapiro (1968:43–44) agrees that the Sirionó system is prescriptive, but does not believe that it is asymmetric. Instead, he suggests that the terminology reflects the symmetric, dyadic properties of a system of avuncular marriage (ibid., 45–47). In Shapiro's model, MBD marriage and ZD marriage coincide, for with consistent ZD marriage, ZD will be equivalent to MBD, while FZD will be structurally equivalent to M (ibid., 49). Consistent avuncular marriage amounts to a form of matrilateral cross-cousin marriage which is compatible with the restricted exchange of symmetric, two-line systems.

Scheffler and Lounsbury (1971:35) propose that the "MBD–FZS-spouse equation rule" (i.e. the equations W=MBD and H=FZS) "does not rest on a prescription of MBD–FZS marriage," but "on nothing more or less than the *right* of each man to claim one or more of his MBDs as a wife or wives." Why, then, is the FZD strictly forbidden but the MBD a rightful spouse? The answer, Scheffler and Lounsbury suggest, lies in the implications of the "parallel-transmission rule." If male Ego is covertly equivalent to his F, and his FZD is covertly equivalent to her M, "then by implication the genealogical relationship of a man to his FZD is also in some significant way 'like' and covertly equivalent to that of a man to his sister" (ibid, 175), and sexual relations with FZD would be incestuous (cf. Holmberg 1950:64).

Lévi-Strauss (1968a) discovers that the Nambikwara and the Tupí-speakers acknowledge an identical marriage preference: the ideal spouse is either a cross-cousin or a ZD. In both cases the marriage amounts to an agreement between male cross-cousins/brothers-in-law, who exchange either sisters or daughters. Ego may claim his ZD as wife in exchange for his Z, or if an exchange of sisters has taken place, the brothers-in-law may continue their exchange by emphasizing each one's right to his ZD. Considering the number of equations in the Sirionó terminology which suggest that the ZD preference was strong even here, it is surprising to find three equations which imply the

opposite: that Ego gives his own ZD in marriage to his WB. These equations are: WBW=ZD, MBW=FZD, and WM=FZD. The first of these, of course, may simply be an extension of the matrilineal WBW=SW, and the other two extensions of FZ=FZD. If not, they suggest a triadic structure, in which Ego's ZD is not reclaimed in exchange for his Z, but passed on to a third party. Apparently, the terminology affords possibilities of both restricted and generalized exchange.

External Relations

As the Sirionó are not warlike, relations between bands are peaceful (Holmberg 1948:458). Yet, contact between groups is rare, and bands are "more endogamous than exogamous" (ibid.; 1950:81).

Conclusions: Tupí

The two-line pattern appears to be fundamental to Tupí kin terminologies. Out of 11 Tupí societies for which there is adequate information, W. Shapiro (1968:41) lists five as Dravidian. Deviations include the generational cousin terminology of the Tapirapé and Mundurucú (vocative only), which may represent a codification of endogamous marriage preferences (cf. Dietschy 1977). Although not evident from the sample of tribes presented here, the generational cousin terminology apparently recurs in several Tupí-speaking tribes, including the Tenetehara, Kamayurá, and Cayuá (Dole 1969:107, 117; Murphy 1956:421; W. Shapiro 1968:41).

Uxorilocal residence appears to have been predominant, except among the recent Parintintin and Tupí-Cawahíb. Yet, all the tribes save the Sirionó emphasize patrilateral rather than matrilateral affiliation, and all, including the Sirionó, have patrilineal succession to chieftainship or some other indication of rank discrepancies between patrilines. Among the Mundurucú, lineal principles may underlie the distinction FM≠ MM. As in some of the Gê tribes, there has been a conscious strategy of virilocal residence in chiefly households, particularly among the Mundurucú, the Tupinambá, and the Guaraní. The Parintintin and Tupí-Cawahíb were predominantly virilocal, and Murphy believes that the Mundurucú may have been so in the past. On the other hand, there are indications that all these groups share a tradition of uxorilocality.

There is a highly significant correlation between local group size, mode of affiliation, and external relationships. The Tapirapé, Mundurucú, Parintintin, Tupí-Cawahíb, Tupinambá, and Guaraní all had large settlements, a decidedly patrilateral ideology of male affiliation, and an extremely aggressive disposition. The Sirionó, on the other hand, live in smaller groups, emphasize matrilateral affiliation, and are generally peaceful. Holmberg (1948:455) suggests that the anomalous, semi-nomadic Sirionó are a devolved remnant of a more complex Tupí culture. They certainly appear to represent a trajectory alternative to that of the main stock of Tupí-speakers. The position of the Sirionó is reminiscent of that of the Nambikwara in relation to other Gê-affiliated tribes.

Dual organization has been reported from the Tapirapé, Mundurucú, and Parintintin, and moiety exogamy from the latter two tribes. Avuncular marriage has been reported from all tribes save the Sirionó and the Tapirapé, and appears to be firmly imprinted in the terminologies of both the Mundurucú (who seem fairly recently to have abandoned ZD marriage) and the Sirionó. The former includes five equations indicative of ZD marriage, the latter no less than eight. In both terminologies, there are also equations suggesting matrilateral cross-cousin marriage. This accords well with the preference for MBD marriage among the Sirionó, and with the observation that consistent ZD marriage actually amounts to a dyadic form of MBD marriage. Lévi-Strauss (1968a:176) suggests that avuncular marriage seems to have been a "preferential union" among the

"ancient Tupí," and Kracke (1984:124, note 7) writes that "Tupí societies are those *par excellence* in which avuncular marriage is practiced."

It is interesting to note that ZD marriage, although strongly implied by the terminology, appears not to have been an explicit preference among the Sirionó. One explanation may be that ZD marriage will not be ideologically emphasized in a society stressing matrilateral affiliation, as the two are obviously incompatible (cf. Lave 1966:196; Rivière 1966a:739). As a strategy leading to privileged patrilocality, avuncular marriage derives its primary rationale from the tension between patrilateral affiliation and uxorilocal residence. An alternative explanation is suggested by the complementary distribution of the two kinds of indications of this marriage type. Nowhere is ZD marriage as consistently codified in the kin terminology as among the Sirionó, and yet this is one of the two tribes in our sample for which no explicit preference for it has been reported. We may be faced with a formal parallel to the manifestations of dyadic reciprocity among the Gê, where alternatively stated rules or institutions appear to replace terminological regularities with the increase in size of local groups. Perhaps these cases illustrate what J. Shapiro (1984:24) means when she proposes that "anthropologists interested in the cross-cultural study of marriage can benefit from the experience of linguists who have found that studying a pattern that is overt, formal, and obligatory in one grammatical system enables them to understand the operation of a similar pattern in another language in which it is relatively covert and less formalized."

Terminological distinctions between elder and younger siblings are reported from both the Tapirapé and the Mundurucú. Among the Mundurucú, the Tupinambá, the Guaraní, and possibly the Tapirapé, differently ranked patrilines have inclined towards rank endogamy. The exchanging pairs of Parintintin patrilines would ideally form endogamous units, although there is now no evidence of hierarchical ordering.

160

Chapter 8
Pano

28. The Amahuaca

Kin Terminology (Table 29)

The list provided by Dole (1979:15, 23) conveys only the focal kin type for each term. Apparently, there is considerable variation in the application of these terms, often due simply to the tendency to play with words (ibid., 21). The equations resulting from such extensions frequently distort the two-line structure of the "formal" terminology. There is, for instance, a tendency to use sibling terms for cross-cousins in the Hawaiian manner (ibid., 20, 33). Most of the play with kin terms, however, merely reflects inversions resulting from the reciprocal use of terms which are not reciprocal in nature, e.g. eSi/ySi, F/S, GP/GC, FB/BS, BSS/FFB, and SpP/CSp. Several of these usages suggest principles of alternating generations. For female Ego, the reference to a FZ with a term meaning BC recalls the identification of FZ and BD in Northern Gê name transmission. The reference to ZS as F is probably secondary to the identification of ZD and FZ, i.e. focal kin types for female affines of the first descending and ascending generations, respectively. Their identification again suggests alternating generations. In practice, both categories are also marriageable, even if such marriages are considered "irregular" (ibid., 32).

Dole (ibid., 22, 29) notes that "a moiety structure is suggested by . . . the reciprocal use of terms for alternate-generation kin types that would be in the same 'line'." Another, strong indication of lineality is the possibility of distinguishing between paternal and maternal grandparents (ibid.,

30). Farabee (1922:110), however, discovered no such distinctions at the second ascending generation. He equates M=MM=FM (*mipui*), MM=FM (*uga*), and FF=MF (*miyawaka*). His equations D=yZ (*tcipi* = Dole's *chipí*) and S=yB (*tcampi*= Dole's *chambí*) suggest patrilineal principles of affiliation.

Local Group Size and Composition

A report from 1686 mentions a village of 12 huts and 150 people (Steward & Métraux 1948:565), but community size has since been drastically reduced. Traditional Amahuaca hamlets were composed of patrilocal extended families, but recent work migration and other factors have encouraged neolocal and uxorilocal residence (Dole 1979:28, 31).

Patterns of Affiliation Other than Residence

Amahuaca individuals belong to one of several named groups which, being more or less localized, are presumably patrilineal (ibid., 28). According to Dole, several terminological usages suggest that the Amahuaca in the past maintained exogamous, unilineal moieties (ibid., 21–22, 29–30), and descriptions of earlier settlements (ibid., 34–35, note 6) support this interpretation. Among such usages is the reciprocal *xotá* (FF/SS, FFB/BSS), which in Cashinahua (*xutá*) signifies "namesake" and accords well with the Amahuaca ideal that a male child should receive the name of his FF or FFB (ibid., 21, 34, note 3).

Table 29
KIN TERMINOLOGY OF THE AMAHUACA
LINGUISTIC FAMILY: Pano
Male Ego, terms of reference.

GEN.	Male	Female
+ 2	FF *ipaxindi* *xotá (xindi)* MF *hochixindi* *(ipaxindi)*	FM *i'axindi* MM *chukaxindi* *(i'axindi)*

	KIN (Lineal kin, parallel collaterals, affines of affines)		*AFFINES* (In-laws, cross collaterals)	
	Male	Female	Male	Female
+ 1	F *ipa* FB *apatsá* *papa*	M *i'a* MZ *i'atsá* *yaxuí*	WF *kuka (p.17)* MB *kuka*	WM *achí (p.17)* FZ *achí*
0	B *witsá,* e *hochi* y *chambí* FBS *witsá,* e *hochi* y *chambí* MZS *witsá,* e *hochi* y *chambí*	Z *pui,* e *chuka* y *chipí* FBD *pui,* e *chuka* y *chipí* MZD *pui,* e *chuka* y *chipí*	WB *i'ra (p.20)* MBS *i'ra* FZS *i'ra* ZH *i'ra (p.20)*	W *ai* MBD *ai* *aitsá (p.26)* FZD *ai* *aitsá (p.26)* BW *aitsá (p. 26)*
− 1	S *wirí* *waki (hondi)* BS *wirí*	D *áiwaki* *waki (xando)* BD *áiwaki*	DH *wawa'ba* *(p.23)* ZS *pi'á*	SW *wawa'a* *(p.23)* ZD *xota'á*

	Male		Female	
− 2	SS	*wawa* *xotá*	SD	*wawa*
	DS	*wawa* *xotá*	DD	*wawa*

SOURCES: Dole 1979:15,17,20,23,26. The term *aitsá* for BW and female cross-cousins means "other wife" (ibid., 26). Farabee (1922:110) gives *mipui* for M=MM=FM, *uga* for MM=FM, *miyawaka* for FF=MF, *tcipi* for D=yZ, and *tcampi* for S=yB.

DEVIATIONS FROM THE TWO-LINE PATTERN	CONCEIVABLE IDEOLOGICAL OR BEHAVIOURAL CORRELATES
Dole: FF=SS, MF=eB, MM=eZ	Alternating generations
FF≠MF, FM≠MM	Lineal principles
Farabee: D=yZ, S=yB	Patrilateral affiliation

Hierarchy

Descriptions of an earlier settlement with two exogamous divisions suggest that each moiety had its own leader (ibid., 34–35, note 6). Farabee (1922:105) claims that succession to chieftainship was hereditary.

Alliance

In addition to a number of terminological features suggesting bilateral cross-cousin marriage (Dole 1979:14, 17, 25, 26), there is "a norm of marriage with a cross-cousin, near or distant," and "people do in fact frequently marry or plan to marry cross-cousins" (ibid., 17). The Amahuaca marriage rule is most frequently expressed in terms of a man choosing his FZD, but informants agree that MBD marriage is also suitable (ibid., 28–29). An ideal marriage unites families of separate Amahuaca groups, who exchange siblings. Marriages conflicting with explicit norms (including ZD and FZ marriage) are treated by Dole (ibid., 31–33) as irregularities resulting from demographic stress.

External Relations

The small Amahuaca family settlements are far apart and today "have little contact with each other" (ibid., 27). Farabee (1922: 108) writes that the Amahuaca once conducted regular war campaigns to capture women, and that they were "noted warriors."

29. The Mayoruna

Kin Terminology (Table 30)

The lineal equation M=ZD contradicts the two-line pattern, but is consistent with the matrilineal equation MB=ZS (*matses*). These equations suggest that a pair of opposite-sex siblings is identified with a corresponding pair in alternate generations, traced through the female line.

A second feature contradicting the two-line structure is the equation FZ=BD (*nachi*). *Nachi* is translated as a "man's aunt/ niece" and a "man's female agnate" (Fields & Merrifield 1980:3, 7). This equation is the mirror image of the MB=ZS equation. In both cases, there is an identification of collaterals in alternate generations, traced through Ego's parent and sibling of the sex opposite to that of the identified individuals. Implicit in both equations is the identification of alternate generations of same-sex lines (M=ZD, F=BS), suggesting parallel affiliation. The identification of FZ and BD also occurs among the Amahuaca, and recalls Northern Gê name transmission. Although similarly suggestive of parallel affiliation as it is among the Northern Gê, cross transmission among the Mayoruna has somewhat different implications. Since FZ and BD are equated even by male Ego, this identification is not merely a reciprocal kin term usage among patrilineally related females, but suggests that a woman is structurally equivalent to her FFZ. For males, the corresponding conclusion is that a man is identified with his MMB. If a woman is equivalent to her FFZ, her brother should be equivalent to his FF, and if a man is identified with his MMB, his sister should be identified with her MM. In a system of bilateral cross-cousin marriage, FFZ is identical to MM and MMB to FF.

Another noteworthy feature of Mayoruna kin terminology is the distinction of paternal and maternal grandparents. The distinction of different categories of kin in second ascending or descending generations is highly indicative of lineal principles. Such distinctions have been reported from the Amahuaca and from Gê-affiliated groups such as the Timbira, Bororo, and Nambikwara.

Local Group Size and Composition

Early reports mention Mayoruna villages of 100 or even 250 people (Steward & Métraux 1948:552). Such early villages would have consisted of three or four houses (ibid., 553). Today, settlements are much smaller.

Table 30
KIN TERMINOLOGY OF THE MAYORUNA
LINGUISTIC FAMILY: Pano
Male Ego, terms of reference.

GEN.	Male		Female	
+ 2	FF *buchido* MF *buchido* *chaido*		FM *shano acho* MM *chichi*	

	KIN (Lineal kin, parallel collaterals, affines of affines)		*AFFINES* (In-laws, cross collaterals)	
	Male	Female	Male	Female
+ 1	F *papa* FB *papa (utsi)* *bo*	M *tita* MZ *tita (utsi)*	WF *cucu* MB *cucu* *matses*	WM *nachi* FZ *nachi*
0	B e *buchi* y *tsidionquit* FBS e *buchi* y *tsidionquit* MZS e *buchi* y *tsidionquit*	Z e *chuchu* y *chibi* FBD e *chuchu* y *chibi* MZD e *chuchu* y *chibi*	MBS *chaí, daues cania* FZS *chaí, daues cania*	W *chido* MBD *chido shanu* FZD *chido shanu*
− 1	S *mado* BS *mado* *bo*	D *champi* BD *champi nachi (p.3)*	ZS *piac matses*	ZD *tita*

	Male		Female	
− 2	SS *baba* DS *baba*		SD *baba* DD *baba*	

SOURCES: Fields & Merrifield 1980:2,3,7–10,27

DEVIATIONS FROM THE TWO-LINE PATTERN	CONCEIVABLE IDEOLOGICAL OR BEHAVIOURAL CORRELATES
M=ZD, MB=ZS, FZ=BD, FB=BS	Alternating generations
FF≠MF, FM≠MM	Lineal principles

Post-marital residence is patrilocal (ibid., 554). The application of the term *matses* ("kinsmen", "our people") to MB and ZS may reflect an early practice of uxorilocality. Support for this hypothesis comes from early reports of Mayoruna boys marrying into Omagua households (Steward & Métraux 1948:552). A likely explanation for the contemporary predominance of virilocality is the frequency with which Mayoruna men are forced to resort to bride-capture in order to obtain a wife (Fields & Merrifield 1980:1, 2, 26).

Patterns of Affiliation Other than Residence

Fields and Merrifield (ibid., 5) write that all Mayoruna belong to one of two patrilineal but agamous moieties: *bedi* (jaguar) or *macu*

Table 31
KIN TERMINOLOGY OF THE SHARANAHUA
LINGUISTIC FAMILY: Pano
Male Ego, terms of reference.

GEN.	Male			Female		
+ 2	FF	*shota* (*ochi*)	MMB *ochi* *andaifo*	FM	*shano* (*bimbiki*)	MFZ *bimbiki*
	MF	*chata* (*chai*)	FMB *chai*	MM	*chichi* (*chipi*)	FFZ *chipi* *yoshafo*

	KIN (Lineal kin, parallel collaterals, affines of affines)			*AFFINES* (In-laws, cross collaterals)		
	Male		Female	Male		Female
+ 1	F	*upa*	M *uwa*	WF (*koka*)		WM (*achi*)
	FB	*upa*	MZ *uwa*	MB *koka*		FZ *achi*
0	B	e *ochi* y *ursto*	Z e *chipi* y *chiko*	WB (*chai*)		W (*bimbiki*)
	FBS	e *ochi* y *ursto*	FBD e *chipi* y *chiko*	MBS *chai*		MBD *bimbiki*
	MZS	e *ochi* y *ursto*	MZD e *chipi* y *chiko*	FZS *chai*		FZD *bimbiki*
− 1	S	*faku* (*upa*)	D *faku* (*achi*)			
	BS	*faku*	BD *faku*	ZS *pia*		ZD *pia*

	Male		Female	
− 2	SS	*shota* (*ursto*)	SD	*shota*
	DS	*fafa*	DD	*fafa*

SOURCES: Siskind 1973:200. Terms in brackets are vocative (ibid., 55–56,62,199).

DEVIATIONS FROM THE TWO-LINE PATTERN	CONCEIVABLE IDEOLOGICAL OR BEHAVIOURAL CORRELATES
FF=B=SS, MF=MBS, MM=Z, FM=FZD, F=S, FZ=D	Alternating generations
FF≠MF, FM≠MM	Lineal principles

(worm). They classify the terminology as Dravidian (two-section), but in fact discover that Mayoruna kin categories fall into a four-section pattern (ibid., 26), where each individual needs only establish his or her point of reference in order to be able to apply the eight fundamental categories. A *buchi* (FF, B) always marries a *shanu* (FM, FZD/MBD), and a *chuchu* (MM, Z) marries a *daues* (MF, FZS/MBS). In adjacent generations, a *bo* (FB, BS) always marries a *tita* (MZ, ZD), and a *nachi* (FZ, BD) marries a *cucu* (MB, ZS). This system of alternating generations is reflected in the kin terminology (ibid., 2–3, 16). It suggests that the Mayoruna have recognized the cyclical merging of disharmonic principles of affiliation, i.e. the patrilineal moieties and uxorilocal residence.

165

Alliance

The Mayoruna prescribe marriage with a woman of the category *shanu*, which generally implies bilateral cross-cousin marriage (ibid., 1, 2, 15, 18). The reference of cross-cousin terms, however, ranges over kinsmen of all even-numbered generation (+2, 0, –2, etc.), and "several men have wives both of their own generation as well as others of the grandchild generation" (ibid., 2–3). An adult Mayoruna may ask his *cucu* (MB) or *nachi* (FZ, BD) for his or her daughter, implying that BDD would be one of the eligible kin-types of the second descending generation.

External Relations

For many years the Mayoruna have been raiding other tribes for women and children (ibid., 2), presumably owing to a shortage of women within the prescribed category of potential spouses.

30. The Sharanahua

Kin Terminology (Table 31)

In the three medial generations, Sharanahua kin terms are perfectly faithful to the two-line pattern. Terms for the second ascending and descending generations, however, allow for distinctions between matrilateral and patrilateral grandkin, which suggests lineal principles of affiliation. When supplemented with terms of address, these categories reveal a consistent principle of alternating generations. Thus, FF, B, and SS are identified, as are MF and MBS. Similarly, MM and Z are equated, and FM is equated with FZD. All these equations duplicate those of the implicit four-section system of the Mayoruna. In both cases, the system of alternating generations implies a recognition of the cyclical merging of male and female lines,

as in a disharmonic combination of residence and affiliation.

FMB is WB (*chai*) to FF, with whom Ego is identified. With cross-cousin marriage, FMB is also MF, FF=MMB, FM=MFZ, and MM=FFZ. The identification of FZ and D (or BD), as among the Amahuaca and Mayoruna, is consistent with the system of alternating generations, and with a principle of parallel affiliation or, as Siskind (1973: 199) puts it, "a world view different for each sex."

Local Group Size and Composition

The Sharanahua settlement of Marcos numbered 89 individuals in 1966 (ibid.,196). Traditions speak of villages of two or three *malocas* sheltering 60 to 90 people (ibid., 42).

Post-marital residence is predominantly uxorilocal (ibid., 63, 77, 80, 81), but some men, emphasizing the patrilineal line, have "successfully avoided uxorilocality and have remained in the same village as their father and brother" (ibid., 202). Siskind speculates that in the past, "given the strong preference for village endogamy, residence would have been at least as often virilocal as uxorilocal" (ibid., 203).

Patterns of Affiliation Other than Residence

Siskind (ibid., 50, 61) suggests that neighbouring Pano peoples represent what were once exogamous, intermarrying groups (cf. the Tukano-speakers.) This accords with the position of Torralba (1981:38–39). As these groups expanded, the preference for marriage within the *maloca* would have led to linguistic endogamy and the differentiation of several patrilineal, exogamous descent groups within each language group.

Siskind (1973:199, 202) writes that "a moiety interpretation seems partially accurate for the Sharanahua," and suggests that "the flexibility of Panoan kinship seems to allow for moieties and group endogamy whenever a group is sufficiently numerous, increased importance of affines and marriages to foreigners when the group is small." She modifies her reference to patrilineal "descent groups" by proposing that members of each sex delineate their kin categories according to separate principles, producing a system of parallel affiliation. This would be consistent with Sharanahua terms of address: women call their children *uwa* and *koka*, while men call them *upa* and *achi*. The system of alternating generations (ibid., 55,62) is consistent with both moieties and parallel affiliation, and also evident in the transmission of personal names from FF or FFB to SS or BSS, and from FFZ (structurally equivalent to MM) to BSD (i.e. DD) (ibid., 61). Torralba (1981:39–40) confirms this mode of name transmission, including the MM–DD link. He also attributes to the Sharanahua a four-section system identical to that of the Cashinahua.

Hierarchy

Sons-in-law and parents-in-law call each other *raisi,* are often foreigners, and treat each other with distance (Siskind 1973:79). Although the term is reciprocal, the son-in-law is obliged to provide meat for his wife's parents for as long as they live (ibid., 82).

Alliance

Marriage is preferably community endogamous (ibid., 61, 66, 203). Potential spouses include bilateral cross-cousins (ibid., 61, 66, 77). There appears to be "a faint preference for patrilateral cross-cousin marriage" (ibid., 202–203), but the structure of Sharanahua society nevertheless assumes that children, "like their father, will marry someone in their mother's descent group" (ibid., 61).

These two ideals are compatible, since marriages ideally involve sister exchange (ibid., 60, 199). Both Siskind (ibid., 199, 202) and Torralba (1981:39–40) attribute a moiety system to the Sharanahua.

External Relations

In the past, there appears to have been continuous warfare and raiding in connection with bride-capture (Siskind 1973:65–66, 203), and *malocas* were fortified.

31. The Cashinahua

Kin Terminology (Table 32)

Siskind (1973:202) notes that the Cashinahua have "almost precisely the same kinship system" as the closely related Sharanahua. Kensinger (1974a:283) classifies it as Dravidian.

Local Group Size and Composition

In 1974, there were 400 people distributed among seven villages ranging in size from 22 to 98 persons (ibid.), which gives an average village size of 57. Three Cashinahua villages studied by Kensinger (1977:236–238) housed 37, 34, and 16 people, respectively. Estimates based on the ideal composition of a village, however, yield between 44 and 92 (ibid., 234).

The ideal Cashinahua village consists of two intermarrying, uxorilocal extended families (ibid., 236). Kensinger (ibid., 239) discovered instances of "patrilocally extended families," but as villages are primarily alliance-organized and endogamous, choice of post-marital residence does not make a crucial difference. D'Ans (1975:28) offers uxorilocality as the rule.

Patterns of Affiliation Other than Residence

The Cashinahua have a four-section system of affiliation and alliance. The two patri-moieties, *inubake* and *duabake*, possibly meaning "sons of the jaguar" and "sons of the snake," respectively (Girard 1958:217), are each subdivided into two generations (Kensinger 1977:235; d'Ans 1975:28–29). The two generations of *inubakebu* are *awabakebu* and *kanabakebu*. These intermarry with the *yawabakebu* and *dunubakebu* generations, respectively, of the *duabakebu* moiety. Kensinger calls these categories "alternating generation namesake groups," as their foundation is the transmission of names and associated artistic designs (Kensinger 1980:6) from FF or FFB to SS or BSS, and from MM/FFZ to DD/BSD. The alternation of generations in each of the two patrilines is geared to the two-generation cycles of two implicit matrilines. Thus, a namesake group can be defined as the group of people who share the same patrilineal moiety *and* the same matri-line (uxorilocal household?). Patrilineally related women constitute named categories within each of the two patrimoieties (*inani-bakebu* within the *inubakebu* moiety, and *banubakebu* within the *duabakebu* moiety). On the other hand, Kensinger (1985b:20, 24, note 2) can also describe the system of classi-fication as if gender is divided by moiety membership, rather than vice versa (i.e., patrimoieties subdivided by gender), produc-ing two male and two female moieties. It would seem possible, then, to question the significance of female membership in the patrimoieties. If the dual division *inubake/duabake* is primarily a male concern, the two sets of alternating generations *awaba-kebu-dunubakebu* and *kanabakebu-yawaba-kebu* may be equally relevant to female identity, producing a parallel system of female matrilines criss-crossing the male patrilines (cf. J. Shapiro 1984:29, note 19). The transfer of medical knowledge, in fact, is an explicit instance of parallel transmission (Kensinger 1974a:285). Parallel affiliation may among the Cashinahua provide a means for reconciling a Dravidian kin termino-logy and dual organization (cf. Conclusions: Pano).

Kensinger (1977:240) notes that the moieties function as social groups only at the level of their local representatives, who "interact and intermarry." The fundamental organizing principle underlying the model of the ideal Cashinahua village involves neither residence nor descent, but the cohesive relationship of alliance between two "focal males," one from each moiety (ibid., 242).

Hierarchy

As among the Sharanahua, Cashinahua sons-in-law are expected to serve their parents-in-law, which generally means uxorilocal residence (d'Ans 1975:28).

Girard (1958:217–218) attributes consider-able authority to Cashinahua chiefs. He claims that the *inubake* moiety is ruled by a polygynous shaman, while the *duabake* moiety has a monogamous, secular chief. These data suggest diarchy, as in the tradi-tional Amahuaca village. "In a sense," writes Kensinger (1974b:4), "each village has two headmen."

Alliance

The ideal Cashinahua marriage involves sister exchange between two men who are related as bilateral cross-cousins (Kensinger 1977:233–236; d'Ans 1975:28). The ideal village is composed of "two patrilines bound in a symmetrical marriage alliance" (Ken-singer 1974a:283). The four "alternating generation namesake groups" function as marriage sections similar to those reported from Australia.

Kensinger (1984b) identifies five distinct rules relating to marriage: (1a) preferential marriage with an actual, genealogically

Table 32
KIN TERMINOLOGY OF THE CASHINAHUA
LINGUISTIC FAMILY: Pano
Male Ego, terms of reference.

GEN.	Male		Female	
+ 2	FF	*huchikuin*	FM	*xanukuin ainkuin*	MFZ	*xanukuin ainkuin*
	MF	*chaikuin*	MM	*chichikuin*	FFZ	*chichikuin*

	KIN (Lineal kin, parallel collaterals, affines of affines)			*AFFINES* (In-laws, cross collaterals)			
	Male		Female		Male		Female
+ 1	F	*epakuin*	M	*ewakuin*	WF	*kukakuin*	WM	*achikuin*
	FB	*epakuin*	MZ	*ewakuin*	MB	*kukakuin*	FZ	*achikuin*
	MZH	*epakuin*	FBW	*ewakuin*	FZH	*kukakuin*	MBW	*achikuin*
0	B	e *huchikuin* betsakuin y *ichukuin*	Z	*chipikuin puikuin ichukuin*	WB	*chaikuin*	W	*ainkuin xanukuin*
					MBS	*chaikuin*	MBD	*ainkuin* e *xanukuin*
					FZS	*chaikuin*	FZD	*ainkuin* e *xanukuin*
					ZH	*chaikuin*		
– 1	S	*bedenkuin bakekuin*	D	*bakekuin*	DH	*daiskuin*	SW	*babawankuin*
					ZS	*daiskuin*	ZD	*babawankuin*

	Male		Female	
– 2	SS	*babakuin betsakuin*	SD	*babakuin puikuin*
	DS	*babakuin chaikuin*	DD	*babakuin ainkuin*

SOURCES: Kensinger 1984b:229.

DEVIATIONS FROM THE TWO-LINE PATTERN	CONCEIVABLE IDEOLOGICAL OR BEHAVIOURAL CORRELATES
FF=B, MF=MBS, FM=MFZ= FZD, B=SS, Z=SD, FZS=DS, MBD=DD	Alternating generations
FF≠MF, FM=MFZ≠MM=FFZ, SS≠DS, SD≠DD	Lineal principles

defined, bilateral first cross-cousin; (1b) prescriptive marriage with a member of the kin class *ainbuaibu/benebu,* i.e. a person of the opposite sex in the opposite moiety and linked marriage section; (2) moiety exogamy; (3) prescribed marriage with a member of a specific marriage section; and (4) village endogamy.

External Relations

Villages are "politically, socially, and economically autonomous" (Kensinger 1974a:283; 1984b:246, note 1). There is a strong preference for village endogamy (1975:11) and an ideal of sororal polygyny (1984b:247, note 5). Kensinger (1977:240) notes that the Cashi-

169

nahua conceive of their society as a well-defined, totally self-contained, closed social unit, where "contact between persons from different societies or villages during day-to-day activities would be unlikely."

Conclusions: Pano

"Disharmonic systems have naturally developed towards organizations with marriage classes, because, in such systems, direct exchange is the simplest and most effective process for ensuring the integration of the group. Of course, this development is not necessary. In South America we know of numerous examples of systems without marriage classes which feature marriage with the bilateral cross-cousin. However, if the elements of the organization into marriage classes are given, in the form of dual organization, then it can be predicted that all development towards integration will be through the subdivision of the two original classes into sections and subsections, as has taken place in Australia."
– C. Lévi-Strauss (1969:442)

The two-line pattern appears to be fundamental to all the Pano terminologies in our sample. Equations suggesting alternating generations also occur in all groups, and are consistent with principles of name transmission and with the system of marriage sections reported from the Mayoruna, Sharanahua, and Cashinahua. Terminological usages which seem anomalous among the Amahuaca, such as the identification of FZ and BD, may be explained within the framework of comparative Panoan ethnography. In conjunction with the equation FF=SS, and with the rule of name transmission from FF to SS, such usages strongly suggest a previous four-section system identical to that of the remaining three peoples in our sample.

Strong principles of lineality are suggested by the distinctions between paternal and maternal grandparents. In the terminologies of the Sharanahua and Cashinahua, the same kind of distinction is made regarding the second descending generation. The recognition of lineality is consistent with the existence of exogamous, patrilineal moieties among the Mayoruna, Sharanahua, and Cashinahua. Traditions suggest that the Amahuaca, too, may have had moieties. Both the Amahuaca and the Cashinahua also appear to have maintained a system of diarchy corresponding to their dual organization. Succession to chieftainship is patrilineal among the Amahuaca.

The co-existence of patrilineal and matrilineal principles, whether a matter of parallel or bilineal affiliation, is implicit in the system of alternating generations. The patrilineal component is obvious in the exogamous patrimoieties, whereas the matrilineal component is consistent with uxorilocal residence among the Sharanahua and Cashinahua. Early reports suggest that the Mayoruna, too, may have practiced uxorilocal residence. We may speculate that even the Amahuaca may have undergone a shift from uxorilocality to virilocality. Ethnographers of the Sharanahua and Cashinahua, however, argue that since villages are largely endogamous and alliance-organized, there need not be any heavy emphasis on one exclusive rule of residence. Local group size is less than 50 for all but the Sharanahua, but communities of over 150 have been attributed to the Amahuaca, Mayoruna, and Sharanahua of past centuries.

All four groups in our sample favour bilateral cross-cousin marriage and sister exchange. The Amahuaca and Sharanahua express a faint preference for FZD marriage. Occasional marriage to a ZD or FZ is reported from the Amahuaca. Groups tend to be endogamous and isolated from each other, but warfare involving bride-capture was apparently widespread in the past.

Since they have been credited with both two-line terminologies *and* exogamous moieties, i.e. both egocentric and socio-centric dualism (Kensinger 1980), the Pano-speakers deserve particular attention. By equating cross-collaterals and affines in generations +1 and 0, their terminologies all qualify as fundamentally Dravidian. As was observed by W. Shapiro (1970), however, the consistent equation of cross-collaterals and affines is logically incongruent with exogamous moieties. Although terminologically defined as an affine (WM), FZ belongs to Ego's own patrilineal moiety. This contradiction may explain why the co-existence of moieties and Dravidian kin terms is such a rare feature. (Outside of the Pano linguistic family, the only other people in our sample to whom it has been attributed are the Parintintin.) The presence of these two logically contradictory schemes of classification, in conjunction with indications of a decrease in village size and an ongoing abandonment of uxorilocality, may indicate that the Pano-speakers represent a state of transition from larger, uxorilocal, moiety-organized villages to small, viri- or ambilocal groups founded on the principle of inherited alliance. If this is the case, these groups illustrate the reversibility of the trajectory through which a terminologically regulated, symmetric alliance structure is recodified in the form of dual organization (cf. the Gê.) The Amahuaca, who even tolerate occasional marriage to a FZ, have obviously departed furthest from the patrilineal moiety model. Oblique marriage (including ZD marriage, also known to occur among the Amahuaca) is alien to a system of alternating generation marriage sections and thus to the remaining three Pano-speaking groups in our sample (cf. Kensinger 1984b:238). Trautmann (1981:207) has suggested that these two possibilities, i.e. marriage with cross-kin of adjacent or alternate generations, represent alternative trajectories of Dravidian classification (cf. Henley 1982:104, for a similar point concerning the Panare.)

The problems concerning the classification of FZ as kin or affine, envisaged on a purely theoretical level but illustrated by the complementary distribution of Dravidian terminologies and patrilineal moieties, appear to be alleviated by the Panoan system of marriage classes in conjunction with an underlying principle of parallel transmission. The emphasis seems to be on the father's sister's marriage class membership, rather than on her membership in Ego's own moiety. Even if FZ is classified with F (Kensinger 1984b: 229) rather than MB, as in classical Dravidian systems, the denial of the Dravidian kin-affine dichotomy in itself neutralizes her contradictory status. For any specific Ego, the "kin-affine" distinction is applicable only to alternate generations. This appears to be the Kariera solution so well known from Australia. From another point of view, parallel transmission in itself neutralizes the kin-versus-affine contradiction by confining kin-affine distinctions to same-sex relationships. The category FZ=WM=MBW would only be "affinal" from the point of view of females such as M or Z. Panoan groups such as the Sharanahua and Cashinahua thus illustrate how parallel affiliation may provide a passage from pure Dravidian, cognatic systems to the recognition of sociocentric, unilineal categories. Even the distinction between different varieties of grandkin, which is intimately linked to alternate generation marriage and which so strongly suggests unilineal principles, may emerge as an extension of the dimension of "crossness" inherent in Dravidian terminologies (Trautmann 1981:188–193; Henley 1982:98).

Chapter 9

Tukano

32. The Cubeo

Kin Terminology (Table 33)

The only equation which contradicts the two-line pattern is BD=ZD=SW. Goldman (1963:125–126) remarks on the "neutral character" of the term *hwainkó*, which does not connote "out-of-the-sib, as does *paní*,", but instead reflects the closeness of the ZD as a likely SW and co-resident.

Himanípako (W) is a teknonym meaning "my children's mother" (ibid.,135). *Baküdyó* (FB) means "like a father" (ibid., 124). For parallel cousins of the same phratry but outside the lineage, Goldman lists *amiyó/ hwainyó* for males and *amikó/hwainkó* for females.

Local Group Size and Composition

Goldman (ibid., 25, 48) lists 29 residence sites on the Cuduiarí River, averaging in size between 30 and 35 people. Post-marital residence is patrilocal (ibid., 27, 90, 115), but if there is ample land daughters are sometimes invited to reside in their natal sib (ibid., 36), and there are "exceptional but not rare cases" of matrilocality (ibid., 42).

Patterns of Affiliation Other than Residence

Goldman found among the Cubeo patrilineal, named descent groups which are normally localized. These sibs are in turn divided among three "unnamed exogamic phratries" (ibid., 90). Within the range of patrilineal consanguinity, uterine brothers form particularly close groups, excluding agnatic brothers by a different mother (ibid., 115–116). MZC, though parallel cousins, often belong to another phratry, which makes them eligible for marriage (ibid., 125–126).

Kin are not defined exclusively according to the principle of patrilineal descent, since a ZD, destined as a SW to be a member of Ego's residence group, is assimilated with the category of BD (*hwainkó*). Despite patriliny a sib can also be established by a woman, as it can recognize female as well as male founder-ancestors (ibid., 96, 123).

In the exogamous phratries, and in the practice of exchange marriages, Goldman (ibid., 288) sees a "potentiality for moiety formation . . . never realized because of geographic distances and the wide ranges of marital choice." A principle of alternating generations is evident from the transmission of honorific names from grandparent to grandchild (ibid., 92).

Hierarchy

Sibs are hierarchically ranked within each phratry (ibid., 26, 90; 1977:176, 178). External signs of high rank include large *malocas* (1963:40) and particular kinds of ornament such as quartz cylinders (ibid., 98, 154). A report from the 1860:s mentions caste-like distinctions between chiefs, nobles, and commoners on the Vaupés River (ibid., 152), and informants claim that in the past all the sibs along a river were united

Table 33
KIN TERMINOLOGY OF THE CUBEO
LINGUISTIC FAMILY: Tukano
Male Ego, terms of reference.

GEN.	Male		Female	
+ 2	FF *nyekundjó* MF *nyekundjó*		FM *nyéko* MM *nyéko*	

	KIN (Lineal kin, parallel collaterals, affines of affines)		AFFINES (In-laws, cross collaterals)	
	Male	Female	Male	Female
+ 1	F *bakü* *hípakü* FB *bakü (dyó)* *hípakü*	M *bakó* *hípako* MZ *bakó* *hípako* FBW *bakó* *hípako*	WF *hipániyo* *paní* MB *hipániyo* FZH *hipániyo*	WM *hipánimo* FZ *hipánimo* MBW *hipánimo*
0	B e *himámikü* y *híyokü* FBS e *himámiko* y *híyokü* MZS e *himámikü* y *híyokü*	Z e *himámiko* y *híyoko* FBD e *himámiko* y *híyoko* MZD e *himámiko* y *híyoko*	WB *hikópwimana* *hikódjumu* MBS *tcimá* FZS *tcimá* ZH *hikódjumu*	W *himanípako* MBD *hítcimako* FZD *hítcimako* BW *hikápenamo*
− 1	S *hímakü* BS *hwainyó*	D *hímako* BD *hwainkó*	DH *paní* ZS *paní*	SW *hwainkó* ZD *hwainkó*

	Male		Female	
− 2	SS *hipanímekü* DS *hipanímekü*		SD *hipanímeko* DD *hipanímeko*	

SOURCES: Goldman 1963:134–135. The term *hikódjumu* for WB derives from p. 129, and the term *paní* ZS from p. 125.

DEVIATIONS FROM THE TWO-LINE PATTERN	CONCEIVABLE IDEOLOGICAL OR BEHAVIOURAL CORRELATES
BD=ZD	Cognatic principles, virilocal residence of ZD as SW

under a single chief (ibid., 157). Today, the Cubeo have but "the skeleton of an aristocratic system" (ibid., 92), a "shadow aristocracy only" (ibid., 99).

Succession to headmanship within a particular household is usually determined by seniority (ibid., 118), the office passing from a father to his eldest son or from a man to his next younger brother (ibid., 154). Within each *maloca*, "lineages occupy residential spaces according to birth-order-defined rank" (Goldman 1977:176; cf. the Barasana, Bora/Miraña, and Bidou 1977:116 on the Tatuyo.) Polygyny is usually a privilege of the headman (Goldman 1963:145), and sib segmentation tends to occur along cleavages between groups of brothers by his different wives (ibid., 116–117). The high-prestige *habókü* status is a position achieved primarily by headmen of higher-ranking sibs, and these sibs tend to consider *habókü* status hereditary (ibid., 152).

173

The Cubeo claim that they have never intermarried with the lower-ranking Makú, even though a sib tradition holds that the Bahúkiwa sib once took Makú wives (ibid., 105). The Makú (also known as Borówa) appear once to have constituted an ethnically distinct servant class subordinate to the Tukanoan and Arawakan tribes in the region (ibid., 106–107). Apparently, the Cubeo found it increasingly difficult to maintain authority over the Makú, and the class structure was dissolved. The tradition of intermarriage with the Makú, however, still "stigmatizes the Bahúkiwa as an inferior sib" (ibid., 7, 96). Goldman warns that his perspective on Cubeo society is unavoidably that of the Bahúkiwa, the sib with which he stayed throughout his fieldwork. From the point of view of a high-ranking sib such as the Hehénewa, Cubeo society would probably be characterized more in terms of hierarchy and authority (ibid., 23). Goldman's Bahúkiwa bias probably also taints the version of sib rank presented in his exposure of Cubeo phratric organization (ibid., 100).

The emphasis on birth order evident from Cubeo sibling terms is consistent with the hierarchy of senior and junior sibs (ibid., 98). Sibling terms are used to convey not only relative seniority but, when used among members of different sibs, also a dimension of respect (ibid., 117). The Tucano, neighbours of the Cubeo, have developed such seniority usages between the sibs of each phratry in a more systematic manner (ibid., 27, 118).

It is noteworthy that the strong ideological emphasis on differences in rank applies to kin only, whereas the relationship between affines is remarkably egalitarian. This is illustrated by the reciprocal use of the term *paní* between father-in-law and son-in-law (ibid., 128).

Alliance

Sibs and phratries are exogamous (ibid., 6, 24, 26, 90, 97). There is also a convention of community exogamy "that has grown out of the tradition of the localized sib" (ibid., 43). The three phratries may originally have been four, since there are traditions which speak of two previously intermarrying groups of sibs which amalgamated with one another (ibid., 93). Even now, although this composite phratry is exogamous, "informants disagree as to the proprieties of intermarriage between the two divisions" (ibid., 103).

Brother-sister exchange marriage is the explicit ideal (ibid., 118, 119, 122, 127, 132), and over time is equivalent to bilateral cross-cousin marriage. The Makú are said by the Cubeo to be "without shame," since they allow parallel cousins to marry (ibid., 106). The only context in which parallel-cousin marriage may occur among the Cubeo is when a MZC belongs to a sib outside the phratry (ibid., 126). There is a strong preference for choosing a wife from one's mother's natal sib, particularly when this is also the *maloca* of one's FZ, i.e. when there was an exchange marriage in the previous generation (ibid., 137).

External Relations

Goldman (ibid., 37) notes that there is a tendency in the north-west Amazon region for particular *malocas* to become rudimentary ceremonial centers for a number of scattered smaller groups. Considering the characteristic fluidity of tribal organization in the region, he suggests that we cannot dismiss the tradition of the phratry as a unit politically consolidated under a single headman (ibid., 93).

The widespread multilingualism of the area is evidence of "the frequency of intermarriage with other linguistic groups and the love of the Indians for travel and intertribal trade" (ibid., 15). Major articles of trade include ornaments serving as insignia of high prestige, such as feather headdresses and quartz cylinders, and there is a certain division of labour between tribes specializing in the manufacture of particular items (ibid., 153–154). Simultaneously, the Cubeo have a tradition of frequent raiding for women or revenge, even of struggling for mastery of the Cuduiarí River. In the past, these raids were apparently associated with cannibalism. The Cubeo have also repeatedly been attacked by Cariban and Arawakan tribes, and annually by the Tukano-speaking Desana (ibid., 162–164).

33. The Barasana

Kin Terminology (Table 34)

There are no equations in the Barasana kin nomenclature which contradict the two-line pattern. The distinction between patrilateral and matrilateral parallel cousins obviously reflects the latter's indeterminate patrilateral affiliation. For female cross-cousins, there is a common category (*tenyo*) as well as an alternative, descriptive usage permitting distinction between the matrilateral and patrilateral variants.

C. Hugh-Jones (1977a:94) describes the Barasana kinship terminology as "a variation on the basic Dravidian type." In her "'Dravidian Box' form" exposition (ibid., 97), however, FZ and MZ occupy inverted positions compared to the classical Dravidian scheme (Dumont 1953a:36). A predictable consequence of replacing the Dravidian notion of "kin" with "agnates", it seems an unnecessary and misleading accommodation to the patrisib system. Linguistically, both F and M (*haku* and *hako*) and FB and MZ (*buamu* and *buamo*) belong together, attesting to the fundamentally Dravidian structure. If "agnates" versus "affines" according to C. Hugh-Jones' diagram truly represents emic Barasana supra-categories, it seems as if their descent system has outgrown their language, producing two alternative dichotomies.

Local Group Size and Composition

C. Hugh-Jones (1977a:28) is convinced that Barasana communities have been constantly diminishing during the past century. She lists 13 longhouse groups with populations ranging between four and 29 and averaging 12 or 13 (ibid., 53). Early travellers in the region, however, saw "both conglomerations of longhouses and also huge houses containing upwards of 75 people" (S. Hugh-Jones 1974:12).

Each longhouse group centers around a set of brothers or patrilateral parallel cousins and their patrilineal descendants (C. Hugh-Jones 1977a:26; 1977b:186–187; S. Hugh-Jones 1974:11; 1977:207). In other words, post-marital residence is patrilocal (C. Hugh-Jones 1977b:190–191).

Patterns of Affiliation Other than Residence

The Barasana reckon patrilineal descent (S. Hugh-Jones 1974:11; C. Hugh-Jones 1977b: 191). As among the Cubeo, named clans or sibs are grouped into unnamed, exogamous categories (Goldman's "phratries"). S. Hugh-Jones (1974:13) writes that names like Barasana, Bará, and Makuna, though "frequently and incorrectly referred to as 'tribes'," are generally used by non-Indians to refer to "exogamic groups each of whose members speak a common language." C. Hugh-Jones (1977a:17–21) notes that anthropologists reporting on Tukanoan social organization have used different sets of terms for a series of levels which appears to be fairly uniform among all Tukanoan groups. Whereas Goldman speaks of sib, phratry, and tribe, the latter category defined by common language, Jackson found among the Bará a level she calls "language-aggregate" (i.e. linguistically defined like Goldman's "tribe") intermediate to sib and phratry. For the Barasana, C. Hugh-Jones employs "exogamous groups" instead of Jackson's

Table 34
KIN TERMINOLOGY OF THE BARASANA
LINGUISTIC FAMILY: Tukano
Male Ego, terms of reference.

GEN.	Male		Female	
+ 2	FF *niku* MF *niku*		FM *niko* MM *niko*	

	KIN (Lineal kin, parallel collaterals, affines of affines)		AFFINES (In-laws, cross collaterals)	
	Male	Female	Male	Female
+ 1	F *haku* FB *buamu* MZH *buamu*	M *hako* MZ *buamo* FBW *buamu*	WF *umaniku* MB *hakoarumu* FZH *hakoarumu*	WM *umaniko* FZ *mekaho* MBW *mekaho*

0	B *e gagu*
	  y bedi
	 FBS *e gagu*
	  y bedi
	
	 MZS *hako-maku*
		Z *e gago*
		  y bedeo
		 FBD *e gago*
		  y bedeo
		
		 MZD *hako-mako*
			WB *tenyu*
			
			 MBS *tenyu*
			
			 FZS *tenyu*
			
			 ZH *tenyu*
				W *manaho*
				
				 MBD *tenyo*
				 hakoarumu-
				 mako
				 FZD *tenyo*
				 mekaho-
				 mako
				 BW *buhibako*

− 1	S *maku* BS *gahe*	D *mako* BD *gahe*	DH *haroagu* *buhi* ZS *haroagu*	SW *haroago* *hēho* ZD *haroago*

	Male		Female	
− 2	SS *hanami* DS *hanami*		SD *hanenyo* DD *hanenyo*	

SOURCES: C. Hugh-Jones 1977a:342–344.

DEVIATIONS FROM THE TWO-LINE PATTERN	CONCEIVABLE IDEOLOGICAL OR BEHAVIOURAL CORRELATES
FBC≠MZC	Indeterminate patrilateral affiliation of MZC

"language-aggregates," since, even though the former are ideally language-bearing units, exceptions are sufficiently numerous to justify "discarding language as a distinctive feature of Exogamous Groups."

The content of shared patrilineal descent within exogamous categories largely focuses on the transmission of ancestral power symbolized by ritual property such as names, dances, chants, myths, ornaments, and other paraphernalia (ibid., 37). Patrilineal "soul-stuff (*usu*)" is transmitted to a child both through the father's semen and through its name (C. Hugh-Jones 1977b:188). The Barasana theory of conception claims that girls are made from blood and boys from semen, so that "there is actually a sense in which blood and semen as reproductive potentialities are passed on in same-sex lines" (C. Hugh-Jones 1977a:196), suggesting an ideology of parallel transmission. There is also a distinct alternation of generations inherent in the transmission of names, which ideally should pass from FF or FFB to SS or BSS, and from FFZ (ideally also MM) to BSD (i.e. DD) (ibid., 49, 196–198; 1977b: 188). This alternation coincides with the cyclical merging of a "socially stressed male line and a socially unrecognized female line," the former accumulating each in its own longhouse while the latter "shuttles back and forth," leaving permanent testimony only in the spatial separation of longhouses (C. Hugh-Jones 1977a: 196, 199; 1977b:187). The repetitive, alternate phases of female continuity are "consistent with the exchange of women between groups" (C. Hugh-Jones 1977a:202). Considered in conjunction with the terminological system, which is "consistent with a 'dual organization' marriage system in which sisters are exchanged between two opposed groups" (ibid., 96), the alternation of generations suggests a potentiality for moiety formation such as that which Goldman ascribes to the Cubeo. Virilocality, however, does not appear to be as conducive to the spatial integration of affines as is uxorilocality (cf. the Gê.)

Hierarchy

Sibs are ranked in terms of relative seniority. Not only sibs, but even sets of sibs, are thought to descend from analogous series of five brothers ranked according to birth order (S. Hugh-Jones 1974:11–12). Each sib is associated with a specialist ritual role. These are, in descending order of rank and seniority: chiefs, dancers/chanters, warriors, shamans, and cigar-lighters/servants. This series implies political order only in terms of the extreme roles of chief and servant (C. Hugh-Jones 1977a:81). The three middle roles do not fit a model of political hierarchy: in terms of power, shamans are superior to dancers/chanters. If political power is not the fundamental organizing principle underlying the hierarchy of specialist roles, C.

Hugh-Jones suggests that the roles are simply modelled after the successive attainment, by siblings of different age, of the various stages in the individual life-cycle. The principle of birth order, she suggests, "is found at every level of organization within an exogamous unit" (ibid., 22). The internal organization of the sib follows the same hierarchical matrix, with "small descent groups founded by a living or recently dead ancestor ordered from first born to last born" (ibid., 25). Even within the *maloca*, brothers occupy family compartments according to birth order and rank (S. Hugh-Jones 1977:207; cf. the Cubeo.)

Turning to the realm of external relationships, C. Hugh-Jones (1977a:93, 125) suggests that there is an increasing amount of interaction with other groups as one moves from servants to chiefs. Whereas servants are allegedly endogamous, chiefs manipulate their relationships with outside groups in order to accumulate wives. Polygyny is the privilege of chiefs and a direct reflection of politico-economic power in that "it is an expression of superior ability to make affinal relations" (ibid., 71). The increment in labour power will yield a surplus of manioc products for investment in rituals serving to expand the chief's prestige. According to C. Hugh-Jones' informants, "both the frequency of polygamy and the number of wives per leader have decreased over the last two generations." S. Hugh-Jones (1974:14) writes that most men practicing polygyny are longhouse headmen. There are several cases of headmen with two wives, and one with three (C. Hugh-Jones 1977a:70–71).

The headman is ideally the eldest of a group of brothers (S. Hugh-Jones 1974: 94–95). The longhouses of particularly accomplished headmen tend to be impressive structures serving as ceremonial centers for smaller houses in the vicinity (ibid., 14). In the past, the frequency of raiding and killing would have been conducive to the maintenance of political alliances embracing numbers of longhouses, and to the emergence of more powerful leaders (C. Hugh-Jones 1977a:39). Acculturation has reduced the amount of violence and consequently encouraged a development away from hierarchy (ibid., 67). Yet, there is some evidence suggesting that rank endogamy is still an ideal (ibid., 102, note 2). In practice, however, C. Hugh-Jones was able to discover such endogamy only in the servant sib corresponding to the warrior sib which hosted her (ibid., 71).

Alliance

C. Hugh-Jones (ibid., 96) points out that although the kin terminology suggests sister exchange between two opposed groups, there are in reality a number of Exogamous Groups from which to choose a spouse. This is the foundation for terminological distinctions between patrilateral and matrilateral cousins, both parallel and cross. A "minimal model of a Vaupés marriage system" requires three Exogamous Groups: Ego's, Ego's mother's, and "a third which also receives women from the second" (ibid., 25, 46, 96–97, 113). People from this third category (hako-rĩa="mother's children") are theoretically unmarriageable, since they as affines of Ego's affines are logically assimilated with kin. Nevertheless, marriage to a matrilateral parallel cousin ("mother's child") is considered less incestuous than marriage to a patrilateral parallel cousin ("sibling"), as the former need not be a member of the same Exogamous Group as Ego (ibid., 101).

The Barasana prescribe marriage to a real or classificatory bilateral cross-cousin (tenyo) and prefer true sister exchange (S. Hugh-Jones 1974:13; 1977:205; C. Hugh-Jones 1977a:101–102; 1977b:186). Zero generation classification of potential spouses is determined by previous marriages in the first ascending generation (C. Hugh-Jones 1977a:99). Within the category of women

classified as tenyo, the ideal spouses are close patrilateral cross-cousins, the next best close matrilateral cross-cousins (ibid., 103; 1977b:186). This preference relates to the fact that FZD marriage implies continuing exchange of women between two groups, while MBD marriage represents a one-way flow of women (C. Hugh-Jones 1977a:105). Furthermore, the former represents Ego's rightful claim, whereas the latter may imply competition with his hako-rĩa, since "mother's sons" are not hierarchically ordered like agnatic brothers, among whom competition is minimized. C. Hugh-Jones also discovered cases of true ZD marriage, "justified by the need to complete an exchange when age and sibling-group structure prevent a sister-exchange" (ibid., 102). Because of bilateral cross-cousin marriage, Ego's FFZ is ideally his MM (ibid., 196).

External Relations

The Barasana and other groups along the Pirá-paraná River were once warlike, but the decline in intergroup hostilities probably began even before the first rubber-tappers arrived (ibid., 14–15, 28, 39, 67). Apparently, higher-ranking groups maintained the most widespread network of external relations, whereas low-ranking servant groups were more or less endogamous (ibid., 93, 106, 125).

34. The Bará

Kin Terminology (Table 35)

Bará terminology maintains the two-line pattern. As among the Barasana, however, matrilateral parallel cousins constitute a category distinct from that of patrilateral parallel cousins and siblings.

178

Local Group Size and Composition

Each longhouse is inhabited by four to eight nuclear families (Jackson 1976:3). Post-marital residence is patrilocal (Jackson 1975a:1, 3, 6; 1977:87).

Patterns of Affiliation Other than Residence

Bará units of patrilineal affiliation, "in ascending order of inclusion, are the local descent group, the sib, the language group, and a possible more inclusive exogamic unit, here called the phratry" (Jackson 1977:85; 1984:158). Jackson points out that although a number of lowland South American societies have recently been reclassified as cognatic instead of unilineal, the cultures of the north-west Amazon remain "a clear-cut case of patrilineality" (1975a:1, 6, 8–9; 1976:3; 1977:102, note 9).

Hierarchy

Among the Bará, as throughout the central north-west Amazon, descent units of different orders of inclusiveness are ranked (Jackson 1975a:13). The ethnically distinct Makú, often engaged as long-term servants of Tukanoans, are assimilated into the hierarchy as the lowest-ranked group of all (Jackson 1976:4, 5, 19). Historically, it appears that Makú were enslaved, traded, and sold by Tukanoans (ibid., 17). Jackson connects this slave trade with "the presence of warfare, much stronger headmen, and rapacious traders and rubber-gatherers" (ibid., 16). Today, the position of the Makú should not be attributed entirely to their historically distinct origins, but viewed in the light of their contemporary status, reproduced in their interaction with other groups (ibid., 6). The model emphasizing the distinct ethnic identity of the Makú can be understood as an ideological justification for their exploitation by the Tukano-speakers (ibid., 25–27).

The hierarchical cosmology of the Bará applies even to the classification of natural phenomena such as all species of fish (ibid., 22).

Headmanship is partly hereditary (ibid., 21), and some informants claim that there is an ideal of rank endogamy (Jackson 1975a: 11).

Alliance

Local descent groups are exogamous (Jackson 1975a:2, 6). The ideal is direct sister exchange, and potential spouses include bilateral cross-cousins (ibid., 8; 1977:86). Within this category, FZD is preferred to MBD, and the same explanation for this preference is given as among the Barasana: FZD marriage implies continued reciprocity between two kin groups over time (Jackson 1977:87, 89).

External Relations

Local exogamy, of course, is conducive to external interaction. In the past, there was frequent warfare and raiding (Jackson 1975a: 8; 1976:16).

The north-west Amazon area has developed some specialization in the production of items for trade. Different language groups hold the right to manufacture specific ceremonial objects (Jackson 1976:4). The Makú specialize in smoked or fresh game, twined baskets, snuff, *curare* poison, blowguns, and pelts, whereas Tukanoans trade cultivated food, coca, tobacco, and second-hand White-manufactured articles (ibid., 7, 12, 30). In the 19th century, Makú slaves were traded for ceremonial objects or to the Whites (ibid., 16–17).

Table 35
KIN TERMINOLOGY OF THE BARÁ
LINGUISTIC FAMILY: Tukano
Male Ego, terms of reference.

GEN.	Male		Female	
+ 2	FF *ñihkü* MF *ñihkü*		FM *ñihkó* MM *ñihkó*	

	KIN (Lineal kin, parallel collaterals, affines of affines)		*AFFINES* (In-laws, cross collaterals)	
	Male	Female	Male	Female
+ 1	F *pahkú* FB *bügü* MZH *bügü*	M *pahkó* MZ *bügó* FBW *bügó*	WF *mehkú* MB *mehkú* FZH *mehkú*	WM *mehkó* FZ *mehkó* MBW *mehkó*
0	B *báü* FBS *báü* MZS *pahkó-mahkú*	Z *bayó* FBD *bayó* MZD *pahkó-mahkó*	MBS *mehkú-mahkú* FZS *mehkó-mahkú*	MBD *mehkú-mahkó* FZD *mehkó-mahkó*
– 1	S *mahkú* BS *mahkú*	D *mahkó* BD *mahkó*	ZS *bayó-mahkú*	ZD *bayó-mahkó*

	Male		Female	
– 2	SS *párami* DS *párami*		SD *párameo* DD *párameo*	

SOURCES: Jackson 1977:88–89.

DEVIATIONS FROM THE TWO-LINE PATTERN	CONCEIVABLE IDEOLOGICAL OR BEHAVIOURAL CORRELATES
FBC≠MZC	Indeterminate patrilateral affiliation of MZC

35. The Makuna

Kin Terminology (Table 36)

Terms for ZCSp and WBC complete a particularly exhaustive illustration of a two-line terminology. As do other Tukano-speakers, however, the Makuna distinguish between siblings and patrilateral parallel cousins, on the one hand, and matrilateral parallel cousins ("mother's children"), on the other.

Owing to the patrilineal nature of Makuna social organization, Århem (1981:37, 341) locates FZ in the category of "kin" and MZ in

that of "affines" (cf. C. Hugh-Jones 1977a: 97). Comparative Tukanoan ethnography, however, suggests that Dumont's (1953a:36) model of the Dravidian kin-affine dichotomy may be applicable: in the terminologies of the Cubeo, Barasana, and Bará, MZ is linguistically cognate to FB, and FZ is assimilated with WM among both the Cubeo and Bará. In fact, Århem (1981:36–37) establishes that the Makuna relationship terminology is "a variant of the general Dravidian type," and that "it is equally possible, but more complicated, to define the same opposition in terms of consanguines versus affines, or cross-relatives versus parallel relatives,

180

without reference to the rules of descent and exogamy in any particular society."

Local Group Size and Composition

Århem (ibid., 218–219) lists 14 residence groups ranging in size from five to 25 and averaging 12 individuals. In the past, settlements were apparently much larger, and early reports mention communities numbering over 100 people (ibid., 54).

Post-marital residence is generally virilocal (ibid., 150, 175, 217, 223, 254), but in the case of gift marriages, the husband is expected to reside uxorilocally for a time before taking his wife back to his own agnatic group (ibid., 163). Århem (ibid., 140–141, 149, 183, 194–195, 209, 212, 239) emphasizes that although the residence group is organized according to principles of patrilineal descent, the more inclusive cluster of residence groups which he calls "local group" is, in fact, alliance-organized.

Patterns of Affiliation Other than Residence

Makuna society is ordered in terms of patrilineal descent (ibid., 115, 136). A set of patrilineal sibs, relating to each other as elder or younger brothers, constitute what Århem calls a "phratric segment" (ibid., 101). Phratric segments are in turn grouped into vaguely defined, exogamous "phratric categories" (ibid., 102). The sibs of each phratric segment are associated with particular specialist roles and ordered in terms of relative seniority (ibid., 113, 136), as among the Barasana.

The Makuna conceive of their 12 sibs as being divided into two intermarrying categories (ibid., 47, 116), and Århem (ibid., 137) notes that marriage statistics from the Komeña territory largely verify this dual conception of society. If the sample is widened to include all marriages recorded,

however, it becomes apparent that the division is triadic rather than dual. Marriages outside Komeña territory confuse the dual division of Komeña sibs, so that two sibs opposed to each other as affines find themselves having geographically more distant affines in common. Instead of being integrated into the dual model, these distant groups are classified as "mother's children" by either of the two sets of Makuna sibs. The "triadic division of social reality" (ibid., 134) is concealed by the dual scheme of classification, which assimilated "mother's children" (affines of Ego's affines) with kin. Århem (ibid., 140) relates both the triadic and the dualistic systems of classification to aspects of Makuna kin terminology. Thus, the triadic division is "modelled upon the categorical distinctions between relatives of Ego's own generation" (i.e. FBS, MZS, MBS/FZS). On the other hand, the dual division is "consistent with the underlying structure of the relationship terminology based on the conceptual opposition between kin and affines." Århem concludes that, "from the point of view of the Makuna, the social reality appears to be, and for all practical purposes is, divided into two rather than three parts – kin and affines." Local groups (i.e. clusters of longhouse residence groups) appear to be organized so as to bring these two categories – kin and affines – closer together (ibid., 296, 299). Over the generations, repeated intermarriage tends to produce "solid and tightly bound alliance segments," which incline toward endogamy (ibid., 194–195). These alliance-ordered local groups generally constitute the politically significant units in disputes (ibid., 209), and in other respects "take on the corporate character and functions usually associated with the unilineal descent group" (ibid., 212).

Århem suggests that moieties may be emerging among the Makuna (ibid., 299). Referring to Goldman's (1963:288) attribution of a "potentiality for moiety formation" to the Cubeo, and to his report that there are

Table 36
KIN TERMINOLOGY OF THE MAKUNA
LINGUISTIC FAMILY: Tukano
Male Ego, terms of reference.

GEN.	Male		Female	
+ 2	FF *ñiku* MF *ñiku*		FM *ñiko* MM *ñiko*	

	KIN (Lineal kin, parallel collaterals, affines of affines)		*AFFINES* (In-laws, cross collaterals)	
	Male	Female	Male	Female
+ 1	F *haku* FB *buamu* MZH *buamu*	M *hako* MZ *gahego* FBW *gahego*	WF *mañiku* MB *mai* FZH *mai*	WM *mañiko* FZ *mekaho* MBW *mekaho*
0	B e *rihoru* y *okabahi* FBS e *rihoru* y *okabahi* MZS *hakomaku*	Z e *rihoro* y *okabahio* FBD e *rihoro* y *okabahio* MZD *hakomako*	WB *teñi* MBS *teñi* FZS *teñi* ZH *teñi*	W *manaho* MBD *teño* *buhibako* FZD *teño* *buhibako* BW *buhibako*
− 1	S *maku* BS *gahe* ZDH *gahe*	D *mako* BD *gahe* ZSW *gahe*	DH *buhi* ZS *harugu* WBS *harugu*	SW *heho* ZD *harugo* WBD *harugo*

	Male		Female	
− 2	SS *hanami* DS *hanami*		SD *haneño* DD *haneño*	

SOURCES: Århem 1981:341–342.

DEVIATIONS FROM THE TWO-LINE PATTERN	CONCEIVABLE IDEOLOGICAL OR BEHAVIOURAL CORRELATES
FBC≠MZC	Indeterminate patrilateral affiliation of MZC

"traces of an earlier moiety organization" (personal communication to Århem, 1979), Århem proposes that moieties may intermittently form and dissolve among groups such as the Makuna, Cubeo, and Piaroa. It is questionable, however, whether the social cohesion associated with true dual organization is likely to develop in virilocal societies. The few virilocal instances of dual organization in our South American sample (cf. Tupí, Pano) appear all to have been uxorilocal in the past.

Makuna names are transmitted patrilineally from grandparents to grandchildren (ibid., 112), suggesting a principle of alternating generations.

Hierarchy

The sibs of a phratric segment are hierarchically ordered according to seniority. Århem (ibid., 102) suggests that such hierarchies are "modelled" on the distinction between elder and younger agnatic brothers in the kin terminology (cf. Goldman 1963:27, 98,

117, 118; Bidou 1977:113). Furthermore, sibs are assigned specialist roles identical to those of the pervasive five-tiered hierarchy of the Barasana: chiefs, chanters, warriors, shamans, and servants (Århem 1981:113, 127). The hierarchy of specialist roles recurs at all levels of the Makuna descent system, so that even names transmitted from grandparents to grandchildren are associated with specific roles, and accordingly bestowed on a set of brothers so as to agree with their order of birth (ibid., 112, note 6, 128). This hierarchical differentiation of agnatic brothers serves to reduce competition for women (ibid., 136). There is, however, a tendency for high-ranking, senior men to practice polygyny (ibid., 170–172).

The order of sib seniority within phratric segments, says Århem (ibid., 120), is "fixed and undisputed." Yet, a case of status change leads him to the conclusion that "circumstances of size, political strength and ritual ownership of land may contribute to the definition and redefinition of phratric hierarchies" (ibid., 130).

Both actual marriage practices and explicit ideals suggest an inclination towards rank endogamy (ibid., note 4).

Alliance

Phratric categories are strictly exogamous (ibid., 103, 131–132). The category of "mother's children," i.e. affines of affines who do not belong to Ego's phratric category, are regarded as a sort of distant "kin" with whom marriage is "discouraged and avoided but not strictly prohibited." The regularly intermarrying komeña sibs "fall into a consistent, dual pattern of two exogamous classes exchanging women" (ibid., 137).

For a male Makuna, marriage is prescribed with a relative of the category buhibako, which includes bilateral cross-cousins (ibid., 146–147, 185). Between 86 and 89% of actual marriages comply with this prescrip-

tion. Marriages outside the prescribed category are usually oblique, but even these spouses belong to sibs classified as affines. In all but one of the aberrant cases, male Ego has married one or two generations down, and all are secondary marriages. A majority of these marriages are to women classified as harugo (ZD/WBD) (ibid., 186). The ideal Makuna marriage entails direct sister exchange between two men related as true cross-cousins (ibid., 147). The Makuna alliance system tends to produce endogamous local groups of regularly intermarrying sib-segments (ibid., 212, 239).

External Relations

Traditions suggest that intense feuding and inter-group hostility may have been characteristic of the area in times past (ibid., 54, 124). According to Makuna informants, the reasons for these hostilities were disputes over women and ceremonial feather headdresses (ibid., 89–90). To this day, conflicts between distant groups always involve small-scale raiding to capture women. Århem (ibid., 149) notes that the "negative reciprocity" underlying bride-capture becomes increasingly applicable with greater affinal and spatial distance between groups.

Conclusions: Tukano

Tukano kin terminologies are generally faithful to the two-line pattern. Jackson (1984:160) concludes that several are "Dravidian in structure." Patrilineal principles, however, tend to transform the first ascending generation "kin-affine" dichotomy into a classification distinguishing "agnates" from "affines" (C. Hugh-Jones 1977a:97; Århem 1981:37, 341). The distinction of siblings according to relative age is consistent with the explicit birth-order hierarchy permeating all levels of descent. The Tukano distinction between patrilateral and matrilateral parallel cousins, well explained by the triadic structure introduced with the category "affines of affines", is duplicated in the early terminologies collected by Nimuendajú among the Gê-speaking Apinayé, Eastern Timbira, and Sherente, and in that of the Carib-speaking Txicáo.

Common to all four cultures in our sample is a local group size average well below 50, although early accounts suggest settlements of between 50 and 150 people. Post-marital residence is virilocal, but initial periods of uxorilocality are reported from the Makuna. Affiliation is strongly patrilateral (cf. Jackson 1975a), but an ideology of parallel transmission is evident at least among the Barasana. A principle of alternating generations is widespread, and has been interpreted as the result of symmetric alliance between pairs of virilocal longhouses.

All four cultures have a system of rank in which patrilineal descent groups of different levels of inclusiveness are ordered according to the birth order of their founders. There is generally an ideal of rank endogamy (cf. Chernela 1985:36, 39; Hill 1985:29, 31–32, note 5). The lowest-ranked category is conceived as an ethnically distinct, endogamous servant class. Polygyny is a privilege of chiefs.

All the Tukano cultures in our sample prescribe marriage to a category including bilateral cross-cousins. Within this category, the Barasana and Bará state a preference for FZD marriage (cf. Jackson 1984:168, but, for a contrary view, Sorensen 1984:181). Instances of avuncular marriage have been reported from the Barasana and Makuna. All four cultures define exogamy by reference to patrilineal descent groups. All have had a warlike inclination in the past, but there has also been an interest in contracting distant alliances and trading ceremonial objects between specialized groups. Traditions suggest extensive chiefdoms and strict hierarchy in times past.

Chapter 10

Yanoama

36. The Yanomamö

Kin Terminology (Table 37)

In the three medial generations, Yanomamö kin terms present a perfect two-line pattern. The second ascending generation, however, allows for lineal equations such as FF=MF =F, FF=MF=eB, FM=MM=M, FM=MM =Z, and possibly FF=MF=MB.

Local Group Size and Composition

The Yanomamö of the Mavaca and Orinoco Rivers live in villages ranging between 40 and 250 people, with an average between 75 and 80 (Chagnon 1968:1). Generally, villages will fission when they reach a population of about 150 (ibid., 40). "Military requirements" relating to raiding techniques suggest that the minimum size of a viable village is between 40 and 50 people. The groups studied by Lizot (1975:625) averaged 54 inhabitants.

Post-marital residence is generally virilocal (Chagnon 1968:68–69; Lizot 1977: 63), but uxorilocal bride-service may last as long as three years (Chagnon 1968:79; Lizot 1977:61, 65). A man's parents-in-law will try to persuade him to prolong his period of uxorilocal residence (Chagnon 1968:93). Another strategy to maximize the size of the local group is to inhibit migration by trying to keep marriages within the group (ibid., 40).

Patterns of Affiliation Other than Residence

The Yanomamö belong to exogamous, patrilineal kin groups called "lineages" by Chagnon (1968:56) and Lizot (1977:57, 62, 63). These lineages tend to segment into localized patrilineal descent groups, which are "corporate with respect to the functions of arranging the marriages of the female members" (Chagnon 1968:68–69). According to Chagnon (ibid., 61), lineages, known as *mashi*, are not named. Lizot (1977:60), however, writes that each lineage is associated with a particular animal image (*noreshi*), which is transmitted patrilineally from F to S in the same manner as a lineage name. *Noreshi* (literally "reflection" or "shadow") are transmitted along parallel, same-sex lines, from F to S and from M to D. Murphy (1979:220–221) questions "the utility of reifying patrifiliation among the Yanomamö into lineages."

Lizot (ibid., 59) reports a different usage of the concept of *mashi*. With the exception of parents, the *mashi* category can only apply to people of the same genealogical level. Moreover, it is used to distinguish same-sex siblings and parallel cousins from those of the opposite sex, which are called *yaiye*. Lizot suggests that *mashi* could be regarded as "une sorte de parentèle (kindred)."

Chagnon (1968:57–58, 61) notes that "villages tend to have two (and only two) politically dominant lineages that intermarry," producing a "dual organization" of communities, but that the occasional intrusion of a third lineage may generate "structural faults" which later determine the boundaries of segmentation. The dual organization of villages tends to be regenerated, and ties of marriage alliance to be stronger than distant agnatic bonds (ibid., 59, 71; J. Shapiro 1974:306). Lizot (1977:68), too, recognizes the importance of inherited affinity as an organizing principle.

Table 37
KIN TERMINOLOGY OF THE YANOMAMÖ
LINGUISTIC FAMILY: Yanoama
Male Ego, terms of reference.

GEN.	Male		Female	
+ 2	FF	ēiwä hayä (šoayä?)	FM	amiwä nayä
	MF	ēiwä hayä (šoayä?)	MM	amiwä nayä

	KIN (Lineal kin, parallel collaterals, affines of affines)				AFFINES (In-laws, cross collaterals)			
	Male		Female		Male		Female	
+ 1	F	hayä	M	nayä	WF	šoayä	WM	yesiyä
	FB	hayä	MZ	nayä	MB	šoayä	FZ	yesiyä
	MZH	hayä	FBW	nayä	FZH	šoayä	MBW	yesiyä
0	B	e eiwä y aiwä	Z	amiwä	WB	šoriwä	W	suwäbiyä
	FBS	e eiwä y aiwä	FBD	amiwä	MBS	šoriwä	MBD	suwäbiyä
	MZS	e eiwä y aiwä	MZD	amiwä	FZS	šoriwä	FZD	suwäbiyä
			WBW	amiwä	ZH	šoriwä	BW	suwäbiyä
– 1	S	ihiruyä	D	thääyä	DH	hekamayä	SW	thathäyä
	BS	ihiruyä	BD	thääyä	ZS	hekamayä	ZD	thathäyä

	Male		Female	
– 2	SS	mōrōši	SD	nakasi
	DS	mōrōši	DD	nakasi

SOURCES: Lizot 1971:28–30,33. Chagnon (1968) confirms *shoriwä* and *suaböya*, but gives *yaiye* instead of *amiwä*. Lizot (1971:31) confirms that *yaiwä*, a general term for opposite-sex siblings, can be used for yZ. Alternatively, the vocative for *nakasi* can be employed.

DEVIATIONS FROM THE TWO-LINE PATTERN	CONCEIVABLE IDEOLOGICAL OR BEHAVIOURAL CORRELATES
FF=F, FM=M	Patrilateral affiliation
FF=eB, MM=Z	Alternating generations

Consistent with the dichotomy of kin and affines within each village, which in Chagnon's usage qualifies as an example of dual organization, are indications of alternating generations. As a result of the reciprocal exchange between kin groups, Yanomamö lineages are alternately wife-givers and wife-takers to each other (Lizot 1977:61).

Hierarchy

Chagnon (1968:66) reports diarchy from the Yanomamö village of Patanowä-teri, where the Sha and Hor lineages each has its own headman. There are indications that headmanship is transmitted patrilineally (ibid., 110).

186

Lizot (1977:61, 65) writes that wife-takers, particularly when residing uxorilocally, are markedly subordinate and inferior to wife-givers, and that bride-service is a very laborious period in a man's life.

Alliance

Chagnon (1968:56, 61) states that Yanomamö patrilineages are exogamous, and that they tend to form intermarrying pairs in each particular village, approximating dual organization. According to Lizot (1977:60, 62), lineage exogamy is maintained by a rule stating that a man may not receive a wife from another man whose *noreshi* (patrilineally inherited animal image) is identical to his own.

For a male, marriage is prescribed with a woman of the category *suaböya* (Lizot's *suwäbiyä*), which includes bilateral cross-cousins (Chagnon 1968:56–57, 61; Lizot 1977:57). Another way of phrasing the marriage rule is to say that "children of men who call each other *shoriwä* (brother-in-law) can marry" (Chagnon 1968:64). Sister exchange is the ideal (ibid., 55; Lizot 1971: 33).

To avoid virilocal residence in a distant village, women prefer to be married to men of their own natal village, ideally a FZS or MBS (Chagnon 1968:69; J. Shapiro 1974: 305). In order to make bride-service and in-law relationships more agreeable, men also prefer endogamous unions (J. Shapiro 1974:305; Lizot 1975:625). A number of factors, however, such as the unequal distribution of women or political necessity, may force a man to deviate from the prescribed ideal and seek a wife in another village (Chagnon 1968:76). According to Lizot (1975:625), in fact, most of the marriages he recorded were village-exogamous.

External Relations

The Yanomamö, Chagnon's "fierce people," have an extremely aggressive reputation. Belligerence is characteristic of relations both within and between villages. The village of Patanowä-teri was raided about 25 times, by about a dozen different groups, in a period of 15 months (Chagnon 1968:40). With increasing village size, internal feuding and fighting become more frequent, and the community is more likely to split into two separate groups (ibid., 40, 120).

In order to feel more secure in the face of enemy threats, groups of Yanomamö engage in trading and feasting for the purpose of contracting military alliances (ibid., 100–102). Such alliances may stop at sporadic reciprocal trading or develop into mutual feasting or even a reciprocal exchange of women.

As in the Upper Xingú and Vaupés regions, each village specializes in the production of particular trade items, such as dogs, drugs, arrowheads and shafts, bows, cotton, hammocks, baskets, and pots, even though each is "economically speaking, capable of self-sufficiency." The implication is that trading is merely an ideological justification for co-operation which is fundamentally military in nature. To confess to a need of military assistance would be to admit vulnerability and perhaps "invite predation from the potential ally." Traditions reveal how easily a peaceful trading relationship can be converted into one of suspicion and regular warfare (ibid., 76).

37. The Yanomam

Kin Terminology (Table 38)

The Yanomam kin nomenclature is a perfect example of the two-line pattern. The equation of second ascending generation kin with first ascending generation affines, and of second descending generation kin with first descending generation affines, recalls the terminologies of the Sirionó, Waiwai, Nambikwara, and Northern Gê. Ramos and Albert (1977:82–83) note that these

187

equations serve to extend the range of "potential affinal relationships."

Local Group Size and Composition

The Yanomam of the Catrimani and Parima Rivers live in communities averaging about 40 people (Ramos & Albert 1977:79). As among the Yanomamö, the preference for endogamous marriages implies that local groups are largely organized on the basis of alliance, rather than in terms of a core of kinsmen supplemented with spouses born elsewhere. Village-exogamous marriages, however, generally involve an initial period of uxorilocal bride-service (ibid., 83). After bride-service, about half of the men who have married outside their natal village return to take up virilocal residence, while half retain uxorilocality. In practice, then, post-marital residence is ambilocal, even if virilocality is preferred by most men.

Patterns of Affiliation Other than Residence

The Yanomam do "not acknowledge either any sort of cumulative sequence of filiation links or any correlated biological symbolization of an extended lineal continuum" (ibid., 83). The only named and "culturally recognized" unit is the local residential group. The emphasis is on living with one's affines (ibid., 84). The common ancestry of particular local groups is traced by referring to the name of an older community which has undergone fission, whereas there is no recognition of supra-local agnatic categories. Consistent with the absence of "any superordinate system of social categorization . . . based on extended genealogical lines" is (a) the equation of all relatives beyond the three medial generations with affines, and (b) the idiosyncratic relationship networks produced by the highly intransitive application of kin terms (ibid., 82–83).

In Yanomam kin nomenclature, descending generations of males are alternately classed as *shori a* and *thani a* (ibid., 80). The equation of the third ascending generation with affines of Ego's generation (*shori a, thuwä a*) suggests three-generation cycles rather than simple alternation.

Hierarchy

Ramos and Albert (ibid., 84) note that village-exogamous marriages among the Yanomam are virilocal mainly when contracted by headmen.

Alliance

The Yanomam prescribe marriage with women of the category *thuwä a* (ibid., 80), which includes all real or classificatory female bilateral cross-cousins. Although there is a preference for endogamous unions, the residential unit is only "semi-endogamous," with about half of the marriages studied village-exogamous (ibid., 83). The intransitive application of kin terms precludes the emergence of a clear kin-affine dichotomy, and creates highly idiosyncratic relationship networks (ibid., 81–83).

External Relations

Although relatively rare at present, raids are "reported historically, including the quite recent past" (ibid., 89, note 8).

38. The Sanumá

Kin Terminology (Table 39)

In the three medial generations, Sanumá kin terms follow the two-line pattern. The

Table 38
KIN TERMINOLOGY OF THE YANOMAM
LINGUISTIC FAMILY: Yanoama
Male Ego, terms of reference.

GEN.	Male		Female	
+ 2	FF *shoayä a* MF *shoayä a*		FM *yayä a* MM *yayä a*	

	KIN (Lineal kin, parallel collaterals, affines of affines)		AFFINES (In-laws, cross collaterals)	
	Male	Female	Male	Female
+ 1	F *hayä a* FB *hayä a* MZH *hayä a*	M *nayä a* MZ *nayä a* FBW *nayä a*	WF *shoayä a* MB *shoayä a* FZH *shoayä a*	WM *yayä a* FZ *yayä a* MBW *yayä a*
0	B *hepara a* FBS *hepara a* MZS *hepara a*	Z *yahu a* FBD *yahu a* MZD *yahu a*	WB *shori a* MBS *shori a* FZS *shori a* ZH *shori a*	W *thuwä a* MBD *thuwä a* FZD *thuwä a* BW *thuwä a*
− 1	S *ihiru a* BS *ihiru a*	D *thäeyä a* BD *thäeyä a*	DH *thani a* ZS *thani a*	SW *thathe a* ZD *thathe a*

	Male		Female	
− 2	SS *thani a* DS *thani a*		SD *thathe a* DD *thathe a*	

SOURCES: Ramos & Albert 1977:79–80.

DEVIATIONS FROM THE TWO-LINE PATTERN	CONCEIVABLE IDEOLOGICAL OR BEHAVIOURAL CORRELATES
None	

second ascending generation, however, is assimilated with first ascending generation kin, and the second descending generation with first descending generation kin. The equations MM=M and DD=D are duplicated by the Bororo.

Local Group Size and Composition

The Sanumá of the Auaris River live in villages averaging between 30 and 50 people (Ramos 1974:172; Ramos & Albert 1977:72). Villages are largely alliance-organized (Ramos 1974:172), but post-marital residence is generally uxorilocal (Taylor & Ramos 1975:129; Ramos & Albert 1977:74; Lizot

1977:63). Uxorilocality, which appears to have developed from the convention that bride-service should last as long as 10 or 12 years (Ramos & Albert 1977:74; cf. the Mundurucú, Murphy 1956:430), is consistent with the recommendation that "a woman should not leave her village to marry because then she would lose the protection of her brothers against a possibly aggressive husband" (ibid., 77).

Patterns of Affiliation Other than Residence

The Sanumá are divided into named, exogamous but non-corporate patrilineal sibs and

189

Table 39

KIN TERMINOLOGY OF THE SANUMÁ
LINGUISTIC FAMILY: Yanoama
Male Ego, terms of reference.

GEN.	Male		Female	
+ 2	FF *hawa* MF *hawa*		FM *nawa* MM *nawa*	

	KIN (Lineal kin, parallel collaterals, affines of affines)		*AFFINES* (In-laws, cross collaterals)	
	Male	Female	Male	Female
+ 1	F *hawa* FB *hawa*	M *nawa* MZ *nawa*	WF *soazea* MB *soazea* FZH *soazea*	WM *saazea* FZ *saazea* MBW *saazea*
0	B e *hebala* y *hoosa* FBS e *hebala* y *hoosa* MZS e *hebala* y *hoosa*	Z *sawa* FBD *sawa* MZD *sawa*	WB *soli* MBS *soli* FZS *soli* ZH *soli*	W *hiziba* MBD *hiziba* FZD *hiziba* BW *hiziba*
− 1	S *ulu* BS *ulu*	D *tewa* BD *tewa*	DH *hizagiba* ZS *hizagiba*	SW *hizagiba* ZD *hizagiba*

	Male		Female	
− 2	SS *ulu* DS *ulu*		SD *tewa* DD *tewa*	

SOURCES: Ramos & Albert 1977:72, 73.

DEVIATIONS FROM THE TWO-LINE PATTERN	CONCEIVABLE IDEOLOGICAL OR BEHAVIOURAL CORRELATES
FF=F, FM=M, S=SS, D=SD MM=M, D=DD	Patrilateral affiliation Matrilateral affiliation, uxori-local residence

lineages (Ramos 1974:172; Taylor & Ramos 1975:129; Ramos & Albert 1977:74, 75). Recruitment to these patrilineal categories is by name transmission from father to children of both sexes (Ramos 1974:171, 173; Taylor & Ramos 1975:129; Ramos & Albert 1977:73). Personal names, as opposed to patronyms, are most often bestowed by maternal kinsmen (Ramos 1974:181, 182). Succession to leadership is patrilineal (Taylor & Ramos 1975:129).

Hierarchy

Among the Sanumá, the elaborate procedure whereby a child is given a *humabi* spirit name is generally reserved for first-borns (Ramos 1974:174, 180). Society is conceived as divided into four basic age grades sub-divided into 11 taxonomic categories (Taylor 1977). The differential status of particular age categories in different lineages suggests an hierarchical arrangement of lineages. Leadership is patrilineally inheritable (Taylor & Ramos 1975:129).

Alliance

The Sanumá prescribe marriage with women of the category *hiziba* (Ramos & Albert 1977:73). As among the Yanomamö and Yanomam, this marriageable category corresponds to Ego's bilateral cross-cousins (ibid.; Ramos 1974:172). Marriage to a *hizagiba* (ZD) is fairly common and "easily tolerated," although considered "rather improper" (Ramos & Albert 1977:73, 76). Of 82 marriages, 43 were with a *hiziba*, 15 with relatives other than cross-cousins, and 24 with non-relatives (ibid., 89, note 6).

Sibs and lineages are exogamous, and "each sib and each lineage stand in a kin or in an affinal relationship to other sibs and lineages," providing a matrix for proper marriages (Ramos 1974:172). Although minor discrepancies may occur, kin terms are used transitively, so that the allocation of different relatives to the two superordinant categories of kin and affines is logical and predictable (Ramos & Albert 1977:76, 87).

Although there is an ideal of village endogamy, shortages of marriageable women prompt men to seek wives elsewhere (ibid., 74). Of a sample of 93 marriages in eight villages, only 31% were village-endogamous, and 69% were exogamous.

External Relations

Whereas Chagnon (1968:40) reports that a single Yanomamö village was raided 25 times in 15 months, Taylor (1977:91) notes that among eight Sanumá villages not a single raid occurred in 23 months.

Sanumá	*Yanomam*	*Yanomamö*
Named social units other than the community	No named social units other than the community	Chagnon and Lizot contradict each other on the issue of whether lineages are named
Grandkin equated with kin	Grandkin equated with affines	Grandfathers equated with either kin or affines
Kin solidarity	Affine solidarity	Both kin and affine solidarity
Transitivity of kin term usage	Intransitivity of kin term usage	Transitivity of kin term usage may be confused upon the introduction of a third lineage

Table 40. The intermediate position of the Yanomamö in some parameters relevant to the Sanumá/Yanomam contrast (cf. Ramos & Albert 1977:87)

Conclusions: Yanoama

All three terminologies in our sample follow the two-line pattern. The only significant differences involve the classification of grandkin. The Yanomamö have the option of equating second ascending generation males with first ascending generation kin *or* affines. They thus occupy a position intermediate to the two extremes represented by the Yanomam and the Sanumá. The latter two are inversions of each other, the Yanomam equating all relatives beyond the three medial generations with affines, the Sanumá equating all such relatives with kin (cf. Table 40).

Common to all three groups is the tension between male preferences for virilocality, on the one hand, and requirements on uxorilocal bride-service, on the other. The Yanomamö represent the virilocal extreme, whereas the Sanumá have advanced furthest in submitting to uxorilocality. This difference correlates with a difference in average local group size. If virilocality for once seems more successful in integrating larger villages, factors such as "military requirements" should also be taken into consideration among the Yanomamö.

All three groups share the tension between an ideal of village endogamy, on the one hand, and the necessity to contract exogamous marriages, on the other. The Sanumá represent the exogamous extreme.

The Yanomamö and Sanumá share named, exogamous patrilineal kin groups and an inclination toward patrilineal succession to leadership. The Yanomam, on the other hand, represent the alliance-organized extreme, recognizing no descent categories whatsoever.

All three groups prescribe bilateral cross-cousin marriage, but ZD marriage appears to be particularly frequent among the Sanumá.

Ramos and Albert (1977:87) have contrasted the Sanumá and the Yanomam on a number of points. In at least four of these, it can be shown that the Yanomamö occupy an ambivalent position intermediate to the other two groups, combining elements of both (Table 40).

The striking difference between the intensity of raiding among the Yanomamö and Sanumá (Taylor 1977:91), finally, undoubtedly relates to their different patterns of post-marital residence.

Chapter 11

Jívaroan

39. The Jívaro

Kin Terminology (Table 41)

The equation M=FZ=MBW (*nuku*) is the only feature to contradict the two-line pattern in Jívaro terms of reference. However, Harner (1972:99) writes that if Ego marries "a daughter of MBW, FZ, or FBW, *tsatsa* is substituted for *nuku* with regard to the bride's mother." In the vocative terminology, the form *nukuá* is used for both *nuku* and *tsatsa,* while *umači* denotes both *umaí* and *wahe.*

Local Group Size and Composition

The Jívaro longhouse (*jivaría*) may formerly have accommodated between 80 and 300 people (Steward & Métraux 1948:623). Steward and Métraux estimate the mid-20th century average at 30 to 40. Harner (1972:77–78) estimates an average of nine persons per house, but sometimes two or even three related households may be located within a few hundred yards of one another, yielding a local group population of up to 27.

The Jívaro have a norm of uxorilocal bride-service, which tends to last until the birth of the first child, whereafter a new house is built near that of the wife's parents (ibid., 78, 79, 95, 96). Uxorilocal residence can be avoided altogether by substituting bride-price for bride-service (ibid., 79), or by resorting to bride-capture (ibid., 116, 186–187). The recent tendency to shorten the period of bride-service (ibid., 199) may represent a development away from uxorilocality. The small size of Jívaro households is consistent with neolocal residence, but the location of the new house can reflect either viri- or uxorilocal preferences, which suggests an attenuated form of ambilocality.

Patterns of Affiliation Other than Residence

Harner (ibid., 78, 111) found no unilineal kin groups among the Jívaro. Instead, "the basic Jívaro kin group is a personal bilateral kindred with a slight patrilineal tendency" (ibid., 97). Name transmission is either patrilineal or parallel (ibid., 85). Owing to the extent of uxorilocal residence, a man normally sides with his affines in disputes against his own consanguineal kin (ibid., 96). The alliance-organized local group is the corporate unit in Jívaro society.

A principle of alternating generations may be inferred from Harner's (1972:85) observation that "if the father's father or the mother's mother are still alive, they may be asked to name the child of their own sex."

Hierarchy

As has been reported from other tribes (cf. the Machiguenga and Barasana), plural wives assure a surplus production of beer and food for entertaining visitors, which serves to heighten a man's status (ibid., 81). Possession of two wives, in fact, is more common than having only one (ibid., 80). Sororal polygyny is the preferred form, and "wives who are sisters usually work out a hierarchical relationship, with the eldest (characteristically the first bride) assuming direction of activities within the house" (ibid., 94).

Table 41
KIN TERMINOLOGY OF THE JÍVARO
LINGUISTIC FAMILY: Jívaroan
Male Ego, terms of reference.

GEN.	Male		Female	
+ 2	FF	*apači* (*apatceru*)	FM	*nukuči* (*mukucuru*)
	MF	*apači* (*apatceru*)	MM	*nukuči* (*mukucuru*)

	KIN (Lineal kin, parallel collaterals, affines of affines)			*AFFINES* (In-laws, cross collaterals)			
	Male		Female		Male		Female	
+ 1	F	*apa* (*aparu*)	M	*nuku* (*nukuru*)	WF	*iči*	WM	*tsatsa*
	FB	*apa*	MZ	*nuku*	MB	*iči*	FZ	*nuku*
	MZH	*apa*	FBW	*nuku*	FZH	*iči*	MBW	*nuku*
0	B	*e yači (yetci)* *y umpá* (*yatsuru*)	Z	*umaí* (*umai*)	WB	*sai*	W	*ekentu, nua* (*éiohiri*)
	FBS	*e yači* *y umpá*	FBD	*umaí*	MBS	*sai*	MBD	*wahe*
	MZS	*e yači* *y umpá*	MZD	*umaí*	FZS	*sai*	FZD	*wahe*
					ZH	*sai*	BW	*wahe*
− 1	S	*uči*	D	*nawanta*	DH	*awe*	SW	*awe*
	BS	*uči*	BD	*nawanta*	ZS	*awe*	ZD	*awe*
	ZDH	*uči*	ZSW	*nawanta*				

	Male		Female	
− 2	SS	*tirani*	SD	*tirani*
	DS	*tirani*	DD	*tirani*

SOURCES: Harner 1972:99–100. Terms in brackets derive from Farabee (1922:126).

DEVIATIONS FROM THE TWO-LINE PATTERN	CONCEIVABLE IDEOLOGICAL OR BEHAVIOURAL CORRELATES
M=FZ=MBW	Cognatic principles

Except for the number of wives, factors which enhance a man's status *(untä*="big man") include his age and his reputation as a killer or shaman (ibid., 110, 111). An outstanding killer (*ti kakaram* = "very powerful one") may accumulate support from most of the men of several neighbourhoods, and from some men in a number of other localities as well (ibid., 115). Such alliances, however, are unstable. Another way to gain prestige and obligations is to engage in formal trading partnerships (*amigri* =

"friends") to secure goods for distribution in the neighbourhood (ibid., 125–126).

Whereas the strategy of an *amigri* trader is to redistribute rather than to accumulate, shamans (*uwišin*) "are invariably the wealthiest persons and usually candidly admit that they supply their services primarily for the purpose of gaining valuables" (ibid., 117). Respecting their supernatural powers, non-shamans almost never ask shamans for gifts. As a result, shamans are usually the only persons who are able to hoard any quantities of goods. As a profession, Jívaro shamans are hierarchically organized (ibid., 118–124). Shamanistic power emanates from spirit servants called *tsentsak* (magical darts), which are purchased from "higher" by "lower" shamans, and payment consists of tribute in the form of material valuables (*kuit*) such as shotguns, hunting dogs, blowguns, *curare*, and feather headbands. The most powerful *tsentsak* derive from the Quechua-speaking Canelos, in the north, and the prestige of shamans generally declines as one moves south. The northern Jívaro and Achuar, through their direct contact with the Canelos, are considered more powerful than their southern neighbours, and so on. Along several such parallel hierarchies culminating in the land of the Canelos, material tribute flows from south to north in compensation for the flow of shamanistic power in the opposite direction. Shamans of a specific neighbourhood are also hierarchically arranged, and recognize a formal leader.

Alliance

Requirements on uxorilocal bride-service help to explain the preference for marriages within the kindred-based neighbourhood (ibid., 95, 131). The Jívaro prescribe marriage with a "cross-cousin (*wahe*) from either parent's side of the family," and slightly over half of actual marriages are with cross-cousins (ibid., 95). Harner (ibid., 99) mentions the possibility of marrying the daughter of a FBW, but we may presume that this will not occur when she is also a FBD, i.e. parallel cousin. Sister exchange is a common practice (ibid., 96).

External Relations

The Jívaro have achieved a very warlike reputation, and are particularly well known for their practice of taking head trophies (*tsantsa*) (cf. Karsten 1920). War raids and head-taking occur between tribes only (usually between Jívaro and Achuar), whereas intra-tribal killings generally take the form of expeditions aimed at the assassination of a single victim (Harner 1972:116, 183). Several neighbourhoods may unite under a single leader (*ti kakaram*) in major military undertakings (ibid., 115).

There is also considerable economic integration on the supra-local level. We have already considered the tribute flows of the inter-tribal shamanistic hierarchies (ibid., 121–122), and the egalitarian exchange of trade goods between formal trading partners (*amigri*) (ibid., 125). Harner (ibid., 126–127, 132) notes that the network of native trading partners in its total extent "apparently stretches from the foot of the Andes in the west to near Iquitos on the Amazon on the east, and from the Río Napo in the north to the Río Marañon on the south." The Achuar, to the east, provide the Jívaro with blowguns, *curare*, and feather ornaments in exchange for steel cutting tools and guns. The Achuar also supply monkeys, parrots, woven kilts, ornamental earsticks, beadwork, and glass beads from the Peruvian Amazon, whereas the Jívaro provide them with much of their salt (ibid., 128).

Oberem (1974) gives a detailed history of trade relations across the Ecuadorian *montaña*. In pre-Hispanic times, highland *caciques* established marital alliances with chiefs of *montaña* tribes such as the Quijo, northern neighbours of the Canelo (ibid., 347). The Inca exchanged axes and salt for gold from the *montaña* (ibid., 347, 353). The Quijo have had the position of middlemen, forwarding highland products to the tribes of the upper Amazon, and vice versa (ibid., 350). Oberem (ibid., 348) suggests that there were professional traders among the Quijo who sold tropical produce such as coca leaves in the highlands in exchange for cotton and other products. Reports from 1763 disclose that the Quijo also travelled downriver, trading gold dust to the Omagua in exchange for salt from the Huallaga River and dart poison manufactured by the Peba or Ticuna (ibid., 349). With shifting emphasis, the tribes of the *montaña* (Yumbo, Kofán, Quijo, Canelo, Jívaro) supplied those of the highlands with gold, wood (planks, agricultural implements), tropical plants (coca, calabashes, *pita* fiber, tobacco, fruit, copal, rubber, resins, cinnamon, and medicinal herbs), tropical animals (tame parrots and monkeys, feather ornaments, bird skins, smoked meat), *pilche* vessels, baskets, hammocks, palm fiber nets, blowguns, and slaves. Many of these products were procured from lowland tribes in exchange for gold dust, maize, and drums, and for highland-derived cloth, metal tools, threads, and beads. The Quijo once produced their own cotton cloth, coca, and even some salt (from plants), but are now dependent on the highlands for cloth and on both the highlands and lowlands for most of their salt. Some salt, however, is obtained from the Jívaro north-east of Macas (ibid., 352, 353). Whereas salt has constantly been a scarce commodity in this part of the *montaña*, its gold dust deposits have been a valuable asset in trade. Trade goods mentioned in the 16th century but no longer exchanged include gold ornaments, coca, and slaves (ibid., 355). Trade in blowguns and dart poison has not decreased, and dart poison has at times served as a medium of exchange.

In the 16th century, the Jívaro exchanged animals and other foodstuffs with highland tribes such as the Cañari, and traded salt downriver (ibid., 348-349). As the Jívaro had hardly any contact with Europeans in the 17th and 18th centuries, we know very little of their trade relations in this period. Today, the Canelo exchange drums, blowgun darts, and dart poison for Jívaro blowguns, dogs, and salt. The only salt production in the *montaña* is that of the Jívaro north-east of Macas, conducted by means of salt water evaporation (ibid., 354). Except for these, the Jívaro generally "trade much less than do the Quijo and Canelo" (ibid., 352).

196

40. The Achuar

Kin Terminology (Table 42)

Achuar terms of reference follow the two-line pattern. Terms of address, however, equate *umaí* and *wahér'* in the generational category *umáru* (Taylor 1982:4, 18). The vocative terminology similarly duplicates the equation M=WM of the Jívaro by including both in the category *nukuá*. Even in the first descending generation, the two-line dichotomy is neutralized: *nowánt* and *awé* are both addressed as *nawánta* (ibid., 5, 18).

Local Group Size and Composition

Among the Achuar, Taylor (ibid., 2) reports "nexi" of about 10 scattered households with total populations averaging around 100 persons. Although sororal polygyny should lead to the dispersion of male siblings (ibid., 9), local "nexi" have an "agnatic inflexion" (ibid., 2), and "it is women rather than men who move from one group to another and who are absorbed by agnatic units" (ibid., 17). Bride-capture (ibid., 10) excludes uxorilocal residence.

Patterns of Affiliation Other than Residence

Taylor (ibid., 2) describes the fundamental social unit as an "endogamous nexus": "a relatively closed set of overlapping, bilateral kindred groups of agnatic inflexion," unnamed but associated with a specific territory. In the same vein, Taylor (ibid., 17) speaks of "agnatic units" and "agnatic territoriality." Within the endogamous kindred groups, rules such as leviratic marriage lend opposed blocks of male siblings, whose children regularly intermarry, a "ghost of 'corporateness'" (ibid., 8).

Table 42
KIN TERMINOLOGY OF THE ACHUAR
LINGUISTIC FAMILY: Jívaroan
Male Ego, terms of reference.

GEN.	Male		Female	
+ 2	FF *apáchi* MF *apáchi*		FM *nukúchi* MM *nukúchi*	

	KIN (Lineal kin, parallel collaterals, affines of affines)		*AFFINES* (In-laws, cross collaterals)	
	Male	Female	Male	Female
+ 1	F *ápa*	M *nukú*	MB *jíich* FZH *jíich*	FZ *tsátsar'* MBW *tsátsar'*
0	B *yachí*	Z *umaí*	MBS *saí* FZS *saí*	MBD *wahér'* FZD *wahér'*
− 1	S *uchíru*	D *nawánt*	DH *awé* ZS *awé*	SW *awé* ZD *awé*

	Male		Female	
− 2	SS *tiránki* DS *tiránki*		SD *tiránki* DD *tiránki*	

SOURCES: Taylor 1982:18.

DEVIATIONS FROM THE TWO-LINE PATTERN	CONCEIVABLE IDEOLOGICAL OR BEHAVIOURAL CORRELATES
None	

Hierarchy

Taylor (ibid., 9) asserts that Jívaroan polygyny is generalized, rather than a chiefly prerogative. Three wives, in fact, is considered the ideal and "correct" maximum. She notes, however, that "great-men often (though by no means always) have more wives than other men" (ibid., 11). *Kakáram*, she says, are "those who are most likely to engage in hyper-polygamy" (ibid., 12). "Far more than a question of prestige or expansion of the domestic labour force," she believes, the accumulation of women on the part of the *kakáram* must be understood as "the result of the capitalization of affinal bonds" (ibid., 11). Marriage alliances connecting *kakáram* belonging to different "nexi" are essentially political marriages designed to expand their networks of affinal kin. This "constitutes the essence of politics and greatmanship among the Jívaroan groups." Very close, "semi-incestuous" marriages such as with a ZD are also a privilege of the *kakáram* (ibid., 12).

Alliance

Taylor (ibid., 1) notes that converse ideals of "close" and "distant" marriage exist side by side among the Achuar. On the one hand, marriage is prescribed with a woman of the category *wahér'*, a daughter of Ego's *jíich*

197

(MB/FZH), i.e. of Ego's father's affine (*sai*), "preferably a true MBD and/or FZD living within the same nexus" (ibid., 2–3). To the extent that this ideal is obeyed, neighbourhoods of "nexi" are fundamentally endogamous local kindred-groups (ibid., 2, 16). On the other hand, hyper-polygamous great-men (*kakáram*) contract exogamous marriages for political reasons (ibid., 11). Pursuing a yet different strategy, men who choose careers as *amígri* traders rather than warriors also seek to marry women from distant "nexi" (ibid., 13). These different kinds of exogamous marriages serve to "prevent the nexus from closing completely and to insure that all local groups remain bound to each other by self-perpetuating bonds of alliance." There is also an endogamous extreme, represented by the marriage of great-men to a ZD, the widow of a classificatory F, or even a classificatory D (ibid., 12). Such "semi-incestuous" marriages, which deprive Ego's real and classificatory children of potential spouses, remain the privilege of "tough old *kakáram* whom the offended parties will not dare attack."

Marriage ideally takes the form of sister exchange (ibid., 3, 17). A stringent rule of leviratic wife inheritance, in conjunction with a preference for sororal polygyny, ensures the continuity of affinal bonds and the relative stability of the kin-affine dichotomy (ibid., 7, 10). On the other hand, two living brothers cannot "redouble" an affinal relation by marrying two sisters (ibid., 9). As a result, male siblings are initially dispersed among different affinal households (cf. the Kayapó.) According to Taylor (ibid., 10), sororal polygyny compensates for the scarcity of marriageable male cross-cousins resulting from the high mortality rates of the warlike Jívaroans.

External Relations

Taylor (ibid., 2) describes the relationship between "relatively closed," endogamous "nexi" as one of "institutional hostility tempered by shifting and uneasy alliances." She notes that the exogamous marriages of great-men (*kakáram*) and *amígri* traders, "by diffusing kin relations and affinal potentialities outside the nexus," provide "every individual with rights of membership and residence in other nexi" (ibid., 13). This fact is important for an understanding of the shifting patterns of feuding and warfare in Jívaroan societies.

41. The Aguaruna

Kin Terminology (Table 43)

The Aguaruna kin terms reported by Larson (1977) follow the two-line pattern. The equation   M=MZ=FBW=FZ=MBW, however, suggests cognatic principles. The classification of zero generation collaterals depends on the categories between which first ascending generation marriages have taken place (ibid., 470, 472). Thus, FZC can be classified as *yátsu/ubá* or *sái/antsú-*, depending on the kinship status of FZH. The possibility of classifying MZC as *sái-/antsú-* may reflect their indeterminate patrilateral affiliation, as among the Tukano-speakers.

Local Group Size and Composition

Larson (1977:469) notes that households never include more than eight to 10 adults and their children. Uxorilocal bride-service can be substituted with bride-price (ibid., 473). Bride-capture is consistent with neo- or virilocal residence.

Patterns of Affiliation Other than Residence

Larson (ibid., 467–469) claims that the Aguaruna have a system of segmentary

Table 43
KIN TERMINOLOGY OF THE AGUARUNA
LINGUISTIC FAMILY: Jívaroan
Male Ego, terms of reference.

GEN.	Male		Female	
+ 2	FF	*apách*	FM	*dukúch*
	MF	*apách*	MM	*dukúch*

	KIN (Lineal kin, parallel collaterals, affines of affines)		*AFFINES* (In-laws, cross collaterals)	
	Male	Female	Male	Female
+ 1	F *ápa*	M *dúku*	WF *weá-*	WM *tsatsá-*
	FB *ápa*	MZ *dúku*	MB *diích*	FZ *dúku*
	MZH *ápa*	FBW *dúku*	FZH *diích*	MBW *dúku*
0	B *yátsu*	Z *ubá*	WB *sái-*	W *antsú-*
	FBS *yátsu*	FBD *ubá*	MBS *sái-*	MBD *wajé- antsú-*
	MZS *yátsu* *sái-*	MZD *ubá* *antsú-*	FZS *sái- yátsu*	FZD *wajé-, ubá antsú-*
			ZH *sái-*	BW *antsú-*
− 1	S *úchi*	D *nawántu*	DH *awé-*	SW *awé-*
	BS *úchi*	BD *nawántu*	ZS *awé-*	ZD *awé-*

	Male		Female	
− 2	SS	*tijágki*	SD	*tijágki*
	DS	*tijágki*	DD	*tijágki*

SOURCES: Larson 1977:469-475. Larson (ibid., 470,472) shows how alternative usages for MZC and FZC reflect the categories involved in first ascending generation marriages.

DEVIATIONS FROM THE TWO-LINE PATTERN	CONCEIVABLE IDEOLOGICAL OR BEHAVIOURAL CORRELATES
M=MZ=FBW=FZ=MBW, Si=FZC	Cognatic principles
MZC=MBC=FZC	Indeterminate patrilateral affiliation of MZC; marriageability of MZC

patrilineages, the smallest unit of which is the patrilineal extended family. The notion of a segmentary lineage system among Jívaroans derives from their capacity to muster increasingly inclusive armies as a conflict escalates. Larson quotes M.W. Stirling on the Jívaroan obligation to revenge one's "lineage," and claims that each "lineage" knows the limits of its territory (ibid., 477, 479). She even translates kin terms according to a "lineage" matrix: *úchi* and *nawántu* allegedly refer to first descending generation relatives of Ego's own lineage, whereas *awé-* denotes relatives belonging to other lineages (ibid., 471, 472). R. Karsten mentions that children frequently receive the names of ancestors (Larson 1977:476–477).

Alliance

Any cross-cousin or matrilateral parallel cousin classified as *antsú-* is marriageable.

199

Patrilateral cross-cousins classified as *ubá* are unmarriageable. Larson (ibid., 471) attributes to the Aguaruna a preference for marriage with a MBD.

Conclusions: Jívaroans

The general agreement between terms listed in the four sources suggests not only that the different Jívaroan groups maintain a virtually identical, two-line terminology, but also that this terminology has remained more or less unaltered during the past half century. Generational equations have been reported from all three groups.

The Jívaro and the Aguaruna have an extremely dispersed settlement pattern, with local longhouse conglomerations rarely reaching a population of 27. Among the Achuar, Taylor has distinguished larger "nexi" of scattered longhouses. These "nexi" average about 100 people.

All three groups share the convention of uxorilocal bride-service and the male attempts to avoid it in favour of viri- or neolocal residence.

The Jívaro and the Achuar are both organized into bilateral, kindred-based social groups with patrilineal tendencies. The Aguaruna allegedly possess segmentary patrilineages. Name transmission among the Jívaro is either patrilineal or parallel. The semi-endogamous kindred groups of the Jívaro and Achuar are basically alliance-organized.

Both the Jívaro and the Achuar prefer to marry within the kindred-based local group. Both prescribe marriage with bilateral cross-cousins, and the ideal is sister exchange. From the Aguaruna, Larson reports a preference for the matrilateral cross-cousin.

The Jívaro and the Achuar both practice sororal polygyny. There is a correlation between number of wives and a man's status. Among the Achuar, close endogamy such as ZD marriage is the prerogative of men of high status.

Chapter 12
Other linguistic families

42. The Piaroa (Saliva)

Kin Terminology (Table 44)

The kin terminology of the Piaroa is a perfect example of the two-line pattern. Kaplan (1984:135) calls it "a straightforward Dravidian-type terminology." An interesting peculiarity, however, is the equation of third ascending generation relatives with elder siblings, and of third descending generation relatives with younger siblings (Kaplan 1975: 129, 130, 199).

Local Group Size and Composition

The Piaroa local group (itso'de) is composed of 14 to 60 people (Kaplan 1972:283; 1973: 559). Post-marital residence is ambilocal, and the choice appears to depend on the relative status of the spouses' parents (Kaplan 1972:283; 1973:561, 562; 1975:134). High-status headmen (ruwang) attract affines to settle in their itso'de (Kaplan 1973:564), thereby increasing its size and prestige even further. Larger groups, by implication, presuppose a higher incidence of uxorilocal residence. Smaller groups are generally founded on the alliance of brothers instead of affines, and, by implication, on virilocal residence. Where marriages comply with the ideal of itso'de endogamy, however, post-marital residence need not imply such a choice. Distant marriages are invariably uxorilocal (Kaplan 1975:139–140).

Patterns of Affiliation Other than Residence

Affiliation is bilateral, and the itso'de ideally a cognatic kinship group (Kaplan 1972:283, 292, 294; 1973:561). The Piaroa nevertheless recognize a patrifilial moiety system distinguishing between "groups of the sky" and "groups of the earth" (Kaplan 1975:203–205). In each moiety there are six to eight subgroups. Those "of the sky" carry the names of birds, fruits of high trees, or a star, while those "of the earth" are named after land animals or "objects of the earth." Apparently, this moiety system has no ritual, economic, or political significance whatsoever.

We have already taken note of the three-generation cycles implicit in the equation of third ascending and descending generation with elder and younger siblings, respectively (ibid., 129, 130, 199).

Finally, Kaplan (ibid., 130) remarks that the two-line terminology implies that, "for men, the crucial links are through men; for women, they are through women." Parallel affiliation, in other words, is congruent with, and follows logically from Dravidian kin terminologies. For male Ego, same-sex kin and same-sex affines constitute two opposed patrilines, whereas for female Ego, same-sex kin and same-sex affines represent two matrilines. The divergence is most obvious in the first descending generation, where children of same-sex siblings are classified as kin and those of opposite-sex siblings as affines. The complementary perspectives of the two sexes, which reverse the positions of BC and ZC as kin or affines, illustrate the difference between a two-line terminology as an Ego-centered, sex-biased system of classification, on the one hand, and unilineal kin groups such as moieties, on the other. A shift from the former to the latter would entail the abandonment, by one of the sexes, of its same-sex criteria for classifying kin.

The significance of same- versus cross-sex

Table 44
KIN TERMINOLOGY OF THE PIAROA
LINGUISTIC FAMILY: Saliva
Male Ego, terms of reference.

GEN.	Male		Female	
+ 2	FF *cha'do* MF *cha'do*		FM *cha'da* MM *cha'da*	

	KIN (Lineal kin, parallel collaterals, affines of affines)		*AFFINES* (In-laws, cross collaterals)	
	Male	Female	Male	Female
+ 1	F *cha'o* FB *cha'o* MZH *cha'o*	M *cha'hu* MZ *cha'hu* FBW *cha'hu*	WF *chiminya* MB *chiminya* FZH *chiminya*	WM *chiminyahu* FZ *chiminyahu* MBW *chiminyahu*
0	B e *chú'buo* y *chihawa* FBS e *chú'buo* y *chihawa* MZS e *chú'buo* y *chihawa*	Z e *chú'bua* y *chihawahu* FBD e *chú'bua* y *chihawahu* MZD e *chú'bua* y *chihawahu*	WB *chisapo* MBS *chisapo* FZS *chisapo* ZH *chisapo*	W *chirekwa* MBD *chirekwa* FZD *chirekwa* BW *chirekwa*
− 1	S *chitti* BS *chitti*	D *chittihu* BD *chittihu*	DH *chuhöri* ZS *chuhöri* WBS *chuhöri*	SW *chuhörihu* ZD *chuhörihu* WBD *chuhörihu*

	Male		Female	
− 2	SS	*chu'do*	SD	*chu'da*
	DS	*chu'do*	DD	*chu'da*

SOURCES: Kaplan 1972:286–287; 1975:199.

DEVIATIONS FROM THE TWO-LINE PATTERN	CONCEIVABLE IDEOLOGICAL OR BEHAVIOURAL CORRELATES
None	

links is observed by Kaplan (ibid., 132), who notes that, "for Ego to delineate the proper marital categories of his kinsmen in relation to himself, the distinction of sex of relative must be made in all categories of his own generation," i.e. "male kin of own generation must be distinguished from female kin." From the consideration of gender in all contexts including the delineation of affinal categories (ibid., 137; cf. also Kaplan 1973:

562), it is apparent that genealogical reckoning is far from superfluous even in societies which have been characterized as organized by alliance rather than by descent.

Hierarchy

The land inhabited by the Piaroa is divided into 13 or 14 political territories (*itso'fha*), each composed of six to seven *itso'de* (Kaplan 1973:559). The political organization of these territories is "based upon the loose and competitive ordering, hierarchical in nature, of *ruwatu* (religio-political leaders)." Competition between headmen (*ruwang itso'de* ="owner of the house") focuses on strategies to maximize the size of local groups (ibid., 562–563). To ensure that all his in-laws move into his *itso'de*, the *ruwang* must "influence marriages so that no member of his *itso'de* marries a person who is linked to a leader of higher status than he." Choice of post-marital residence usually depends upon "the respective power positions of the fathers-in-law" (Kaplan 1975:134). The centripetal pressure of influential headmen thus prompts lesser leaders always to contract alliances with their inferiors, in order to maintain and expand the size of their *itso'de*. A son-in-law from outside the territory will always settle uxorilocally, assuring his father-in-law of a subordinate and himself of a protector (ibid., 140). Although a man's total number of followers enhances his political status, there is no correlation between status and number of wives (ibid., 144).

Alliance

The local group (*itso'de*) is ideally endogamous (Kaplan 1972:283–284, 294; 1973:561, 563), and may have been so more consistently in the past (Kaplan 1975:140). Marriage is prescribed with women belonging to the category *chirekwa*, which includes the MBD and FZD, but the rule is most frequently stated in terms of marriage with a child of one's parent's affines (a child of father's *chisapo* = WB/ZH or mother's *chóbiya* =HZ/BW), or with a child of first ascending generation affines (a child of *chiminya* or *chiminyahu*) (Kaplan 1972:285, 287, 288; 1973:560; 1975:132, 133). Marriages are usually arranged by two adult affines,

primarily *chisapomu* (brothers-in-law), who exchange children (Kaplan 1972:287; 1973:560; 1975:133). Although Kaplan (1972:288; 1973:560) emphasizes that the Piaroa themselves do not recognize categories such as "bilateral cross-cousins," she admits that their ideal of kindred endogamy "does have genealogical denotations," i.e. marriage to MBC or FZC (1973:561). In fact, "since the immediate kindred is of only first cousin depth, the only type of marriage permissible, given the positive marriage rule, is with the child of either parent's cross-sex sibling." Children of cross-sex siblings of Ego's parents are thus the potential spouses of Ego and his siblings (ibid., 563), and Kaplan (ibid., 564) even considers it "appropriate to ask if the preference to marry 'close' (*tuku*) is not indeed *for the Piaroa* the preference to marry one's cross-cousin." At a later date (Kaplan 1975:127), she attributes to the Piaroa "a straight-forward system of prescriptive bilateral marriage (following the definition given by Maybury-Lewis of such a system, 1965: 221)." According to this definition, "a man must marry a woman whom he addresses by a relationship term denoting a category of relatives which includes the joint specification MBD/FZD" (Maybury-Lewis 1965: 221).

Occasionally, a Piaroa man marries an affine of the first descending generation (*chuhörihu* = ZD) (Kaplan 1972:569). Such "incorrect" marriages are always secondary unions (Kaplan 1975:133). Kaplan (ibid., 140) suggests that, since these unions are also a matter of exchange between *chisapomu*, the reason why spouses are sought in the first descending generation is that by middle age, the sisters of Ego's *chisapomu* would all be married. Instead of exchanging children, one of the *chisapomu* marries the other's daughter (Kaplan 1972:569; 1975: 133). The compatibility of ZD marriage with a symmetric brother-in-law relationship has been similarly demonstrated among the Nambikwara (Lévi-Strauss 1968a).

Out of 16 Piaroa marriages on which Kaplan has full data, in all but two the bride and groom were able to claim that their spouses belonged to the prescribed category (*chirekwo*/*chirekwa*) (Kaplan 1975:137). The two exceptions were oblique marriages, i.e. between a man and his *chuhörihu*. The ideal of direct exchange, finally, is founded on the observation that, "when such marriages occur neither of the grooms need pay bride-service, nor must they give a flow of small gifts to the father of the bride" (ibid., 135).

External Relations

The strong preference for local group endogamy suggests that the *itso'de* are introversive, fairly isolated units. Yet, the hierarchical integration of political territories (*itso'fha*) indicates significant regional interaction.

43. The Witoto (Witoto)

Kin Terminology (Table 45)

The Witoto recognize a number of terminological equations and distinctions which deviate from the two-line pattern. The distinctions MB≠FZH, FZ≠MBW, DH≠ZS, and SW≠ZD all contradict symmetric alliance. In addition to the Hawaiian equation of siblings and cross-cousins, generational equations assimilate MZ=FZ, BW=WBW, BC=WBC, DH=ZDH, and SW=ZSW. Many of these equations suggest an endogamous, cognatic category. The equation BC=SC, on the other hand, suggests patrilineal continuities. The range of *enaize*/*enaizeño*, by equating WBC=DC, would also accommodate ZD marriage.

Farabee's half a century older list equates MF=MB and FM=FZ.

Local Group Size and Composition

The population of a *maloca* varies between 50 and over 200 (Gasché 1977:144). The Witoto claim that their *malocas* were generally larger in the past, and Farabee (1922:137) maintains that they were able to accommodate as many as 100 families. He mentions groups of 400 people (ibid., 141), whereas Steward (1948c:755) gives a community average of about 100.

Post-marital residence is predominantly virilocal (Gasché 1977:141, 142, 145, 146; Steward 1948c:755; Farabee 1922:142), but Gasché (1977:145) notes a uxorilocal tendency among men without firm patrilineal ties of their own, e.g. refugees or displaced survivors of an epidemic.

Patterns of Affiliation Other than Residence

Although consanguinity is reckoned bilaterally, the Witoto recognize named patrilineages (Gasché 1977:142, 147, 149). Each lineage is associated with a specific "semantic field," from which derive its name, the personal names of its members, and its "emblem" (*jekiraingo*) (ibid., 146, 148). Farabee (1922:142) lists personal names specific to particular "sub-tribes", and Steward (1948c:756) also notes that there are "sets of group names." More than 50 named groups are mentioned in the literature (Gasché 1977:160, note 9; Steward 1948c: 755–756). Such Witoto "sub-tribes" range from 25 to 500 persons.

Lineages generally comprise no more than three *malocas*, at the most, and Gasché (1977:147–148) attributes this limit to genealogical amnesia inherent in the system of naming. Each headman transmits his own name to his successor, whereas names given to heads of new *malocas* tend to be innovations within the semantic field of the lineage. The segmentation of lineages corre-

Table 45
KIN TERMINOLOGY OF THE WITOTO
LINGUISTIC FAMILY: Witoto
Male Ego, terms of reference.

GEN.	Male		Female	
+ 2	FF *uzuma* (*iusuma*) MF *uzuma* (*iusuma*)		FM *uzungo* (*iusunu*) MM *uzungo* (*iusunu*)	

	KIN (Lineal kin, parallel collaterals, affines of affines)		*AFFINES* (In-laws, cross collaterals)	
	Male	Female	Male	Female
+ 1	F *mooma* (*mota*) FB *izo* MZH *mookama*	M *eiño* (*e'i*) MZ *ii* FBW *eikango*	WF *jĩfai* MB *billama* (*iusuma*) FZH *mookama*	WM *jĩfaiño* FZ *ii* (*iusunu*) MBW *eikango*
0	B *ama* (*ama*) FBS *ama* MZS *ama* WZH *rífema*	Z *miringo* (*bunu*) FBD *miringo* MZD *miringo* WBW *ofaiño*	WB *oima* MBS *ama* FZS *ama* ZH *oima*	W *aĩ* (*kwi'ai*) MBD *miringo* FZD *miringo* BW *ofaiño*
− 1	S *jitoo* (*hito*) BS *enaize* ZDH *ñekore*	D *jiza* (*hisa*) BD *enaizeño* ZSW *mio*	DH *ñekore* ZS *komoma* WBS *enaize*	SW *mio* ZD *komongo* WBD *enaizeño*

	Male		Female	
− 2	SS *enaize* DS *enaize*		SD *enaizeño* DD *enaizeño*	

SOURCES: Gasché 1977:150. Terms in brackets derive from Farabee (1922:149). Farabee gives
iusuma for "uncle" and *iusunu* for "aunt", but does not specify whether parallel or
cross-collaterals are intended.

DEVIATIONS FROM THE TWO-LINE PATTERN	CONCEIVABLE IDEOLOGICAL OR BEHAVIOURAL CORRELATES
MB≠FZH, FZ≠MBW, DH≠ZS, SW≠ZD	Absence of symmetric alliance
B=FBS=MZS=MBS=FZS, Z=FBD=MZD=MBD=FZD, MZ=FZ, BW=WBW, BC=WBC, DH=ZDH, SW=ZSW, MZH=FZH, FBW=MBW	Cognatic principles
BC=SC	Patrilateral affiliation
WBC=DC	Avuncular marriage

205

sponds to the segmentation of such semantic fields.

Whereas Farabee (1922:137) refers to the named subdivisions of the Witoto as "sub-tribes," Steward (1948c:755) suggests that they are "sibs" comparable with those of the neighbouring Tukano-speakers. Each residential unit is simultaneously a ceremonial unit, since it is associated with one kind of ceremonial career only. Each career, however, may be celebrated in several *malocas* (Gasché 1977:145–146).

Succession is patrilineal to the offices of chief, sub-chief, and shaman/"medicine man", and to the three ceremonial roles of *lladiko*, *zikii*, and *lluai* (Gasché 1977:144; Steward 1948c:756, 760; Farabee 1922:137, 145). If there are no male heirs, sons-in-law prepared to reside uxorilocally may succeed their fathers-in-law (Gasché 1977:145). The transmission of an office through a daughter is best accomplished by marrying her to a co-resident deriving from an alien *maloca* (ibid.; Steward 1948c:757).

Hierarchy

In each *maloca*, the core of patrilineal kinsmen (*jofo nani* = "masters of the house") are of superior status (Gasché 1977:142–143). Residents deriving from other *malocas* (*jaieniki* = "orphans" or "commoners") are inferior, and prisoners of war may temporarily constitute yet a third category of *maloca* inhabitants.

Members of the patrilineal core are distinguished according to birth order, with the senior male (F, eB) its chief (*illaima*), and his descendants recognized as such (*illaini*). The Witoto concept of *erofene* ("born after") is applied to the relation between eldest son and father in the same way as it is used for the relation between younger and elder brothers. Birth order determines not only which son is to succeed his father, but also, where sons are

absent, which daughter's husband will succeed his father-in-law (ibid., 144–145).

The three ceremonial roles (*lladiko*, *zikii*, and *lluai*) are also envisaged in terms of a birth-order hierarchy, with *lladiko* representing the firstborn and most prestigious. Since each *maloca* is specifically associated with only one of these three roles, it is possible to distinguish three categories of *malocas* arranged in accordance with the hierarchy of roles. As each *maloca* upon segmentation can yield *malocas* of the same status only, the ceremonial hierarchy is not a product of the process of segmentation (ibid., 145, 148). Farabee's (1922:146) mention of a "leader of songs, *nugoitimoi*," suggests that the Witoto may have recognized yet other ceremonial roles.

Chieftainship is inherited patrilineally, and polygyny is recognized as the privilege of chiefs and shamans (ibid., 137, 141; Steward 1948c:756, 758). Farabee's (1922: 141) claim that "the sons of chiefs must always marry the daughters of other chiefs" indicates an ideal of rank endogamy. He writes that "the greatest of the medicine men lives in the house with the chief" (ibid., 145), which suggests a dichotomy of sacred versus secular power. Each village has "two or more sub-chiefs" (ibid., 137). Farabee (ibid., 141) writes that chiefs and sub-chiefs wear particular kinds of ornaments (lip plugs and necklaces) as marks of distinction.

Alliance

The Witoto express an ideal of local exogamy (Gasché 1977:141; Steward 1948c:757; Farabee 1922:141). Steward (1948c:757) writes that "an exception to the rule of local exogamy is that when the chief needs a successor, his daughter weds a man who has been adopted into the community." Steward (ibid., 756) believes that the Witoto fail to extend the ideal of exogamy beyond the local community, but Gasché (1977:147, 156–158) has shown that the preference for marriage with non-kin ("c'est-à-dire avec une personne qui ne soit pas frère ou soeur") implies avoidance of at least four separate lineages: those of F/FF, M/MF, FM and MM. The explicit prohibition of certain lineages is paralleled by a prohibition of marriages with "close kin" (*nanoka*). Collateral ties weaken with genealogical distance, however, and the ideal of exogamy proves on closer scrutiny to be an ideal of marriage with distant kin (ibid., 153, 155). Lineages which need not be avoided apparently include those of FFZH, FZH, FBW, MBW, and MZC (ibid., 156–157). For marriage to be possible with women of these lineages (e.g. FZD), the latter must not be congruent with those which are prohibited. For example, the lineage of FFZH must not be identical to that of FM, that of FZH or FBW to that of M, or that of MBW or MZC to that of F. In other words, symmetric alliance would be precluded in a number of cases, in order for Gasché's list of eligible lineages to hold.

Although Gasché (ibid., 157–158) does mention unions involving "un frère et une soeur mariés à un frère et une soeur," he confirms that the Witoto "politique d'alliance diversifiée" generally keeps the number of marriages uniting two lineages very low. As among the similarly organized Tukano-speakers, the category of MZC lends the system a triadic aspect. Gasché (1977:153) notes that the named patrilineages, while to some extent codifying the proximity of parallel kin descending from a set of brothers, tend to separate the descendants of a set of sisters. We have seen that, for members of the lineage of MZC to be eligible for marriage, this lineage must not be congruent to that of F. In other words, MZ must not have married into the same lineage as M. Gasché does mention marriages of "deux frères mariés à deux soeurs," but once again the "politique d'alliance diversifiée" keeps such marriages to a minimum. Instead, the marriages of two sisters will generally unite a second and third lineage as *rifema*, or "co-alliés" (ibid., 160,

note 18), a concept which corresponds precisely to the category of MZC as "affines of affines" among Tukano-speakers. As among the latter, marriage to a MZD is acceptable (Steward 1948c:757).

External Relations

Farabee (1922:146) claims that the Witoto are not a warlike people, yet describes their habit of taking head trophies and their cannibalistic practices. Steward (1948c: 756) notes that "considerable hostility has prevailed between the Witotoan tribes and even between communities of the Witoto." Motives causing war include the desires to take prisoners, and for vengeance against shamans. Some villages are protected by trenches in which sharp, poisoned stakes are concealed (ibid., 753, 756).

Trade between communities is minimal "because of a high degree of self-sufficiency and because of intertribal strife" (ibid.. 755). Nevertheless, the Witoto trade tobacco and hammocks for Menimehe pottery, Carijona poisons, and mats and other woven products from the neighbouring Bora.

44. The Bora and Miraña (Miraña)

Kin Terminology (Table 46)

Steward (1948c:750) treats Bora and Miraña as dialects of Witoto, but this is denied by Rowe (1974:49). Guyot (1977:167) merely notes that the kin nomenclature of the Bora and Miraña does not "contradict" that of the Witoto, with whom the Bora intermarry.

The kin terminology of the Bora and Miraña deviates in several respects from the two-line pattern. In the first ascending generation, parallel aunts and uncles are

Table 46
KIN TERMINOLOGY OF THE BORA AND MIRAÑA
LINGUISTIC FAMILY: Miraña
Male Ego, terms of reference.

GEN.	Male		Female	
+ 2	FF *ta?di* MF *ta?di*		FM *ta?dže* MM *ta?dže*	

	KIN (Lineal kin, parallel collaterals, affines of affines)		*AFFINES* (In-laws, cross collaterals)	
	Male	Female	Male	Female
+ 1	F *kani* FB *na?ni* MZH *na?ni*	M *tsixi* MZ *me?e* *ba?be* FBW *me?e*	WF *na?ni* MB *na?ni* *ba?be* FZH *na?ni*	WM *me?e* FZ *me?e* MBW *me?e*
0	B e *kani* y *ñabe, ñama* FBS *ñama* MZS *ñama*	Z e *bi?hi* y *ñadže,* *ñama* FBD *ñama* MZD *ñama*	WB *a?tjo* MBS *ñama* FZS *ñama* ZH *kani*	W *ta?ba* MBD *ñama* FZD *ñama* BW *a?tjonidže*
− 1	S *iči* BS *domigwe*	D *idzi* BD *domidže*	DH *axa* ZS *domigwe*	SW *axa* ZD *domidže*

	Male		Female	
− 2	SS *ačigwa* DS *ačigwa*		SD *akigwa* DD *akigwa*	

SOURCES: Guyot 1977:167–168. For S and D, there are alternative terms which distinguish between elder and younger sons and daughters.

DEVIATIONS FROM THE TWO-LINE PATTERN	CONCEIVABLE IDEOLOGICAL OR BEHAVIOURAL CORRELATES
FB=MB, MZ=FZ, B=ZH, BC=ZC, FBC=MZC=MBC=FZC	Cognatic principles
F=eB	Patrilateral affiliation
DH≠ZS, SW≠ZD	Absence of symmetric alliance

equated with cross aunts and uncles. There appears to be a special term (*ba?be*) for mother's siblings of both sexes. In Ego's generation, parallel cousins are equated with cross-cousins in the Hawaiian manner, and B is equated with ZH. In the first descending generation, BC are accordingly equated with ZC. Although not indicated in Table 46, distinctions of seniority are made among both Ego's siblings and his children (Guyot 1977:167). The equation F=eB suggests patrilineal principles. The distinctions DH≠ ZS and SW≠ZD suggest an absence of symmetric alliance.

Local Group Size and Composition

Steward (1948c:755) suggests an average community size of 300 among the Bora. Post-marital residence is virilocal (Guyot 1977: 166, 169, 172).

Patterns of Affiliation Other than Residence

Steward (1948c:755–756) cites descriptions of Miraña communities as "kin" groups, and a list of 20 named Bora "kin", suggesting that careful fieldwork is needed to clarify the nature of such groups. Guyot (1977:163, 170) speaks of named "groupes de filiation" reproduced by means of patrilineal name transmission.

Through three basic types of name transmission (ibid., 164–166), a set of brothers is succeeded by their eldest sons. Positions in the birth-order hierarchy are associated with specific specialist roles. There are also roles inherited by females, such as that of artist, which is transmitted from a paternal aunt (FZ) to her brother's eldest daughter.

Whereas elder brothers generally transmit the names of paternal ancestors, "assurant ainsi l'existence de la lignée" (ibid., 163–165), a younger brother may give his eldest son the name of an ancestor from either the mother's or the father's side (ibid., 166). The equation B=ZH (*kani*) applies only to eldest B and the husband of eldest Z, both of whom represent the status of firstborns within the agnatic line (ibid., 167). The inclusion of matrilateral ancestors, and even brothers-in-law, in categories referred to as kin, suggest that the "kin" groups of the Bora and Miraña are focused more on the continuity of a senior patriline of chiefs, than on the delineation of a patrilineal lineage.

Hierarchy

Succession to statuses and roles among the Bora and Miraña is determined by a birth-order hierarchy reminiscent of that of the Witoto and Tukano-speakers (ibid., 164). It is noteworthy that the second eldest brother is generally associated with the role of shaman (*čakomi*) and typically opposed to the firstborn as his more or less hostile rival for authority (ibid., 165). In fact, Guyot speaks of a "complémentarité de deux autorités": that of the headman (chief) and that of the shaman (ibid., 166).

Another feature worthy of notice is the equation eB=eZH represented by the term *kani* (ibid., 167). In a system of bilateral cross-cousin marriage, this equation is consistent with the Hawaiian equation of siblings and cross-cousins. We have suggested that generational cousin terms may serve to delineate endogamous strata in societies with permanent status differences. The Bora and Miraña do lend support for such an interpretation, since the category *kani* assimilates two male affines of identical high status (i.e. that of firstborns.)

The internal, spatial organization of each *maloca* expresses the hierarchical relationship between a chief and his sons or brothers (ibid., 163–164; cf. the Cubeo.)

Alliance

The Bora and Miraña express an ideal of local exogamy but a preference for tribal or linguistic endogamy (ibid., 166, 169). Nevertheless, the Bora migrants of the Igaraparaná have established ceremonial partnerships and relations of intermarriage with their previous enemies, the Witoto.

In accordance with Dole's (1969) predictions, the generational kin terminology of the Bora and Miraña is complemented with a prohibition against marriage with cousins (Guyot 1977:167). This prohibition appears to include even second cousins, as Guyot claims that Ego's descendants of the first and second descending generations are prohibited from contracting alliances with the group into which Ego's own generation mates have married.

As among the Witoto, the policy of diversifying a group's relations of alliance means that brothers rarely marry women from the same group. From a genealogical analysis of a family of 10 children born around the beginning of the century, Guyot concludes that only two brothers married sisters from the same affinal group. An exception to the rule of diversification is the sororal polygyny practiced by some chiefs.

Among the Bora, Guyot suggests that the same group into which the eldest sister marries provides the elder brothers with ceremonial partners (ibid., 169). As ceremonial partnerships are ideally transmitted from F to S, it seems that alliances, at least at the status level of firstborns, would have been repeated in successive generations. Among the Miraña, separate groups provide ceremonial partners for the eldest brother (chief) and the next eldest brother (shaman), one situated upstream and the other down-stream. This again confirms the ideal of diversification.

External Relations

Steward's (1948c:756) judgement on the Witoto is meant to apply to the Bora and Miraña as well. The Bora, in fact, are specifically mentioned as having practiced cannibalism on war victims. In recent times, however, the Bora have established some peaceful exchange with the Witoto.

45. The Trumaí (Trumaí)

Kin Terminology (Table 47)

The Trumaí kin nomenclature presented in Table 47 represents an attempt to integrate the vocative terminologies provided by Quain, Oberg, and Wagley (Murphy &

Quain 1955:49–51). In most cases, there is agreement between two or even all three authors, but some terms rely exclusively on one of them. These are *takwai* for yB (Quain), used by Oberg and Wagley for female Ego's yZ and female parallel cousins; *ha-dif* and *ha-difletsi* for male parallel cousins and BW, respectively (Oberg); and *ha-pat* for S (Wagley). The use of *ha-doho* for second ascending generation relatives also derives exclusively from Wagley, as does the consistent use of the prefix *ha-* (first person possessive.)

Although our reconstruction of Trumaí kin terminology remains uncertain, it appears to follow the two-line pattern. Wagley's report that the term *ha-doho* is used by male Ego for both grandparents and grandchildren suggests a principle of alternating generations.

Local Group Size and Composition

In 1938, the dwindling population of the Trumaí village was 43. Ten years later, it had dropped to 25 (Murphy & Quain 1955:20). Had not peace been enforced since the building of an airfield in the area, a village of 25 would not have been viable, i.e. secure from predation from other groups (ibid., 14).

Post-marital residence was generally virilocal (ibid., 16, 44).

Patterns of Affiliation Other than Residence

Due to virilocality, "there was a tendency for patrilineally related males to live together, but this did not result in the establishment of a patrilineal lineage" (ibid., 44). Nevertheless, Upper Xingú villages generally recognized "the right of the father's village over the children" (ibid., 48). A man's property was inherited primarily by his brother or son, but a ZS or a BS (in that order) could also have a claim (ibid., 41–42).

210

Table 47
KIN TERMINOLOGY OF THE TRUMAÍ
LINGUISTIC FAMILY: Trumaí
Male Ego, terms of address.

GEN.	Male		Female	
+ 2	FF	*ha-yeí* *ha-doho*	FM	*ha-tsetá* *ha-doho*
	MF	*ha-yeí* *ha-doho*	MM	*ha-tsetá* *ha-doho*

	KIN (Lineal kin, parallel collaterals, affines of affines)		*AFFINES* (In-laws, cross collaterals)	
	Male	Female	Male	Female
+ 1	F *ha-papa* FB *ha-taték*	M *ha-tsive* MZ *kokó*	MB *wawé*	FZ *ha-káte*
0	B *ha-pisí* y *takwai* FBS *ha-dif* MZS *ha-dif*	Z *ha-dufle* FBD *ha-dufle* MZD *ha-dufle*	WB *ha-eshlá* MBS *ha-mipiné* FZS *ha-mipiné* ZH *ha-eshlá*	W *ha-detsi* MBD *ha-mipiné* FZD *ha-mipiné* BW *ha-difletsi*
− 1	S *ha-pat* BS *waremó*	D *ha-faxlo* BD *ha-faxlo*	ZS *detá*	ZD *ha-dak*

	Male		Female	
− 2	SS	*ha-doho*	SD	*ha-doho*
	DS	*ha-doho*	DD	*ha-doho*

SOURCES: Murphy & Quain 1955:49–51.

DEVIATIONS FROM THE TWO-LINE PATTERN	CONCEIVABLE IDEOLOGICAL OR BEHAVIOURAL CORRELATES
GP=GC	Alternating generations

The office of chief was generally inherited patrilineally, but there is evidence that it could "pass matrilineally if there are no male heirs available" (ibid., 42, 56). The transmission of status, such as membership in the *aek* or *camara* status classes, was predominantly patrilineal, although matrilineal transmission did occur (ibid., 60).

"Manifestly," write Murphy and Quain (ibid., 57), "patrilineality was very fluid." A man's ties to his MB were equally strong, including gift-giving claims and traveling partnerships (ibid., 54). Gift-giving obligations also bound together the four houses of the Trumaí village, two by two (ibid., 46). The fact that the two pairs of connected houses represented different architectural traditions suggests that each of these "moiety-like" divisions may have derived from a previously separate village. Murphy and Quain suggest that the residents of the pair of smaller, "true" Trumaí-type houses may have been the descendants of inhabitants of a southern village, whereas the other two houses show strong influence from Kamayurá building traditions.

There is ample evidence for a principle of alternating generations. We have seen that grandparents and grandchildren may have been equated in the reciprocal use of the term *ha-doho*. The ceremonial *ole* songs were inherited "either through the mother's brother or the mother's father" (ibid., 42). "Since cross-cousin marriage was practiced," the transmission from MB to ZS meant that "the *ole* songs returned to the direct patrilineal line every other generation." Such an arrangement implies that a man's *ole* songs derive from his FF, rather than his MF. A man's second name, however, was inherited from his MF (ibid., 53), as a Trumaí was unable to mention his son's second name in order to avoid that of his father-in-law. This situation recalls that of the nearby Kalapalo, where each parent transmits to a child the name of one of his or her own parents, depending on sex, and where each will call the child only by the names he or she has given it, since the others are subject to affinal name avoidance (Basso 1973:85–86).

Murphy and Quain (1955:42) write that the combination of matrilineal and patrilineal elements is "characteristic of the bilaterality in upper Xingú culture."

Hierarchy

Trumaí leadership was weak (ibid., 15, 55), yet there was considerable jealousy of the chief's status (ibid., 45). Beneath the Trumaí chieftain, two sub-chiefs were recognized (ibid., 54), suggesting an element of diarchy. One of the sub-chiefs was a shaman, the other the chief curer of the village (ibid., 61).

The chief told Quain that "he did not plant because he was a chief" (ibid., 56), which suggests traditions from a stratified society in which high-status citizens were exempt from manual labour. The Trumaí recognized two status categories: *aek,* which included the chief, the two sub-chiefs, and their families, and *camara,* a term which probably derives from the Brazilian concept of *camarados* (workers) (ibid., 60). Two Trumaí men refused to help build Quain's house "on the grounds that he was only a *camara,* or person of low status" (ibid., 57). Status appears to have been hereditary, but its transmission

ambilineal. Murphy and Quain (ibid., 60, 61) write that "the significance of being *aek* had probably declined with the weakening of leadership patterns and the lessened importance of the sub-chiefs," but that it is possible that "before the Trumaí had declined to their present low estate, prestige and authority were more clearly patterned," as in the Tupí-speaking Kamayurá village with which the Trumaí intermarried.

Murphy and Quain note that dominance appeared to correlate with the energy with which a man indulged in ceremonial trading (ibid., 43).

In the only polygynous marriage reported from the Trumaí, the second wife accepted a position subordinate to that of the first (ibid., 47).

The status of three foreign women in the village (a Suyá, a Mehinacu, and a Kamayurá) was lower than that of the Trumaí women (ibid., 13).

Alliance

The "most acceptable" marriages were between cross-cousins (ibid., 42, 51, 52). Although one informant claimed that true cross-cousins should not marry, Quain's genealogies indicate that such marriages were common. The Trumaí would not accept, as do the Kamayurá, marriage with a ZD.

Polygyny, if practiced, should preferably be sororal (ibid, 47, 52). Consistent with the two-line terminology is the chief's complaint that "all the women in the village were prohibited to him, as they were his wife's cross-cousins" (ibid., 48).

External Relations

The villages of the Upper Xingú tribes (cf. the Kuikuru, Kalapalo, and Mehinacu) maintain extensive contact with each other and "a rather distrustful peace" (ibid., 7, 10). The Trumaí were once "feared" by their neighbours, but at the time of Quain's fieldwork they themselves lived in fear of more numerous and powerful tribes (ibid., 10, 15). The capture of women, looting, and vengeance are the most common motives for warfare in the region (ibid., 14). In the past, inter-tribal alliances were formed between the Kamayurá, Mehinacu, Waurá, and Trumaí, to revenge attacks from the ferocious Suyá (ibid., 11). Contemporary co-operation, however, is restricted to intermarriage and trade (ibid., 16–17).

The Trumaí were incorporated into the Upper Xingú system of craft specialization (ibid., 18–19). Tradition had institutionalized an Arawak monopoly on pottery production, and a Kamayurá monopoly on a highly prized type of bow. The Trumaí, once active manufacturers of stone axes, came to specialize in the preparation of salt. Basso (1973:56) adds that stone axes manufactured by the Gê-speaking Suyá entered the Upper Xingú trade network *via* the Trumaí, suggesting some peaceful contact between these traditional enemies.

46. The Warao (Warao)

Kin Terminology (Table 48)

The kin terminology of the Warao deviates in several respects from the two-line pattern. In the first ascending generation, spouses of cross-collaterals can be classed together with parallel collaterals (FZH=FB, MBW=MZ). In Ego's generation, Hawaiian cousin equations merge siblings, parallel cousins, and cross-cousins all in the same category. A Warao terminology published in 1825 distinguishes between siblings and "cousins" (*hesenga*), but Suárez suggests that this datum is erroneous (Suárez 1972:53, 65–67). The distinctions WB≠ZH, DH≠ZS, and

SW≠ZD suggest an absence of symmetric alliance.

Local Group Size and Composition

Local groups of Warao vary in size between 15 and 100 individuals (ibid., 46). Reports from the 18th and early 19th centuries, however, mention settlements with streets, plazas, and houses holding as many as 150 people (Kirchhoff 1948:872). Post-marital residence is uxorilocal (Suárez 1972:46, 72, 79, 82, 84, 102).

Patterns of Affiliation Other than Residence

Affiliation is essentially bilateral (ibid., 72, 85). However, matrilateral affiliation is evident from the observation that, "in cases of intertribal marriage only the children of Warrau mothers were considered Warrau" (Kirchhoff 1948:874). Some authors (e.g. Steward & Faron 1959:443) have attributed matrilineal lineages to the Warao (Suárez 1972:72), but Suárez notes that such an interpretation is incompatible with the practice of ZD marriage (ibid., 85). She refutes the existence of unilineal descent groups among the contemporary Warao, suggesting instead that the accent on uterine relations derives from the practice of uxorilocal residence (ibid., 83–85, 102).

Suárez suggests that the Warao have previously maintained a "two-section system of prescriptive alliance," but that there has been a gradual loss of lineal principles in favour of "un sistema cognático y preferencial" (ibid., 77, 78, 96, 101, 103). This distinction between "two-section systems" and "cognatic systems" is unfortunate, as it suggests that a two-section kin terminology is to some extent diagnostic of unilineality. In reality, two-line terminologies in South America generally appear in conjunction with cognatic descent reckoning (cf. Chapter 20).

Table 48
KIN TERMINOLOGY OF THE WARAO
LINGUISTIC FAMILY: Warao
Male Ego, terms of reference.

GEN.	Male		Female	
+ 2	FF nobo		FM natu	
	MF nobo		MM natu	

	KIN (Lineal kin, parallel collaterals, affines of affines)		AFFINES (In-laws, cross collaterals)	
	Male	Female	Male	Female
+ 1	F dima	M dani	WF dahi	WM dabai
	FB e dehota y dimuka	MZ e danihota y danikatida	MB daku	FZ dakatai
	MZH e dehota y dimuka	FBW e danihota y danikatida	FZH daku, e dehota, y dimuka	MBW dakatai, e danihota y danikatida
0	B e dahe y daka	Z e dakoi y dakoi-sanuka	WB dami-sanuka	W tida
	FBS e dahe y daka	FBD e dakoi y dakoi-sanuka	MBS e dahe y daka	MBD e dakoi y dakoi-sanuka
	MZS e dahe y daka	MZD e dakoi y dakoi-sanuka	FZS e dahe y daka	FZD e dakoi y dakoi-sanuka
			ZH damitu	BW behetida
– 1	S auka	D aukatida	DH dawa	SW natohorani
	BS auka	BD aukatida	ZS e hido y hido-sanuka	ZD e hido y hido-sanuka

	Male	Female	
– 2	SS natoro	SD natoro	
	DS natoro	DD natoro	

SOURCES: Suárez 1972:73–74.

DEVIATIONS FROM THE TWO-LINE PATTERN	CONCEIVABLE IDEOLOGICAL OR BEHAVIOURAL CORRELATES
FB=MZH=FZH, MZ=FBW=MBW, B=FBS=MZS=MBS=FZS, Z=FBD=MZD=MBD=FZD	Cognatic principles
WB≠ZH, DH≠ZS, SW≠ZD	Absence of symmetric alliance

Hierarchy

Kirchhoff (1948:874) suggests that the authority of headmen may have been greater in the past, when settlements were larger.

Steward and Faron (1959:441–442) note that the Warao have "a priest-temple-idol cult and social classes that are more like those of chiefdoms than the patterns of the nomads or village farmers," and suggest that they may have suffered deculturation upon being displaced from their original habitat. Wilbert's description of "classes of chiefs, priests, shamans, and magicians, and several groups of laborers that functioned only in connection with temple festivals" (ibid., 443) recalls the specialist roles of the Tukano-speakers.

Suárez (1972:49, 82–83) writes that the Warao distinguish two types of status: chiefs (*kobenahoro*, etc.) and workers (*nebu*). Recruitment of chiefs is not hereditary, nor are there any restrictions on intermarriage between the two categories. The observation that the supreme chiefs of three different local groups are closely related (ibid., 89), however, suggests hereditary succession or permanent status differences. As two of these chiefs relate as cross-cousins, i.e. prototypical affines, there may also be an ideal of rank endogamy.

Suárez (ibid., 49) writes that the Warao local group has one, two, or three chiefs, of which the *kobenahoro* has supreme authority. In the cluster of three local groups studied by Suárez, there are two "jefes principales" (ibid., 80). Another indication of diarchy is the distinction between sacred and secular leaders (Steward & Faron 1959: 441).

Kirchhoff (1948:874) notes that chiefs have more wives than other men, and that polygyny generally is sororal. Suárez claims that polygyny was formerly the exclusive privilege of chiefs, whose numerous daughters would attract sons-in-law to reside uxorilocally and thus reinforce their political power (ibid., 51, 80, 86).

Alliance

The Warao have an ideal of local endogamy (ibid., 72, 85–88). Marriage is possible with both cross-cousins and parallel cousins on either side, and with ZD. Suárez claims that her data on 75 Warao marriages indicate a predominance of symmetric alliance (ibid., 94–96, 101), and suggests that this supports her hypothesis that the Warao have formerly maintained a "two-section system of prescriptive alliance" (ibid., 104). Of 20 unambiguous cases of "symmetric" alliance (in Suárez' idiosyncratic definition, marriages with cross-collaterals, i.e. marriages which align with an implicit, genealogical dichotomy of the population into two sections), seven are with bilateral cross-cousins, four with MBD, two with FZD, six with ZD, and one with a MBD who is simultaneously a ZD (ibid., 95). A total of 13 marriages are classified as "non-symmetric" or even "asymmetric" (i.e. internal to one of the implicit sections), but one of these (with a FZ) ought to belong in the so-called "symmetric" category. As many as 27 marriages (of a total of 75) cannot be unambiguously classified in one or the other category, another 10 are exogamous, and 5 are "undefinable." Exogamous and undefinable marriages together amount to 20% of the total sample.

External Relations

In 1596 Sir Walter Raleigh found Warao chiefs warring against each other and against other tribes, especially Caribs (Kirchhoff 1948:878). The Warao were pushed by the Caribs from the plains and highlands into the Orinoco delta (Morey & Marwitt 1978:255).

In the middle of the 18th century, the Warao engaged in institutionalized barter, particularly of hammocks and palm starch (Kirchhoff 1948:874). More recently, there has been trade in smoked fish, canoes, and cassava sifters. Kirchhoff adds that "it appears as if trade goods were stored in some villages," which suggests accumulation and hoarding of wealth.

For fear of witchcraft, contemporary Warao tend to avoid contact with distant groups (Suárez 1972:88).

47. The Kadiwéu (Guaycurú)

Kin Terminology (Table 49)

Kadiwéu kin terminology deviates in several respects from the two-line pattern. In the first ascending generation, F and FB are equated with MB. In Ego's generation, siblings and parallel cousins are equated with cross-cousins in the Hawaiian manner. The distinctions MB≠FZH, FZ≠MBW, WB≠ZH, DH≠ZS, and SW≠ZD all suggest an absence of symmetric alliance.

Local Group Size and Composition

Ribeiro (1974:167) lists four groups of Kadiwéu ranging in size between 11 and 94 and averaging 50 people. Post-marital residence is uxorilocal (ibid., 171, 178).

Patterns of Affiliation Other than Residence

Kadiwéu reckon kinship bilaterally (ibid., 172). They possess "no institution based on unilineal exogamous divisions." By virtue of the division of labour by sex, "boys are more attached to their father and girls to their mother" (ibid., 180), suggesting an element of parallel affiliation.

Hierarchy

Relationships between older and younger brothers are markedly asymmetrical (ibid., 180). A son-in-law's respect for his parents-in-law is so great that these categories of people never speak to each other (ibid., 181–182). The most characteristic form of social asymmetry among the Kadiwéu, however, is the relation of servitude between captured "slaves" and their captors (ibid., 168, 172, 176–177). Ribeiro writes that "Kadiwéu social structure is based on an ethnic division into two strata: masters and slaves, the slave stratum consisting of individuals captured or bought from other tribes and of their descendants in the first and second generations." Some slaves are treated as lower status members of the family, and kin terms implying consanguinity are used between slaves and masters. This recalls the Makú servants of the north-west Amazon, as does the evidence of a recent decline in the significance of these status distinctions. The fact that there is "some disapproval" (ibid., 178) of sexual relationships between the two strata suggests an ideal of rank endogamy.

Alliance

Ribeiro's only mention of regularities in the choice of marriage partners is his observation that a woman's first sexual experiences are generally with "boys of the group from which will come her future husband" (ibid., 170), suggesting local group exogamy and a pre-determined pattern of intermarriage between groups.

Ribeiro notes that marriage between persons who call each other "sibling" is prohibited. Marriage between "socially determined 'siblings'", e.g. between god-children and the children of their godparents, is "permitted with some disapproval" (ibid., 170, 178).

External Relations

The warlike Kadiwéu constantly menaced the Spanish settlements in Paraguay until the end of the 18th century (ibid., 167). These activities had ended altogether by the beginning of the 20th century. Ribeiro writes that the Kadiwéu "still preserve many of the characteristics of the lordly people, the celebrated Indian Cavaliers, who dominated almost all the tribes of the Chaco, enslaving many of them."

Table 49
KIN TERMINOLOGY OF THE KADIWÉU
LINGUISTIC FAMILY: Guaycurú
Male Ego, terms of reference.

GEN.	Male			Female		
+ 2	FF	*iné-lôkud* *ie-mé*		FM	*iá-mît*	
	MF	*iné-lôkud* *ie-mé*		MM	*iá-mît*	

	KIN (Lineal kin, parallel collaterals, affines of affines)			*AFFINES* (In-laws, cross collaterals)		
	Male		Female	Male		Female
+ 1	F *iá-tád*		M *ié-déd* *é-iodôd*	WF *iô-txí-hádit*		WM *iô-txí-hát*
	FB *iá-tád*		MZ *ié-déd* *é-iodôd*	MB *iá-tád*		FZ *iá-djiôdo*
	MZH *iá-nín-húdi*		FBW *iá-nín-hôdot*	FZH *iá-nín-húdi*		MBW *iá-nín-hôdot*
0	B *in-niô-txuá*	Z *in-niô-álo*		WB *ié-déu-dít*	W *iô-dauát* *iô-txá-háua*	
	FBS *in-niô-txuá*	FBD *in-niô-álo*		MBS *in-niô-txuá*	MBD *in-niô-álo*	
	MZS *in-niô-txuá*	MZD *in-niô-álo*		FZS *in-niô-txuá*	FZD *in-niô-álo*	
				ZH *iá-níu-údit*	BW *i-lát*	
− 1	S *iôn-niguít*	D *iôn-nát*		DH *ihá-dít*	SW *ihá-tét*	
	BS *iôn-niguít*	BD *iôn-nát*		ZS *ité-txeguít*	ZD *ité-txét*	

	Male		Female	
− 2	SS	*í-uá-lúdi*	SD	*í-uá-téti*
	DS	*í-uá-lúdi*	DD	*í-uá-téti*

SOURCES: Ribeiro 1974:173–174.

DEVIATIONS FROM THE TWO-LINE PATTERN	CONCEIVABLE IDEOLOGICAL OR BEHAVIOURAL CORRELATES
F=FB=MB, B=FBS=MZS=MBS= FZS, Z=FBD=MZD=MBD=FZD, MZH=FZH, FBW=MBW	Cognatic principles
MB≠FZH, FZ≠MBW, WB≠ZH, DH≠ZS, SW≠ZD	Absence of symmetric alliance

217

48. The Cuiva (Guahibo)

Kin Terminology (Table 50)

The kin terminology of the Cuiva represents a particularly complete documentation of the two-line pattern.

Beyond the age of about 10, a child is incorporated into a system of alternative kin term usages which equates alternate generations (Arcand 1977:25). A male Ego's son's children are equated with zero generation affines, while his daughter's children are equated with kin. Reciprocally, his FF is equated with affines, his MF with kin. The resultant distinction between two kinds of grandparents and two kinds of grandchildren suggests lineal principles of classification. Logically consistent with the equations connecting generations +2, 0, and –2 are the principles by which generations +1 and –1 are equated: for male Ego, female kin of the first ascending generation are equated with those of the first descending generation, and female affines of the first ascending generation with those of the first descending generation, but male kin of the first ascending generation are equated with first descending generation affines, and male affines of the first ascending generation are equated with first descending generation kin. This alternation cannot be explained as the cyclical merging of patrilines and matrilines (which would produce the characteristic FF=B=SS, and so on), but instead suggests a system where affiliation is alternately reckoned through males and through females (ibid., 29–30).

Local Group Size and Composition

The tree bands of Cuiva visited by Arcand numbered respectively 211, 179 and 149 members (Arcand 1972:4). These maximal bands, however, are assembled for only one-fourth of the year (ibid., 5). During another fourth of the year bands divide into two separate groups of roughly equal size (from 70 to 105 people), and during the remaining half of the year the Cuiva live in small groups of between 10 and 40 individuals. Each band is composed of about 10 to 15 such units, averaging about 20 people in each.

Post-marital residence is uxorilocal (ibid.; 1977:29).

Patterns of Affiliation Other than Residence

The Cuiva do not think of themselves as being organized in terms of any system of descent lines (Arcand 1972:4; 1977:28). Yet, the terminological equations of alternate generations suggest a four-section system reproduced along "lines of descent running from a man, to his daughter, her son, his daughter, and so on" (Arcand 1977:30). Arcand notes that "these cycles of male-to-female descent do correspond to a very real ethnographic fact: they are a feature of the terminology itself." *Pentapin/pentapiyo* always marry *pamoyo/pécotsiwa*, and *péyung/péyunyo* always marry *pérobi/pécopinyo*. Offspring of *pentapin* are always *péyung/péyunyo*, offspring of *pamoyo* are *pérobi/pécopinyo*, offspring of *péyung* are *pamoyo/pécotsiwa*, and offspring of *pérobi* are *pentapin/pentapiyo*. The four-section system of marriage alliance is strongly reminiscent of that of Pano-speakers, but specific lines follow four-generation cycles rather than a simple principle of alternating generations.

Hierarchy

Aboriginal Guahibo war parties were "divided into squads under a powerful head chief" (Morey & Marwitt 1978:253). The Guahiban-speaking Chiricoa recognized a paramount chief with authority over several local groups.

218

Table 50
KIN TERMINOLOGY OF THE CUIVA
LINGUISTIC FAMILY: Guahibo
Male Ego, terms of reference.

GEN.	Male		Female	
+ 2	FF	*amo* (*pamoyo*)	FM	*akwé* (*pentapiyo*)
	MF	*amo* (*pentapin*)	MM	*akwé* (*pécotsiwa*)

	KIN (Lineal kin, parallel collaterals, affines of affines)		*AFFINES* (In-laws, cross collaterals)	
	Male	Female	Male	Female
+ 1	F *aha*	M *èna*	WF *ahuyo*	WM *amio*
	FB *ahon* (*pérobi*)	MZ *énowa* (*péyunyo*)	MB *ahuyo* (*péyung*)	FZ *amio* (*pécopinyo*)
	MZH *ahon*	FBW *énowa*	FZH *ahuyo*	MBW *amio*
0	B e *pentapin* y *péapin*	Z e *pentapiyo* y *péapiyo*	WB *pamoyo*	W *piyowa*
	FBS e *pentapin* y *péapin*	FBD e *pentapiyo* y *péapiyo*	MBS *pamoyo*	MBD *pécotsiwa*
	MZS e *pentapin* y *péapin*	MZD e *pentapiyo* y *péapiyo*	FZS *pamoyo*	FZD *pécotsiwa*
	WZH e *pentapin* y *péapin*	WBW e *pentapiyo* y *péapiyo*	ZH *pamoyo*	BW *pécotsiwa*
− 1	S *péhanto*	D *péhantiyo*	DH *pérobi*	SW *pécopinyo*
	BS *péyung* (*ahuyo*)	BD *péyunyo* (*énowa*)	ZS *pérobi* (*ahon*)	ZD *pécopinyo* (*amio*)
			WBS *pérobi*	WBD *pécopinyo*

	Male		Female	
− 2	SS	*pémomo* (*pamoyo*)	SD	*pémoyo* (*pécotsiwa*)
	DS	*pémomo* (*péapin*)	DD	*pémoyo* (*péapiyo*)

SOURCES: Arcand 1977:22–23. Terms in brackets are alternative usages applied to relatives beyond the age of about 10 (ibid., 25–27).

DEVIATIONS FROM THE TWO-LINE PATTERN	CONCEIVABLE IDEOLOGICAL OR BEHAVIOURAL CORRELATES
FF≠MF, FM≠MM, SS≠DS, SD≠DD	Lineal principles
FF=MBS=FZS=SS, MF=B=DS, FM=Z=DD, MM=MBD=FZD=SD, FB=ZS, MZ=BD, MB=BS, FZ=ZD	Alternating generations: alternate patrilateral and matrilateral affiliation

Alliance

Marriage is prescribed with a woman of the category *pécotsiwa* (Arcand 1977:24), which includes bilateral cross-cousins as well as classificatory MM and SD.

External Relations

The aboriginal Guahibo annually raided riverine villages such as those of the Achagua, collecting tribute and slaves, annexing conquered territories, and occasionally even allying themselves with the Carib (Morey & Marwitt 1978:252–253).

The Cuiva have suffered four centuries of violent contacts with the outside world, and many bands have been dispersed by warfare and disease (Arcand 1972:4). As contacts with settlers have generally been violent, the Cuiva have earned an exceedingly ferocious reputation (ibid., 7–11; Morey 1972:64, 66; Morey & Marwitt 1978:253).

Trade and alliances link villages, as when "Guahibo villagers serve as middlemen for their Sikuani kinsmen to whom they trade garden produce, tools, fishhooks, utensils and clothing, for game, wild plant foods, *paricá*, and hammocks" (Morey 1972:65).

Part III
General Correlations:
A Tentative Typology of
Lowland Societies

"Instead of typologies we need a series of relevant elements, like descent, classification, exchange, residence, filiation, marriage, and so on; these need to be rigorously defined as analytic categories and then combined and recombined into various combinations and permutations, in different sizes, shapes, constellations."
– D.M. Schneider (1965:78)
"A direct consequence of the approach that I am advocating is that comparison becomes far more difficult, and on any large and detailed scale perhaps impracticable..."
– R. Needham (1971c:13)

It is with some hesitation that we now venture to formulate some general conclusions on lowland South American social organization. As the implied level of generalization necessarily strips the ethnography of most of the cultural detail which determines the trajectories of permutation, such conclusions must remain unpretentious and tentative. The parameters chosen for comparison must be increasingly abstract as wider syntheses are attempted, and the subtle variation within single linguistic families must yield to much cruder classification. At this point, the subjective vehicles of cultural transformation are lost from sight. Hermeneutics yield to statistics, emics to etics, and cultural codes to formal principles. Such reductionism may have its temporary justifications, but the reader should be warned that information is bound to be distorted in the process. In choosing crucial parameters and delineating the various alternatives, the author is inevitably constrained by his *own* categories. Due to the uncertainties involved in classifying ethnographic data, imprecise and inexhaustive as they inevitably are, it has not seemed meaningful to restate numerical observations in terms of more sophisticated statistical relationships.

Chapter 13
Possible Trajectories of Lowland South American Social Organization

"Our investigation . . . is directed not towards *phenomena*, but, as one might say, towards the *'possibilities'* of phenomena."
  – L. Wittgenstein (quoted in Needham 1971c:32)

". . . The Guiana region may hold a special place by representing the Lowland culture in its simplest form. ... The proposed relationship is one of logical possibilities, and the Guiana sub-culture, as it so happens, exhibits the simplest of such possibilities."
  – P.G. Rivière (1984:102)

In order to facilitate comparison, we have tabulated some fundamental information on the 48 cultures in our sample (Table 51). The parameters chosen for this tabulation are:
I.   Other denotations of the term used for MBD
II.   Other denotations of the term used for FZD
III.   Average local group size
IV.   Patterns of post-marital residence
V.   Principles of affiliation other than residence
VI.   Indications of principles of alternating generations
VII. Distinction of siblings according to relative age
VIII. Indications of hierarchy
IX.   Preferred and/or actual spouses for male Ego
X.   Nature of external relations

The alternatives relevant to each parameter are listed in Table 52.

When arranged linguistically, the groups immediately reveal significant patterns and differences. Many of these have been mentioned in the conclusions for separate linguis-

tic families, but a few comparative statements can be made at this point (cf. also Table 53.) Crow equations, for instance, are almost exclusively found among Gê-speaking peoples such as the Eastern Timbira, Apinayé, and Bororo, and Omaha equations only among Northern and Central Gê. The Dravidian equation of both cross-cousins with the category of "spouse" is predominant among Caribs, Pano, and Yanoama, but almost absent among Gê and Tupí. Large or formerly large villages are typical of the Gê and Tupí, whereas those of the Caribs, Tukano, Pano, Yanoama, and Jívaroans are usually smaller. Gê and Tupí are generally uxorilocal, Caribs ambilocal and Tukano virilocal. The Eastern Timbira recognize matrilateral affiliation of males, whereas Central and Southern Gê, Tupí, Tukano, Pano, Yanoama, and Jívaroans emphasize patrilateral ties. Arawak and Caribs, on the other hand, are more purely bilateral. Named unilineal groups occur among the Gê, Tupí, Pano, Tukano, and Yanoama, but moieties only among the former three. Two-generation cycles of alternating generations are common among the Gê, Tukano, Pano, and Arawak, but rare among Caribs. Birth-order hierarchies of names and ceremonial roles are reported from the Gê, Tupí, and Tukano, whereas hierarchy seems to be weak among Caribs and Pano. Among the Tupí, Tukano, Arawak, and Jívaroans, high social status is associated with polygyny, feasting, or the control of external exchange. Indications of rank endogamy are strongly suggested among Gê, Arawak, Tupí, and Tukano, but apparently absent among the Caribs,

Linguistic Family	Culture	I.	II.	III.	IV.	V.	IV.	VII.	VIII.	IX.	X.
GÊ	1. Krahó	4	7	3	1	1456	1	2	7	12	2
	2. Ramkokamekra	4	7	1	1	1456	1	1	45	5	13
	3. Krîkatí	45	9	3	1	1456	4	2	127	5	2
	4. Apinayé	457	567	24	1	1456	1	1	17	25	23
	5. Kayapó	5	6	1	1	246	4	2	1	6	13
	6. Suyá	5	4	3	13	246	1	2	123	12	1
	7. Shavante	68	68	1	13	2456	1	1	17	25	1
	8. Sherente	25	46	34	1	256	1	1	17	2	134
	9. Caingang	2	2	24	16	256	4	2	237	1234	1
	10. Bororo	246	7	1	1	1456	1	1	1247	124	24
	11. Karajá	2	2	34	1	2456	1	2	17	123	13
	12. Nambikwara	16	16	2	4	134	4	1	6	123	35
ARAWAK	13. Machiguenga	8	8	2	1	34	1	2	467	1234	234
	14. Mehinacu	28	28	3	25	34	1	1	36	5	3
CARIB	15. Trio	146	56	2	13	234	1	1	8	1234	5
	16. Kalapalo	1	1	3	4	34	1	1	36	12	3
	17. Kuikuru	2	2	3	345	3	4	2	36	12	3
	18. Karinya	16	16	1	4	13	4	1	8	123	3
	19. Barama River	16	16	2	256	13	4	1	8	123	5
	20. Pemon	128	128	2	345	3	4	2	4	123	4
	21. Waiwai	13	134	2	45	134	4	1	3	1234	2
	22. Txicáo	134	7	3	1	134	4	1	5	1	1
TUPÍ	23. Tapirapé	2	2	1	1	2456	4	1	167	5	1
	24. Mundurucú	26	9	34	135	2456	2	1	12467	123	13
	25. Parintintin/ Tupí-Cawahíb	1	1	1	25	256	4	2	34	123	14
	26. Tupinambá/ Guaraní	9	9	1	13	25	4	2	3467	123	134
	27. Sirionó	1	7	3	1	14	4	2	36	1	25
PANO	28. Amahuaca	1	1	24	26	256	1	1	3	1234	15
	29. Mayoruna	1	1	24	2	256	1	1	8	12	1
	30. Sharanahua	1	1	34	13	2456	1	1	8	12	1
	31. Cashinahua	1	1	2	1	2456	1	1	8	12	5
TUKANO	32. Cubeo	8	8	2	2	25	1	1	124567	12	134
	33. Barasana	8	8	2	2	245	1	1	12467	123	134
	34. Bará	9	9	2	2	25	4	2	23567	12	13
	35. Makuna	1	1	2	25	25	1	1	1267	123	1
YANOAMA	36. Yanomamö	1	1	3	25	2345	4	1	3	12	13
	37. Yanomam	1	1	2	345	3	12	2	8	12	1
	38. Sanumá	1	1	2	1	25	4	1	23	123	2
JÍVAROAN	39. Jívaro	1	1	24	456	234	1	1	46	12	134
	40. Achuar	8	8	3	2	23	4	2	6	12	14
	41. Aguaruna	8	8	2	256	25	4	2	8	12	14
OTHER	42. Piaroa	1	1	2	45	23456	2	1	46	123	4
	43. Witoto	2	2	34	2	25	4	2	23467	5	1
	44. Bora/Miraña	2	2	1	2	245	4	1	12	5	1
	45. Trumaí	8	8	2	2	234	1	1	3456	12	13
	46. Warao	2	2	34	1	13	4	1	4567	1234	134
	47. Kadiwéu	2	2	2	1	34	4	2	57	5	14
	48. Cuiva	1	1	123	1	3	3	1	4	12	1

Table 51 Fundamental ethnographic information on the 48 lowland South American cultures in our sample.

I./II. Other denotations of the term used for MBD/FZD:
1. W or BW (I + II: Dravidian)
2. Z (Hawaiian)
3. MBW
4. D (I: Crow)
5. M (I: Omaha)
6. ZD (II: Omaha)
7. FZ (II: Crow)
8. Other cross-cousin, but not W or BW (Iroquois)
9. No other, or no information

III. Average local group size:
1. Large (over 150)
2. Small (less than 50)
3. Intermediate
4. Formerly large

IV. Patterns of post-marital residence:
1. Uxorilocal
2. Virilocal
3. Preferred or privileged viriloacality
4. Ambilocal, alliance-organized
5. Uxorilocal bride-service
6. Neolocal

V. Principles of affiliation other than residence:
1. Matrilateral inclination
2. Patrilateral inclination
3. Bilateral
4. Parallel or cross transmission
5. Named unilineal groups
6. Moieties, i.e. dual organization

VI. Indications of principles of alternating generations:
1. 2-generation cycles
2. 3-generation cycles
3. 4-generation cycles
4. No information

VII. Distinction of siblings according to relative age:
1. Present
2. No information

VIII. Indications of hierarchy:
1. Great names associated with high-status roles
2. Birth-order hierarchy
3. Other accounts of hereditary succession
4. Hierarchy of leaders
5. Permanent stratification or spouse-giver/spouse-taker relationships
6. Status achieved through control of exchange, through polygyny, through feasting, or through attraction of a large number of co-residents
7. Indications of rank endogamy
8. No information

IX. Preferred and/or actual spouses for male Ego:
1. MBD
2. FZD
3. ZD
4. FZ
5. Kindred exogamy, i.e. all first cousins prohibited
6. No information

X. Nature of external relations:
1. Aggressive or formerly aggressive
2. Peaceful
3. Pronounced interest in trade; frequent interaction
4. Regional hierarchy, i.e. political integration
5. Isolated

Table 52 Key to Table 51

Pano, Yanoama and Jívaroans. The category of marriageable women includes both cross-cousins, and often ZD, among most Tupí, Arawak, Caribs, Tukano, Pano, Yanoama, and Jívaroans, whereas the Northern and Central Gê generally have unilateral preferences and in some cases even extend exogamic prohibitions to all first cousins. Avuncular marriage is particularly common among Caribs and Tupí, whereas alternate

Para-meter	GÊ	ARAWAK	CARIB	TUPÍ	PANO	TUKANO	YANOAMA	JÍVAROAN
I–II.	Crow-Omaha	Iroquois	Dravidian		Dravidian	Iroquois	Dravidian	Iroquois
III.	Large		Small	Large	Small	Small	Small	Small
IV.	Uxorilocal		Ambilocal	Uxorilocal		Virilocal		
V.	Unilateral Named groups Moieties	Bilateral	Bilateral	Patrilateral Named groups Moieties	Patrilateral Named groups Moieties	Patrilateral Named groups	Patrilateral Named groups	Patrilateral
VI.	Alternation	Alternation			Alternation	Alternation		
VIII.	Birth-order hierarchy			Birth-order hierarchy		Birth-order hierarchy		
		Achieved status		Achieved status		Achieved status		Achieved status
	Rank endogamy	Rank endogamy		Rank endogamy		Rank endogamy		
IX.	Unilateral cross-cousin marriage or kindred exogamy	Bilateral cross-cousin marriage	Bilateral cross-cousin marriage; avuncular marriage	Bilateral cross-cousin marriage; avuncular marriage	Bilateral cross-cousin marriage; alternate generation marriage	Bilateral cross-cousin marriage	Bilateral cross-cousin marriage	Bilateral cross-cousin marriage
X.	Integrated		Isolated	Aggressive Integrated	Aggressive Isolated	Aggressive Integrated	Aggressive	Aggressive Integrated

Table 53 Characteristic features of linguistic families in the sample.

generation marriage is peculiar to Panoans. The Central and Southern Gê, Tupí, Tukano, Pano, Yanoama, and Jívaroans have been notoriously aggressive in their external relations, whereas the Eastern Timbira, Caribs, and Arawak in our sample have been less devoted to warfare. Several Gê-speaking groups, the Xingú Caribs, the Tukano, and the Jívaroans have shown a strong interest in trade, and a measure of regional integration has been achieved among some Gê, Tupí, Tukano, and Jívaroans. Isolated groups, on the other hand, are found particularly among Caribs and Pano.

We may also make some observations on the correlation between the factors of residence and affiliation, on the one hand, and the remainder of our parameters, on the other. Some of these correlations are summarized in Table 54.

The two cross-cousins are terminologically distinguished only in societies practicing uxorilocal residence. In ambilocal and virilocal societies, MBD and FZD appear to be universally equated, either as a separate category (Iroquois) or together with W/BW (Dravidian), Z (Hawaiian), or ZD. The classical Dravidian equation of cross-cousins and potential spouses is particularly prominent in ambilocal societies. All instances of Crow-type cousin terms occur in societies which are uxorilocal and in other respects matrilaterally inclined. All instances of Omaha cousin terms derive from societies which are uxorilocal but patrilaterally inclined.

Large or formerly large villages are frequent among uxorilocal groups with inclinations toward unilateral affiliation, whereas ambilocal and virilocal villages are generally smaller.

Parallel affiliation is particularly emphasized in uxorilocal societies. Named social divisions occur among most tribes tending toward unilateral affiliation, but moieties are particularly prominent among uxorilocal societies. Cases of virilocal moiety systems, in fact, all belong to linguistic families (Tupí, Pano) the mainstreams of which have previously been uxorilocal.

In ambilocal and virilocal societies, high status appears more often to be achieved

225

Parameter	AMBILOCAL	UXORILOCAL		VIRILOCAL
III.	Small	Large		Small
V.	Bilateral affiliation	Dual organization Parallel affiliation particularly pronounced		Patrilateral affiliation
VIII.	Achieved status	Hereditary status		Achieved or hereditary status
IX.	Bilateral cross-cousin marriage	Unilateral cross-cousin preferences Extended exogamy		Bilateral cross-cousin marriage
		Predominantly matrilateral affiliation	Predominantly patrilateral affiliation	
	Avuncular marriage		Avuncular marriage	Avuncular marriage
X.	Peaceful	Peaceful	Aggressive	Aggressive
I–II.	Dravidian	Crow	Omaha	Iroquois

Table 54 Various features characteristically associated with some fundamental forms of residence and affiliation

(e.g. through trade, polygyny, feasting.) In uxorilocal societies, prestige is generally inherited in the form of specific names and accompanying ceremonial roles. The virilocal tribes of the north-west Amazon (Tukano, Witoto, Bora/Miraña) duplicate the birth-order role hierarchies of many uxorilocal groups. Indications of rank endogamy are particularly explicit among societies with named unilineal divisions. On the other hand, none have been reported from ambilocal groups.

In consonance with the terminological evidence, marriage is enjoined with both cross-cousins in all ambilocal and almost all virilocal societies, whereas uxorilocal groups often express unilateral preferences. ZD marriage is also common in ambilocal and patrilaterally inclined groups, whereas among societies which are both uxorilocal and matrilaterally inclined, it has been reported only from the Warao. Prohibitions against marriage with first cousins have apparently occurred among several uxorilocal groups, but are rare among virilocal societies.

Patrilateral affiliation of males appears generally to be associated with aggressive external relations, whereas ambilocal and matrilaterally inclined groups are less preoccupied with warfare.

The Implications of Unilocal Residence

"The variable is the degree of control that each society exercises over its women." . . . ". . . Virilocal residence represents considerable risk, for when control over a woman is surrendered there is no mechanism that assures replacement."
– P.G. Rivière (1984:106–107, 105)

We may now offer a very tentative and admittedly speculative interpretation of some of the various transformational trajectories traced by the indigenous peoples of lowland South America. It is obvious that socio-structural variation among these peoples represents a spectrum of potentialities defined by a cultural repertoire which is, to a large extent, shared by them all (cf. Rivière 1973:3; 1984:102). This point of view is strengthened as new linguistic connections between widely separate groups are being discerned (cf. Chapter 3.)

A number of writers have suggested that the simplest type of society conceivable is the locally endogamous group within which marital alliance is regulated by a terminological dichotomy of kin and affines. We would expect this type of society to be inwardly egalitarian and outwardly isolated or at least unaggressive. Endogamous marriages such as with the ZD would be commonplace, and as the entire group is organized around the co-residence of affines, there would be no emphasis on any unilocal rule of post-marital residence (cf. Rivière 1984: 40). In our ethnographic sample, this ideal type is approached by groups such as the Nambikwara, Yanomam, and Piaroa.

Beyond this logical starting-point, a major structural "option" is represented by the adoption of unilocal residence. As a corollary to our interpretation of ambilocality in endogamous local groups, we suggest that unilocal residence becomes a relevant concern only when a certain proportion of marriages are exogamous to the local group. We need not here enter into a discussion of the factors (demographic expansion or decline, trade, political integration, etc.) contributing to the articulation of different local groups. Such articulation has been a fact throughout most of the South American lowlands, and it has complicated the maintenance of reciprocity in marital alliance (cf. J. Shapiro 1984:11; Jackson 1984:176; Rivière 1984:105–107). For obvious reasons, direct exchange of women (sisters or daughters) between groups is often impracticable. Alternative means of assuring reciprocity might be for the husband either to pay bride-price or to submit to uxorilocal bride-service. Bride-price, however, is a rare phenomenon in lowland South America, sporadically reported only from eastern Brazil (Basso 1984:41–42; Dole 1984:52; Kracke 1984:105; for an inverted,

"groom-price" variant, cf. W. Crocker 1984: 64–65, 67, 69, 90, note 15, 92, note 28) and the Jívaroans on the border between Ecuador and Peru (Harner 1972:79; Larson 1977: 473). Apparently, there is a fundamental economic multicentricity inhibiting the exchange of women for goods (cf. Jackson 1984:163–164). J. Shapiro (1984:27) notes that "bride service, rather than bride wealth, is the general practice in the region." In response to this obligation, generally unattractive to males, two radically different strategies may be followed. The first is to staunchly retain virilocality. This can be accomplished by arranging exchange marriages between virilocal groups, by marrying a ZD if ZH has been persuaded to reside uxorilocally, or by acquiring women through violent bride-capture. This type of society, exemplified in our sample by the Tukano-speakers, Yanomamö, and Achuar, would tend to produce small, competitive groups. Competition for women would be associated with privileged polygyny and a measure of social hierarchy. The second strategy is to yield, in greater or lesser measure, to uxorilocality. This is an alternative with far-reaching structural ramifications, as exemplified by the Gê (cf. Turner 1979a). Where bride-service has been institutionalized into a rule of permanent uxorilocal residence, we may expect a tendency to draw affines spatially closer, in order for male kin to be able to retain continuous social bonds. The result would be large villages, where kin and affines, though spatially distinct, reside immediately contiguous to each other. Here, then, is a rationale for exogamous moieties. Dual organization, we suggest, represents the reconciliation of exogamy and uxorilocal residence.

Uxorilocality provides the only context in lowland South America where males may reckon matrilateral affiliation. The "matriliny" of the Eastern Timbira and Bororo reflects the matrilineal continuity of females in uxorilocal households. Generally, uxorilocality appears to involve parallel affiliation of the sexes, so that localized female matrilines co-exist with dispersed, "ceremonial" male patrilines. The strong male/female dualism in these societies represents the refusal of patrilateral kin to yield to the matrilateral slant implicit in uxorilocality. The recognition of lineal bonds of both kinds has left unilateral marks in both kin terminologies and marriage preferences. Crow-Omaha equations occur only in uxorilocal societies, and unilateral cross-cousin preferences have been reported from the Ramkokamekra, Apinayé, Central Gê, Suyá, Txicáo, and Sirionó.

The large, moiety-organized, uxorilocal villages, finally, provide a setting conducive to hierarchy at both the household and the village level (cf. Turner 1979a). In bringing together male affines in the same household, uxorilocality puts the newly married male in a characteristically subordinate position. The extended exogamy of Gê villages implies that these affines are at best only distantly related, suggesting that formal relations of dominance and submission will be more pronounced than in the familiar contexts of bride-service among Caribs, Yanoama, or Jívaroans. As each married male will uphold close ties with his natal household across the plaza, pairs of affinal households will tend to maintain enduring bonds. There is often an explicit preference for unions which reinforce such bonds, whether expressed as marriage with women of the household of one's MB or of that of one's FZ. Owing to the size of these households, the distinction between MBD and FZD, and the preference for one of these, will not contradict the practice of repeated intermarriage between households or domestic groups. The result is a number of endogamous enclaves superimposed on the exogamic dichotomy codified in the village layout. Such endogamous strata are a prerequisite for hierarchy in symmetric alliance systems.

The ambiguity concerning the social affiliation of males represents a constant tension in uxorilocal societies. Here, too, is a crucial junction at which separate structural trajectories originate. We have seen that the Eastern Timbira and Bororo have yielded most consistently to matrilateral affiliation. A larger number of societies, however, have counterbalanced uxorilocality by emphasizing patrilateral affiliation. These include the Kayapó, Sherente, Karajá, Tapirapé, Cashinahua, and Sanumá.

Uxorilocal societies with elements of matrilateral male affiliation tend to make Crow-type equations such as MBD = D and FZD = FZ, whereas those with an emphasis on patrilateral affiliation may have Omaha equations such as MBD = M and FZD = ZD. Tribes such as the Txicáo, Sirionó, and Trio illustrate that his is a regularity not exclusively confined to the Gê. In consonance with the terminological differences, ZD marriage is commonplace in the latter category, but in the former is reported only for the Warao, who also lack the Crow cousin terms. Inversely, FZ marriage occurs in at least two cases in the former category, whereas in the latter it would only have occurred among the deculturated Aweikoma-Caingang, who also lack Omaha cousin terms.

Uxorilocal societies with matrilateral affiliation of males are notably peaceful in their relations with other groups, whereas those with an emphasis on patrilateral affiliation are decidedly more aggressive. Apparently, matrilateral affiliation counteracts the build-up of patrilateral loyalties which would be conducive to factionalism and feuding. Where patrilateral affiliation is emphasized, these forces are set free. The wish to consolidate patrilateral loyalties has stimulated strategic virilocality in certain dominant households of uxorilocal tribes such as the Suyá, Shavante, Mundurucú, Tupinambá, Sharanahua, and Trio. At least among the Mundurucú and Tupinambá, this has been associated with privileged polygyny. Finally, we have reasons to believe that predominantly virilocal Pano- and Tupí-speaking groups such as the Mayoruna, Amahuaca, Parintintin, Tupí-Cawahíb, and Guaraní may have been uxorilocal in the past. Several of these tribes appear to have increasingly chosen bride-capture instead of bride-service.

Let us reconsider the evidence. Ambilocal and unambiguously virilocal groups each have fairly straightforward ways of approaching the problem of reciprocity. The former tend to conceive of marriage exchange as an internal affair, involving a minimum of risk. Hence the ephemeral and egocentric nature of the kin-affine division in cognatic, Dravidian systems. As bride-service is generally an obligation between close kinsmen, it is not very deterring. Virilocal groups, on the other hand, recognize alliance as an external exchange and resort to various strategies for handling it profitably. Exogamous, patrilineal descent is logically concomitant to viewing marriage exchange as external to the virilocal group.

The differences between various kinds of uxorilocal societies appear to be associated with their conceptions of endogamy and exogamy. I believe that at least five different permutations of uxorilocality can be discerned. First, there are the endogamous groups typical of Guiana (Rivière 1984), which present a continuum ranging from almost undifferentiated ambilocality to an ever greater emphasis on uxorilocal bride-service. As long as marriage is conceived of as an essentially internal process, the cognatic, Dravidian ideology is maintained. The Gê, on the other hand, follow the Tukanoans in viewing marriage as external, yet retain uxorilocality. The Dravidian terminology has been replaced with exogamous marriage preferences and unilineal moieties. Kin and affines are conceptually and spatially distinguished, yet dual organization and male ceremonialism guarantees their tight articulation (cf. Turner 1979a; Rivière 1984:97). The conceptual integration of kin and affines in Dravidian systems has been replaced with an emphasis on their spatial contiguity, but their delineation as enduring, sociocentric units requires unilineality. The Gê illustrate that this combination of uxorilocality

and exogamy works with integrative, male ceremonialism based on either matrilateral (Bororo, Eastern Timbira) or patrilateral (Central Gê, Kayapó, Karajá) affiliation.

By drawing together affines in large villages, the combination of uxorilocality and exogamy is self-reinforcing. The abandonment of sister exchange is associated with the application of distinct affinal terms, yielding an Iroquois relationship terminology. As there is no longer any behavioural foundation for the automatic equation of cross-cousins and affines, the matrilateral and patrilateral cross-cousins may be distinguished from each other on the basis of household affiliation or succession to ceremonial roles, producing Crow-Omaha equations.

We have seen that the combination of uxorilocality and exogamy provides a setting conducive to the development of both exogamous moieties and Crow-Omaha kin terminologies. On the other hand, we have found instances of dual organization (Sharanahua, Cashinahua) and Crow-type relationship terms (Txicáo, Sirionó) where uxorilocality combines with close endogamy rather than exogamy. In addition to the endogamous uxorilocality of Guiana and the two variants (matrilateral and patrilateral) of exogamous uxorilocality among the Gê, these two categories form our fourth and fifth permutations along the uxorilocal trajectory. Both are interesting in that they have already struck us as anomalous and contradictory, each in its own way. Along with the Parintintin and Mayoruna, the Sharanahua and Cashinahua are unique in combining exogamous patrimoieties and a Dravidian terminology, whereas the Txicáo and Sirionó are the only lowland South American peoples suggesting prescriptive, asymmetric alliance. I believe that both these trajectories may be the result of demographically enforced endogamy. In other words, I suggest that both originated in a previous context of exogamy akin to that of the Gê. The Panoan marriage sections may be an accommodation to the contradictory status of FZ in a context where residual patrimoiety exogamy is articulated with a revitalized Dravidian terminology (cf. Conclusions: Pano). The Txicáo and Sirionó, on the other hand, suggest regression to the kind of conditions which the Northern Gê (possibly with the exception of the Suyá) at some time seem to have left behind, i.e. somewhat smaller local groups and a high proportion of marriages with the actual MBD.

Having committed ourselves to the hypothesis that dual organization tends to develop in uxorilocal societies, it is gratifying to note that the few moiety systems in our sample which are *not* straightforwardly uxorilocal (Mayoruna, Parintintin) all appear to have been uxorilocal in the past.

Let us reiterate this necessarily panoramic exposition in typological terms. Before we venture further, however, two cautions are apposite. In the first place, we cannot assume that empirical instances ever agree entirely with the ideal types envisaged in these speculations. Specific groups may hover at any point along a continuum, and it is conceivable that they may oscillate back and forth along reversible trajectories. Far from a model of unilineal evolution, the argument here deals only with structural possibilities. In the second place, our typology of theoretical "stages" correlates only vaguely with the classification of linguistic families. As can be seen in Fig. 13, much of the variation within a single linguistic family can be comprehended against the background provided by these conceivable "stages".

We have isolated eight different "permutations" along the ramified trajectories of transformation precipitated by supra-local alliance and the shift to a sociocentric conception of exogamy. These are illustrated in Fig. 13.

If our argument hinges on varying ideals and practices relating to the social definition of "affines", we can only hint at the kind of factors which may have generated this variation. A single group may apply various conceptions of the kin-affine dichotomy at various ranges of social distance (Århem 1981: 147–152; Rivière 1984:104–106), illustrating that these different models of "affinity" spring from a common conceptual source, much as the various phenotypic responses of a single genotype. Regional variation in emphasis on particular models (egocentric "alliance endogamy" versus sociocentric, unilineal exogamy) may reflect differences in demographic and political conditions. Local group endogamy and introversion is expectable in connection with very low population densities or with threatening political surroundings which cannot be effectively controlled by means of inter-group alliances. The Tukano-speakers, on the other hand, stress local exogamy and the expansion of political alliances. Political aspirations and strategies will differ in relation to the nature of supra-local interaction. In the north-west Amazon, virilocality, polygyny, and bride-capture may serve as instruments for political expansion, whereas a Guiana headman can augment his status only through mediation, i.e. by managing to keep the local group from segmenting (Rivière 1984:73-75). For the Tukano, the crucial matter is control over women and agnates, whereas for a Guiana headman, it is control over affines. Thus, Tukano-speakers can classify their relatives in an exclusive, unilineal fashion, whereas kin-affine polarities in Guiana have to be reconciled and finally denied. Alliance, residence, and ideology all form a coherent whole. Although it is beyond the scope of this book, which seeks to chart the cultural permutations rather than explain them, it would probably be worthwhile to investigate how different conceptions of the kin-affine dichotomy correlate with varying experiences of European encroachment and indigenous warfare. If the combination of generalized reciprocity and uxorilocal bride-service is feasible only within a restricted social range (Århem 1981:149,163,177; Rivière 1984:105-108), it is possible that the difference between more or less uxorilocal Guiana Caribs and virilocal Tukanoans

AMBILOCAL
Small local groups
Egalitarian
Unaggressive
Bilateral cross-
    cousin marriage
Avuncular marriage
Bilateral affiliation
Ex.: Nambikwara
        Yanomam

ENDOGAMOUS/UXORILOCAL 1
(Bride-service of
varying duration)
Ex.: Pemon
        Waiwai

VIRILOCAL 1
Small local groups
Hierarchy/privileged
polygyny
Aggressive/bride-capture
Bilateral cross-cousin
marriage
Avuncular marriage
Patrilineal descent
Ex.: Tukano
        Yanomamö

EXOGAMOUS/UXORILOCAL
Large local groups
Hierarchy
Unilateral cross-
    cousin marriage
Extended exogamy
Dual organization
Parallel affiliation

MATRILATERAL MALE
AFFILIATION
Unaggressive
FZ marriage

Crow equations
Ex.: Bororo
        Eastern Timbira

PATRILATERAL MALE
AFFILIATION
Aggressive
Avuncular marriage
Privileged virilocality
Privileged polygyny
Omaha equations
Ex.: Sherente
        Kayapó

ENDOGAMOUS/UXORILOCAL 2
Formerly exogamous

Matrilateral cross-
cousin marriage

Parallel affiliation
Crow equations

Ex.: Txicáo
        Sirionó

ENDOGAMOUS/UXORILOCAL 3
Formerly exogamous
Small local grups
Egalitarian
Bilateral cross-
cousin marriage
Dual organization
Parallel affiliation
Alternate generation
marriage
Ex.: Sharanahua
        Cashinahua

VIRILOCAL 2
Formerly uxorilocal
Dual organization
Ex.: Mayoruna
        Parintintin

Fig. 13 Trajectories of transformation precipitated by supra-local alliance

reflects a difference in the degree to which supra-local, indigenous exchange networks have been atomized into locally endogamous groups.

If our characterization of the "ideal types" in Fig. 13 is justified, Table 51 should permit us to demonstrate additional correlations between the relevant aspects of social organization. In fact, of the nine ambilocal societies in our sample, all recognize bilateral affiliation, all practice bilateral cross-cousin marriage, and none have indications of rank endogamy. All but one of these nine have bifurcate merging (Dravidian or Iroquois) cousin terms, and six have local groups averaging less than 50 people. We may also note that 13 of the 15 virilocal societies in our sample have been characteristically aggressive in their external relations, whereas seven of the eight societies classified as peaceful feature uxori-local residence. Of the 21 cultures said to have large or formerly large local groups, two-thirds are uxorilocal.

The ethnographic information compiled in Table 51 reveals a number of additional correlations. Where relevant, but without pretending to exhaust the data, we shall discuss some of these in subsequent chapters as we summarize our main theoretical conclusions. If the purpose of the present chapter was to sketch the more tangible aspects of socio-structural transformations in lowland South America, our primary concern henceforth will be with the cosmological correlates (or, if you will, vehicles) of these transformations.

Part IV
Theoretical Conclusions: Structural Congruities in Social Classification

"Structuralists, in general, see comparison to be possible only in terms of fairly abstract notions of formal relations. 'Culturological' or 'symbolic' approaches tend to entail interpretive schemata that are intended as specific to one society. Insights gained from these kinds of studies must now be formulated in terms appropriate to focused and specific comparative research."

   – J. Shapiro (1984:13)

This comparative and analytical inquiry has doubtless raised more questions of a theoretical nature than can be answered at this point. We shall, however, summarize our position with respect to several classical issues in South American ethnography. Topic by topic, we shall discuss features such as bilateral, bilineal, parallel, and unilateral affiliation; alternating generations; lineal Crow-Omaha kin equations; unilateral and oblique marriage preferences; generational (Hawaiian) cousin terms; the relation between two-line kin terminologies, dual organization, and symmetric alliance; and the conceptual and structural foundations of social hierarchy. Each section contains a condensed review of anthropological debate on the subject, focused wherever possible on its application to South America. Finally, we shall return to the relation between code and behaviour in social organization, and to the locus of social structure.

Chapter 14
Bilateral, Bilineal, and Parallel Affiliation

"It is conceivable that the idea of sex affiliation might be a very primitive one, preceding the idea of rigid descent in either one line or the other."
  – F.E. Williams (1932:81)
  "A world view different for each sex seems far more usual in primitive societies than a moiety system."
  – J. Siskind (1973:199,note3)

We have employed the concept of "affiliation" so as to encompass all kinds of socially recognized ties by which individuals succeed to the identities of members of previous generations. Concepts such as "succession" to social roles or "transmission" of statuses would have done just as well. Under this topic, we have discussed such diverse phenomena as post-marital residence, name transmission, succession to ceremonial roles, inheritance, ideologies of procreation, and recruitment to named groups. These phenomena reflect fundamental concepts concerning the nature of continuity in human society. Needham (1971c:10) distinguishes six "elementary modes of descent" (patrilineal, matrilineal, bilineal, alternating, parallel, and cognatic, i.e. bilateral), but points out that a particular society may apply separate principles to different aspects of behaviour. Instead of arranging societies according to typologies (cf. Murdock 1949: 226–257), we should thus approach each as a specific combination of principles patterning residence, succession, inheritance, and so on (cf. Schneider 1965:73,78; Scheffler 1971:253–254). In Table 51, the multiple values assigned to single societies under parameters IV and V illustrate that this is the

course we have chosen. In a number of cases, recourse to more detailed ethnographic information would doubtless have extended the number of detectable, co-existent principles.

Murdock's (1949:194) statistics suggest that, compared with other continents, indigenous South America shows a strong predominance of bilateral (as opposed to matrilineal, patrilineal, or double, i.e. bilineal) "descent". Out of an early sample of 21 South American societies, 14 were classified as bilateral. In a more recent, expanded sample (Murdock 1981:134), 55 out of a total of 81 are said to reckon "descent" bilaterally.

There appears to be widespread agreement, however, that "descent" is a concept best avoided in describing patterns of affiliation in South America (cf. e.g. Kaplan 1977:9; Murphy 1979; Rivière 1980:536–539). "Descent" tends to connote "descent groups", a mode of conceptualizing social continuity that is rare on this continent (but cf. Jackson 1975a on the north-west Amazon.) We have used "affiliation" as the more general concept, of which descent, like name transmission, is a special case. We have found that bilateral principles of affiliation (in the sense of a relatively low emphasis on unilateral ties) are predominant in 20 out of 48 societies in our South American sample.

It is difficult to say to what extent this bilaterality also involves bilineal principles (Murdock's "double descent"; cf. Lipkind 1948:186 on the Karajá.) If we view residence as the expression of a principle of affiliation, all societies combining unilocal post-marital residence with another, disharmonic mode of affiliation should qualify as bilineal. In our sample of 48, there are 14 instances of such disharmonic systems, all but one of which combine uxorilocal residence and patrilateral affiliation. Properly speaking, these societies generally reveal a pattern of affiliation that is more parallel than bilineal. Uxorilocal residence is a form of matrilateral affiliation which primarily involves the female sphere, whereas the patrilaterality of ceremonial relations mainly concerns males. There is evidently a widespread discrepancy between male and female modes of reckoning affiliation. Parallel affiliation has been reported in one form or another from 28 of the 48 societies in our sample.

Parallel Affiliation

Parallel affiliation was first described by Williams (1932) for the Koiari-speaking Idutu-bia of Papua. "Sex affiliation" here appeared in some contexts to complement a system of fundamentally patrilineal descent, and to codify a practice of cross-cousin marriage (ibid., 58,75–81). Williams found that the link between a girl and her mother expressed the expectation that the girl upon marriage would go to the virilocal group in which her mother was born, and marry a classificatory MBS. He suggests, finally, that "the idea of sex affiliation might be a very primitive one, preceding the idea of rigid descent in either one line or the other," and underlying "the system described as bilateral descent."

Parallel affiliation did not gain renown, however, until Nimuendajú (1939:31) attributed a system of "parallel descent" to the Apinayé. The so-called kiyé, in fact, were presented as exogamous descent groups founded on the principle of parallel affiliation. Maybury-Lewis (1960a) found Nimuendajú's account "anomalous" and suggested that he had misinterpreted the field data. The work of da Matta (1973,1979,1982),

carried out several decades later, has been marshalled in support of Maybury-Lewis' position (Maybury-Lewis 1979c:304). Yet, da Matta (1982:120,125) did recognize among the Apinayé a sociological identification, reflected in the kin terminology, "between genitor and son and between genetrix and daughter." Meanwhile, "parallel transmission" and "sex affiliation" have been attributed to an increasing number of South American cultures (e.g. Wagley & Galvao 1948:171; Maybury-Lewis 1967:303; Lave 1971:345, note 4, 1979:18; Turner 1971: 367; Scheffler & Lounsbury 1971: 179; Siskind 1973:199; Dietschy 1977; Lizot 1977:60; Kensinger 1977:235; W.Crocker 1977:272, 1979:247,1984; Zuidema 1967; Hickman & Stewart 1977:48-51; Belote & Belote 1977:107; Collins 1981:204–221; Whitten & Whitten 1984:196–197,219). Scheffler and Lounsbury (1971:179–190), in particular, insist that a principle of "parallel transmission of kin-class status" is apparent in the kin terminologies of several South American peoples, and point to other features of social organization among the Apinayé, Kayapó, Nambikwara, and Inca, which suggest an underlying "notion of an essential identity between same-sex parent and child." In the opinion of these authors, the characteristic principle of "cross transmission" among the Northern Gê, according to which male names should pass from MB to ZS and female names from FZ to BD, "might equally be a consequence of a posited essential identity of same-sex parent and child" (ibid., 188–189). Lévi-Strauss (1973c:110), too, attributes both the parallel affiliation of the Apinayé and the cross transmission of the Kayapó and Eastern Timbira to a common principle of sex affiliation.

In response to Scheffler and Lounsbury, Lave (1973) rejects their articulation of parallel and cross transmission. She notes that name transmission is fundamentally opposed to parenthood and even "kinship" (ibid.,315). For this reason, naming "can hardly be used as evidence of sociological correlates to the Lounsbury-Scheffler parallel transmission principle; rather the opposite, in fact." We submit that these opposed perspectives are compatible. The cross transmission of personal names codifies a regularity in social organization which can be described in terms both of sex affiliation and of the opposition of naming and parenthood. The first perspective takes as point of departure the articulation of uxorilocal residence and a recognized continuity of patrilineally related males. Occasional recognition of male patriliny has been implied among uxorilocal Northern Gê tribes such as the Ramkokamekra (W. Crocker 1977:266), Krĩkatí (Lave 1971:345,note 4; 1979:18), Apinayé (Nimuendajú 1939:29–31; da Matta 1982: 120, 125), Kayapó (Turner 1971:367–368; 1979:183), and Suyá (Seeger 1977:203). Whereas male name transmission is a recognition, or reflection, of the matrilineal continuity of uxorilocal households, female name transmission recognizes the dispersed lines of patrilineally related males. When name-receivers succeed to the status of their name-givers, they succeed to the position of adult, opposite-sex siblings of the fundamental female matrilines and male patrilines. To use a figure of speech, the lines of matrilineally related males and patrilineally related females are structural "shadows" of the system of parallel affiliation.

To account for Lave's point that name transmission among the Northern Gê belongs to the sphere of ceremonial activities, and is diametrically opposed to domestic relationships, we should consider how naming may be articulated with alliance. Northern Gê name transmission, in fact, is formally congruent with symmetric alliance. Lave (1979:20,21,31) notes that naming is ideally a reciprocal exchange between cross-sex siblings, as is bilateral cross-cousin marriage (cf. J. Shapiro 1985:3,6–7). Several terminological indications suggest that the Eastern Timbira tribes have codified a male preference for MBD marriage. Among the Suyá, this preference is explicit. In this context, the name-givers (male Ego's MB and female Ego's FZ) are prototypical affines, diametrically opposed to true "kin" (male Ego's F and female Ego's M). This structure, which in fact articulates cross-cousin marriage and parallel affiliation, is most consistently codified in Dravidian kin terminologies (cf. Dumont 1953a, 1957). If cross-cousin marriage preferences and parallel affiliation have been fundamental to the Northern Gê, name-giving may represent a codification of these principles which can be seen as an alternative to, or permutation of, Dravidian terminologies. The connection between name transmission and marriage arrangements seems fundamental and pervasive (cf. the Sherente). By naming it, a Kagwahiv brother explicitly claims his sister's child for betrothal to his own (Kracke 1984:107–108,113).

It is significant that Dumont (1957:29,33) discovered a systematic connection between South Indian Dravidian systems and the ceremonial role of the maternal uncle. His observation that ceremonial gifts and functions are "essentially affinal" and "the most conspicuous feature of alliance as an enduring marriage institution" agrees well with the fundamental opposition between parents and name-givers among the Krĩkatí. The strong element of succession inherent in the transmission of names and associated ceremonial roles does not contradict the affinal nature of the avuncular relationship. Owing to uxorilocal residence, male Ego would succeed his MB both as brother vis-à-vis the female matriline of his natal household, and as head of his post-marital household. We have seen that the kin terminology of the Carib-speaking Txicáo most consistently codifies the implications of a combination of uxorilocal residence and MBD marriage. Among the Kagwahiv, naming and adoption into avunculocal residence similarly combines with cross-cousin marriage as a culturally standardized mode of succession (Kracke 1984:113). Affinity and succession would be one, and it is obvious that a concept of matrilineal "descent" would only confuse the matter (but cf. de Heusch 1981:61, on identical conditions among the Bemba of Zambia.)

It appears that parallel affiliation in combination with different ideals pertaining to exogamy or endogamy may generate inclinations toward either form of unilateral cross-cousin marriage. Scheffler and Lounsbury (1971:175) suggest that parallel transmission among the Sirionó would have been conducive to matrilateral cross-cousin marriage, and a similar interpretation has here been advanced for the Txicáo. If endogamy rather than exogamy were emphasized, we should expect a duplication of the Papuan preference for the patrilateral cross-cousin, as among the Karajá, Bororo, and Sherente. Alternatively phrased structural connections between sex affiliation and patrilateral cross-cousin marriage have been recognized by Lévi-Strauss (1973c:110–111) and de Heusch (1981:65–67, 75–76).

We have suggested (cf. the Kalapalo and the Piaroa) that parallel affiliation is immanent in Dravidian kin terminologies, where, from the point of view of each sex, the kin-affine division is focused on the opposition of two same-sex lines (patrilines of men for male Ego, matrilines of women for female Ego; cf. Henley 1982:96). Another way of looking at this is to say, in Emeneau's words, that no man may marry any woman who is related to him "through a wholly male line or through a wholly female line" (Trautmann 1981:78). The articulation of parallel affiliation and Dravidian kin terms is evident among groups such as the Nambikwara, Waiwai, Kalapalo, Yanomamö, Piaroa, and Jívaro. If the two features are congruent, the principle of parallel affiliation nevertheless persists in a wide range of societies, the kin terminologies of which have diverged considerably from the Dravidian pattern (e.g. most of the Gê and Tupí.) We submit that the structural congruity of these two features, both of which are peculiarly characteristic of South America (cf. Scheffler & Lounsbury 1971:179–190; Rivière 1973), is not fortuitous. Parallel affiliation appears to be a recodification, phrased in genealogical terms, of regularities inherent in the alliance-focused, Dravidian mode of classification. This mode of affiliation, moreover, has achieved its most tangible manifestations in societies combining uxorilocal residence and a ceremonial life emphasizing the patrilateral succession of males.

Chapter 15
Unilateral Affiliation

"Unilineally phrased ideologies, it seems to me, are often devices for legitimating closure and cognatically phrased ideologies devices for legitimating openness of groups or access to their resources."
– H.W. Scheffler (1966:550)

Whereas both bilateral and parallel principles of affiliation represent sexual symmetry and equilibrium, a unilateral reckoning of affiliation by both sexes suggests a kind of cosmological imbalance. A unilateral inclination implies that one of the sexes would abandon its own perspective, so to speak, in favour of a reification of the bias of the other.

Murdock (1949:59) claims that his statistics "fully validate" the hypothesis, propounded by Lowie and Linton, that rules of post-marital residence can be instrumental in establishing unilineal "descent". Unilocal residence may give rise to clans, defined as integrated, localized cores of "unilinearly related adults of one sex together with their spouses and children" (ibid., 68, 75), and "lineages and sibs invariably arise out of clans by the extension of the recognition of unilinear affiliation from the sex which forms the core of the clan to their siblings of opposite sex who have moved away in marriage" (ibid., 74). Murdock asserts that there is overwhelming evidence for "the nearly universal derivation of lineages and sibs from clans, and of clans from unilocal extended families and exogamous demes" (ibid., 78).

When applied to South America, of course, Murdock's argument is impaired by his preoccupation with "descent groups" and "kin groups" of various kinds. Unilinearly constituted, named groups occur in only 27 of the 48 societies in our sample. In 23 of these, male Ego succeeds his F or FF, while in the remaining four (Krahó, Ramkokamekra,

Krîkatí, Bororo), he succeeds his MB. Rarely do these groups enrol members of both sexes, and even more rarely are they exogamous (cf. ibid., 47–48). We have suggested that the classification of people in terms of descent groups is only one of a number of possible ways of expressing affiliation. Consequently, descent groups should not *per se* be reified into socio-structural objects of analysis. Instead, our emphasis should be on the abstract principles of affiliation of which descent groups are merely sporadic expressions. Once this qualification has been established, we are ready to concede that unilocal residence is a likely point of origin for various, less tangible codifications of unilateral affiliation. The hypothesis gains support, for instance, from the correlation between virilocality and patrilateral affiliation. Of the 23 societies in our sample which are predominantly virilocal or express a strong male ideal of virilocal residence, as many as 19 have been credited with other forms of patrilateral affiliation.

If unilateral slants in the reckoning of affiliation originate in unilocal residence, the symmetry of bilateral and/or parallel affiliation would be jeopardized in connection with the abandonment of local group endogamy. It is at this point, whether related to demography or processes of politico-economic integration, that a structural "choice" would have to be made between viri-, uxori-, or ambilocality. The different trajectories which these alternatives may engender have been discussed in Chapter 13. Although recent centuries have surely seen the transformation widely reversed, it is probable that endogamous, alliance-organized local groups with Dravidian terminologies have often yielded historically to networks of intermarrying communities recognizing dispersed lines of affiliation. Conditions favouring unilateral affiliation would include an inclination toward kindred or local group exogamy, providing incentives to extended genealogical reckoning. It is noteworthy that, out of the 27 societies in our sample which recognize named unilineal groups, frequent external interaction has been attributed to as many as 24, whether through feuding, trade, or some measure of political integration. Out of nine societies prohibiting marriage to any first-degree cousins, seven recognize named unilineal groups.

The distinction between parallel and cross-collaterals is congruent with unilateral modes of affiliation such as unilineal descent. It is, however, equally congruent with symmetric alliance, irrespective of the mode of affiliation (cf. Dumont 1953a; Kaplan 1972,1973, 1975.) We may conclude that this feature of kin classification may arise in altogether cognatic, symmetric alliance systems, but that under certain conditions it may in turn be conducive to unilateral affiliation, even to the recognition of unilineal descent groups (cf. Århem 1981). The zero-generation cross/parallel distinction, which in Dravidian systems expresses a transient, egocentric kin-affine dichotomy, provides a cognitive stepping stone to more permanent, sociocentric delineations. Alliance theorists (cf. particularly Leach 1961a) have demonstrated that unilineal descent itself is an inevitable by-product of the classification of relatives into enduring categories of kin versus affines. It is a cultural illusion requiring the renunciation of consanguinity vis-à-vis one of Ego's parents and one half of his or her social universe. In Chapter 13, we suggested that this reinterpretation of marriage, as "external" rather than "internal", is more likely to appear in connection with higher frequencies of locally exogamous unions. Dual organization, however, represents a cohesive reaction to the combination of exogamy and uxorilocal residence. Thus, whereas Gê moieties and Tukano patrisibs reflect a similar conception of marriage and affi-

nity, the patterns of post-marital residence produce two very different kinds of society.

Another terminological feature which has been interpreted as a reflection of unilineal principles is the distinction between different kinds of grandkin. This feature, however, need not be more diagnostic of unilateral affiliation than the cross/parallel distinction in the three medial generations. Trautmann (1981:188–193) has shown how a dichotomy of grandkin may simply represent the logical extension of the egocentric cross/parallel polarity geared to symmetric alliance. Precisely as the Dravidian opposition F/M versus MB/FZ must be distinguished from the patrilineal polarity F/FZ versus MB/M (cf. W. Shapiro 1970:384–385; Trautmann 1981:176), Trautmann (1981:191) distinguishes between the patrilateral/matrilateral dichotomy FF/FM versus MF/MM and the cross/parallel distinction FF/MM versus MF/FM. The latter polarity is the grandkin classification most likely to be encountered in cognatic, Dravidian systems, and is in our sample often reflected in ideals relating to alternate generation name transmission from FF to SS and from MM to DD. Although the ethnography rarely permits us to establish whether this is indeed the semantic essence of grandkin distinctions (but cf. Henley 1982:98), we might observe that where such distinctions occur, they need not contradict a fundamentally cognatic conception of kinship. On the other hand, if the extension of cross/parallel distinctions to grandkin is geared to alternate generation marriage (ibid.), which in turn may be an accommodation to the contradictory status of FZ in societies combining patrilateral affiliation and close endogamy (cf. Pano: Conclusions), the dichotomy of grandkin would be indirectly associated with an emergent unilineality. By retaining internal divisions rather than denying them, the terminological recognition of grandkin dichotomies seems less immediately congruent, though not incompatible, with cognatic, Dravidian systems.

Chapter 16
Alternating Generations

"We may even risk the evolutionary surmise that alternating generations are more primitive than a continuous flow of generations."
   – L. Dumont (1966:238)

It has long been recognized that the various types of "section" system of Australia may be associated with bilineal affiliation (e.g., Lawrence 1937), generally a combination of virilocal residence ("patriclans") and implicit, usually unnamed, exogamous matrimoieties (Murdock 1949:51–56). The identification of Ego with specific members of the second ascending generation is congruent with the cyclical merging of patrilineal and matrilineal categories in symmetric alliance systems. Lévi-Strauss (1969:219; 1973c:110–111) shows that alternating generations may also be associated with consistent patrilateral cross-cousin marriage, illustrating a "phenomenon of convergence" in social transformation (but cf. Korn 1973:117–121, 141, for an empirically based objection.)

Dumont (1966) doubts that systems of alternating generations in Australia should be reduced to bilineal affiliation. He claims (ibid., 249, note 5) that Australians nowhere explicitly recognize a *double* set of moieties. Citing Josselin de Jong, Layard, and Lane, Dumont suggests that the unnamed, "implicit" moieties are structural epiphenomena generated by symmetric alliance, and asks why such epiphenomena should be considered essential to the theory of alternation (ibid., 235; cf. Fox 1967:190-194). Apparently, we are dealing with two congruent, emic conceptualizations of symmetric alliance. Rather than referring to bilineality as an explanation, we should simply note that it represents an alternative interpretation of structural regularities generated by symmetric alliance. As such, the bilineal model is congruent with alternating generations but not necessarily its foundation. Dumont even speculates that the phenomenon of circular (as distinct from lineal) genealogical time is primordial (1966:238–239). Korn (1973:111, 121–123) similarly demonstrates that bilineal affiliation is not universally associated with alternating generations. In fact, nor are "marriage sections," which to Dumont (1966:249) were "the real agent" of alternation. Trautmann (1981:197–199) finds that an extension of the cross/parallel distinction to the second ascending and descending generations, as occurs in some Dravidian systems, may reflect the permissibility of alternate generation marriages. Adjacent and alternate generation marriages seem to represent alternative, mutually exclusive means of expanding the number of genealogically close, potential spouses in Dravidian systems (ibid., 207, 235–236; Henley 1982:94–95,104). Marriage with a male Ego's own DD would be the result of an exchange of daughters between that man and his DH (Henley 1982:117–118; J.-P. Dumont 1978:83). Trautmann (1981:237, 436–437) remarks that Dravidian systems accommodating marriage between alternate generations are structurally indistinguishable from the Kariera-type systems of Australia: "all that is missing" is the sociocentric, Kariera marriage classes.

Murdock (1949:56) asserts that "true bilinear kin groups or sections have never been reported outside of Australia and a limited area in Melanesia." The Gê tribes of Brazil, he continues, "despite occasional allegations to the contrary . . . bear no relationship to those of Australia." It is certainly true that alternating generations among the Gê are not "marriage classes" in the explicit sense reported from Australia. Yet, alternation among the Gê, as expressed in kin terminologies and modes of name transmission, does appear to be associated with the cyclical merging of completementary lines of affiliation. We would agree with Lévi-Strauss' (1973c:109) suggestion that "alternate generations and sex affiliation seem structurally linked" among the Gê. Even if affiliation is overtly parallel rather than bilineal, Northern Gê name transmission illustrates that opposite-sex continuities (male Ego's sister's matriline or female Ego's brother's patriline) are also recognized at some level. We have found that male patrilines tend to oscillate between affinally related uxorilocal households among the Gê, so that alternate generations of patrilineally related men will be associated with opposite sides of the village plaza, while alternate generations of matrilineally related women will marry men of opposite patrilines. Out of 22 societies in our sample which show evidence of alternation (two-generation cycles), parallel affiliation has been attributed to 15. This supports the contention that alternating generations and parallel affiliation may be "structurally linked".

If we consider the Pano-speaking tribes, Murdock's denial of marriage classes outside of Australia and Melanesia can be decisively refuted. Among the Mayoruna, Sharanuahua, and Cashinuahua, the articulation of uxorilocal residence and exogamous patrilineal moieties provides a matrix for their four-section systems of named marriage classes. We have suggested that Panoan marriage classes represent an accommodation to the contradictory status of FZ as both consanguine (according to the patrimoiety model) and affine (according to the Dravidian terminology) in strongly endogamous societies featuring dual organization. The Kariera-type marriage classes circumvent the requirements on consistent,

sociocentric dualism by recognizing the kin-affine dichotomy in alternate generations only. Such systems of alternating generations thus seem half-way between cognatic "alliance endogamy" and unilineal descent.

In conclusion, the alternation evident in Gê name transmission and in the four-section systems of the Pano-speakers appears to be associated with the cyclical merging of disharmonic (or parallel) principles of affiliation. The other structural foundation envisaged by Lévi-Strauss, i.e. patrilateral cross-cousin marriage, may be a secondary codification of the same arrangement. In Chapter 14, we noted that an emphasis on endogamy would establish a connection between patrilateral cross-cousin marriage and the principle of parallel transmission itself. Preferential marriage with a FZD has been indicated for the Gê-speaking Apinayé, Sherente, Shavante, Bororo, and Karajá, and for the Pano-speaking Amahuaca and Sharanahua. The combination of an emergent alternation and patrilateral cross-cousin marriage is also evident among Tukano- and Arawak-speaking tribes such as the Barasana, Bará, and Machiguenga.

The mode of affiliation which Needham (1971c:10) and Maybury-Lewis (1960a:191) call "alternating", and of which the "ropes" attributed by Mead to the Mundugumor of New Guinea are the classical example (cf. Lévi-Strauss 1973c:88), implies that boys in some sense succeed their mothers, whereas girls follow their fathers. In our South American sample, similarly inverted principles of sex affiliation have been reported from the Cuiva, where they appear to produce four-generation cycles.

The kin terminologies of the Mundurucú, Yanomam, and Piaroa, finally, appear to express three-generation cycles. It is difficult to see any structural foundation for these cycles common to all three tribes. For instance, whereas the Mundurucú equate male Ego and his FFF, the Yanomam classify FFF as a zero generation affine.

Chapter 17
Lineal Equations

"It would . . . form an intriguing investigation, on the part of someone better versed in South American ethnography than I, to reconstruct the possible course of historical and structural development by which Sirionó society has reached its present form. The lineal terminology equations might seem to make a two-section derivation unlikely, but there do exist two-section systems with limited lineal equations (e.g. the Nambikwara of the Mato Grosso, to the north of the Sirionó . . .), though not of 'Omaha' or 'Crow' type; so that the Sirionó equations . . . are not necessarily entirely inconsistent with an earlier symmetric system."

R. Needham (1961:253).

In an assumption derived from Kroeber, Murdock (1949:133) lists six "inherent distinctions" of fundamental significance in the classification of relatives beyond the nuclear family, plus three "subsidiary criteria". Dumont (1953a:39) demonstrates that Dravidian, two-line kin terminologies can be reduced to the recognition of three of these fundamental distinctions (generation, sex, affinity), plus Murdock's subsidiary criterion of relative age (cf. Trautmann 1981:230–231). Dumont (1953a:36) notes that in Dravidian systems, "the generations are as a rule absolutely distinguished; there is no assimilation of relatives belonging to different generations" (cf. Trautmann 1981: 233). Bearing in mind that two-line kin terminologies have been advanced as a "structural definition" of the lowland South American culture area (Rivière 1973), it should be important to investigate the significance of various lineal equations in our sample of terminologies. Having in the previous chapter discussed equations of relatives belonging

to alternate generations, we turn now to equations assimilating generations adjacent to each other.

In our sample of 48 lowland South American societies, 22 recognize consecutive, lineal equations among 18 fundamental genealogical positions. These 22 groups represent several linguistic families: Gê, Tupí, Carib, Yanoama, Witoto, and Bora/ Miraña. Figure 14 illustrates the fundamental types of lineal equation encountered in our sample, the number of connecting lines denoting the frequency with which they occur. Table 55 indicates which groups recognize specific equations, or inversely which equations are recognized by specific groups.

One of Murdock's (1949:52) "most definite conclusions" was that "kin groups are the primary determinants of both kinship terminology and marriage rules." In finding significant correlations between the occurrence of Crow- and Omaha-type kin equations and matrilineal and patrilineal kin groups, respectively (ibid., 166–168), he drew the conclusion that group membership was reflected in the terminology. Once again, we are prepared to accept his argument only if the concept of "kin groups" is replaced by less tangible principles of classification. We have already noted that Crow- and Omaha-type kin equations in our sample correlate with uxorilocality combined with matrilateral and patrilateral principles of affiliation, respectively. Of the seven societies in our sample which equate MBD = D, for instance, six combine uxorilocal residence with an emphasis on the matrilateral affiliation of males.

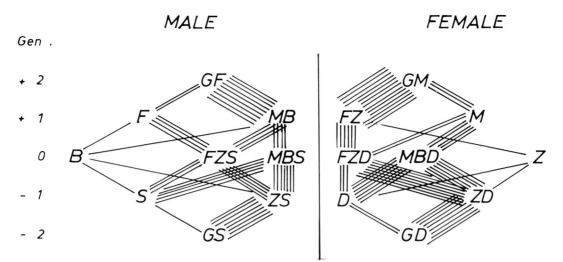

MALE   FEMALE

Fig. 14. Frequency of lineal equations in the sample.

Lineal Equations Not Involving Ego's Generation

Not all lineal equations reflect a recognition of lineal continuity, however. The most common lineal equations assimilate a general grandparent or grandchild category with cross-collaterals of the first ascending or descending generation, respectively. Since different kinds of grandparents or grandchildren are generally not distinguished, these equations tell us nothing about lineality. (Viz. if the implicit combination MF = MB and FM = FZ is not taken as a sign of parallel affiliation.) Instead, they allow us to conclude that kin-affine distinctions in the three medial generations tend to be neutralized in the second ascending and descending generations. By widening affinal categories, this should serve to obstruct a genealogical extension of exogamy. On the other hand, the Yanomamö, Sanumá, and Bororo equate grandparents with parents instead of uncles and aunts, and grandchildren with children instead of sister's children, which suggests extended exogamy and a more rigid codification of lineal principles. In the case of the Bororo, lineality may also underlie the distinction between different kinds of grandparents and grandchildren, a feature elsewhere reported only from the early Ramkokamekra and Apinayé, the Nambikwara, the Mundurucú, and the Pano-speaking Amahuaca, Mayoruna, Sharanahua, and Cashinahua (but cf. Chapter 15 for an alternative interpretation.)

Lévi-Strauss (1969:121) writes that "most of the kinship systems of South American tribes practicing cross-cousin marriage identify grandparents with parents-in-law, and that, from a "purely feminine perspective," this phenomenon is "easily explained by the practice of avuncular marriage." Although he appears to have overestimated the statistical occurrence of these identifications, Lévi-Strauss is correct in noting their congruity with oblique marriage. If FZ marriage is also considered, this congruity is no longer a matter merely of the feminine perspective. We would choose to say that the equation WP = PP, deriving from the strategy of expanding Ego's affinal categories, may be congruent and associated with oblique marriage, rather than the form of marriage simply "explaining" the terminology. The further

243

Table 55 column headers (left to right, each an equation):

1. GF = F
2. GF = MB
3. AG: GM = FZ
4. AG: GM = M
5. C: F = B
6. F = FZS
7. F = B
8. C: MB = B
9. O: MB = FZS
10. MB = MBS
11. C: FZ = FZS
12. O: FZ = FZD
13. FZ = Z
14. M = FZD
15. O: M = MBD
16. B = S
17. B = ZS
18. C: FZS = ZS
19. O: FZS = S
20. C: MBS = S
21. MBS = ZS
22. O: FZD = D
23. FZD = ZD
24. C: MBD = D
25. MBD = ZD
26. Z = D
27. Z = ZD
28. AG: S = GS
29. AG: ZS = GS
30. D = GD
31. AG: ZD = GD

		GF=F	GF=MB	AG: GM=FZ	AG: GM=M	C: F=B	F=FZS	F=B	C: MB=B	O: MB=FZS	MB=MBS	C: FZ=FZS	O: FZ=FZD	FZ=Z	M=FZD	O: M=MBD	B=S	B=ZS	C: FZS=ZS	O: FZS=S	C: MBS=S	MBS=ZS	O: FZD=D	FZD=ZD	C: MBD=D	MBD=ZD	Z=D	Z=ZD	AG: S=GS	AG: ZS=GS	D=GD	AG: ZD=GD
1.	Krahó	x		x				x					x				x							x							x	x
2.	Ramkoka-mekra	x		x				x					x				x							x							x	x
3.	Krîkatí	(x)		(x)				x					x				x							(x)							(x)	(x)
4.	Apinayé	x		x				x	x				x	x	x		x							x							x	x
5.	Kayapó	x		x					x				x				x					x		x							x	x
6.	Suyá	x		x							x					x	x					x		x							x	
7.	Shavante						x		x		x		x				x					x									x	
8.	Sherente						x	x			x	x				x						x									x	
10.	Bororo	x	x			x	x	x					x				x							x			x					
12.	Nambikwara						x		x	x														x							x	x
15.	Trio						x	x	x				x	x	x	x				x				x							x	
18.	Karinya						x		x	x														x							x	
19.	Barama R.C.						x		x	x														x							x	
21.	Waiwai	x		x						x				x					x					x							x	
22.	Txicáo	x		x	x			x					x		x	x					x	x		x							x	
24.	Mundurucú						x		x				x							x				x							x	
27.	Sirionó								x				x				x			x				x							x	x
36.	Yanomamö																										x				x	x	x
37.	Yanomam	x		x																						x				x	x	x
38.	Sanumá		x		x																					x				x		x
43.	Witoto																													x	x	
44.	Bora/Miraña																												x			

Table 55 Distribution of lineal equations in the sample. O = Crow, O = Omaha, AG = Affinal grandkin equations. (Where terminologies are incomplete, the list may be inexhaustive. Marks in brackets for the Krîkatí are assumptions based on comparative Timbira kinship.)

codification of oblique marriage in additional, lineal equations will be discussed shortly.

Discussing the equation of grandparents and parents-in-law among the Kuma, Scheffler (1971:250) admits having "no ready structural (that is, formal or sociological) explanation for this arrangement, but it seems obvious that it has nothing whatsoever to do with 'alliance systems' of any sort." Scheffler notes that these equations are inconsistent with an interpretation positing two corporate, exogamous sections. We have used the labels "two-section" and "two-line" system merely to characterize the fundamental properties of the kin terminology, not to suggest that its kin-affine division corresponds to recognizable social groups. In this usage, the equation of grandparents and parents-in-law is not incompatible with a "two-section" system. In fact, it may represent an important strategy for expanding Ego's affinal categories in groups such as the Nambikwara, Waiwai, Yanomam, Sirionó, and Trio, all of whom have kin terminologies based on the two-line pattern.

244

Lineal Equations Involving Ego's Generation

Within the three medial generations, most of the recurring lineal equations appear to express either matrilateral or patrilateral succession. The crucial parameter is the classification of cross-cousins in relation to adjacent generations, i.e. as either lineal or cross-collateral relatives. Even if particular societies appear to incline towards either Crow- or Omaha-type cousin equations, the Krīkatí, Apinayé, and Trio illustrate that both alternatives may co-exist in the same population (Lave 1979:22; da Matta 1973: 291; 1979:123; 1982:126–127,129). Once again we may conclude that it is wiser to deal with combinations and permutations of underlying principles than with typologies. We have seen that the combination of Crow and Omaha elements in Northern Gê name transmission may reflect principles of parallel affiliation. Crow-Omaha equations, although harbouring the potential of fully unilateral systems, may thus originate in symmetrical contexts.

Ten years after Murdock's (1949) statistical exercises, Lane and Lane (1959:258) suggested that "Crow-Omaha systems of terminology may be associated not only with matrilineal and patrilineal sibs respectively, but also with matrilateral cross-cousin marriage." Whereas Dakota-Iroquois systems seem "especially well adapted to regularized sister-exchange marriage" (ibid., 260), in Crow-Omaha systems such marriage would be precluded (ibid., 256-257). The hypothesis that Crow-Omaha systems reflect kin type alignments resulting from matrilateral cross-cousin marriage receives support from Eyde and Postal (1961), who believe that the feeble statistical correlation between the two features is due to the "self extinguishing" nature of matrilateral marriage (ibid.,756–757). Moore (1963), on the other hand, suggests that "either Crow or Omaha terms may be found in combination with

either asymmetrical marriage, depending upon the antecedent oblique marriage" (ibid.,307). Oblique marriages "illustrate a kind of sexual succession," suggesting "of which close relative (or relatives) in the generation above a young man or woman is the younger counterpart" (ibid.,299). If the older partner of an oblique marriage (or sexual relationship) is replaced by his or her same-sex child, matrilateral cross-cousin marriage would develop in societies permitting marriage or sexual relations between male Ego and his WBD or MBW, while patrilateral cross-cousin marriage would be associated with marriage or sexual relations with ZD or FZ (ibid.,304–305).

Moore seems to suggest, as we have done, that Crow-Omaha equations are associated with sex affiliation. She claims that differences between the sex-biased perspectives of male and female speakers are "the key to the concepts which underlie Crow-Omaha categories," i.e. the identification of "children of the linear sex . . . with the kinship position of the parent through whom linearity is traced," and of children of opposite sex with "the kinship position of the linear parent's sibling of opposite sex" (ibid., 307, 308). The identification of father and son in an Omaha context would allow MBD marriage to develop from WBD marriage, but also FZD marriage from ZD marriage. Inversely, the identification of mother and daughter in a Crow context would allow FZD marriage to develop from FZ marriage, but also MBD marriage from MBW marriage. In fact, the congruities recognized by Moore do not imply any necessary chronological relationship between the associated forms of oblique and asymmetric marriage (ibid., 309). It is equally conceivable that oblique marriages might develop secondarily within a system of preferential unilateral cross-cousin marriage. The structural connection between lineal equations and oblique marriage, finally, has also been suggested by Needham (1966a:27; 1972:24).

Lounsbury (1964a) contrasts his own "formal" or "structural" (ibid., 351, 387, note 2) account of Crow-Omaha systems with the "causal" (functional, historical, etc.) accounts of his predecessors. A "formal" account should show how terminological data are "the lawful and expectable consequences of an underlying principle that may be presumed to be at work at their source" (ibid., 351). Rejecting, as we have done, the notion that Crow-Omaha equations necessarily reflect the constitution of corporate unilineal descent groups (cf. Tax 1937:12–13; Radcliffe-Brown 1952:70–78; Murdock 1949:52, 166–168), Lounsbury (1964a: 383–386) nevertheless suggests that the "skewing rules" underlying Crow-Omaha extensions express laws of matrilineal or patrilineal succession. Indeed, if systems of social classification codify information on social structure, it is logical to assume that cross-generational equations should tell us something about its continuity over time.

Dole (1972:146–148) has found a correlation between Crow-Omaha kinship nomenclatures and exogamous unilineal kin groups. Echoing Lowie and White, she suggests that small, exogamous, unilocal groups with bilateral cross-cousin marriage and a bifurcate merging (Dakota-Iroquois) terminology have tended to develop into larger villages with unilineal kin group exogamy, frequent oblique marriage, and "cross generation" (Crow-Omaha) nomenclatures.

In sum, the numerous anthropologists who have struggled to account for lineal equations of the Crow-Omaha type have emphasized their congruity with specific forms of marriage and/or specific principles of affiliation. Some (e.g. Lane & Lane 1959; Eyde & Postal 1961) have followed Kohler, Rivers, Gifford, Seligman, and Lévi-Strauss in emphasizing marriage, while others (e.g. Murdock 1949; Lounsbury 1964; Dole 1972) have emulated Durkheim, Lowie, Tax, White, and Radcliffe-Brown in stressing principles of lineal affiliation. (For a brief survey of some of these positions, cf. Radcliffe-Brown 1952:

56–57.) Moore (1963:308), by discussing the identification of children with relatives of a higher generation as the "core" of both oblique marriages and Crow-Omaha kin equations, has come close to a synthesis of these two approaches. Her concept of "sexual succession" (ibid., 299) expresses the fact that alliance and affiliation may be inextricably linked.

Linel Equations and Descent

Unfortunately, even Moore professes that "Crow and Omaha terminology express relationships within lineage," and "the oblique and asymmetrical marriages can be seen as aspects of the rights of one lineage to the women of another" (ibid., 308). Moore here explicitly adopts the view of Lévi-Strauss, whose discussion (1969:xxxvi-xlii) of Crow-Omaha systems is phrased entirely in terms of corporate "lines" or "lineages". Lévi-Strauss claims, for instance, that "Crow-Omaha systems always have more than four lines, there being seven clans among the Cherokee; ten among the Omaha; thirteen among the Crow, and presumably more at one time; twelve phratries and about fifty clans among the Hopi; and thirty to forty clans among the Seniang." In the same vein, the Omaha equation WBD = MBD of the Miwok is explained in terms of a "collection of patrilineages, interconnected by a system of generalized exchange" (ibid., 368).

Similarly, in discussing the Crow-type lineal equations of what he perceives as the "two-section system" of Mota, in the Banks Islands, Needham (1960b:24) claims that lineal equations occur exclusively in lineal descent systems. In order to account for the lineal equations of the Sirionó, he suggests (Needham 1961:253) that "a possible development might be from a two-section system via exogamous moieties and internal differentiation of lines." In a more recent contribution, Needham (1971c:19) suggests that, "where we find lineal terminological equations, . . . we can be fairly confident that we shall find in the sphere of institutions some explicit expression of a mode of descent," but that "this can never be an absolute inference, . . . for there is no telling to what extent rights of other kinds may prove to be transmitted by different modes . . ." Echoing a recommendation made by Lowie as early as 1917, Needham (ibid.,16–17) suggests that we speak of principles of classification rather than of "types" of kinship system (cf. also Rivière 1980:537). Once this perspective is adopted, it will become clear that Crow-Omaha kin equations cannot be expected to reflect specific types of descent group.

In responding to an alternative interpretation of the "Mota problem" offered by Keesing, Needham (1964b) makes several concessions. He admits that he was mistaken in treating Mota society as a two-section system (ibid.,302), and even concludes that "Crow-Omaha lineal terminological equations are not found in two-section systems, and are in fact . . . inconsistent with symmetric alliance" (ibid., 312). Other kinds of lineal equation, he notes, may nevertheless occur in two-section systems. To exemplify, he specifically mentions the Nambikwara and the Trio. In Table 55, it can be seen that both these tribes do, in fact, make Crow-Omaha equations, but that a more fundamental similarity is the equation MBC = ZC, which in both groups appears to be geared to oblique (ZD) marriage.

In South America, Crow-Omaha kin equations are particularly prominent among Gê-speakers. Rivière (1980:537) notes that Gê concepts concerning the transmission of "social personae" (i.e. the succession to social roles) "throw new light, or shadow, on the whole vexed question of Crow-Omaha terminologies." Crow-Omaha equations among the Gê appear to reflect "matrilineal" and "patrilineal" principles of social succession, and Rivière asks, with da Matta, "if the Northern Gê do not in fact have unilineal

descent disguised as name transmission" (ibid., 538). However, da Matta (1979:127) argues that instead of a trans-generational continuum, the Northern Gê recognize only the duality between name-giver and name-receiver, i.e. the constituent fragments of a continuity attained through substitution. Rivière (1980:539) accepts this ethnographic distinction, but adds that the scheme of continuity reproduced by these peoples is "just as effective as unilineal descent" in achieving the succession of social personae "in orderly linear progression." A similar judgement, of course, could be made for the "inherited affinity" of alliance-organized, Dravidian systems such as that of the Piaroa. Marriage rules tend to reproduce, through substitution, pairs of theoretical "lines" articulated in alliance.

Transformations

In addition to so-called Crow-Omaha equations, we have noted that several other types of lineal equation occur in our sample (Fig. 14, Table 55). Of these, the assimilation of grandparents with uncles and aunts and of grandchildren with sister's children is more widespread than any equation of the Crow-Omaha type. Within the three medial generations, the equation MBC = ZC is just as common as the Crow-type equivalence MBC = C; the equation FZC = C, though rarer than the Omaha equation FZC = ZC, occurs in three different cultures; and the equation MB = FZS is encountered as frequently as the Omaha-type MB=MBS or the Crow-type F = FZS.

The equation of grandparents with uncles and aunts and of grandchildren with sister's children occurs in 14 and 9 societies respectively. In the case of the Yanomam, Ramos and Albert (1977:82–83) note that these equations have "the effect of equating all distant relatives with cross collaterals (affines)," which is "hardly compatible with any superordinate system of social categorization which might be based on extended genealogical lines." The expanded range of "potential affinal relationships" may thus provide the rationale for these equations among fundamentally cognatic, alliance-organized groups such as the ambilocal Nambikwara, Waiwai, and Yanomam, and the uxorilocal Txicáo, Sirionó, and Trio. The Northern Gê tribes which exhibit this type of equation (Krahó, Ramkokamekra, Apinayé, Kayapó, Suyá) do not recognize "extended genealogical lines" either, but their transmission of personal names from MB to ZS and from FZ to BD does produce lineal continuities in social succession. We have noted that the structural equivalence of FF and MB among the Northern Gê is consistent with matrilateral affiliation in a symmetric alliance system. It thus appears as if a codification originally geared to the expansion of affinal categories in alliance-organized societies may subsequently have provided leeway for matrilateral trajectories. Finally, the occurrence of these affinal grandkin equations among the Mundurucú and the Witoto, both of whom recognize patrilineal descent groups, remains to be explained. The former equate MM and FZ in a category distinct from FM, suggesting that membership in sibs or moieties is indeed the foundation for this classification. According to an early report, the Witoto previously equated grandparents with uncles and aunts, implying that their contemporary system of named patrilineages may be a recent derivation from a society organized fundamentally in terms of alliance.

If originally associated with the neutralization of consanguinity in alliance-organized societies, the widespread equation of grandparents with uncles and aunts and of grandchildren with sister's children in itself may be conducive to lineal equations within the three medial generations. Merely as a matter of logical consistency, the equation DC = ZC should imply that ZC = FZC (Omaha), and SC = ZC that C = FZC. Similarly, the equations M = MBD and MB = MBS (both Oma-

ha) can be generated from the equation MP = WP (i.e. MF = MB and MM = FZ), and the equations FZ = FZD, F = FZS, and C = MBC (all Crow) from FP = WP (i.e. FF = MB and FM = FZ). The assumption underlying these permutations is simply that the principles of succession implicit in one equation are applicable to all other, structurally equivalent relationships. Thus, if DC may be equivalent to ZC, the implicit patrilineal succession of D to the position of Z should apply also to the relationship between Z and FZ, and thus between ZC and FZC. If SC may be equivalent to ZC, the equation C = FZC is simply the result of raising the implicit relationship between a male and his FZ one generation. Similarly, if MB succeeds MF and FZ succeeds MM, the implication is that MBS/FZS succeeds MB, Z succeeds FZ, and MBD/FZD succeeds M. If MB succeeds FF and FZ succeeds FM, the implication is that MBS/FZS succeeds F, Z succeeds M, and MBD/FZD succeeds FZ. In this latter case, male Ego would succeed his MB, and his C would succeed MBC.

Since different kinds of grandparents and grandchildren are only rarely distinguished, the system of classification allows for increasing emphasis on either the patrilineal or matrilineal implications of the grandkin equations. The structural implications of lineal equations in the three medial generations are not exclusively related to lineal affiliation, however. For instance, the equations MB = FZS, M = FZD, FZS = S, and MBD = ZD carry no intrinsic implications for affiliation, and the equations MBS = ZS and FZD = D do so only if articulated with a rule of bilateral cross-cousin marriage. As has been proposed (e.g. for the Nambikwara, Mundurucú, Sirionó, and Trio), the frequency of these equations indicates that we are dealing with the codification of a feature other than affiliation, i.e. oblique marriage. The equations M = FZD, MB = FZS, and MBC = ZC are all congruent with ZD marriage, whereas the equation FZC = C suggests marriage with the FZ.

Correlations

Although our sample is of limited scale, it may be worthwhile to consider whatever correlations can be discovered between specific lineal equations and various features which have been offered as their foundation. In order to evaluate the interpretations of Crow-Omaha kin equations reviewed so far, the following conclusions appear to be particularly relevant:

1. Few of the lineal equations encountered in our sample can be said to be generally diagnostic of the existence of unilineal descent groups. In fact, the linguistic families in which descent groups are most prominent (i.e. Tukano, Pano) lack lineal equations altogether. However, equations which may be geared to descent groups include those of grandparents with parents and of grandchildren with children among the Yanomamö, Sanumá, and Bororo, that of MM = FZ among the Mundurucú, and that of F = B among the Bora/Miraña.

2. The following equations occur only in societies emphasizing matrilateral affiliation or, in the case of the Trio, uxorilocal residence: F = FZS (Crow), MB = B, FZ = FZD (Crow), B = ZS, MBS = S (Crow), MBD = D (Crow), and Z = ZD.

3. The following equations occur only in societies emphasizing patrilateral affiliation: F = B, MB = MBS (Omaha), M = MBD (Omaha), and FZS = ZS (Omaha).

4. Of the four societies in our sample which equate MB = FZS, at least two (Mundurucú, Trio) have been credited with ZD marriage. Of the two societies which equate M = FZD, ZD marriage has been attributed to at least one (Waiwai).

5. Of the seven societies in our sample which equate MBC = ZC, at least five (Nambikwara, Mundurucú, Trio, Karinya, Barama River Carib) have practiced ZD marriage. A sixth, the Sirionó, has been credited with MBD marriage, which will in fact be generated as a result of consistent ZD marriage. Moreover, the Sirionó not only retain an unusual number of equations suggestive of avuncular marriage, but also belong to a linguistic family (Tupí) in which ZD marriage has been particularly prominent. It is possible that the Sirionó, like the Mundurucú, have abandoned ZD marriage only recently (cf. W. Shapiro 1966: 83–85, note 4, 5; 1968), retaining the "MBD-FZS Spouse Equation Rule" (Scheffler & Lounsbury 1971) as one of its many structural vestiges. The Shavante, Nambikwara, Karinya, and Barama River Caribs equate both MBD and FZD with ZD, which simply amounts to an assimilation of zero generation and first descending generation, female affines in a two-line system. If the equation FZD = ZD is "focal", and MBD = ZD simply an "extension", this feature may derive from patrilineal principles of affiliation, such as have been attributed to the Shavante. In the case of the cognatic Nambikwara, Karinya, and Barama River Caribs, however, the codification of avuncular marriage appears to be primary, and the patrilineal implications of the Omaha equation FZD = ZD merely an epiphenomenon. This difference is further suggested by the fact that these three groups do not recognize, as do the Shavante, the corresponding Omaha equation FZS = ZS.

6. Of the three societies in our sample which equate FZC = C, FZ marriage has been attributed to at least one (Waiwai).

7. Of the 12 groups in our sample which recognize genuine Crow-Omaha equations, 10 appear to express unilateral cross-cousin marriage preferences. These unilateral inclinations are summarized in Table 56. Of the eight groups with Crow equations, five appear to incline towards MBD marriage and two towards FZD marriage. Of the seven groups with Omaha equations, two appear to favour MBD marriage and three FZD marriage.

Conclusions

In conclusion, we must begin by rejecting Murdock's conviction (implicit also in the

Culture	Type of lineal equations	Unilateral marriage preferences		Explicit preference
		Prescribed in terminology	Suggested, e.g. by terminology	
Trio	Crow-Omaha	MBD/FZD		
Sirionó	Crow	MBD		
Txicáo	Crow	MBD		
Krahó	Crow		MBD	
Ramkokamekra	Crow		MBD	
Krĩkatí	Crow-Omaha		MBD	
Suyá	Omaha			MBD
Kayapó	Omaha			?
Apinayé	Crow-Omaha			FZD
Shavante	Omaha			FZD
Sherente	Omaha			FZD
Bororo	Crow			FZD

Table 56 Correlation of Crow-Omaha kin equations and unilateral marriage preferences.

work of Lévi-Strauss, Needham, Moore, Dole, etc.) that corporate "kin groups" are the primary determinants of lineal kin equations. On the other hand, Crow-Omaha equations in lowland South America do appear to reflect underlying *concepts* (Lounsbury's "underlying principles") of matrilateral and patrilateral affiliation. As all instances of Crow-Omaha equations derive from uxorilocal societies, it seems that uxorilocal residence is conducive to the emergence of such unilateral principles, whether matrilateral or patrilateral (cf. Conclusions: Gê and Chapter 13).

Crow-Omaha equations can be generated from the assimilation of grandkin with first ascending and descending generation cross-collaterals, a feature associated with the strategy of expanding Ego's affinal categories in alliance-organized two-line systems. The partial abandonment of generation as a criterion for classification may also be associated with a greater emphasis on relative age, since, for instance, the lineal continuum of males denoted by the category MB = MBS or FZS = ZS is more usefully subdivided by age than by generation. Moreover, we have suggested that the co-existence of Crow and Omaha equations, as in Northern Gê name transmission, may reflect fundamentally

parallel concepts of affiliation, such as are also inherent in two-line kin terminologies.

Some suggestions made by Lane and Lane (1959), Eyde and Postal (1961), and Moore (1963) are supported by our data. The Txicáo illustrate the congruity between Crow kin alignments and matrilateral cross-cousin marriage. Marriage with the daughter of one's MB (i.e. of one's father's affine) is a fundamental preference even in two-line systems. The Txicáo, Sirionó, and Suyá all explicitly favour this type of marriage. The Krahó, Ramkokamekra, and Krĩkatí, on the other hand, may well be examples of the "self extinguishing" nature of MBD marriage in Crow contexts. Among these Eastern Timbira tribes, several terminological suggestions of MBD marriage are contradicted by a dislike for marriage to any first cousins. Among the Apinayé, Shavante, Sherente, and Bororo, the MBD preference has become inverted in favour of cross-cousins *other* than the MBD, yielding a tendency towards FZD marriage.

Moore's suggestion that unilateral cross-cousin preferences may be associated with specific combinations of oblique marriage patterns and principles of affiliation articulates the hypotheses of Lane and Lane and of Eyde and Postal with those of Kohler, Ri-

Affiliation	Marriage: Oblique	Asymmetric	South American approximations
Matrilateral for females	MBW	MBD	Txicáo
Matrilateral for females	FZ	FZD	Bororo
Patrilateral for males	WBD	MBD	Suyá
Patrilateral for males	ZD	FZD	Sherente

Table 57 Four configurations of affiliation and alliance envisaged by S.F. Moore (1963).

vers, Gifford, and Seligman. Whereas Kohler and Rivers noted that marriage with the MBW would be congruent with the Crow equation MBC = C, Moore suggests that MBW marriage in combination with matrilateral succession of females will tend to produce MBD marriage. Whereas Kohler, Gifford, and Seligman remarked that marriage with the WBD would be congruent with the Omaha equations MBD = M and MBS = MB, Moore suggests that WBD marriage in combination with patrilateral succession of males will tend to produce MBD marriage. In a system of bilateral cross-cousin marriage, MBW will be equivalent to FZ, and WBD to ZD. Moore comments that FZ marriage in combination with female matrifiliation, and ZD marriage in combination with male patrifiliation, would both be conducive to FZD marriage. It seems that all these possibilities are permutations which may unfold as the result of differential emphasis on relationships inherent in simple two-line systems, without any recourse to unilineal descent. We shall return to the discussion of Crow-Omaha equations in the next chapter.

The four trajectories envisaged by Moore are illustrated in Table 57, where we have also indicated that these structural types may be approximated by the Txicáo, Bororo, Suyá, and Sherente respectively. The Txicáo prescribe marriage with MBW or MBD, and the matrilateral affiliation of females is the result of uxorilocal residence. The Bororo rate FZ and FZD marriage as the most preferable, and are strongly inclined towards matrilateral affiliation. The Suyá prefer marriage with MBD, and include WBD in the marriageable category *hron* (W = BW = WBD). Leadership is inherited patrilineally, and political factions are usually composed of co-resident agnates. The patrilineal Sherente, finally, may marry a FZD but not a MBD, and FZD is equated, in the Omaha fashion, with ZD *(kremzú)*.

It is noteworthy that parallel affiliation has been posited for all four groups serving as examples in Table 57. We have suggested that parallel affiliation in combination with exogamous marriage ideals will be conducive to MBD marriage, whereas in conjunction with endogamy the same principles of affiliation will favour the FZD. Indeed, ideals of rank endogamy have been attributed to both the Bororo and the Sherente.

251

Chapter 18
Unilateral Marriage

"Prescriptive alliance is, of course, found in a fair number of societies (in South America), but not asymmetric alliance. The characteristic form, without exception outside the Sirionó, is symmetric alliance in the form of the two-section system, whether or not marked by exogamous moieties. I think that on formal grounds alone asymmetric alliance may be derived from symmetric . . ."
    – R. Needham (1961:253)

"It seems reasonable to say that the bilateral rule is related to the others as theme to variation, the matrilateral and patrilateral variants of it being derivable formally, and perhaps therefore derived historically, by secondary restrictions on it."
    – T.R. Trautmann (1981:205-206)

Whereas two-line terminologies prescribe marriage with bilateral cross-cousins (symmetric alliance), a number of societies throughout the world express preferences for marriage with either the MBD or the FZD. Lévi-Strauss (1969:438–455) has demonstrated that a statistical preponderance of one or the other type of unilateral cross-cousin marriage will yield radically different structures of exchange. Matrilateral cross-cousin marriage will result in longer cycles of reciprocity, i.e. generalized exchange, whereas the patrilateral variant reverses the flow of spouses in every generation, producing shorter cycles akin to the restricted exchange of bilateral marriage (cf. Leach 1961b:59,61–62; Needham 1962:15). Generalized exchange, in maintaining linear alignments of spouse-givers and spouse-takers, may be conducive to the emergence of social hierarchy (cf. Leach 1961b:84).

Needham (1958b:200–201; 1962:8–11,15–16) finds that Lévi-Strauss' formal analyses "do not make sense" unless applied to marriages rigidly prescribed between groups in a lineal descent system. The association of elementary alliance structures with lineal descent systems is obvious throughout the work of Lévi-Strauss (1969:105; cf. also Leach 1961b:56; Needham 1961:239), but the strict distinction between prescription and preference advocated by Needham has been rejected by, among others, Schneider (1965), de Heusch (1981), and Lévi-Strauss himself (1969: xxx-xxxv), for whom structures of exchange can be detected in statistical tendencies in human behaviour as well as in systems of classification. Needham's perspective, however, leads him to the conclusion that "a prescriptive marriage system based on exclusive patrilateral cross-cousin marriage cannot exist in theory and does not exist in fact" (1958b:217). Since patrilateral and matrilateral cross-cousins would not be structurally distinguishable in terms of descent group membership, Needham argues that a system of terminologically prescribed patrilateral cross-cousin marriage could not be perpetuated. Although recognizing that "preferential marriage with the FZD may well have the asymmetrical features and social consequences of Lévi-Strauss' 'short cycle' in the relations between individual families," he claims that these characteristics and relations cannot be those of a total system (ibid.,210–211). If FZD marriage was practiced consistently, FZD would be identical to MMBDD, i.e. a classificatory matrilateral cross-cousin (Needham 1962:109–110). Needham (1958b:217) concludes that there can only be "two basic modes of exchange of women by the prescriptive regulation of marriage: direct (with section-systems) and indirect (with matrilateral cross-cousin marriage)." This position, rephrased in terms of symmetric versus asymmetric alliance, is reiterated by Maybury-Lewis (1965a:217–218,224) and Needham (1971c:20).

We are currently more interested in the emergent structural properties of unilateral cross-cousin marriage than in the way in which such marriage practices are codified in the system of classification (prescription or preference, descent groups or relationship categories.) For the time being, however, we may recall that the Sherente, Apinayé, and Bororo all distinguish terminologically between the patrilateral and matrilateral cross-cousin, favouring marriage with the former rather than the latter. Furthermore, the periodic inversions inherent in patrilateral cross-cousin marriage appear to be fundamental to Sherente culture. We must disregard genealogical categories such as "classificatory matrilateral cross-cousin" and accept that other rules may be operative. Instead of alliances between lineal descent groups, the Gê are often concerned with marrying "across the plaza" or into the father's natal household. Genealogical amnesia and a considerable liberty to reclassify one's relatives would also undermine the logical obstacles to patrilateral cross-cousin marriage envisaged by Needham.

Determinants of Unilateral Cross-Cousin Marriage

Lévi-Strauss (1969:215–219,266,441,493) suggests that beyond the level of integration represented by simple moiety exogamy, systems of unilateral cross-cousin marriage will be associated with "harmonic regimes", i.e. where unilineal descent and unilocal residence are aligned, whereas bilateral marriage (restricted exchange) will be associated with disharmonic regimes. This, "the only falsifiable hypothesis" in Lévi-Strauss' entire book (Korn 1973:140–141), has been rephrased in less committing terms

by Scheffler (1970:255) and somewhat modified by Dumont (1957) and de Heusch (1981). Even if Korn (1973:24–26,35,141), by arguing that the Aranda combine restricted exchange with an harmonic regime, claims to have falsified it, we shall have reason to return to Lévi-Strauss' pivotal formulation.

Homans and Schneider (1955) offer an alternative interpretation based on the structures of inter-personal sentiments which Radcliffe-Brown assumed to be characteristic of patrilineal and matrilineal societies respectively. Their conclusion is that matrilateral cross-cousin marriage will be associated with patrilineal societies, and patrilateral marriage with matrilineal. Needham's (1962) monograph is essentially a refutation of the psychological reductionism underlying the theory of unilateral cross-cousin marriage advanced by Homans and Schneider. In its place, Needham advocates a structural approach along the lines suggested by Lévi-Strauss.

In comparing several South Indian groups, Dumont (1957:19–21) demonstrates that the interrelation assumed by Lévi-Strauss is on the whole confirmed. In his sample of six groups representing different variations of a common cultural stock, only the two groups which incline toward full consonance between rules of succession/inheritance, descent, and residence practice matrilateral marriage. Dumont, however, modifies Lévi-Strauss' formulation by letting patrilateral rather than bilateral cross-cousin marriage represent restricted exchange (cf. Trautmann 1981:204–205). De Heusch (1981:71, 77) similarly suggests that patrilateral cross-cousin marriage may be associated with disharmonic, matrilineal systems. In fact, this modification, which agrees with Needham's and Maybury-Lewis' symmetric/asymmetric dichotomy, seems immanent in Lévi-Strauss' reasoning, for whereas harmonic regimes are said to *require* unilateral marriage (1969: 218), disharmonic regimes are not said to *outrule* it. Even if he does not go so far as to classify patrilateral cross-cousin marriage as restricted rather than generalized exchange, Lévi-Strauss (ibid.) concedes that "the transition from patrilateral systems to the formula for restricted exchange (is) easier than it is for matrilateral systems."

The Lanes (1959:262) account for unilateral cross-cousin marriage as the result of asymmetrical extensions of incest taboos in symmetric alliance systems. This tautological statement does not provide any attempt at explanation of either unilateral inclination. Moreover, as pointed out by Eyde and Postal (1961:769, note 8), it ignores the point of view of a female Ego, for whom unilateral marriage is always in the direction opposite to that for a male.

Eyde and Postal (ibid.,750) propose an alternative theory for the development of unilateral cross-cousin marriage. They suggest that a matrilineal, matrilocal symmetric alliance system, if subjected to pressures which increase the need for co-operation (e.g. economic, military) among the males of a residence group, will either shift toward avunculocality or enjoin a girl's marriage to her FZS (i.e. matrilateral cross-cousin marriage, from the male point of view.) Similarly, a patrilineal, patrilocal society, if subjected to pressures which increase the need for cooperation among the females of a residence group, will either shift to amitalocality or enjoin a boy's marriage to his MBD (matrilateral cross-cousin marriage.) The development of matrilateral marriage is thus explained in terms of "the desires of individuals to have same-sex members of their own lineages reside with them" (ibid., 753).

Eyde and Postal (ibid., 755) predict that matrilateral cross-cousin marriage would develop more frequently in matrilineal than in patrilineal societies. The factual correlation between matrilateral marriage and patrilineal descent is explained as the result of the "self extinguishing" nature of MBD marriage. Lineal kin equations generated by this form of marriage will identify MBD with incestuous categories: either with Ego's M

(Omaha) or with his D (Crow). The extension of incest taboos would tend to pursue the extension of kin terms, finally resulting in the prohibition of MBD marriage (ibid., 756–757,766). Matrilateral cross-cousin marriage, Eyde and Postal predict, will be extinguished more rapidly in matrilineal than in patrilineal societies. The prohibition of MBD marriage in matrilineal Crow contexts may eventually produce a statistical predominance of FZD marriage, i.e. patrilateral cross-cousin marriage (ibid.,761,764). Finally, "maximal extension of incest taboos will tend to prohibit all first cross-cousin marriage." The authors conclude that patrilateral cross-cousin marriage "develops for the most part as a result of the extinction of marriage with MBD," whereas matrilateral cross-cousin marriage is "a reasonable response to the problems of residential co-operation in unilineal societies" (ibid.,767). In the previous chapter we suggested that the "self extinguishing" properties of MBD marriage in Crow contexts has been operative among the Eastern Timbira tribes, and that these may even be responsible for an inclination towards FZD marriage among the closely related Apinayé.

In the preceding chapter we also discussed Moore's (1963) suggestion that the two forms of unilateral cross-cousin marriage would be associated with specific combinations of oblique marriages and principles of "sexual succession". MBD marriage would be associated with marriage to the MBW or WBD, FZD marriage with marriage to the FZ or ZD (cf. Trautmann 1981:206–207, 212–213; de Heusch 1981:41–48). The observation, made by de Sousberghe, Philipson, and others (cf. Leach 1961b:59–60, note 2; Rivière 1966a; W. Shapiro 1968:49; de Heusch 1981:42–43), that consistent FZ or ZD marriage will be equivalent to MBD marriage implies that the structure associated with patrilateral cross-cousin marriage carries "the seeds of the matrilateral form," and suggests "a possible explanation for the prevalence of the matrilateral type" (Moore 1963:306). Finally, Moore (ibid.,309) notes that "the historical sequence" could go either way, from an emphasis on oblique marriage to an emphasis on cousin marriage, or vice versa.

Discussion

It is evident that Lévi-Strauss, Homans and Schneider, Eyde and Postal, and Moore are all concerned with the relationship between unilateral marriage and unilateral affiliation. Irrespective of the way in which this relationship is explained (whether in terms of the articulation of descent groups, in terms of structurally determined sentiments, in terms of strategies related to residence and same-sex cooperation, or in terms of sexual succession), the crucial parameter is always seen as the way in which members of Ego's generation are affiliated with those of the first ascending generation. No doubt, none of these four approaches is entirely mistaken; each can probably be applied to some specific ethnographic instance. In fact, it may well be that two or more of these interpretations, by amounting to the same thing, are often applicable to a single society. Lévi-Strauss and Moore talk about the structural possibility of combining particular types of marriage and affiliation, while Homans/Schneider and Eyde/Postal emphasize the motives of individual actors. The former deal with universal constraints, the latter with specific, cultural incentives.

In which respects do the four models differ? First, whereas Lévi-Strauss considers the structural effects of two juxtaposed principles of affiliation (disharmonic systems), the remaining authors have taken only single unilineal principles into account. It is interesting to deduce what these latter theorists would predict for disharmonic systems, where both descent and residence serve as matrices for sentiments, cooperation, and succession. Homans and Schneider's emphasis on the locus of jural authority as a determinant of sentiments suggests that they would consider residence irrelevant (cf. Homans & Schneider 1955:55). For Eyde and Postal, disharmonic systems should represent an alternative solution to the problem of articulating same-sex units of co-operation of the sex opposite to that through which descent is reckoned. The need to articulate closely related males in a matrilineal society could be satisfied by virilocality rather than avunculocality or matrilateral cross-cousin marriage. Inversely, the need to articulate closely related females in a patrilineal society could be satisfied by uxorilocality rather than amita-locality or matrilateral marriage. It is gratifying to note that the premises with which Eyde and Postal have been concerned (same-sex co-operation in relation to unilocal residence) generate the same conclusion as has emerged from Lévi-Strauss' structural analyses: disharmonic systems and matrilateral cross-cousin marriage are two mutually exclusive alternatives.

If disharmonic systems were the point of departure. Eyde and Postal's concern would be with strategies for the residential articulation of lineage mates of the lineal sex. In order for male Ego to stay together with his patrilineal kin in a uxorilocal society, he should marry his classificatory M, Z, or ZD. In order for female Ego to remain with her matrilineal kin in a virilocal society, she should marry her classificatory F, B, or BS (i.e. male Ego must marry his classificatory FZ, Z, or D.) It is not difficult to see that both systems will tend to encourage oblique marriage: ZD marriage in the former, and FZ marriage in the latter.

This finally brings us to Moore's perspective. Her conclusion agrees with that of Lévi-Strauss in predicting that both types of unilateral marriage will occur in both patrilineal and matrilineal systems. But what would she say about disharmonic systems? Assuming that children of the sex through which descent is traced succeed their same-sex parent, Moore suggests that MBD marriage would be associated with WBD marriage, and FZD marriage with ZD marriage, in a patrilineal society, whereas MBD marriage would be linked with MBW marriage, and FZD marriage with FZ marriage, in a matrilineal society. Since both WBD marriage and MBW marriage are secondary unions which cannot amount to a significant proportion of all marriages, and since neither appears to be geared to the problem of staying with one's kin in a disharmonic system, we are left with a connection between FZD/ZD marriage and patriliny, and between FZ/FZD marriage and matriliny. Again it is gratifying to see the different approaches converge. We have suggested that oblique marriages (particularly to ZD or FZ) tend to be associated with disharmonic systems. In both types of disharmonic system, the expectable version of oblique marriage will be structurally compatible with patrilateral cross-cousin marriage, the variant of unilateral marriage which according to Lévi-Strauss is structurally closest to a disharmonic regime. Furthermore, if disharmonic systems are expressions of bilineal or parallel principles of affiliation (cf. Chapter 14), the preference for the FZD would accord with an ideal of close, endogamous marriage (cf. Scheffler & Lounsbury 1971: 175).

We may conclude that the approaches of Lévi-Strauss, Eyde and Postal, and Moore are convergent with respect to the incongruity of matrilateral cross-cousin marriage and disharmonic systems. In emphasizing descent and jural authority, while ignoring disharmonic rules of residence, Homans and Schneider fail to make this important observation. If Lévi-Strauss and Moore have outlined the structural constraints, it seems that the cultural incentives have been better defined by Eyde and Postal than by Homans and Schneider.

By focusing on the use of strategic marriage to ensure the cohesion of social groups, Eyde and Postal may have addressed a consideration central to an understanding of the emic foundation of Crow-Omaha kin equations. In a patrilineal but uxorilocal society, the localized female matriline composed of classificatory M, Z, and ZD defines male Ego's alternatives in contracting a marriage endogamous to the household. In a matrilineal but virilocal society, female Ego can marry endogamously only if she is classificatory FZ, Z, or D to her spouse. In the former case, the Omaha equation ZD = FZD would serve to underscore the distinction between Z and ZD and to legitimize marriage into one's natal household. In the latter case, the Crow equation FZ = FZD would similarly accentuate the distinction between FZ and Z. These distinctions are crucial, because although belonging to separate descent lines, in terms of residence ZD succeeds Z and Z succeeds FZ respectively. A synthesis of Eyde and Postal's and Moore's hypotheses would predict that whereas the equations ZD = FZD and FZ = FZD would encourage patrilateral cross-cousin marriage, the corresponding Crow-Omaha equations M = MBD and D = MBD would in the long run not be conducive to actual MBD marriage. The logic underlying the Crow-Omaha "raising" or "lowering" of cross-cousins, it seems, may be connected to the fact that a preference for endogamy in disharmonic patrilineal systems would favour marriage into the first descending generation (Omaha: ZD = FZD), whereas in disharmonic matrilineal systems it would mean marrying into the first ascending (Crow: FZ = FZD). An inversion of this pattern would imply marrying either a classificatory M or D. The third alternative, that of marrying a classificatory Z (parallel cousin), may underlie some terminologies featuring Hawaiian (generational) cousin terms. A common basis for Crow-Omaha and Hawaiian nomenclatures, then, is the assimilation of the matrilineal series M/Z/ZD and the patrilineal series FZ/Z/D with "cross-cousins", i.e. prototypical affines. Much as Eyde and Postal argue with respect to the "self extinguishing" trajectory of MBD marriage in societies with Crow cousin terms, we have suggested that Hawaiian cousin terms in themselves will tend to precipitate a prohibition of all first cousin marriage: hence Murdock's (1949:228) correlation between Hawaiian nomenclatures and a "bilateral extension of incest taboos" (cf. Dole 1969: 114). But even if marriage to classificatory "sisters" in societies with Hawaiian cousin terms in the long run tends to be "self-extinguishing", as the consanguineal content of terms for zero generation females is increasingly accentuated, we have here a possible foundation for preferential marriage with a distant "sister" among the Karajá, Tapirapé, and early Apinayé (cf. Chapter 20 and Dietschy 1977).

Matrilateral Cross-Cousin Marriage

If the Crow-Omaha identification of MBD with M or D is not *per se* conducive to matrilateral cross-cousin marriage, but rather the opposite, we should consider how this marriage rule might come about. Even if there are no linear arrangements of wife-giving and wife-taking descent groups, no intimate avuncular relationship, and no pressures for same-sex co-operation other than that achieved by the system of affiliation, the matrilateral preference may be seen as yet another trajectory emanating from the structure of reciprocity encoded in two-line terminologies. In Dravidian systems, the marriage rule is often phrased so as to enjoin male Ego's marriage to the daughter of his father's same-sex affine, and female Ego's marriage to the son of her mother's same-sex affine. The ideal of duplicating the alliance of one's same-sex parent represents the articulation of inherited affinity and parallel succession, two principles inherent in Dravidian systems. The prototype for a father's same-sex affine is his WB, i.e. Ego's MB, and the prototype for a mother's same-sex affine is her HZ, i.e. Ego's FZ. These focal preferences may be the origin of what

Scheffler and Lounsbury (1971) have called the MBD-FZS-Spouse Equation Rule.

It is important to observe that a system of symmetric alliance, or bilateral cross-cousin marriage, may rest on two separate, distinguishable principles. First, that male Ego ought to duplicate the alliance of his F by marrying the daughter of his FWB. Second, the ideal of sister exchange. By visualizing these two ideals as distinct principles, which jointly may generate bilateral cross-cousin marriage, we are in a position to reconstruct the conditions under which unilateral marriage may emerge. If marriage to a MBD is the genealogical implication of the focal Dravidian marriage rule, and her simultaneous status as FZD merely the logical result of continued sister exchange, we would expect an abandonment of sister exchange to be a sufficient explanation for the transition from bilateral to matrilateral cross-cousin marriage. If the exchange of women is fundamentally a relationship between men, it will be seen why male Ego, even in a Dravidian system, is primarily interested in the status of his WF (MB), rather than in that of his WM (FZ). A preference for the *MBD* would emphasize exogamy and the dimension of inherited affinity, whereas a preference for the *FZD* would emphasize the consanguineal dimension, or at least the ideal of close marriage. An abandonment of sister exchange, we suggest, is likely to take place as small, endogamous local groups yield to larger villages with a wider range of potential marriage partners.

Let us now reconsider the data in our sample in order to evaluate Lévi-Strauss' proposition that matrilateral cross-cousin marriage will be associated with harmonic systems, whereas disharmonic systems will be linked to bilateral or patrilateral marriage. Of the four societies prescribing (Sirionó, Txicáo) or favouring (Suyá, Aguaruna) MBD marriage, all but the Aguaruna combine uxorilocal residence with matrilateral affiliation. (The Suyá are an ambiguous case, but male name transmission is, after all, matrilineal.) The Aguaruna combine virilocal residence with patrilateral affiliation. In other words, all four are harmonic systems. Among the Gê, the predominantly Crow-oriented Eastern Timbira combine matrilateral marriage preferences with harmonic regimes founded on uxorilocal residence and matrilateral affiliation (cf. Table 56). Patrilateral marriage preferences occur in the disharmonic (uxorilocal but patrilateral) systems of the Omaha-oriented Central Gê. Northern Gê groups other than the Eastern Timbira (i.e. Apinayé, Kayapó and Suyá) seem in various respects transitional, whereas the Bororo, who prefer patrilateral marriage, may qualify as disharmonic by virtue of their patrilateral ceremonialism (C. Crocker 1977).

Finally, we should consider the characteristic structures of exchange which Lévi-Strauss envisaged as concomitant to the two forms of unilateral cross-cousin marriage. We have seen that FZD marriage is generally associated with some form of short-cycle alternation among the Apinayé, Sherente, Shavante, Bororo, Karajá, Amahuaca, Sharanahua, Barasana, Bará, and Machiguenga. MBD marriage, on the other hand, appears only rarely to have generated structures of "generalized exchange" in the societies where it is enjoined. The Sirionó certainly do not recognize any triadic arrangement of wife-givers and wife-takers. We can only speculate as to whether the MBD preference among the Ramkokamekra and Suyá may occasionally have generated cycles of generalized exchange between uxorilocal households. The cyclical arrangement of Apinayé *kiyé* and Sherente men's associations do suggest a codification of such patterns prior to the predictable "self extinction" of the MBD preference. The spatial alignments of Txicáo kin terms (Fig. 12), however, remain the only clear indication of a linear arrangement of uxorilocal households articulated by generalized exchange.

258

Chapter 19
Oblique Marriage

"Since oblique marriages are secondary marriages, Murdock, Lévi-Strauss and others have dismissed them as peripheral to kinship systems with low incidence and influence. Infrequent they may be, but the information they can yield about a kinship system is considerable. They illustrate a kind of sexual succession. They suggest of which close relative (or relatives) in the generation above a young man or woman is the younger counterpart."
– S.F. Moore (1963:299)

We have discussed oblique marriages (particularly with ZD and FZ) in terms of their congruity with specific constellations of affiliation, lineal equations, and unilateral cross-cousin marriage. Lévi-Strauss (1969:368) interprets WBD marriage among the Miwok as an expression of the claims, in a system of generalized exchange, of one patrilineage on the women of another. The notion of lineage, says Lévi-Strauss (ibid.,361-362), has here been "strongly enough implanted as to take priority over the notion of generation."

Moore (1963) is primarily interested in considering oblique marriages as "possible antecedents" of unilateral cross-cousin marriage (ibid.,304), and in their relationship to Crow-Omaha kin equations. Between 1887 and 1917, this latter relationship was discussed by Kohler, Rivers, Gifford, and Seligman, whose contributions jointly suggested that Crow equations would be generated by MBW marriage, and Omaha equations by marriage to WBD (cf. the account of Radcliffe-Brown 1952:56). Moore's point that oblique marriage may be congruent with principles of parallel succession agrees with the Whittens' (1984) observation that cross-generational marriages among the Canelos Quichua express the wish of both men and women to perpetuate soul and body substances transmitted along parallel, male and female lines.

By far the most common form of oblique marriage in South America is that with ZD. Lave (1966:185, 194) concludes that ZD marriage "does not occur as a prescriptive rule." However, if prescription is defined as the equation of a specific category of kin with the category of potential spouses, we have seen that ZD marriage is in fact prescribed, if not exclusively, in four of the societies in our sample (Nambikwara, Trio, Karinya, Barama River Carib).

Lave (ibid., 196–197) further concludes that ZD marriage would structurally amount to a system of direct exchange between patrilineal "descent groups", and that the ZD preference would be unlikely where descent is matrilineal. She also suggests that ZD marriage is compatible with a simple two-line terminology (cf. Needham 1972:16), but that distinctions based on relative age will be likely to appear as an alternative to classification by generation. Ultimately, ZD marriage will yield a distinction of cross-cousins, most likely classifying FZD with M and MBD with ZD (i.e., an inversion of Omaha equations.)

Rivière (1966a:740) envisages the "hypothetical possibility" of a system in which marriage is prescribed with a category of women including MBD and ZD, but prohibited with FZD. The distinction between MBD and FZD would be diagnostic of this type of prescriptive alliance (ibid., 739). Rivière agrees with Lave on the congruity between ZD marriage, on the one hand, and direct exchange, two-line terminologies, and "patrilineal descent", on the other. He suggests, however, that ZD marriage "could exist in a society with a lineal descent terminology but with no firm rule of descent." Citing Lévi-Strauss, da Matta (1970:551) notes that bilateral cross-cousin marriage and ZD marriage are different possibilities "given in a single principle of organization," in which "women run through a short cycle" (cf. Lévi-Strauss 1968a;Kaplan 1984:153, note 13). In emic terms, a two-line terminology accommodates marriage with the daughter of father's "brother-in-law" (MBD/FZD) or of his own "brother-in-law" (ZD), rather than focusing on consanguineal links (Kaplan 1984:140).

In an expanded note on the same topic, Riviére (1966b:551) points out that ZD marriage among the Trio does not involve corporate groups articulated in alliance. The local community is mainly endogamous and "women are exchanged within the unit rather than outside, with other similar units." However, the kin terminology of the Trio is not a typical two-line system, but equates FZD = M and MBD = ZD (ibid.,553). Rivière remarks that the Trio terminology thus "does exactly the opposite to what Lévi-Strauss expects when he writes that the South American system whereby the grandparents, parents-in-law, and cross-aunts, and cross-uncles are equated, is a means for resolving the terminological conflicts resulting from oblique marriages." This observation agrees with our suggestion that the equation of grandparents and first ascending generation affines, though possibly encouraging oblique marriage, derives primarily from other considerations (i.e. the expansion of affinal categories.)

Whereas Lave (1966:199, note 10) thinks that ZD marriage is "more closely related to bilateral cross-cousin marriage than to any other form of prescriptive marriage," Rivière (1966a:738; 1966b:554) agrees with Lévi-Strauss that ZD marriage shares the "discontinuous" aspect of patrilateral cross-cousin marriage, i.e. the characteristic reversal of the flow of women in alternate generations. In ZD marriage among the Trio, Rivière (1966b:555) recognizes "the embryonic form of the type of arrangement which . . . might allow a small-scale system of patrilateral cross-cousin marriage to work."

W. Shapiro (1966:83) suggests that the equation ZC = MBC is "the most common reflection of avuncular marriage on kinship terminology." He notes that this equation has been found among the Barama River Caribs, Mundurucú, Sirionó, Tukuna, and Tupinambá. Direct evidence for ZD marriage is "unequivocal" for all of these but the Sirionó and Tukuna. The multiple terminological indications, and the fact that ZD marriage has been reported for several other Tupí peoples (e.g. Mundurucú, Tupinambá, Cayuá, Kamayurá), gives Shapiro "good reason to believe that the institution in question is either practiced today by the Sirionó or else once was" (ibid.,84-85, 87). This position is reiterated in an expanded article (W. Shapiro 1968), where Shapiro suggests that ZD marriage among the Mundurucú and Cayuá has subsequently been abandoned, although the terminological correlates are preserved, and suggests a similar trajectory for the Sirionó (ibid.,49).

Shapiro (ibid.,43-44) suggests, as we have done, that a system such as that of the Tupinambá, which assimilates cross-cousins and ZD into a single category of potential spouses, could well be called *prescriptive* ZD marriage. On the other hand, he agrees with Rivière that although such a system "can be seen as one of reciprocal marriage between two patrilines . . . this does not necessarily mean that a society so analyzed . . . has patrilineal descent groups" (ibid.,45).

In the preceding chapter we suggested that ZD marriage will be associated with disharmonic societies combining patrilateral affiliation with uxorilocal residence. Of the 18 societies which have been reported to practice ZD marriage, six are fairly straightforward cases of such disharmonic systems (Caingang, Karajá, Mundurucú, Trio, Sanumá, Tupinambá/Guaraní). In addition, nine societies combine elements of male patrilaterality (bilateral or parallel affiliation) with sporadic uxorilocality or bride-service (Nambikwara, Parintintin/Tupí-Cawahíb, Waiwai, Karinya, Barama River Carib, Pemon, Machiguenga, Piaroa, Warao), providing a setting in which similar conflicts between patrilateral and affinal loyalties may arise. On the surface of it, the remaining three are harmonic, patrilineal/virilocal systems (Amahuaca, Makuna, Barasana). The Amahuaca, however, may have been uxorilocal in the past, and the Makuna are known to practice occasional bride-service. Although we have encountered no positive evidence in its favour, it is not inconceivable that the avoidance of bride-service has been a consideration relevant also to the Barasana, close neighbours and relatives of the Makuna.

In sum, out of 18 societies in which marriages with ZD occur, at least 16 practice general or sporadic uxorilocality, and another has probably done so in the past. These figures support the suggestion that ZD marriage is a likely strategy where there is a conflict between male patrilateral loyalties and requirements on uxorilocal residence.

Chapter 20
Generational Equations

"Les Karajá disent qu'on peut épouser 'chaque soeur', toutes les cousines, parallèles et croisées, étant des 'soeurs' (lerã) dans un système appelé 'bifurcate generation' par Dole (1969). Les soeurs propres sont naturellement exclues . . ."
— H. Dietschy (1977:299)

If lineal equations override the distinction of generations characteristic of two-line terminologies, generational equations disregard the distinction of affinity by assimilating parallel- and cross-collateral relatives. Since these equations assimilate relatives from the entire range of Ego's personal kindred, we have tentatively proposed that they may be based on "cognatic principles." In this chapter, however, we shall primarily be concerned with showing that the delineation of the personal kindred could theoretically provide a matrix for either exogamous or endogamous marriage practices.

Dole (1969) presents the transition from bifurcate merging to what she calls "bifurcate generation" (i.e. a cross/parallel bifurcation at the first ascending generation level in conjunction with a generation terminology at the zero generation level) as a general phenomenon in societies where local or kin group exogamy has yielded to increasing endogamy. With demographic decline, Dole argues, remnants of formerly exogamous local groups tend to amalgamate, so that the distinction between consanguineal and affinal categories will be blurred (ibid.,110). "As members of the same group, cross-cousins will tend to be equated with siblings and parallel cousins" (ibid.,111), even where bifurcating terms are used for the first ascending generation. The use of bifurcating avuncular and nepotic terms, Dole suggests, will tend to continue "as long as cross-cousin marriage remains an ideal union." Thus, potential spouses can be defined with reference to the first ascending generation, even where zero generation terms make no such distinctions. Dole speculates that the amalgamation of consanguineal and affinal kinsmen will finally tend to result in the abandonment of cross-cousin marriage, i.e. an expansion of exogamy (ibid.,114). Her major point, however, is that "the principal determinant of generation cousin terms is kin group endogamy brought about by ambilocal residence." This kind of development, she suggests, has occurred throughout the world. In South America, examples include the post-Columbian Inca; the Carib-speaking Kuikuru and Kalapalo; Tupí-speakers such as the Tapirapé, Tenetehara, and Kamayurá; the Trumai and the Warao. These are contrasted with tribes where fully bifurcating nomenclatures correlate with the existence of exogamous kin groups, e.g. the Shavante, Bororo, Ramkokamekra, Cashinahua, Machiguenga, and Mundurucú. To this category Dole adds peoples whose residence rules "imply" local kin group exogamy, "if practiced regularly" (ibid., 118), e.g. the Piaroa, Sherente, Sirionó, and Yanomamö. Finally, where the co-existence of bifurcation and ambilocal residence or kin group endogamy contradicts Dole's hypothesis, e.g. among the Barama River Caribs, Nambikwara, Trio, and Waiwai, she suggests that we "may expect that the cousin terms of these peoples will change to the generation pattern when cross-cousin marriage is no longer commonly practiced."

A major weakness in Dole's theory is the fact that there are numerous examples of peoples lacking rules of unilocal residence or local exogamy, yet by virtue of their two-line terminology maintaining a pattern of cross-cousin marriage. We have suggested that two-line terminologies, instead of being associated with unilineal kin groups, represent an *alternative* to such organization, i.e. as different codifications of a similar pattern of exchange. Groups such as the Nambikwara, Kalapalo, and Piaroa illustrate how cross-cousin marriage and local endogamy can be perfectly compatible, as long as the two-line terminology is intact.

Even though there may be considerable disagreement with respect to the characterization of particular cultures in Dole's lists, it does seem plausible that generational cousin terms could be associated with endogamy. Endogamy is not, however, necessarily the result of demographic disturbances. We have come across reports of several groups in which the equation of cross-cousins with siblings or parallel cousins co-exists with indications of endogamous divisions wholly independent of residence. These include the Apinayé, Sherente, Bororo, Karajá, Caingang, Tapirapé, Warao, Kadiwéu, and Witoto. Apparently, the foundation for such internal, endogamous subdivisions of local groups is an emphasis on social hierarchy (cf. Chapter 22).

For a group adhering to an ideal of local endogamy, the problem in terms of kin classification is how to distinguish marriageable from non-marriageable individuals. This is effectively accomplished with a two-line terminology and requires no recourse to corporate kin groups. For an endogamous *subdivision* of a local group, however, the problem of classification would come to focus on the outer boundaries of the endogamous group, rather than on its internal divisions. Thus, all generation mates of Ego's bilateral kindred would be classed together, as distinct from non-kinsmen. Within this expanded "sibling" category, of course, Ego can easily isolate those unions which, due to consanguineal over-proximity, would be considered incestuous (cf. the

Karajá). Of course, much as Eyde and Postal (1961:756-757) suggest for Crow-Omaha kin equations, Hawaiian cousin terms are probably in the long run conducive to an expansion of exogamy (Murdock 1949:228; Dole 1969:114).

Dole's hypothesis (cf. Dole 1984 for a somewhat modified version) has received the support of W. Shapiro (1968:52), Thomas (1971:9), and others. Needham (1972:27-28), however, is not convinced. He notes that there is no inherent contradiction between co-residence and the distinction between parallel and cross-collaterals, and that Dole fails to explain why such distinctions are maintained in the generations adjacent to Ego's. Basso (1970:407-409, 411-412) objects that generational and bifurcating cousin terms may co-exist in the same population, which simply employs them in different speech contexts, the former to emphasize consanguinity, the latter to stress affinity. Thomas (1978), in fact, views generational equations as an expression of the struggle to suppress the social distance implied by "the quality of being an affine" in societies favouring close endogamy (cf. also Kaplan 1972; Henley 1982:101-102; Schwerin 1982; Pollock 1985:15). Basso (1970:412) observes that "a term marking a specific affinal category is never uttered within the hearing of such an affine of the speaker." Indeed, generational equations are considerably more common in vocative than in referential terminologies (cf., e.g., Conclusions: Tupí), suggesting that terms of address frequently "constitute a separate semantic field" (cf. Trautmann 1981:36).

While by no means denying that the generational cousin terms of the Kuikuru represent the collapse of a two-line terminology, we would hesitate to draw the general conclusion that the disappearance of the cross/parallel dichotomy is everywhere associated with demographic disturbance. The presence of Hawaiian equations in groups emphasizing social hierarchy suggests that generational cousin terms may also be associated with the delimitation of endoga-mous strata.

Dole's wish to correlate bifurcating nomenclatures with exogamous kin groups, and generational with local group endogamy, is founded on a preconceived model of unilineal descent which appears out of place in South American ethnography. Whereas exogamous kin groups are rare on this continent, two-line terminologies are predominant in most linguistic families. Dole's assumption that members of the same local group will tend to be terminologically equated does not agree with the ethnographic evidence (cf. J. Shapiro 1984:9). This objection can be resolved if the focus is shifted from local group endogamy to *kindred* endogamy. While local group endogamy will usually entail a two-line division of marriageable and non-marriageable kin, kindred endogamy implies that a primary distinction would be between kin and non-kin. These two contexts would correspond to bifurcating and generational nomenclatures respectively. Kindred endogamy, where non-congruent with local group endogamy, suggests large local groups and a social hierarchy reproduced by means of rank endogamy. Such conditions, however, would have dissolved rapidly upon European contact.

Suárez (1972) has discussed the Hawaiian cousin terms of the Warao, reiterating Rivers' and Lowie's theses that such equations develop secondarily from systems featuring bifurcation of the Dakota-Iroquois type. She suggests that the high proportion of marriages with cross-collaterals indicates that Warao society originally had a two-section nomenclature articulating "lines" occupying simultaneously the status of "wife-givers" and "wife-takers" (ibid.,110), and interprets the shift to Hawaiian cousin terms as a reflection of the transition to cognation (ibid., 96, 101, 103-104). Suárez (ibid., 77) explicitly refers to a passage from Needham (1967:45-46) suggesting that the "lineal principle" inherent in two-section terminologies may yield to cognation (cf. Needham 1972:32-33, 36). We have seen, however, that there need be no contradiction whatsoever between two-section terminologies and cognation. Needham's premise, adopted by Suárez, that two-section systems will be associated with "lineality", is misleading. It appears as if the problem reduces to the unfortunate assumption that prescriptive terminologies can only be found in connection with unilineality. This assumption has guided Suárez to the misconception that a former two-line terminology among the Warao could not have been compatible with cognation.

Our suggestion that Hawaiian cousin terms may in some cases be associated with endogamous subgroups accords well with the position of Dietschy (1977). He attributes to the Karajá, Tapirapé, and Apinayé a combination of sex affiliation and subgroup endogamy by which potential wives (including cross-cousins) tend to be equated with sisters. We have suggested that the criterion of affinality in contexts such as these will be superseded by the importance of defining the outer boundary of the endogamous category. The Karajá and Tapirapé combine Hawaiian cousin terms with a rule enjoining marriage with a distant "Z". Dietschy (1977:299) asserts, of course, that true sisters are naturally prohibited. Nimuendajú's (1939) list of Apinayé kin terms similarly disregards the criterion of affinality, equating parallel cousins and cross-cousins. Parallel affiliation to the endogamous subgroups implies that Ego's wife should belong to the same category as his Z and M. This may explain the Hawaiian equation Z = MBD = FZD. It would also be congruent with the equations M = MBD and M = FZD, both of which da Matta found among the Apinayé.

Our data do not support Dole's interpretation of generational cousin terms. Of the nine societies in our sample which are ambilocal, only two have Hawaiian cousin terms. Not one of the six groups classified as isolated (and presumably to a large extent endogamous) have these terms. Nor does Suarez' hypothesis gain support from our data. Named unilineal groups are present in seven of the 11 societies with Hawaiian cousin terms, whereas bifurcate merging terms (Dravidian or Iroquois) are employed by 14 of the 20 groups which have been characterized as predominantly cognatic. On the other hand, our data confirm the suggestion that generational cousin terms will tend to extend the reaches of exogamy.

Of the 11 cultures featuring Hawaiian cousin terms, five express a dislike for marriage to any first cousins. It is significant that three of the five groups which combine Hawaiian cousin terms and first cross-cousin marriage are thought to have had an ideal of rank endogamy. In accordance with our predictions, evidence from all but one of the six groups combining Hawaiian cousin terms and indications of rank endogamy suggest that they have traditionally lived in very large villages.

Chapter 21

Two-Line Terminologies, Dual Organization, and Symmetric Alliance

"Perry identifies cross-cousin marriage with dual organization, and he claims to explain them both historically. But Morgan and Tylor are no different, for when they analyzed cross-cousin marriage they saw it simply as a residue of exogamous customs and dual organization. What should have been done, on the contrary, was to treat cross-cousin marriage, rules of exogamy, and dual organization as so many examples of one basic structure."
— C. Lévi-Strauss (1969:123)
"The irony is that in the very societies where the prescriptive marriage rule is of such overwhelming importance to the organization of groups within them, there is no evidence of a dual organization . . . "
— J. Kaplan (1981:160)

We have found not only that two-line kin terminologies are widespread in lowland South America, but also that the various deviations from this pattern generally can be understood as transformations of features immanent in its classificatory logic. We shall now address the nature of the mutual congruity of two-line terminologies, dual organization (i.e. systems of exogamous moieties), and bilateral cross-cousin marriage (symmetric alliance, direct exchange).

Dual Organization

In 1914, Rivers (1968:82-83, 88) suggested, as had Morgan, Tylor, and Frazer, that the "classificatory system . . . arose in that special variety of the clan-organization in which a community consists of two exogamous moieties, forming the social structure usually known as the dual organization." In 1917, Lowie proposed that bifurcate merging nomenclatures developed in connection with dual organization, whereas lineal equations of the Crow-Omaha type were a subsequent trajectory (Dole 1972:148). Lévi-Strauss (1969:72, 98, 128) agrees that the specific nature of " 'the classificatory kinship system' . . . is very readily accounted for by dual organization." He suggests, however, that dual organization is not primarily an institution but a formulation of the principle of reciprocity, i.e. "a principle of organization, capable of widely varying . . . applications" (ibid.,75). Two-line terminologies, furthermore, may be "an expression, in terms of kinship, of the social organization based on moieties" (ibid.,98). Or, inversely, "dual organization is the expression, on an institutional plane, of a system of kinship which itself derives from certain rules of alliance" (i.e. cross-cousin marriage) (ibid.,99). Whereas Tylor, Rivers, and Perry argued that cross-cousin marriage probably derives from dual organization, Lévi-Strauss does not believe that the relationship between these two features can be interpreted "simply as a derivation." Disregarding their chronological succession, Lévi-Strauss concludes that both dual organization and cross-cousin marriage are "systems of reciprocity, and both result in a dichotomous terminology which is broadly similar in both cases" (ibid.,102, 123). Finally, Lévi-Strauss (ibid.,129-133) demonstrates that cross-cousin marriage, with its inherent distinction between parallel- and cross-collaterals, is logically concomitant to the practice of direct sister exchange between two groups.

Instead of stating that dual organization

is not an institution but a principle, of which two-line terminologies and cross-cousin marriage are alternative expressions, I believe it would be more consistent to say that dual organization and two-line terminologies are two systems of classification codifying an identical structure of bilateral cross-cousin marriage. To speak of "the social organization based on moieties" duplicates the confusion, obvious in River's reference to "the social structure usually known as the dual organization," of moiety divisions and social structure. Moiety divisions, like two-line terminologies, are systems of classification. The underlying structure of reciprocity reflected in both may be referred to as symmetric alliance.

In two subsequent articles, Lévi-Strauss (1963d; 1963e) suggested that dual organization among Gê-speakers may be no more than illusory native representations of a social reality which is actually asymmetrical and triadic. This conclusion is based on the occurrence of lineal kin equations, unilateral cross-cousin marriage, a cyclical ceremonial organization reminiscent of generalized exchange, indications of endogamous subgroups, and concentric dualism in village layouts. Maybury-Lewis (1960b) responded by accusing Lévi-Strauss of a number of "methodological weaknesses," including errors of ethnographic interpretation, lack of precise definitions, comparison of incomparables, and ignorance of the distinction between social and symbolic dualism. He rejects Lévi-Strauss' view that dual organizations are expressions of a principle of reciprocity, suggesting instead that they express "a universal tendency to think in antitheses" (ibid.,41-42). Maybury-Lewis reiterates this mentalistic position in several subsequent publications (1967:298; 1968b; 1974; 1979c:312). Precisely because it refers to an allegedly universal feature, however, this approach does not help to explain the occurrence of dual organization in particular societies (cf. Ortiz 1969:132). In fact, Maybury-Lewis (1967:297) threatens to

regress to the sort of vacuous generalization propounded by Murdock (1949:90; 1965), whose account of exogamous moiety systems goes no further than to suggest that they are instances of a very general phenomenon of dual organization, "whereby aggression generated by in-group disciplines may be drained off internally in socially regulated and harmless ways instead of being translated into out-group hostility and warfare."

In analyzing the dual organization of the Tewa Pueblos of New Mexico, Ortiz (1969) rejects both Lévi-Strauss' denial of dualism as such (ibid.,136) and Maybury-Lewis' attempt to "explain a variable by a constant" (ibid., 132). Ortiz' fundamental problem is "how a society can be united and divided at the same time" (ibid.,137). This approach need not directly grapple with the conditions for features with which dual organization is generally associated (but which Ortiz (ibid., 130) will not accept as "defining criteria"), such as unilineal descent and reciprocal marriage rules. Unilateral affiliation and two-line terminologies, however, represent two alternative solutions to Ortiz' very problem (cf. Kaplan 1981:163-164; 1984: 150). Much as has been done for the Gê (Maybury-Lewis 1979a), Ortiz' book demonstrates how the opposition between Tewa moieties is continually overridden, mediated, transcended, and equalized over time.

Two-Line Terminologies and Descent

Dumont (1953a; 1957:24-29) showed that the two-line, Dravidian kin terminology is a codification of cross-cousin marriage, and that this demonstration does not require any notion of unilineal descent or dual organization. The inheritance of same-sex affinal relationships from one's parents automatically identifies cross-cousins as potential spouses, i.e. "terminological affines" (1953a:37). Radcliffe-Brown (1953) was bewildered by Dumont's disinterest in genealogical reckoning, but his arguments were effectively countered in a rejoinder by Dumont (1953b).

Referring to Dumont, Needham in an early article (1960a:81) proposes that although the principle of affinal alliance may be more fundamental than even descent, "corporate lineal descent groups" are the building-blocks of any prescriptive system. Systems based on prescriptive alliance, he implies, constitute a particular type of lineal descent system (ibid.,105). In fact, "prescriptive alliance is practiced and is possible only in lineal descent systems" (Needham 1960b:24). He explicitly asserts that symmetric alliance is "wholly inconsistent with a cognatic terminology *or society*" (1964a:237; italics mine). On the other hand, he concedes that we cannot infer from the "lineal character" of a two-section terminology "that there will be any definite rule of descent" (1966b:142), that prescriptive asymmetric alliance does "not require descent groups of any kind," and that the lineal *categories* of a descent terminology" need not correspond to any such groups (1964a:237-238). It does not seem useful, however, to speak of "descent terminologies", or terminologies "constituted by descent lines" (Needham 1971b:c), where no descent groups are present.

Needham's concessions in the case of the Sirionó contradict much of what he says elsewhere on the conditions for prescriptive alliance. He appears to accept, for instance, Suarez' (1972) assumption that a former two-section terminology among the Warao would have been incompatible with cognation (Needham 1972). Lave (1966:187) notes that the Sirionó would be an exception to the rule that prescriptive alliance implies "corporate descent groups of one sort or another." Needham's exceptional treatment of the Sirionó would lead to the kind of misleading notions illustrated by W. Shapiro (1970:381, 387, note 4) in consistently using "patrilineal" to characterize the "the organization of relationship categories" in two-

section systems. Needham (1971b:c) himself ridicules Buchler and Selby (1968:135) for making precisely this mistake, i.e. classing Dravidian systems as "patrilineal". Clearly, the fact that the Sirionó combine a marriage prescription with a complete absence of unilineal descent groups exposed a fundamental weakness in the theory of prescriptive alliance (Scheffler 1970:262, 264; 1974:782, note 35; Scheffler & Lounsbury 1971:18-33). This weakness is particularly evident in the case of the numerous South American systems which combine prescriptive symmetric alliance and bilateral affiliation (cognation), which according to Needham (1964a:237) are two "wholly inconsistent" features. Consequently, Rivière (1973:7), though dealing with prescriptive terminologies, has avoided the "potentially misleading" notion of alliance, "for it has had the tendency to make anthropologists think that prescriptive alliance entails relationships between identifiable groups, and furthermore (and worse) that these groups are in some way representative of the relationship categories."

Kaplan (1972, 1973, 1975) provides a detailed demonstration of Dumont's point that unilineal principles are not at all necessary for prescriptive, two-line systems. Schwerin (1982:7) also notes that there is no "need to resort to dual organization" to understand these systems.

Dravidian and Iroquois

Dole (1972:150-154) distinguishes between a general class of bifurcate merging (Murdock's Iroquois) terminologies, which differentiate descendants of parallel from cross-collaterals only in Ego's generation, and a Cross-Cousin subtype, which more consistently codifies the structural dichotomy generated by cross-cousin marriage. This subtype was named Cross-Cousin by Hocart, but had earlier been designated as Tamil by Morgan and as Fijian by Fison (ibid.,151). In modern literature, it is most

268

commonly referred to as Dravidian (Dumont 1953a, 1953b), or as a two-section (Needham 1958b, 1960a, 1960b) or two-line (Needham 1966b:142, note 2; 1972; Rivière 1973, 1977) terminology. Dole (1972:154) notes that "the Cross-Cousin pattern shows a high correlation with the obligatory, preferential, and regular marriage of first cross-cousins or their classificatory equivalents," and suggests that this terminology, "together with the associated preferential cross-cousin marriage, may be the normal pattern for relatively primitive societies that are able to maintain regular and stable intergroup (sic) alliances."

Scheffler (1971:240) also addresses the difference between Dravidian and Iroquois kin terminologies. With Lounsbury (1964b: 1079, note 4) and Pospisil, he notes the "prevalent failure" to distinguish between these two types (cf. Buchler & Selby 1968: 244), both of which have erroneously been interpreted as a single type of system codifying membership in unilineal descent groups. Buchler and Selby (1968:233; cf. Kaplan 1975:127-128, note 1) distinguish the two systems from each other on the basis of whether there are any special affinal terms, the same criterion as is used by Needham (e.g., 1973) to define two-section systems as founded on prescriptive symmetric alliance. In fact, they are prepared to use the label "terminology of symmetric marriage systems" interchangeably with "Dravidian terminology". In Dravidian systems, the affinal content of cross-collateral kin categories is primary, and marriage exchanges are governed by the terminological code (Buchler & Selby 1968:234). In Iroquois systems, on the other hand, the consanguineal content is primary, the affinal content derivative, and marriage exchanges are governed by "various social institutions" (ibid.). Scheffler emphasizes the greater internal consistency of the Dravidian system. He suggests that the fundamental difference between Dravidian and Iroquois is that in the former the consideration of the relative

sex of linking kin is relevant at all generational levels (i.e. the "sibling" versus "cousin" distinction is never neutralized but maintained indefinitely), whereas in the latter only the first ascending generation is considered (1971:242, 244). In other words, the two systems extend the "cross versus parallel" distinction in separate ways (ibid., 233, 247, 252).

All these definitions of Dravidian versus Iroquois share a common implication: Dravidian terminologies are more consistently geared to the practice of bilateral cross-cousin marriage (cf. Trautmann 1981: 85; J. Shapiro 1984:2-3). The Iroquois pattern appears to be a trajectory of this system of classification, in which the immediate, functional consistency associated with cross-cousin marriage has been lost.

Egocentric versus Sociocentric Dualism

> "Unilineal institutions, as we know, do not generate superclasses that exactly correspond to cross/parallel discriminations."
> – T.R. Trautmann (1981:197)

Needham distinguishes between two-section systems of prescriptive alliance, on the one hand, and dual organization, on the other, commenting that although the two "forms of social organization" may coincide, there is no necessary connection between them (1960a:82). This position is reiterated in a later context (Needham 1967:45), where it is supplemented by the suggestion that "because the simple two-section system provides a latitude which the exogamous moieties restrict, the former system developed from the latter." Such a concern with chronological succession, uninteresting to Lévi-Strauss, echoes the early evolutionists.

W. Shapiro (1970) rejects Needham's conviction that two-section terminologies and systems of exogamous moieties are isomorphic and may coincide in particular societies. This would be true only for the

Kariera type, which is more or less confined to Australia. Shapiro claims that the Dravidian-type Beaver terminology "lacks a lineal structure altogether," noting that its "social correlates must be sought elsewhere" than in exogamous moieties. This, of course, is a matter of how we define "lineality". It is true that two-line terminologies of the Beaver type seem incompatible with unilateral affiliation for both sexes. On the other hand, we have shown that this type of terminology implicitly opposes two affinally related male patrilines or, from the perspective of female Ego, two female matrilines. Lineality, in other words, is parallel rather than unilineal, categorical rather than institutional, and egocentric rather than sociocentric. Rivière (1973, 1977) may thus be justified in speaking of "two-line terminologies" (cf. Needham 1966b:142, note 2; 1972) as a defining feature of lowland South American cultures. However, since lineality in Dravidian systems is merely a logical consequence of a system of classification focused on specific marriage arrangements, it would be misleading to refer to these systems as "lineal terminologies," as if lineality itself were the fundamental, defining feature. We have seen that this usage has occasioned considerable confusion when applied to Dravidian terminologies in cognatic societies. Since the categorical opposition of kin and affines is a more fundamental feature of Dravidian systems, perhaps Kaplan's concept of a "kin-affine terminology" is a better designation (cf. Kaplan 1972:285; 1975:127; Schwerin 1982:8). Even Kaplan (1975:128), however, refers to the relationship nomenclature of the Piaroa as "a two-line system which is a variation on the Dravidian."

Rivière claims that some two-line terminologies in South America form a "consistent fit" with grosser social units such as moieties (1973:4; cf. Kracke 1984:101). Kensinger (1979b:83) similarly suggests that two-line terminologies may at times be "used to express the social categories created by . . . social groups" such as moieties or even the marriage sections of the Cashinahua. As W. Shapiro has shown, however, the classification of all first ascending generation cross-collaterals (i.e. *both* MB and FZ) as "affines" (ibid., 9) seems incompatible with either patrilineal or matrilineal moieties. In a patrilineal system, FZ would be classed as kin rather than affine, as would MB in a matrilineal system. Rivière rightly emphasizes that the "lines have nothing to do with descent but are a feature of the terminology" (ibid.,7-8; 1977:39). Dravidian terminologies are not codifications of unilineal moiety systems. Instead, both modes of classification codify an underlying structure of direct exchange. Both result in some form of "lineal" continuity, but as W. Shapiro has shown, the nature of this "lineality" is somewhat different depending on whether affiliation is unilateral or bilateral.

Like Dumont, Yalman (1962:548, 556, 563) suggests that Dravidian terminologies "regulate marriage and sexual relations inside bilateral and largely endogamous 'kindreds'," implying "consistent and regular cross-cousin marriage." In contrast to the emphasis of Rivers, Lévi-Strauss, Murdock, Radcliffe-Brown, and Leach on "lines", lineages, or lineal exogamy, Yalman suggests that even Australian systems such as the Kariera or Murngin may be understood in terms of the regulation of marriage within largely endogamous, bilateral kindreds. Scheffler (1971:243, note 12), too, believes that the Australian systems are "little more than simple variants of the basic Dravidian-type pattern" (cf. also Buchler & Selby 1968:148). Dumont (1966) and Trautmann (1981:237, 436-437) have argued that even the "alternating generations" of Australian section systems may be generated by the underlying logic of Dravidian classification. W. Shapiro (1970), however, insists that two-section terminologies will exhibit different structures if associated with two named super-categories (such as the exogamous moieties of the Kariera and other Australian systems) than if it has no corresponding "sociocentric basis," as among the Beaver Indians, who have a Dravidian, two-line terminology but no moieties. In fact, he holds that the only structural similarity between the Kariera and the Beaver is the opposition between Z/B and W/WB on the zero generation level (ibid., 385). Whereas the former includes FZ in the "lineal" (i.e. "kin") and M in the "affinal" category, the latter reverses their positions (cf. Trautmann 1981:176). Shapiro (1970:386) has observed that a confusion of these two types "pervades much of the literature on two-section systems." Keesing (1975:108) has subsequently illustrated this observation by including FZ = WM (*sic*) in the Dravidian category of "kin", while classifying M as "affine". The ethnography only rarely clarifies the nature of the kin-affine dichotomy in the first ascending generation, but there does seem to be a difference in this respect between completely cognatic peoples and those featuring patrilineal descent groups of some kind (e.g., Tukano- and Pano-speakers). We have suggested (cf. Conclusions: Pano and Chapter 16) that marriage class systems, by permitting Ego to acknowledge kin-affine dichotomies in alternate generations only, represent a reconciliation, perhaps even a stepping stone, between the cross/parallel logic of Dravidian classification and patrilineal descent.

Rivière (1973:10) mentions several "variations" commonly found in connection with two-line terminologies in lowland South America. These include distinctions of relative age, failure to distinguish between siblings of opposite sex, lineal equations, and "the absence *at some level* of the distinction between two lines," i.e. generational equations (italics mine). None of these variations, however, threaten the "fundamental structure of the terminologies." In 1977, a special symposium (Kensinger 1979a) was arranged with the explicit aim of exploring lowland South American correlations between such terminological variations on the two-line

theme and various features of social organization. Schwerin (1982:6) agrees that "the Dravidian system provides a starting point for the analysis of South American systems" (cf. also Henley 1982:89; Kensinger 1984a; Balée 1985).

In this book, we have also been concerned with the possible social correlates of teminological variation in lowland South America. We have seen that a number of factors may generate equations or distinctions deviating from the classical Dravidian pattern. These factors include various patterns of affiliation (including post-marital residence), marriage practices and social stratification. Furthermore, modifications in the terminology generated by one specific feature of social organization may in themselves be conducive to behavioural modification in other spheres of organization, so that the terminology serves as an information-processing code interacting in a *systemic* way with actual behaviour. We may conclude, with Kaplan (1977:394), that the variation forthcoming from the basic two-line terminology is indeed "startling".

Conclusions

Scheffler (1971:231) discusses two types of theory which have been advanced to account for the structure of Dravidian kin terminologies: (1) those relating it to cross-cousin marriage, and (2) those attributing it to dual organization. In the latter category he includes the "two-section" (kin-affine) interpretation, apparently understanding Needham's model to presuppose "affiliation" (ibid.,233) to discrete (if implicit) "social structural entities" (ibid.,235). We have seen that Needham's emphasis on the role of lineal descent in prescriptive alliance systems indeed gives the impression of such an assumption. On the other hand, Needham would undoubtedly agree with Scheffler's (ibid.,234) objection that "the alleged implicit moieties or sections are only analytical artefacts of the system of kin classification, and it is that system that accounts for them rather than vice versa."

Finding that Dravidian kin terminologies may be associated with a wide range of marriage preferences and patterns of affiliation, Scheffler (ibid.,237) concludes that "the presence of Dravidian-type systems of kin classification is not in the least dependent on the presence of any sort of marriage rule" (but cf. the response of Trautmann 1981:60-62), or on "the presence of descent-ordered groups or categories." He rejects Lévi-Strauss' (1969:128) conviction that the cross/parallel distinction coincides "perfectly with dual organization" as downright "false" (Scheffler 1971:242, note 11). His fundamental arguments for this position are: (1) that in Dravidian systems men and women use the same terms for their joint offspring, which is inconsistent with a system of classification based on moiety affiliation, and (2) that moieties are not "invariant structural features" of societies with Dravidian terminologies (ibid.,233-234, 241; Lounsbury 1964b:1079, note 4).

Scheffler's conclusion that Dravidian terminologies are not determined by dual organization is obviously correct, but his arguments are not as effective as those of W. Shapiro (1970). The first objection could be countered with a perspective suggested by Scheffler himself: "It might be supposed that each term has a different meaning for male as opposed to female speakers" (ibid.,234). In fact, we have reasons to believe that this is precisely the case for a Dravidian-type terminology such as that of the Piaroa. Speaker's sex is crucial to the delineation of same-sex, kin-affine categories, evidencing a *parallel* rather than unilineal mode of classification. Female Ego among the Piaroa uses the same terms (*chiminya/chiminyahu* = +1 affines) for her HP as male Ego uses for his WP. Correspondingly, female Ego's *chuhöri/chuhörihu* (-1 affines) include BC = HZC = BWC, whereas the same terms used by male Ego include ZC = WBC = ZHC =

CSp. Inversely, terms for offspring (*chitti/chittihu* = -1 kin) include BC for male Ego but ZC for a female. Theoretically, *chitti* could mean "-1 male, own moiety" for male Ego, but "-1 male, opposite moiety" for a female. There is no inherent contradiction between the factor of relative sex in Dravidian terminologies and the recognition of unilineal moieties (cf. Kaplan 1984:151, note 2, for another formulation.) In fact, the sex-biased, parallel views of the social universe inherent in Dravidian terminologies may represent the link between egocentric and sociocentric dualism (cf. Conclusions: Pano). Scheffler's second objection should be viewed in the light of Lévi-Strauss' own suggestion, consistent with Rivers' observations on Melanesia, that as their "functional value (viz, to establish a system of reciprocity) is identical," cross-cousin marriage appears precisely where dual organization is missing (Lévi-Strauss 1969:103). By reproducing the old error of mistaking the emic model of dual organization for actual social structure, Scheffler misses this point altogether. In failing to recognize that systems of classification are mere interpretations of structural regularities of a more objective nature, Scheffler denies that the two theories of Dravidian systems can be "reconciled and made complementary" in the sense suggested by Lévi-Strauss (Scheffler 1971:231-232). He states that "the disagreement about this matter is a disagreement about how particular societies order social relationships." Instead, we would say that the difference is a matter of how an underlying social order is *expressed*.

A comparison of the implications of cross/parallel extensions in Iroquois- and Dravidian-type systems (cf. ibid.,241, Table I) reveals that whereas the former's disregard for the sex of linking relatives in genealogical levels beyond the first ascending generation implies that the terminology in itself could not produce a consistent alignment with any type of lineal descent system, the consistency of Dravidian systems implies that all cousins classified as siblings would belong to Ego's own moiety, whether patrilineal or matrilineal, if the symmetric alliance structure had been codified in the form of dual organization. In this respect, i.e. zero generation affinality, Dravidian terminologies and dual organization are indeed congruent. Their incongruity in the first ascending generation, demonstrated for the Beaver Indians by W. Shapiro (1970), is another matter. If we accept Scheffler's (1971:243, note 12) suggestion that Australian systems like that of the Kariera are simply variants of the Dravidian pattern, and Shapiro's demonstration that the Kariera system is congruent with a system of unilineal moieties, we might conclude that Kariera-type systems represent a trajectory of Dravidian systems adapted to unilineal descent. We have indicated why a system of alternating generation marriage classes would be crucial to this transformation.

Scheffler (ibid.,245, 252) concludes that his analysis of Dravidian-type systems is "compatible with, but does not require, the bilateral cross-cousin marriage theory of such systems," and that the most that may be said is that where "affinal relatives are classified as though they were kin of certain categories or types to begin with, there may be some sort of expectation about marriage to particular types or categories of kinswomen (and – men)." This cautious approach to the relationship between classification and behaviour illustrates the extreme emphasis of so-called cognitive anthropologists on formal analysis. Scheffler's reservations concerning the direct connection between Dravidian terminologies and marriage practices has been criticized for lacking "the historical framework" (Trautmann 1981:236) and for neglecting the emic meaning of kin terms as revealed by the social contexts in which they are used, thus presenting analyses which are simply "uninteresting to the social anthropologist" (Kaplan 1984:135, 153, note 11).

Kaplan (1973) shows that the inheritance of alliance relationships implicit in Dravidian kin terminologies may serve to maintain group cohesion rather than distinguish different alliance units. Following Dumont, Yalman, and Rivière, she rejects the assumption that marriage prescriptions will be associated with unilineal descent (ibid., 556), demonstrating how the cognatic Piaroa reproduce "alliance-based kinship groups" by emphasizing three congruent ideals: (1) local group endogamy, (2) genealogical kindred endogamy (i.e. cross-cousin marriage), and (3) the replication of the alliance relationships of one's parents (ibid., 565-568). Kaplan admits that the second of these ideals tends to be congruent with the first and implicit in the third, suggesting only that "each has considerably different implications for an interpretation of social organization." A single mode of organization, in other words, may be conceptualized according to three different emic models. We might add that the imposition of dual organization on this same symmetric alliance structure would merely amount to yet a fourth mode of classification, requiring no behavioural modifications (cf. Kaplan 1984:151, note 2). Patrilineal moieties are actually present among the Piaroa, but these have no connection with marriage practices. Were they exogamous, we would expect FZ to be classified as a kinswoman rather than an affine in the kin-affine dichotomy, i.e. according to a Kariera rather than a classical Dravidian pattern. In order for the reclassification of the FZ to entail as little semantic dissonance as possible, we would expect to find either distinct affinal terms (as among Gê and some Tukano) or a system of alternating generation marriage classes (as among Panoans.)

In conclusion, we may broadly distinguish five different approaches to the relation between two-line terminologies, dual organization, and symmetric alliance:

1. Rivers, Morgan, Tylor, Frazer, Perry, and Lowie held that dual organization was responsible for both the terminology and

the practice of cross-cousin marriage. More recently, Needham has suggested that two-section terminologies develop subsequent to dual organization.

2. Dumont, Yalman, Rivière, Kaplan, Trautmann, and Schwerin have argued that two-line terminologies codify cross-cousin marriage, without any influence from dual organization. In his detailed survey of Dravidian systems in India, Trautmann (1981:3, 23-24, 60-62, 214-215, 229) hypothesizes that "bilateral cross-cousin marriage is *ancestral* to all particular cognate Dravidian systems we find in the ethnographic present."

3. Lévi-Strauss suggests that two-line terminologies may be generated both by dual organization and by cross-cousin marriage, both of which are expressions of an underlying principle of direct reciprocity.

4. Maybury-Lewis dissociates dual organization and two-line terminologies from marriage practices, attributing both to the antithetical nature of human thought. This extreme mentalistic position represents a trajectory of some ideas propounded by Needham and Lévi-Strauss. Ortiz also dissociates dual organization from marriage practices.

5. W. Shapiro, Dole, and Scheffler distinguish between different types of two-line terminology, to which different conclusions apply. Shapiro finds that the Kariera type is congruent with dual organization (unilineal descent), whereas the Dravidian-type terminology of the Beaver is not. Dole notes that the Dravidian Cross-Cousin type is most consistent with cross-cousin marriage, whereas bifurcate merging (Iroquois) may represent a subsequent development. Scheffler claims that neither Dravidian nor Iroquois systems are compatible with dual organization, but observes that both are consistent with cross-cousin marriage. In sum, there is agreement on the association between two-line terminologies and cross-cousin marriage, but some hesitation to relate these terminologies to dual organization.

The position adopted by the present author represents a combination of positions 2, 3, and 5. It has been assumed that both two-line terminologies and dual organization are systems of classification codifying a structure which we may describe in etic terms as direct exchange, or symmetric alliance, and that this structure may be expressed in terms of yet other models (e.g. rules enjoining sister exchange, bilateral cross-cousin marriage, replication of alliances over the generations, etc.) The congruity between these different models has inspired both historical and functionalist explanations, but these have generally been founded on a recurrent confusion of classification and organization. Thus, the early evolutionists explained one mode of classification (kin terminology) as the survival of another (dual organization), which they regarded as an actual "social structure". Lévi-Strauss realized that these different features were merely incomplete reflections, or interpretations, of a structural reality which remains only partially visible to its actors. Precisely as predicted by Lévi-Strauss (1969:103), dual organization and prescriptive symmetric alliance appear to have a complementary distribution in lowland South America. There is a correlation between dual organization, large villages and extended exogamy, on the one hand, and between cognation, two-line terminologies, small and isolated groups, and bilateral cross-cousin marriage, on the other. Of the 19 instances of dual organization, 14 are associated with large or formerly large villages, while only six equate the two cross-cousins with potential spouses in the Dravidian manner. (Four of these six are Pano-speakers, whose marriage class systems are unique in South America. Outside the Pano family, the Parintintin are the only people in our sample who combine Dravidian classification and exogamous moieties. The sixth case is the Piaroa, whose moieties have nothing to do with marriage.) Of the 23 cultures the local groups of which average less than 50, on the other hand, as many as 18 equate cross-cousins and potential spouses. Of the 33 cultures in which bilateral, true cross-cousin marriage is enjoined, 23 have local groups averaging less than 50 and 21 reckon bilateral affiliation. Of the six groups classified as isolated, finally, all but one (Sirionó) practice bilateral cross-cousin marriage.

Rivière (1984:108) proposes that the mechanism of exchange inherent in two-line terminologies "only works within a restricted social range." Schwerin (1982:439) similarly suggests that the Dravidian kin-affine (or Kin Integration) system works only in small groups. If the population of the local group "expands much beyond 100 members, the system begins to break down." This hypothesis is consistent with the correlations just presented. Dual organization, we have suggested, is an alternative expression of kin-affine duality associated with large, cohesive, uxorilocal villages.

Ethnographers of the South American lowlands have approached the relationship between two-line terminologies, dual organization, and symmetric alliance in various ways. Some have seen dual organization as more or less implicit in the terminology (Chagnon 1968:57, note 4; Siskind 1973:199, note 3; Jackson 1975a:8; C. Hugh-Jones 1977a:96; Dole 1979:29). Others have regarded dual organization as a potential trajectory of two-line terminologies (Lévi-Strauss 1945:39; Oberg 1973:205; Goldman 1963:288; Århem 1981:299). A few have been content merely with positing their structural compatibility (Rivière 1973:4; Kensinger 1979b:82; Maybury-Lewis 1979b: 224). Yet others have made a point of altogether dissociating two-line terminologies from dual organization (Basso 1973:90; Kaplan 1972, 1973, 1975; Schwerin 1982:2, 7).

W. Shapiro, Dole, and Scheffler are obviously justified in distinguishing different variants of two-line terminologies. At one end of the spectrum are those systems which most consistently codify bilateral cross-cousin marriage (symmetric alliance.) These fully Dravidian systems rarely accompany dual organization. Towards the other end are a number of variants featuring an attenuated two-line structure only. Societies recognizing dual organization generally have kin terminologies of the latter kind. It appears not only that a consistent terminological codification of symmetric alliance will be superfluous in a system of exogamous moieties, but that unilineal principles of affiliation actually contradict the logic of Dravidian kin terminologies. Those rare societies where ego- and sociocentric dualism occur as alternative, context-specific models, e.g. the Cashinahua (Kensinger 1980, 1984b) and Parintintin (Kracke 1984), represent a presumably transient juncture, likely with time to yield more consistently to either alternative. While equifinal in terms of alliance, Dravidian terminologies and dual organization codify two separate principles of affiliation. Their congruity pertains to objective structures of exchange, i.e. social organization, whereas their incompatibility is a logical matter relating to classification. Shapiro and Scheffler have emphasized the latter aspect and paid too little attention to the former. Instead of simply juxtaposing two modes of classification and focusing on their differences, we should concentrate on the behavioural implications which they may initially have in common. Semantic differences which are less relevant to exchange (such as whether FZ is classified as "kin" or "affine") should not be allowed to obscure the crucial issue, i.e. the ideal, behavioural equifinality of two-line kin terminologies and exogamous moieties. The common denominator of these two features is not the way in which social categories are constituted, but the way in which prestations are exchanged. In other words, the difference is less a matter of what people are actually doing than of how they think of it.

275

Chapter 22
Hierarchy

"No doubt, in the majority of cases, hierarchy will be identified in some way with power, but there is no necessity for this, as the case of India will show."
– L. Dumont (1972:55)

The question of indigenous social stratification in the South American lowlands is an intriguing one. The almost exclusive reliance on organic materials, which rapidly deteriorate in the tropical forest, seriously impairs archaeological research. In contrast to the civilizations of the highlands and the arid Peruvian coast, even highly integrated, stratified polities might thus have expanded, declined, and vanished without trace.

Ecological Considerations

Meggers (1954, 1957, 1971) has suggested that the resort to slash- and burn agriculture in tropical forest environments imposes absolute constraints on the development of "advanced" culture. Her conclusions in favour of environmental determinism are supported "by the fact that no advanced culture has developed in the Amazon basin or has been maintained there by a subsistence pattern dominated by slash-and burn agriculture" (1957:83). Carneiro (1973), on the other hand, claims that Meggers has underestimated the productive potential of shifting cultivation. He shows that the Kuikuru of the Upper Xingú could have supported villages of 2,000 persons. Clastres (1977:76-78) similarly asserts that the Guaraní were quite capable of maintaining high population densities, and Reichel-Dolmatoff (1973:29-30) notes that the brand-tillage agriculture of sub-Andean chiefdoms in Colombia "did not lead to rapid soil depletion but proved to be a highly efficient agricultural system." In the same vein, Dumond (1969:344) argues that the development of centralized, stratified systems such as that of the Classic Maya "is by no means impossible under conditions of shifting cultivation." He notes that significant ceremonial centers pre-date intensive agriculture in Mesoamerica, and concludes that "centralization and urbanization tend to pre-date the appearance of intensive cultivation and of heavy population growth" (ibid.,345). Where feasible, population growth would nevertheless stimulate the emergence of intensive agriculture.

In fact, remains of more intensive agricultural systems are being discovered in several regions of lowland South America. In the lowlands of Bolivia, Ecuador, Colombia, and Surinam, extensive areas of raised agricultural fields represent deliberate attempts to "expand the ecological conditions present in the limited areas of riverine flood plains" (Lathrap 1970:160-163). In the Llanos de Mojos alone, W. M. Denevan estimates that a total of 50,000 acres of ridged fields may have supported half a million people. In the Upper Xingú, impressive ditches and other earthworks (Villas Boas & Villas Boas 1974:19) have been encountered. On Marajó Island, Meggers and Evans (1973) interpret the mounds associated with Marajoara Phase pottery as evidence of advanced social stratification. An archaeological survey in the Ariari River region of the southwestern Colombian *llanos* has revealed "extensive sites covering several acres with considerable depth of occupation," suggesting "large indigenous concentrations . . . not previously considered to be characteristic of this region" (Morey & Marwitt 1978:252, note 3).

Ethnohistorical Evidence

If earthworks constitute the major archaeological evidence of indigenous stratification, historical accounts confirm the existence of impressive lowland chiefdoms at the time of the European conquest. According to the chronicle of Gaspar de Carvajal, a Spanish expedition down the Napo River in 1542 encountered an extensive "kingdom" known as Aparia the Lesser. Lathrap (1972:18) suggest that this culture would have been akin to the "vigorous Omagua state" further upriver. Carvajal (1934) reports very high population densities, with villages crowding the river banks and some settlements extending several miles. The ruler of the Omagua was considered divine, and his authority was recognized for more than a hundred leagues along the river. Like several contemporary peoples in the north-west Amazon, the Omagua distinguished a class of servants, or slaves. According to Lathrap, both the Omagua and Aparia the Lesser would have been descendants of Aparia the Greater, near the mouth of the Napo. These westernmost outposts of Tupí migration would still have been "pushing against the peoples of the Andean foothills when Gonzalo Pizarro arrived in 1541" (Lathrap 1972:20). Lathrap's hypothesis of upstream migration, which contradicts Meggers' and Evans' (1973) account of Marajoara culture as an Andean intrusion, is consistent with the oral traditions of both the Omagua and other people of the north-west Amazon (e.g. the Tukano-speakers). Rather than attributing the emergence of social stratification in the lowlands to Andean stimuli, this theory views tropical forest culture as an autonomous source of such developments (cf. Lathrap 1971; Morey & Marwitt 1978:251-254).

Synthesizing data from the *Handbook of South American Indians*, Steward and Faron (1959:174-261) list a number of historical chiefdoms encountered in the lowlands of Colombia, Venezuela, and Bolivia. Here, along the fringes of the Andes, indigenous social stratification has been easier to document than in the remote interior of the Amazon basin. The Arawak-speaking Mojo, for instance, were said to have had villages of up to 400 houses ruled by a class of hereditary nobility (ibid.,252-257). In the more remote parts of the Amazon basin, epidemics deriving from European colonists would have ravaged the indigenous population long before European exploration. Clastres' (1977:64–82) population estimates for the Guaraní illustrate the devastating implications of this assumption. The Guaraní appear to have dwindled from 1,500,000 in 1539 to 200,000 in 1650. Wachtel's estimates for the Inca suggest a drop from 10 million in 1530 to one million in 1600. If a decline of similar proportions can be postulated for more or less uncontacted cultures in remote areas of the Amazon basin, we may expect that this would have involved a complete breakdown of indigenous social structures prior to any documentation.

Long-Distance Exchange

One of the first features of social organization to deteriorate under the impact of the European invasion would have been indigenous exchange networks. As in other parts of the world, control of external exchange is to this day an important foundation for prestige in the South American lowlands. Particularly conspicuous examples in our sample include the Kalapalo and other groups of the Upper Xingú, the Tukano-speakers of the north-west Amazon, and the Machiguenga, Jívaroans, and other tribes along the eastern fringe of the Andes. Reichel-Dolmatoff (1973:33) writes that "most Sub-Andean Indians were great traders and it seems that in many cases wealth – and with it social rank and political control – was based not so much on surplus food production, stability of food supply, or war honors, as on successful trade of such industrial products as gold, cotton cloth, and salt." Recently, there has been a surge of interest in reconstructing indigenous trade routes in the tropical forests of South America (Gade 1972, Lathrap 1973a, Oberem 1974, Camino 1977, Myers 1983). Of particular interest is the frequently attested articulation of highland and lowland trade networks, whereby tropical forest products found their way across the Andes to the Peruvian coast, and metal objects from the highlands far into the eastern lowlands (cf. MacNeish, Patterson & Browman 1975; Métraux 1948a:75-76). Considering how local prestige hierarchies may have been based on the control of such long-distance exchange, we may assume not only that epidemics would have been likely to strike precisely those polities which had this basis for hierarchy, but also that the abandonment of trade routes by one population could have precipitated social collapse in another. The rapid Spanish conquest of the Andes may thus have set off a chain reaction with far-ranging consequences for the indigenous peoples of the Amazon basin. In advocating units of analysis transcending the "tribe", recognizing "social systems that embrace both highlands and lowlands," Nugent (1982:231, 238) appears to anticipate such an interpretation.

Ethnography

Lévi-Strauss (1945:41, 44; 1963c:104-110) concludes that the simpler cultures of lowland South America have devolved from a level of complexity intermediate to their present status and that of the Andean civilizations. The common heritage of these divergent trajectories, he suggests, is particularly obvious in the pervasive institution of dual organization. The hypothesis that lowland

South American band societies are the product of cultural devolution has been reiterated by Martin (1969), Lathrap (1973b), Clastres (1977:69), and Nugent (1982). Morey and Marwitt (1978:255-256) conclude that "there is a substantial body of evidence that indicates that both the size and complexity of many aboriginal cultures occupying the floodplains of the major rivers have been badly underestimated – not by early travellers and explorers, but by their ethnographic successors."

Have we found any ethnographical indications, then, that contemporary lowland cultures have previously maintained more complex social systems? In fact, for 40 of the 48 societies in our sample, we have encountered reports of social hierarchy in one form or another. In 14 cases, name transmission implies succession to differentially ranked roles, and in 15, other modes of hereditary succession are mentioned. Birth-order hierarchies are emphasized in at least 12 groups. Hierarchies of greater and lesser leaders are reported from 15 groups, and class stratification or possible wife-giver/wife-taker relationships (cf. the Txicáo) from seven. Competition for prestige, through trade, feasting, and/or polygyny, occurs in at least 19 cases in our sample. An ideal of rank endogamy also appears to have been operative in 19 cases. Taken together, these numbers indicate that concepts of social hierarchy are integral to the traditional ideology of many lowland groups.

Symmetric Alliance

Lévi-Strauss has shown that dual organization and the structurally congruent practice of bilateral cross-cousin marriage are based on a principle of direct reciprocity. Since debts immediately cancel each other out, sister exchange is a transaction between equals. This is often the conscious rationale with which exchange marriages are motivated, whether the debts thus neutralized would

278

have involved bride-service, bride-price, or simply deference. Whereas asymmetric alliance in other parts of the world (notably South-East Asia) has tended to generate hierarchies of wife-givers and wife-takers (cf. Leach 1954, 1961b), hierarchy in South America cannot be explained by the structural implications of unilateral marriage. Contrary to what has sometimes been assumed (cf. Lounsbury 1978), even the highly stratified Inca empire of the Pre-Columbian Andes appears to have favoured symmetric alliance (Zuidema 1977). South American instances of matrilateral marriage preferences are few and scattered: an ideal of MBD marriage has been suggested for the Sirionó, Txicáo, Suyá, Aguaruna, Mapuche (Faron 1961, 1962) and 16th century Chibcha (Villamarin & Villamarin 1975). In none of the lowland cases, however, does matrilateral cross-cousin marriage appear to be geared to social hierarchy, although the Txicáo may possibly be an exception.

Diarchy

"Why do societies affected by a high degree of endogamy so urgently need to mystify themselves and see themselves as governed by exogamous institutions?"
– C. Lévi-Strauss (1963d:131)

The problem posed by Lévi-Strauss is why dual organization, if a manifestation of immediate reciprocity, should occur "at both the extreme levels – the higher and the lower of the South American scale of cultures" (1945:47). If the institution of dual organization is a codification of reciprocity, it would be expected to disagree entirely with the asymmetric principles of exchange characteristic of stratified societies. Lévi-Strauss suggests that "the problem of dual organization in South America is to be taken as a whole" (ibid.,42, note 7). Moiety divisions are as characteristic of the Andean Quechua and Aymará as of the Gê, Tupí, and Pano. Yet, the differences in terms of social complexity between the Andean empires and the villages of the Pano are enormous. Why does a vast, hierarchical empire cling to a cosmology which seems more at home in the kin-affine duality of endogamous local groups?

The answer may lie in the phenomenon of diarchy. The existence of two chiefs, one for each moiety, is characteristic of the Gê and other lowland peoples featuring dual organization. The opposition of the two leaders is commonly associated with the opposition of sacred and secular (cf. Lévi-Strauss 1969:69; Needham 1960a:100). Even though Andean moiety oppositions such as Hanan-Hurin (Upper-Lower) are often expressed in asymmetric terms, the hierarchical dimension in reality *intersects* the moiety division (cf. Ortiz 1969 for a detailed demonstration of the same phenomenon). Each moiety, in effect, has its own hierarchical organization, as could be exemplified by the double *varayoq* structures of Andean villages such as Chuschi (B.J. Isbell 1977:86). According to ethnohistorical sources, diarchy was also practiced among the Inca of Cuzco (Duviols 1979), the Guanaca of Colombia (Hernández 1946:945), the Chipaya of Carangas (La Barre 1946:583), the Lupaqa of the Titicaca basin (Murra 1968:117), and "most other peoples in the Andes" (ibid.). The horizontal, ceremonially and spatially more conspicuous moiety divisions would have neutralized the vertical dimension of political and economic stratification, augmenting moiety allegiance and minimizing tensions between strata. The same relationship between horizontal and vertical dimensions has been observed by Houdart-Morizot (1976:264) in the contemporary Andean village of Cuenca. I have offered a similar interpretation (Hornborg 1983) of ethnographic data from the Pampas River area of Peru (Palomino 1970, 1971; Earls 1971).

Against this background, the occurrence of dual organization among stratified societies no longer presents a paradox. On the

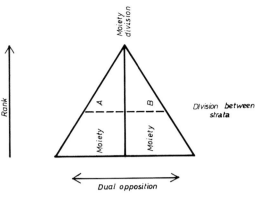

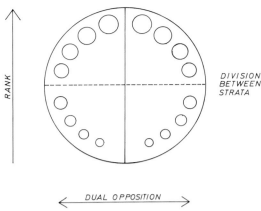

Fig. 15. The articulation of dualism and hierarchy underlying the phenomenon of diarchy.

Fig. 16. Spatial representation of the articulation of dualism and hierarchy common to several indigenous cultures of South America.

contrary, by maintaining the illusion of reciprocity, dual organization may well have *facilitated* the growth of hierarchical systems among populations traditionally "opposed" to the State (cf. Clastres 1977). Dual organization can serve to conceal hierarchy, so that there need be little cognitive dissonance between egalitarian ideals and a highly stratified social reality. Nevertheless, the recognition that the moiety division is intersected by another, asymmetric dimension is implicit in the cosmology of South America and particularly of the Andes. The two perpendicular axes of egalitarianism and hierarchy constitute a system of classification fundamental to lowland peoples such as the Bororo (C. Crocker 1969, 1971), Barasana (C. Hugh-Jones 1979:104-105), and Cashinahua (Kensinger 1985b; J. Shapiro 1985), and pervasive throughout the highlands, where it has been formalized for Pomabamba by Morissette and Racine (1973:181), and for Pinchimuro by Gow (1978:207). This cosmological structure has also been recognized in Andamarca by Ossio (1978:388), in Chaupiwaranga by Fonseca (1981:178), and in ethnohistorical material from the North Coast of Peru by Netherly (1977:110).

Utilizing the symbols of European cultural traditions, the articulation of dualism and hierarchy could be represented as a vertically bisected pyramid (Fig. 15). In the symbolic code of indigenous South America, however, diarchy is often expressed spatially in site layouts by opposing two halves along the circumferences of which differentially ranked entities are arranged into two corresponding, mirror-image hierarchies (Hornborg 1982; Fig.16).

Dual organization is at once a tangible imprint of reciprocity and a condition conducive to its own negation, i.e. asymmetry. Once the function of establishing reciprocity is left to a pair of sociocentric moieties, an increment in genealogical exogamy may be expected to yield more severely hierarchical in-law relationships. In addition, the sheer numerical expansion with which dual organization is most often associated would encourage the formation of viable, endogamous "castes". If the metaphor is permitted, the paradox of dual organization is that of an evacuated pupa: it becomes obsolete precisely when it most rigidly expresses the form of its previous contents.

280

Rank Endogamy and Relative Age

If dualism and hierarchy can be reconciled in the form of diarchy, it remains to be shown how hierarchy can be compatible with symmetric alliance. Dumont (1957:7-12) demonstrates how in southern India the "tendency to graded statuses" in Dravidian systems is based on different degrees of endogamy. Differences of status are expressed in terms of relative age, but their foundation may also be the different kinds of union from which a person is born. Irrespective of the level of inclusiveness (caste, sub-caste, or kindred), the children of an orthodox, endogamous marriage reproduce the status of their parents, whereas offspring of secondary or "irregular" unions (e.g. to younger sisters of the first wife, or to concubines) will be of lower rank. There is also "a tendency, among the people connected with chieftainship, to express or attain a higher status by setting themselves a higher degree of endogamy than is generally required" (ibid.,10-11). In some castes, "junior" sons will typically be assigned the role of servants in chiefly households. The eldest son of the first or principal wife "ranks above a hierarchy of sons born from secondary unions between persons of unequal status" (ibid.,12). Some castes are "made up of two endogamous sections, respectively great and little, pure and mixed" (ibid., note 6). Dumont notes that the mechanism of relative endogamy responsible for the caste system pervades "the whole sphere of kinship" (ibid.,7), and Yalman (1962:550) similarly suggests that Sinhalese kindred may be described as "micro-castes".

Zuidema (1969) proposes that identical mechanisms have been operative in Inca Peru and among the ancestors of the Apinayé. The extreme endogamy of chiefs would provide a common rationale for ZD marriage among the Tupí, on the one hand, and the union between the Inca king and his full sister, on the other (ibid.,136). Similar principles appear to underlie Métraux' (1948d:419) datum that the chief of the Arawak-speaking Bauré of lowland Bolivia transmitted his title to his eldest son only "if he had been born of a noble woman, that is, if his mother were a chief's daughter." The ranked sibs and lineages of the Cubeo tend to form as the sons of a single, polygynous headman are divided into sets of uterine brothers, so that the sons of one wife are opposed to those of another (Goldman 1963:115-117). Steward and Faron (1959: 188) note that, "among a few northern Andean chiefdoms, such as the Chibcha, chiefs tended to preserve the purity of their family line through marriage to their sisters or their sisters' daughters, a practice similar to the marriage of the Inca emperor to his sister," and suggest that "this custom was probably also practiced by nobles, whose status was strongly fixed by heredity." The endogamous "Z" marriage of the Inca ruler may have been geared to their concepts of parallel transmission (Zuidema 1967; Scheffler & Lounsbury 1971:184-185) and Hawaiian cousin terms (Zuidema 1977) in the manner suggested by Dietschy (1977) for the Karajá, Tapirapé, and Apinayé. Zuidema's conclusion that the Inca had a caste system would still be valid. Sarmiento de Gamboa (1908:31) explains the Hanan/ Hurin division of the Inca province of Cañar in terms of primary and secondary sons of a legendary ancestor: the five sons born by his primary wife founded Hanansaya, while Hurinsaya was formed by the five sons of his concubine.

The ethnic composition of several contemporary, four-*ayllu* villages in the Department of Ayacucho (Palomino 1971) suggests that similar principles of relative endogamy may still be operative (Hornborg 1983). Precisely as in southern India, dual divisions here reflect the opposition of pure and mixed strata. As in the days of the Inca, Hanan (Upper) is opposed to Hurin (Lower), and Collana (Highest, Foremost) to Chawpi (Middle) and Cayao (Commoners). The fact that one *ayllu* may refer to another as "younger brothers" (Palomino 1970:67; Earls 1971:76) suggests an idiom of relative age.

Lévi-Strauss (1963d) discovered that marriage rules among the Bororo and Apinayé would generate endogamous subdivisions of society. Among the former, C. Crocker (1969:47) notes that hierarchical concepts of relative age are "a major organisational principle." Much as in the birth-order hierarchies of the north-west Amazon, the highest ranked lineage is termed "our elder brother", and those of lower rank are described as "younger" (cf. Goldman 1963:27, 98, 117-118; Bidou 1977:113; Århem 1981:102; Hill 1985; Chernela 1985: 35; Kelly 1985; Kensinger 1985b; Pollock 1985:10; Price 1985:16; J. Shapiro 1985). Lévi-Strauss (1936:278) remarks that among the Bororo the age hierarchy correlates with clear differences in material wealth.

The idiom of relative age is integral to Dravidian systems in India (Dumont 1953a: 36; 1957:11-12) and South America (Rivière 1973:10, 12; Basso 1985). Distinctions of relative age have been reported from at least 30 of the 48 lowland cultures in our South American sample. Murdock (1949:110) discovered an "appreciable tendency" toward an association between distinctions of relative age and bilateral descent. Needham (1966a:31) suggests that "in a lineal descent system categories will be preponderant, whereas in a cognatic society there will be a lesser emphasis on categories in favour of social distinctions based most generally on relative age" (cf. also Needham 1972:23-24). In a later context (1971b:cv), Needham notes that the correlation "seems to be borne out." Rivière (1966c:59) demonstrates that the Trio employ distinctions of relative age precisely in those contexts where cognatic classification is emphasized, even though relationships are basically classified in terms of genealogically defined categories. Indeed, even if unilateral principles have gained some prominence in 15 of the 30 groups in our

sample distinguishing relative age, bilateral affiliation remains fundamental to most of these.

Lave (1966:191) suggests that the distinction of relative age may be an effect of oblique (ZD) marriage, particularly if "a distinction is made between the marriage-ability of elder and younger sisters' children, and if elder and younger brothers follow different marriage preferences." Lave (ibid.,192) notes that there are numerous references to such marriage preferences in the literature. We have seen that birth order is a crucial consideration in South Indian marriages (Dumont 1957:11-12). The emphasis on birth order in Suyá and Krĩkatí name transmission may reflect a similar ideology. The reciprocal exchange of name-giving services between cross-sex Krĩkatí siblings, formally reminiscent of bilateral cross-cousin marriage, articulates pairs of siblings according to birth order, e.g. firstborn son and firstborn daughter, and so on. These distinctions of relative age are integral to the system of classification as a whole, not the effect specifically of oblique marriage. Lave (1966:194) concludes that "age-based differences in status appear to be especially important where ZD marriage occurs." Viewing this correlation from the opposite angle, we suggest that endogamous unions such as ZD marriage represent a mechanism for status differentiation in Dravidian, symmetric alliance systems, where such differentiation is generally expressed in terms of relative age. Significantly, ZD marriage is almost exclusively confined to lowland South America and the Dravidian peoples of India (Kirchhoff 1932:58-62; Trautmann 1981:206-207).

Dravidian terminologies are conducive to social hierarchy not only by furnishing the idiom of relative age. In conjunction with an increase in social scale, the very principle of repetitive alliance in itself would encourage the emergence of endogamous enclaves. Segregation in turn leads naturally to boundary maintenance phrased in hierarchical terms.

Ethnic Hierarchies

If relative age and/or birth-order-determined specialist roles is the idiom in which hierarchy is generally expressed in indigenous South America, the practice of rank endogamy has provided the foundation for yet another representation of status differences, one based on putative ethnic distinctions. The Indian parallels are once again obvious. Each endogamous subgroup or "caste" will develop its own ideological identity, and the endogamous extremes at the top and bottom of the scale are most likely to be regarded as ethnically altogether distinct. Andean examples include the alien Collana *ayllus* of many Quechua villages (Palomino 1971) and the inferior Uru enclaves of the Titicaca basin (Murra 1968:126-127). In the lowlands, we have seen that the Sherente think of two of their clans (the Prase' and Krozake') as the remnants of an alien tribe, and that Tukano-speakers justify their exploitation of the endogamous Makú by referring to their inferior ethnic origins (Jackson 1976:6, 25-27). Ethnic rank endogamy has been particularly emphasized in the north-west Amazon (cf. Hill 1985:29, 31-32, note 5) and among some Chaco peoples, such as the Kadiwéu and Tereno (Steward & Faron 1959:303).

Endogamy and hierarchy seem everywhere in South America to be conceived of in an egocentric, *relative* sense, so that notions of higher and lower tend to follow a concentric model coinciding with levels of social inclusiveness (cf. Dumont 1972). Andean concepts such as Hanan/Hurin and the tripartite hierarchy Collana/Payan/Cayao were applicable at any level of socio-political integration, whether the local village or the Inca empire as a whole (Zuidema 1964). The Tukanoan hierarchy of specialist roles is equally adjustable to context and scale.

Implicitly, the highest-ranked segment is identified with the social totality, as when phratric names among the Arawak-speaking Wakuénai are equivalent to the names of the highest-ranked sib in each phratry (Hill 1985:27). The descending order of lower statuses seems to be conceived of as a scale of increasingly marginal and attenuated levels of membership in society. Hence the extraneous (non-social or ethnically distinct) aspects of low-status strata such as the Makú (cf. Goldman 1963:7, 96, 105-107; Jackson 1976).

Highland-Lowland Parallels

"Perhaps a close study of social conditions in the tropical forest could shed specific light on the spectacular historical developments in the Andes."
– I. Goldman (1963:5)

In 1948, Steward (1948b:508) accentuated the role of the Ceja de la Montaña as "an effective barrier between the Highland and jungle peoples" of South America. An increasing amount of evidence, however, suggests that indigenous populations of the highlands and lowlands not only have interacted in long-distance exchange networks, but in several respects even represent a common cultural tradition. The entire complex of dual organization, diarchy, rank endogamy, distinctions of relative age, and ethnic stratification appears to be a fundamental potentiality of both areas. Scattered lowland evidence, particularly from Tukano and Gê, suggests widespread themes of hierarchical classification, of which the Andean kingdoms may simply represent the most conspicuous elaboration. The five age-grades of Inca Cuzco, for instance, are formally reminiscent of the five-tiered birth-order hierarchy of the Tukano-speakers. The occurrence in the lowlands of special stools for dignitaries reminds Steward and Faron (1959:315) of Andean thrones.

Particularly striking parallels between

highland and lowland cultures can be recognized in the spatial representation of social organization as expressed in site layouts and ritual (Hornborg 1982). The dual, mirror-image hierarchies (Fig.16) embodied in the circles of ranked, uxorilocal households among the Bororo, Sherente, and other Gê-speakers (cf. Eastern Timbira age-sets, Lave 1977:316; 1979:33) certainly resemble the *ceque* system of Inca Cuzco (Zuidema 1964: 21-23). Lowie even compared the Bororo village layout with Bandelier's reconstruction of Tiahuanaco (Lévi-Strauss 1963c:106). The radial, circular conception of social space is characteristic of other ancient sites (Chiripa, Pucara; cf. Lathrap *et al.* 1977:10-11) in the Titicaca Basin, and may even account for the circular, sunken plaza of the earliest phase of occupation at Chavín de Huántar. It is formally reproduced in the internal organization of *malocas* in the northwest Amazon (Goldman 1977:176; S. Hugh-Jones 1977:207; Guyot 1977:163-164; Bidou 1977:116), and in ritual contexts from Andean peoples as separate as the Mapuche (Tom Dillehay, personal communication, 1982) and the Quechua of the Department of Ayacucho (Ossio 1978:394). The symbolic codes by which social dimensions are plotted in physical space suggest a "grammar" for reconciling contradictory aspects of social classification. The pervasive, mirror-image hierarchies of indigenous South America represent a remarkably tangible illustration of the articulation of dualism and hierarchy.

Chapter 23
Code, Behaviour, and Structure: Concluding Remarks

"Social anthropology . . . is primarily the empirical investigation of human understanding by means of the comparative study of cultural categories."
– R. Needham (1966b:141)

"The question is very simply whether there are unarticulated an unstated lineages existing in behavioural reality, or whether such groups may really have their locus only in the conceptual system of the anthropological observer."
– R. F. Murphy (1979:218)

Human knowledge can only be a representation, or model, of a reality from which it must always be distinguished. The social sciences are confronted with a further complication; instead of the simple dichotomy of model and reality, we have three levels: an ultimately inaccessible reality, the observer's (etic) model, and in addition the participant's (emic) model of social structure. Ethnography is the documentation of emic *representations*, not of the objects (behaviours or institutions) for which they stand (Sperber 1985). As Trautmann (1981: 32) remarks, "the rendering of one cultural set in the terms of another is an enterprise of a fundamentally different sort from the natural-scientific one of rendering nature in terms of a cultural set." Emic models have commonly been confused with objective reality, as when "moiety systems" are presented as a type of social structure. Once we accept that such native categories do not necessarily correspond to objective entities of social organization, we are faced with the problem of in which terms societies can most accurately be described.

Process as Structure

Whereas models, emic or etic, have generally been phrased in terms of morphology (i.e. the constitution of social groups or categories), the invariant features of social organization are fundamentally processual (i.e. regularities in the flow of energy, matter, and information.) This has been recognized in Lévi-Strauss' distinction between restricted and generalized exchange, and in Needham's and Maybury-Lewis' similar division into symmetric and asymmetric alliance systems. None of these authors, however, has abandoned the premise that structures of exchange can only be recognized where they articulate corporate unilineal descent groups (cf. Schneider 1965:49-50; Scheffler 1970:262; Scheffler & Lounsbury 1971:14-33). It is only rarely (cf. Kaplan 1975) that regularities in alliance have been studied independently of morphology.

Following the tradition of the early evolutionists, Murdock (1949:52) concluded that "kin groups are the primary determinants of both kinship terminology and marriage rules." This interpretation is again based on a morphological definition of social structure, according to which social process (i.e. exchange) is determined by the constitution of objectively conceived social groups. To be sure, where conceptions of descent groups are present they often appear to provide a cultural matrix for the flow of prestations. But as they are ultimately products of classification, such groups may represent a codification, in morphological terms, of a social reality which is processual and consequently less tangible (cf. Lévi-Strauss 1969:323 on the priority of marriage exchange over rules of descent.) To use an expression employed by Williams (1932:80) in relating sex affiliation to direct exchange, the rules of affiliation may evolve out of the system of exchange "as a sort of wisdom after the event" (i.e. as a rationalization).

A morphological definition of social structure also underlies Needham's conception of prescriptive alliance systems. It was most explicitly revealed in his early reminder (1958b:200, note 5) that his formal analyses deal *only* with a system of structural relations between *groups* in a lineal descent system." Similarly, Lave (1966:187) claims that, "were the marriage rule prescriptive, corporate descent groups of one sort or another could be postulated with virtual certainty." Needham's (1961, 1964a) treatment of the Sirionó illustrates some of the difficulties in this approach. In classifying the cognatic Sirionó as an instance of prescriptive, asymmetric alliance, Needham was obliged to argue that they recognized matrilineal descent *categories*, explicitly asserting also that symmetric alliance is "wholly inconsistent with a cognatic terminology *or society*" (1964a:237; italics mine). In a similar vein, Suárez (1972) believes that a former two-section terminology among the cognatic Warao would have been diagnostic of unilineality, and Dole (1969) posits a functional relationship between bifurcate merging cousin terms and unilocal residence. These interpretations do not seem to recognize that cross/parallel distinctions may be an emergent feature of alliance-oriented, Dravidian kin terminologies even in societies entirely ignorant of unilineal principles. Instead of assuming that such distinctions are proof of lineal descent categories, we should be content with noting that the two features are in some respects formally congruent, suggesting that lineal descent is indeed a potential trajectory of Dravidian terminologies. Whether we choose to say that we are pursuing Lévi-Strauss' "unconscious categories" or Lounsbury's (1964a:351; 1964b:1091) "underlying principles," the point is that a system of classification codifying one behavioural regularity (visualized by anthropologists as symmetric alliance) by virtue of its own unintentional logic may sometimes generate another (the corporate behaviour of unilineal descent groups). This conclusion seems immanent in much of the recent ethnography from lowland South America, particularly in Århem's (1981) discussion of the interacting principles of affinality and lineality inherent in two-line terminologies (cf. also Dreyfus 1977). We would agree with Yalman's (1965:442) suggestion that our investigation should be not of "the morphology of social groups, but of the principles on which they are formed," for "such principles may be seen in operation as it were behind both social groupings and . . . concepts." Problems begin, however, when these principles are given designations (e.g., "matrilineal" or "descent" categories) which suggest a necessary connection with specific phenomena of social organization.

The assumption of corporate descent groups was responsible not only for the Sirionó controversy (Needham 1961, 1964a; Postal & Eyde 1963), but also for the so-called "Apinayé anomaly" (Maybury-Lewis 1960a). Da Matta (1982:120, 125) confirms that the Apinayé do recognize a form of parallel affiliation, but Nimuendajú's (1939) foremost mistake was to envisage the parallel lines as corporate descent groups (*kiyé*).

Yet another problem raised by the descent group assumption is the concomitant rejection of prescriptive patrilateral cross-cousin marriage (Needham 1958b, 1962; Maybury-Lewis 1965a). If the criterion of descent group membership is abandoned as a matrix for relationship categories, the logical problems envisaged by Needham and Maybury-Lewis disappear (cf. Schneider 1965:77). The short cycles of exchange attributed by Lévi-Strauss to this form of marriage could very well represent a fundamental aspect of social organization, particularly in South America, where descent groups are rare and alliances may be orchestrated by systems of relationship categories unfettered by the logical and practical constraints of corporate descent group formation (cf. J. Shapiro 1984:10-11).

Social Classification and Social Structure

Needham proposes that prescription "may best be defined by reference to the terminology of social classification" (1973: 175), and that such a prescriptive terminology is "constituted by the regularity of a constant relation that articulates lines and categories" (1971c:32). His conviction has been that only prescriptive systems have significant "structural entailments" in terms of symmetric or asymmetric alliance (1958a: 75). Needham thus appears to reject the structural significance of alliance in non-prescriptive systems where a statistically high proportion of marriages unite relatives of specific genealogical positions. Although recognizing that the Garo, Kachin, and Mapuche all marry asymmetrically, whereas only the Kachin express an asymmetric prescription, he goes no further than to concede that "this comparison could conceivably prove interesting in some theoretical context or other" (1973:173). Contrary to Lévi-Strauss (1969:xxxiii), who visualizes structures of exchange as emergent regularities in behaviour, Needham is explicitly concerned with the study of social categories, i.e. "elementary structures – not of kinship, but of classification" (1973: 174, 179). He suggests, in fact, that all social anthropology will be able to do is to comprehend such different schemes of classification (1971c:32).

In addressing the problem of how classification relates to social structure, Durkheim and Mauss (1963:82) concluded that "the social relations of men" provide the "prototype" for the system of classification. Needham (1963:xxvi) adopts the contrary view that "where correspondences between social and symbolic forms are found it is the social organization which is itself an aspect of the classification." The problems raised by this disagreement are fundamental to an understanding of the question which first brought us into this field of investigation, i.e. the relationship between the terminological dualism of Dravidian kin nomenclatures and the corporate dualism of dual organization.

Needham's contribution is to show that even phenomena thought by previous writers to represent "social structure" (e.g. dual organization) are really products of classification. But it would be unwise to stop here. If dual organization is but a means of *classifying* an epistemologically inaccessible order of phenomena which might qualify as objective social reality, how should this assumed reality be approached? Any models of it which we may produce would obviously remain confined to the level of classification. This is not tantamount to saying that social structure is a mental model (cf. Leach 1964: 4–5; Maybury-Lewis 1967:239). If we presuppose that social systems, like any other living systems converting solar energy, have an objective existence outside (though not independent of) men's consciousness of them, we must conclude that it is as justified to assume an ontological "social structure" as it is to speak of the structure of a cell, an organism, or an ecosystem. The analogy suggests that the attempt to delineate invariant features of social organization should concentrate on processes, dynamics, and metabolism, rather than on static morphological models. Against this background, it is easy to see why the emphasis on exchange underlying alliance theory, even though it generally suffers from a certain morphological bias, has proven to hold more promise than descent theory (cf. Jackson 1984:162 for an appropriate view of marriage alliance.)

But even if our perspective is shifted from groups to regularities in exchange, the methodological problems remain. How should social reality be approached?

Lévi-Strauss (1973b:79–81) treats "social

structure" as an objective reality, knowledge of which can only be gained indirectly. Much as the electronic microscope, by revealing the molecular structure of matter, helps to explain the way matter is perceived by the eye, structural analysis may help us to understand our way of perceiving social relations. In advocating perhaps too close an analogy with linguistics (cf. 1963b:33–34), Lévi-Strauss' "ultimate motive" is to search for "those unconscious categories" which generate social organization. His conviction that social structure is somehow embedded in the human unconscious (e.g. as principles of reciprocity) may be true to a degree, but does not provide an exhaustive account. Emergent, "unintentional" properties of social systems (e.g. the long cycles of reciprocity generated by a preference for matrilateral cross-cousin marriage) can perfectly well remain opaque to the actors concerned, both consciously and unconsciously. Various aspects of such ontological structures will certainly tend to be reflected in the subjective apprehension of society, but individual human minds and social reality must nevertheless be recognized as two conceptually distinct levels.

Structural Congruities: Some Methodological Implications

> "The strength of the thread does not reside in the fact that some one fibre runs through its whole length, but in the overlapping of many fibres."
> – L. Wittgenstein (quoted in Needham 1971c:30)

The two contradictory perspectives represented by Durkheim and Mauss, on the one hand, and Needham, Leach, and Maybury-Lewis, on the other, can be reconciled only through what Berger and Luckmann (1966: 208) call "a systematic accounting of the dialectical relation between the structural realities and the human enterprise of constructing reality." Such an account must reckon with two complementary processes of human thought: inductive model-building from empirical experience, on the one hand, and transformative deduction from previously established models, on the other. To unravel the ethnographical tracks of these complementary processes, the same medium must be used as was applied in their construction. Introspective though it may seem, deductive analysis must be employed in order to discover sequences of models which may appear as structurally contiguous links in a transformative process.

Though often difficult to discover as long as phenomena remain couched in the idioms of specific cultures (or anthropologists; cf. Rivière 1984:5), congruities underlying two or more native models may be depicted in etic diagrams representing their mutual juncture, or route of transformation. Thus, symmetric alliance is the anthropologist's label for that behavioural regularity which appears to constitute the common foundation for several cultural models, including ideals of sister exchange, two-line kin terminologies, and dual organization. To be sure, the "underlying structure" we may claim to have captured in our diagram remains but a model, but the fact that it subsumes several alternative apprehensions of a single reality suggests that it will correspond more concisely to that reality than any one of the emic models which it incorporates (cf. Fig.1).

In their contributions to the discourse on the relationship between classification and social organization, neither Durkheim and Mauss nor Needham questioned the notion that emic categories such as moieties constitute the "social structure" of the people concerned. Consequently, in relating social and symbolic dualism, they are really discussing the relationship between different aspects of emic classification. Similarly beside the point was the attempt by Lawrence (1937), Murdock and others to explain one aspect of native Australian classification (alternating generations) by reference to another, more sporadic interpretation (bilineal affiliation), rather than simply acknowledging their congruity. Even the model of "marriage sections" can be dispensed with (cf. Chapter 16). A third example, of course, was the early evolutionists' conviction that bifurcate merging (Dravidian-Iroquois) kin terminologies can be traced to dual organization. Both dual organization and kin terminologies are sets of cultural categories, i.e. products of classification, and it was Lévi-Strauss who first suggested that we look elsewhere for social structure. In not recognizing this fundamental point, anthropological debates over functional relationships or historical sequences are doomed to infertility. One particular mode of social classification can neither imply nor exclude another, only harmonize with it to a greater or lesser extent, indicating the greater or lesser *likelihood* of statistical associations. This is why, in Sperber's (1985:30-31) words, "a cultural anthropology . . . must be an epidemiology of ideas," the study of "why some ideas are more contagious than others." The co-existence of *contradictory* models, of course, poses particularly interesting problems for the study of structural transformations.

Table 58 illustrates the overlapping congruities of several features of social classification which are widespread in lowland South America. Here is a continuum of "serial likenesses" (Needham 1971c:13) such as have preoccupied structuralists for decades. To be included in the Table, the relationship between two features should be one of implication rather than mere compatibility. A number of additional, ethnographically exemplifiable congruities could undoubtedly be indicated, but I have deliberately restricted the number of examples to the clearest and most "immediate" connections. Of the 48 cultures in our sample, I have nevertheless required as many as 20 to complete the ramified continuum which they jointly represent. Each position in the Table represents a transformative link, and the cluster of positions occupied by a particular culture (e.g. 42 = Piaroa, 1 = Krahó, 8 = Sherente) defines what might be called its "transformational space".

There can be no doubt that Dravidian, two-line kin terminologies are fundamental to social classification in the South American lowlands. While itself a codification of sister exchange or bilateral cross-cousin marriage (symmetric alliance), Dravidian classification harbours a number of inherent, logical regularities which appear to have stimulated a wide range of permutations. Its consistent distinction between male and female perspectives yields an implicit system of parallel (i.e. sex) affiliation, which in turn appears to be linked to such features as cross transmission, Crow-Omaha equations, and oblique and unilateral cross-cousin marriage. Different trajectories would unfold as the terminological system is juxtaposed with other factors, such as patterns of post-marital residence, local group size, or the nature and degree of regional integration. In conjunction with uxorilocal residence and larger local groups, for instance, its emphasis on inherited affinal bonds would have been conducive to such diverse phenomena as MBD marriage, dual organization, and ideals of rank endogamy. Its preoccupation with relative age, finally, may have provided the foundations for pervasive concepts of hierarchy based on birth order. Chapters 13 to 22 explore some of these possibilities.

In our sample of 48 lowland South American cultures, we have found statistical support for a number of these proposed relationships. More important than their meticulous verification, however, is the methodological approach by which systems of classification are treated as information-processing subsystems interacting dialectically with the more elusive realities of social organization. The indeterminate relationship between model and behaviour, because it permits a particular form of organization to

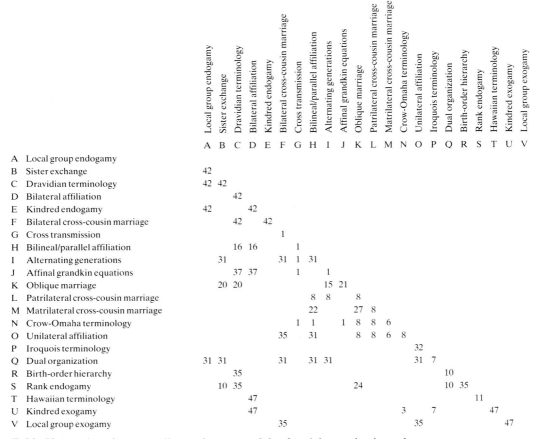

Column headers (A–V):
A Local group endogamy · B Sister exchange · C Dravidian terminology · D Bilateral affiliation · E Kindred endogamy · F Bilateral cross-cousin marriage · G Cross transmission · H Bilineal/parallel affiliation · I Alternating generations · J Affinal grandkin equations · K Oblique marriage · L Patrilateral cross-cousin marriage · M Matrilateral cross-cousin marriage · N Crow-Omaha terminology · O Unilateral affiliation · P Iroquois terminology · Q Dual organization · R Birth-order hierarchy · S Rank endogamy · T Hawaiian terminology · U Kindred exogamy · V Local group exogamy

	A	B	C	D	E	F	G	H	I	J	K	L	M	N	O	P	Q	R	S	T	U	V
A Local group endogamy																						
B Sister exchange	42																					
C Dravidian terminology	42	42																				
D Bilateral affiliation			42																			
E Kindred endogamy	42		42																			
F Bilateral cross-cousin marriage			42	42																		
G Cross transmission						1																
H Bilineal/parallel affiliation			16	16			1															
I Alternating generations		31				31	1	31														
J Affinal grandkin equations			37	37			1		1													
K Oblique marriage		20	20						15	21												
L Patrilateral cross-cousin marriage								8	8		8											
M Matrilateral cross-cousin marriage								22			27	8										
N Crow-Omaha terminology							1	1		1	8	8	6									
O Unilateral affiliation						35		31			8	8	6	8								
P Iroquois terminology															32							
Q Dual organization	31	31				31		31	31						31	7						
R Birth-order hierarchy			35														10					
S Rank endogamy		10	35										24				10	35				
T Hawaiian terminology				47															11			
U Kindred exogamy				47											3		7			47		
V Local group exogamy						35									35						47	

Table 58 A series of structurally contiguous models of social organization relevant to the indigenous cultures of lowland South America. Numbers represent cultures from the sample where the congruity of indicated features is particularly well demonstrated.

be apprehended in alternative ways, is a continuous source of social change.

A particularly interesting case is that of the Gê. Rivière (1973:28, note 1) observes that the Gê-speaking peoples stand apart from other lowland South American groups. They generally lack, for instance, the Dravidian, two-line kin terminology which Rivière suggests is diagnostic of Tropical Forest culture. On the other hand, we have shown that the Gê possess a number of traits which are *inherent* in Dravidian systems: dualism, parallel affiliation, MBD marriage, distinc-

tions of relative age, and even an implicit lineality. Rivière (1980:538–539) suggests that Gê name transmission is a "scheme of continuity, just as effective as unilineal descent." He notes that such systems of transmission are superfluous in the Guianas. In the two-line terminology of the Trio, Rivière (1969:79) discovered a "conceptual vertical cohesion" between certain lines of kin. We propose that the "incipient unilinea-rity" (W. Crocker 1977) of the Gê represents a transformation of the lineal continuity implicit in two-line terminologies. We have suggested that growth in village size would be conducive to the loss of a two-line terminology. But if a simple, kin-affine distinction could not be maintained in the huge villages of the Gê, many of the ideological principles immanent in the obsolete terminology have been all the more elaborated. Nowhere, in fact, is the "Dravidian" emphasis on dualism (between affines and between the sexes) and birth-order hierarchy more pronounced.

Dravidian kin terms distinguish kin from affines in an egocentric and transient manner, whereas unilineal sibs or moieties are sociocentric and enduring. The former model tends to suppress affinity, whereas the latter underscores it. By applying separate affinal terms, the Gê introduce new semantic boundaries corresponding to the qualitatively different relationships implied by affinity in the context of larger villages and extended genealogical exogamy (cf. Rivière 1984:61, 75). To say that Carib-speakers "suppress affinity" (e.g., Thomas 1979:79; Kaplan 1981:161; 1984:129), however, may be slightly beside the mark, since it is not consanguinity but the denial of consanguinity which is the fiction (Lévi-Strauss 1963d:131). Under which conditions is the rigid separation of kin and affines most crucial? Why is it important to introduce the unilineal illusion, i.e. the fiction that one is not marrying one's own kind? These are perennial concerns to which we may not have contributed very much, save, I hope, some indications of the cognitive continuities and discontinuities with which such a shift seems to be associated. Its prerequisites are tentatively outlined in Chapter 13, while its various structural repercussions are discussed throughout Part IV.

To the original question of the relationship between Dravidian terminologies and dual organization, we would reply that both are codifications of symmetric alliance. As they represent *alternative* modes of classification reflecting a common structure of exchange, their complementary distribution does not warrant a rejection of their logical affinity (cf. Scheffler 1971:233–234, 241), but is only to be expected.

To the more general question of how classification relates to social structure, we would respond that the relationship is obviously dialectical. It is insufficient to say either that social structure determines classification (Durkheim and Mauss) or that social structure is an aspect of classification (Needham). Social structure can only be surmised through the systems of classification in which it is imperfectly reflected, and by which it is indeterminately reproduced. We must assume its objective existence but at the same time be content with perceiving it only through the juxtaposition of its various subjective manifestations.

References

Adams, K.J. (1977), Oblique Marriage among the Barama River Caribs. In Albert et al. 1977:11–17.

– (1979), Barama River Carib Kinship: Brother-brother and Mother-daughter Identity Merging in a Two-Section System. In Kensinger 1979a:3–12.

Albert, B., et al., eds. (1977), Actes du XLIIe Congrès International des Américanistes II. Paris: Société des Américanistes.

– (1978), Actes du XLIIe Congrès International des Américanistes IV. Paris: Société des Américanistes.

Albisetti, C. (1953), Analecta et additamenta. Anthropos 48:625–630.

Albisetti, C. & Venturelli, A.J. (1962), Enciclopédia Bororo I. São Paulo: Escolas Profissionais Salesianas.

Arcand, B. (1972), The Urgent Situation of the Cuiva Indians of Colombia. I.W.G.I.A. Document 7. Copenhagen: International Work Group for Indigenous Affairs.

– (1977), The Logic of Kinship: An example from the Cuiva. In Albert et al. 1977: 19–34.

Århem, K. (1981), Makuna Social Organization: A Study in Descent, Alliance, and the Formation of Corporate Groups in the North-Western Amazon. Uppsala Studies in Cultural Anthropology 4. Stockholm: Almqvist & Wiksell.

Avalos de Matos, R. & Ravines, R., eds. (1972), Historia, etnohistoria y etnología de la selva Sudamericana. Actas y Memorias del XXXIX Congreso Internacional de Americanistas 4. Lima: Instituto de Estudios Peruanos.

Balée, W. (1985), Review of Marriage Practices in Lowland South America, edited by Kenneth M. Kensinger, American Anthropologist 87:419–420.

Bamberger, J. (1974), Naming and the Transmission of Status in a Central Brazilian Society. Ethnology XIII:363–378.

– (1979), Exit and Voice in Central Brazil: The Politics of Flight in Kayapó Society. In Maybury-Lewis 1979a:130–146.

Banton, M., ed. (1965), The Relevance of Models for Social Anthropology. A.S.A. Monographs 1. London: Tavistock Publications.

Basso, E.B. (1970), Xingu Carib Kinship Terminology and Marriage: Another View. Southwestern Journal of Anthropology 26:402–416.

– (1973), The Kalapalo Indians of Central Brazil. New York: Holt, Rinehart and Winston.

– (1975), Kalapalo Affinity: Its Cultural and Social Contexts. American Ethnologist 2: 207–228.

– ed. (1977), Carib-Speaking Indians: Culture, Society and Language. Anthropological Papers of the University of Arizona 28. Tucson: The University of Arizona Press.

– (1984), A Husband for His Daughter, a Wife for Her Son: Strategies for Selecting a Set of In-Laws among the Kalapalo. In Kensinger 1984a:33–44.

– (1985), Comment on Siblingship in Lowland South America. In Kensinger 1985a: 46–48.

Bateson, G. (1973), Pathologies of Epistemology. In Steps to an Ecology of Mind, pp.454–463. Frogmore: Paladin.

Belote, J. & Belote, L. (1977), The Limitation of Obligation in Saraguro Kinship. In Bolton & Mayer 1977: 106–116.

Benson, E.P., ed. (1971), Dumbarton Oaks Conference on Chavín. Washington: Dumbarton Oaks Research Library and Collection.

Berger, P.L. & Luckmann, T. (1966), *The Social Construction of Reality*. Harmondsworth: Penguin Books.

Bidou, P. (1977), Naitre et Étre Tatuyo. In Albert *et al.* 1977:105–120.

Bolton, R. & Mayer, E., eds. (1977), *Andean Kinship and Marriage*. Special Publication of the American Anthropological Association 7. Washington: American Anthropological Association.

Buchler, I.R. & Selby, H.A. (1968), *Kinship and Social Organization: An Introduction to Theory and Method*. New York: The MacMillan Company.

Camino, A. (1977), Trueque, correrías e intercambios entre los Quechuas andinos y los Piro y Machiguenga de la montaña peruana. *Amazonia Peruana* 1:2, pp. 123–140.

Carneiro, R.L. (1973), Slash-and-Burn Cultivation among the Kuikuru and Its Implications for Cultural Development in the Amazon Basin. In Gross 1973: 98–123.

Carvajal, G. de (1934), *The Discovery of the Amazon*. American Geographical Society Special Publication 17. New York: American Geographical Society.

Casevitz, F.–M. (1977), Du proche au loin: étude du fonctionnement des systèmes de la parenté et de l'alliance Matsiguenga. In Albert *et al.* 1977:121–140.

Castelli, A. *et al.*, eds. (1981), *Etnohistoria y antropología Andina,* Segunda jornada del Museo Nacional de Historia. Lima: Centro de Proyección Cristiana.

Chagnon, N.A. (1968), *Yanomamö: The Fierce People*. New York: Holt, Rinehart and Winston.

Chernela, J.M. (1985), The Sibling Relationship among the Uanano of the Northwest Amazon: The Case of Nicho. In Kensinger 1985a:33–40.

Clastres, P. (1977), *Society Against the State*. Oxford: Basil Blackwell.

Collins, J.L. (1981), *Kinship and Seasonal Migration among the Aymara of Southern Peru: Human Adaptation to Energy Scarcity*. Ph.D. dissertation. University of Florida.

Crocker, J.C. (1969), Reciprocity and Hierarchy among the Eastern Bororo. *Man* 4:44–58.

– (1971) The Dialectics of Bororo Social Inversions. In Maybury-Lewis 1971a:387–391.

– (1977), Why are the Bororo Matrilineal? In Albert *et al.* 1977:245–258.

– (1979), Selves and Alters among the Eastern Bororo. In Maybury-Lewis 1979a:249–300.

Crocker, W.H. (1977), Canela "Group" Recruitment and Perpetuity: Incipient "Unilineality"? In Albert *et al.* 1977: 259–275.

– (1979), Canela Kinship and the Question of Matrilineality. In Margolis & Carter 1979:225–249.

– (1984), Canela Marriage: Factors in Change. In Kensinger 1984a:63–98.

Da Matta, R. (1970), Review of *Marriage among the Trio: A Principle of Social Organization,* by Peter Rivière. *Man* 5:550–551.

– (1973), A Reconsideration of Apinayé Social Morphology. In Gross 1973:277–291.

– (1979), The Apinayé Relationship System: Terminology and Ideology. In Maybury-Lewis 1979a:83–127.

– (1982), *A Divided World*. Cambridge: Harvard University Press.

D'Ans, A.–M. (1974), Estructura semántica del parentesco Machiguenga (Arawak). *Revista del Museo Nacional* XL:343–361. Lima.

– (1975), *La Verdadera biblia de los Cashinahua: Mitos, leyendas y tradiciones de la selva peruana*. Miraflores: Mosca Azul Editores.

Dietschy, H. (1977), Espace social et "affiliation par sexe" au Brésil Central (Karajá, Tapirapé, Apinayé, Mundurucú). In Albert *et al.* 1977:297–308.

Dole, G.E. (1969), Generation Kinship Nomenclature as an Adaptation to

Endogamy. *Southwestern Journal of Anthropology* 25:105–123.

– (1972), Developmental Sequences of Kinship Patterns. In Reining 1972:134–166.

– (1979), Pattern and Variation in Amahuaca Kin Terminology. In Kensinger 1979a:13–36.

– (1984), The Structure of Kuikuru Marriage. In Kensinger 1984a:45–62.

Dreyfus, S. (1977), Propositions pour un modèle Sud-Américain de l'alliance symétrique. In Albert *et al.* 1977:379-385.

Dumond, D.E. (1969), Swidden Agriculture and the Rise of Maya Civilization. In Vayda 1969:332–349.

Dumont, J.–P. (1978), *The Headman and I: Ambiguity and Ambivalence in the Field-working Experience*. Austin: Univeristy of Texas Press.

Dumont, L. (1953a), The Dravidian Kinship Terminology as an Expression of Marriage. *Man* 53:34-39.

– (1953b), Dravidian Kinship Terminology. *Man* 53:143.

– (1957), Hierarchy and Marriage Alliance in South Indian Kinship. *Occasional Papers of the Royal Anthropological Institute of Great Britain and Ireland*.

– (1961), Descent, Filiation and Affinity. *Man* 61:24-25.

– (1966), Descent or Intermarriage? A Relational View of Australian Section Systems. *Southwestern Journal of Anthropology* 22:231-250.

– (1972), *Homo Hierarchicus: The Caste System and its Implications*. London: Paladin.

Durbin, M. (1977), A Survey of the Carib Language Family. In Basso 1977:23-38.

Durkheim, E. & Mauss, M. (1963), *Primitive Classification*. London: Cohen & West.

Duviols, P. (1979), La Dinastía de los Incas: Monarquia o diarquia? Argumentos heuristicos a favor de una tesis estructuralista. *Journal de la Société des Américanistes* 68.

Earls, J. (1971), The Structure of Modern Andean Social Categories. *Journal of the Steward Anthropological Society* 3:69-106.

Eggan, F., ed. (1937), *Social Anthropology of North American Tribes*. Chicago: The University of Chicago Press.

Eyde, D.B. & Postal, P.M. (1961), Avunculocality and Incest: The Development of Unilateral Cross-Cousin Marriage and Crow-Omaha Kinship Systems. *American Anthropologist* 63:747-771.

Farabee, W.C. (1922), *Indian Tribes of Eastern Peru*. Papers of the Peabody Museum of American Archaeology and Ethnology, Harvard University X. Cambridge.

Faron, L.C. (1961), *Mapuche Social Structure*. Illinois Studies in Anthropology 1. Urbana: University of Illinois Press.

– (1962), Matrilateral Marriage among the Mapuche (Araucanians) of Central Chile. *Sociologus* 12:54-65.

Fields, H.L. & Merrifield, W.R. (1980), Mayoruna (Panoan) Kinship. *Ethnology* XIX:1-28.

Fock, N. (1963), *Waiwai: Religion and Society of an Amazonian Tribe*. National-muséets Skrifter, Etnografisk Raekke VIII. Copenhagen: The National Museum.

Fonseca Martel, C. (1981), Los Ayllus y los marcas de Chaupiwaranga. In Castelli *et al.* 1981:167-188.

Fox, R. (1967), *Kinship and Marriage: An Anthropological Perspective*. Harmondsworth: Penguin Books.

Gade, D.W. (1972), Comercio y colonización en la zona de contacto entre la sierra y las tierras bajas del valle del Urubamba en el Perú. In Avalos & Ravines 1972:207-221.

Gasché, J. (1977), Les fondements de l'organisation sociale des indiens Witoto et l'illusion exogamique. In Albert *et al.* 1977:141-161.

Girard, R. (1958), *Indios selvaticos de la Amazonia Peruana*. Mexico: Libro Mex Editores.

Goldman, I. (1963), *The Cubeo: Indians of the Northwest Amazon*. Illinois Studies in Anthropology 2. Urbana: The University of Illinois Press.

– (1977), Time, Space, and Descent: The Cubeo Example. In Albert *et al.* 1977: 175-183.

Gow, D.D. (1978), Verticality and Andean Cosmology: Quadripartition, Opposition, and Mediation. In Albert *et al.* 1978: 199-211.

Gregor, T. (1973), Privacy and Extra-Marital Affairs in a Tropical Forest Community. In Gross 1973:242-260.

– (1974), Publicity, Privacy, and Mehinacu Marriage. *Ethnology* XIII:333-349.

– (1977), *Mehinaku: The Drama of Daily Life in a Brazilian Indian Village*. Chicago: The University of Chicago Press.

Gross, D.R., ed. (1973), *Peoples and Cultures of Native South America: An Anthropological Reader*. Garden City: Doubleday/The Natural History Press.

– (1979), A New Approach to Central Brazilian Social Organization. In Margolis & Carter 1979:321-342.

Guyot, M. (1977), Structure et évolution chez les indiens Bora et Miraña, Amazonie Colombienne. In Albert *et al.* 1977:163-173.

Harner, M.J. (1972), *The Jívaro: People of the Sacred Waterfalls*. Garden City: Anchor Press/Doubleday.

Henley, P. (1982), *The Panare: Tradition and Change on the Amazonian Frontier*. New Haven: Yale University Press.

Henry, J. (1941), *Jungle People: A Kaingáng Tribe of the Highlands of Brazil*. New York: Vintage Books.

Hernández de Alba, G. (1946), The Highland Tribes of Southern Colombia. In Steward 1946b:910–974.

Heusch, L. de (1981), A Defence and Illustration of the Structures of Kinship. In *Why Marry Her? Society and Symbolic Structures*, pp. 29-81. Cambridge: Cambridge University Press.

Hickman, J.M. & Stuart, W.T. (1977), Descent, Alliance, and Moiety in Chucuito, Peru: An Explanatory Sketch of Aymara Social Organization. In Bolton & Mayer 1977:43-59.

Hill, J.D. (1985), Agnatic Sibling Relations and Rank in Northern Arawakan Myth and Social Life. In Kensinger 1985a:25-32.

Holmberg, A. (1948), The Sirionó. In Steward 1948a:455-464.

– (1950), *Nomads of the Long Bow: The Sirionó of Eastern Bolivia*. Institute of Social Anthropology Publication 10. Washington: Smithsonian Institution.

Homans, G.C. & Schneider, D.M. (1955), *Marriage, Authority, and Final Causes: A Study of Unilateral Cross-Cousin Marriage*. Glencoe: The Free Press.

Hornborg, A. (1982), Possible Affinities Between Highland and Lowland Conceptions of Social Space in South America (originally submitted under the title Possible Affinities Between Highland and Lowland Forms of Dual Organization in South America). Paper presented at the 44th International Congress of Americanists. Manchester.

– (1983), Dual Organization and Hierarchy in the Andes: A Model for the Logic of Village Quadripartition in the Pampas River Area of Peru. In Fock, N., ed., *Hvad kan vi laere af andre kulturer?* pp. 194-203. Copenhagen: Institut for etnologi og antropologi.

Horton, D. (1948), The Mundurucú. In Steward 1948a:271-282.

Houdart-Morizot, M.–F. (1976), *Tradition et pouvoir à Cuenca, communauté Andine*. Travaux de l'Institut Français d'Etudes Andines XV. Lima.

Hugh-Jones, C. (1977a), *Social Classification among the South American Indians of the Vaupés Region of Colombia*. Ph.D. dissertation. University of Cambridge.

– (1977b), Skin and Soul: The Round and the Straight. Social Time and Social Space in Pirá-Paraná Society. In Albert *et al.* 1977:185-204.

– (1979), *From the Milk River: Spatial and*

Temporal Processes in Northwest Amazonia. Cambridge: Cambridge University Press.

Hugh-Jones, S. (1974), *Male Initiation and Cosmology among the Barasana Indians of the Vaupés Area of Colombia.* Ph.D. dissertation. University of Cambridge.

– (1977), Like the Leaves on the Forest Floor . . . : Space and Time in Barasana Ritual. In Albert *et al.* 1977:205-215.

Isbell, B.J. (1977), "Those Who Love Me": An Analysis of Andean Kinship and Reciprocity Within a Ritual Context. In Bolton & Mayer 1977:81-105.

Jackson, J.E. (1975a), Patrilineal Organization in the Northwest Amazon. Paper presented at the 74th Annual Meeting of the American Anthropological Association. San Francisco.

– (1975b), Recent Ethnography of Indigenous Northern Lowland South America. *Annual Review of Anthropology* 4:307-340.

– (1976), Relations Between Tukanoans and Makú of the Central Northwest Amazon. MS. Massachusetts Institute of Technology.

– (1977), Bará Zero Generation Terminology and Marriage. *Ethnology* XVI:83-104.

– (1984), Vaupés Marriage Practices. In Kensinger 1984a:156-179.

Johnson, O.R. (1979), Kinship Decisions among the Machiguenga: The Dravidian System in a Small Scale Society. In Kensinger 1979:54-62.

– (1980), The Social Context of Intimacy and Avoidance: A Videotape Study of Machiguenga Meals. *Ethnology* XIX: 353-366.

Johnson, O.R. & Johnson, A. (1975), Male/ Female Relations and the Organization of Work in a Machiguenga Community. *American Ethnologist* 2:634-648.

Kaplan, J.O. (1972), Cognation, Endogamy, and Teknonymy: The Piaroa Example. *Southwestern Journal of Anthropology* 28:282-297.

– (1973), Endogamy and the Marriage Alliance: A Note on Continuity in Kindred-Based Groups. *Man* 8:555-570.

– (1975), *The Piaroa – a People of the Orinoco Basin: A Study in Kinship and Marriage.* Oxford: Clarendon Press.

– (1977), Comments. In Albert *et al.* 1977: 387-394.

– (1981), Review Article: Amazonian Anthropology. *Journal of Latin American Studies* 13:151-164.

– (1984), Dualisms as an Expression of Differences and Danger: Marriage Exchange and Reciprocity among the Piaroa of Venezuela. In Kensinger 1984a:127-155.

Karsten, R. (1920), *Blodshämnd, krig och segerfester bland Jibaro-indianerna i östra Ecuador.* Helsingfors: Holger Schildts.

Keesing, R.M. (1975), *Kin Groups and Social Structure.* New York: Holt, Rinehart and Winston.

Kelly, R.C. (1985), Sibling Relations in Lowland South America: A Commentary on Symposium Papers. In Kensinger 1985a: 41-45.

Kensinger, K.M. (1974a), Cashinahua Medicine and Medicine Men. In Lyon 1974:283-288.

– (1974b), Leadership and Factionalism in Cashinahua Society. Paper presented at the 73rd Annual Meeting of the American Anthropological Association. Mexico City.

– (1975), Studying the Cashinahua. In *The Cashinahua of Eastern Peru.* Haffenreffer Museum of Anthropology, Brown University, Studies in Anthropology and Material Culture, vol.1., pp. 9-86. Providence, R.I.

– (1977), Cashinahua Notions of Social Time and Social Space. In Albert *et al.* 1977: 233-244.

– ed. (1979a), *Social Correlates of Kin Terminology.* Working Papers on South American Indians 1. Bennington: Bennington College.

– (1979b), Comments. In Kensinger 1979a:81-84.

– (1980), The Dialectics of Person and Self

in Cashinahua Society. Paper presented at the 79th Annual Meeting of the American Anthropological Association. Washington, D.C.

– ed. (1984a), *Marriage Practices in Lowland South America*. Illinois Studies in Anthropology No.14. Urbana: University of Illinois Press.

– (1984b), An Emic Model of Cashinahua Marriage. In Kensinger 1984a:221–251.

– ed. (1985a), *The Sibling Relationship in Lowland South America*. Working Papers on South American Indians 7. Bennington: Bennington College.

– (1985b), Cashinahua Siblingship. In Kensinger 1985a: 20–24.

Kirchhoff, P. (1932), Verwandschaftsbezeichnungen und Verwandtenheirat. *Zeitschrift für Ethnologie* 64:41-71.

– (1948), The Warrau. In Steward 1948a: 869-882.

Korn, F. (1973), *Elementary Structures Reconsidered: Lévi-Strauss on Kinship*. London: Tavistock Publications.

Kracke, W.H. (1984), Kagwahiv Moieties: Form without Function? In Kensinger 1984a:99-124.

LaBarre, W. (1946), The Uru-Chipaya. In Steward 1946b:575-585.

Lane, R. & Lane. B. (1959), On the Development of Dakota-Iroquois and Crow-Omaha Kinship Terminologies. *Southwestern Journal of Anthropology* 15:254-265.

Larson, M.L. (1977), Organización socio-política de los Aguaruna (Jíbaro): Sistema de linajes segmentarios. *Revista del Museo Nacional* XLIII: 467-489. Lima.

Lathrap, D.W. (1970), *The Upper Amazon.* London: Thames and Hudson.

– (1971), The Tropical Forest and the Cultural Context of Chavín. In Benson 1971:73-100.

– (1972), Alternative Models of Population Movements in the Tropical Lowlands of South America. In Avalos & Ravines 1972:13-23.

– (1973a), The Antiquity and Importance of Long-Distance Trade Relationships in the Moist Tropics of Pre-Columbian South America. *World Archaeology* 5:170-186.

– (1973b), The "Hunting" Economies of the Tropical Forest Zone of South America: An Attempt at Historical Perspective. In Gross 1973:83-95. (Originally published in Lee & DeVore 1968:23-29.)

Lathrap, D.W., Marcos, J.G., & Zeidler, J.A. (1977), Real Alto: An Ancient Ceremonial Center. *Archaeology* 30:1, pp.2-13.

Lave, J.C. (1966), A Formal Analysis of Preferential Marriage with the Sister's Daughter. *Man* 1:185-200.

– (1971), Some Suggestions for the Interpretation of Residence, Descent, and Exogamy among the Eastern Timbira. In Maybury-Lewis 1971a:341-345.

– (1973), A Comment on *"A Study in Structural Semantics: The Sirionó Kinship system."* *American Anthropologist* 75: 314-317.

– (1977), Eastern Timbira Moiety Systems in Time and Space: A Complex Structure. In Albert *et al.* 1977:309-321.

– (1979), Cycles and Trends in Krîkatí Naming Practices. In Maybury-Lewis 1979a:16-44.

Lawrence, W.E. (1937), Alternating Generations in Australia. In Murdock, G.P., ed., *Studies in the Science of Society*, pp.319-354. New Haven: Yale University Press.

Leach, E.R. (1954), *Political Systems of Highland Burma*. London School of Economics Monographs on Social Anthropology 44. London: University of London/ The Athlone Press.

– (1961a), *Rethinking Anthropology*. London School of Economics Monographs on Social Anthropology 22. London: University of London/The Athlone Press.

– (1961b), The Structural Implications of Matrilateral Cross-Cousin Marriage. In Leach 1961a:54-104.

Lee, R.B. & DeVore, I., eds. (1968), *Man the Hunter*. Chicago: Aldine Publishing Company.

Lévi-Strauss, C. (1936), Contribution à

l'étude de l'organisation sociale des Indiens Bororo. *Journal de la Société des Américanistes* XXVIII:269-305.

– (1944), Reciprocity and Hierarchy. *American Anthropologist* 46:266-268.

– (1945), On Dual Organization in South America. *America Indigena* IV:37-47.

– (1948a), The Tupí-Cawahíb. In Steward 1948a:299-306.

– (1948b), The Nambicuara. In Steward 1948a:361-370.

– (1948c), *La Vie familiale et sociale des Indiens Nambikwara*. Paris: Société des Américanistes.

– (1957), Le Symbolisme cosmique dans la structure sociale et l'organisation ceremonielle de plusieurs populations Nord et Sud-Americaines. In *Le Symbolisme cosmique des monuments religieux*. Serie Orientale Roma XIV:47-56.

– (1963a), *Structural Anthropology*. London: Allen Lane/The Penguin Press.

– (1963b), Structural Analysis in Linguistics and in Anthropology. In Lévi-Strauss 1963a:31-54.

– (1963c), The Concept of Archaism in Anthropology. In Lévi-Strauss 1963a:101–119.

– (1963d), Social Structures of Central and Eastern Brazil. In Lévi-Strauss 1963a:120-131.

– (1963e), Do Dual Organizations Exist? In Lévi-Strauss 1963a:132-163.

– (1963f), Social Structure. In Lévi-Strauss 1963a:277-323.

– (1963g), The Place of Anthropology in the Social Sciences and Problems Raised in Teaching It. In Lévi-Strauss 1963a:346-381.

– (1968a), The Social Use of Kinship Terms among Brazilian Indians. In Bohannan. P. & Middleton, J., eds., *Marriage, Family, and Residence*, pp. 169-183. Garden City: The Natural History Press.

– (1968b), The Concept of Primitiveness. In Lee & DeVore 1968:349-352.

– (1969), *The Elementary Structures of Kinship*. London: Eyre & Spottiswoode.

– (1973a), *Structural Anthropology 2*. Harmondsworth: Penguin Books.

– (1973b), The Meaning and Use of the Notion of Model. In Lévi-Strauss 1973a:71-81.

– (1973c), Reflections on the Atom of Kinship. In Lévi-Strauss 1973a:82-112.

Lipkind, W. (1948), The Carajá. In Steward 1948a:179-192.

Lizot, J. (1971), Remarques sur le vocabulaire de parenté Yanõmami. *L'Homme* 11: 25-38.

– (1975), Alliance or Descent: Some Amazonian Contrasts. *Man* 10:625.

– (1977), Descendance et affinité chez les Yanõmami: antinomie et complémentarité. In Albert *et al.* 1977:55-70.

Lounsbury, F.G. (1962), Review of *Structure and Sentiment: A Test Case in Social Anthropology*, by Rodney Needham, *American Anthropologist* 64:1302-1310.

– (1964a), A Formal Account of the Crow- and Omaha-Type Kinship Terminologies. In Goodenough, W.H., ed., *Explorations in Cultural Anthropology: Essays in Honour of G.P. Murdock*, pp.351-393. New York: McGraw-Hill.

– (1964b), The Structural Analysis of Kinship Semantics. *Proceedings of the Ninth International Congress of Linguists*, Cambridge, Mass., 1962, ed. H.G. Lunt. The Hague: Mouton.

– (1978), Aspects du système de parenté Inca. In *Anthropologie Historique des Sociétés Andines* (Numéro Spécial). Annales Économies, Sociétés, Civilisations 33: 991-1005.

Lowie, R.H. (1946a), The Bororo. In Steward 1946a:419-434.

– (1946b), The Northwestern and Central Gê. In Steward 1946a:477-517.

Lyon, P.J., ed. (1974), *Native South Americans: Ethnology of the Least Known Continent*. Boston: Little, Brown and Company.

MacNeish, R.S., Patterson, T.C., & Browman, D.L. (1975), *The Central Peruvian Prehistoric Interaction Sphere*. Papers of the Robert S. Peabody Foundation for Archaeology 7. Andover: Phillips Academy.

Margolis, M.L. & Carter, W.E., eds. (1979), *Brazil: Anthropological Perspectives. Essays in Honor of Charles Wagley.* New York: Columbia University Press.

Martin, M.K. (1969), South American Foragers: A Case Study in Cultural Devolution. *American Anthropologist* 71:243-260.

Mason. J.A. (1950), The Languages of South American Indians. In Steward 1950:157-317.

Maybury-Lewis, D.H.P. (1958), Kinship and Social Organisation in Central Brazil. *Proceedings of the 32nd International Congress of Americanists,* pp.123-136. Copenhagen.

– (1960a), Parallel Descent and the Apinayé Anomaly. *Southwestern Journal of Anthropology* 16:191-216.

– (1960b), The Analysis of Dual Organizations: A Methodological Critique. *Bijdragen tot de Taal-, Land- en Volkenkunde* 116:17-44.

– (1965a), Prescriptive Marriage Systems. *Southwestern Journal of Anthropology* 21:207-230.

– (1965b), Some Crucial Distinctions in Central Brazilian Ethnology. *Anthropos* 60:340-358.

– (1967), *Akwẽ-Shavante Society.* Oxford: Clarendon Press.

– ed. (1971a), Recent Research in Central Brazil. *Akten XXXVIII Amerikanistenkongress* 3:333-391. Stuttgart.

– (1971b), Some Principles of Social Organization among the Central Gê. In Maybury-Lewis 1971a:381-386.

– (1974), The Akwe-Shavante: A Test Case of "Dual Organization" in Central Brazil. *Actas del XXXV Congreso Internacional de Americanistas* 3: 135-136. Mexico.

– ed. (1979a), *Dialectical Societies: The Gê and Bororo of Central Brazil.* Cambridge: Harvard University Press.

– (1979b), Cultural Categories of the Central Gê. In Maybury-Lewis 1979a:218-246.

– (1979c), Conclusion: Kinship, Ideology, and Culture. In Maybury-Lewis 1979a: 301-312.

Meggers, B.J. (1954), Environmental Limitation on the Development of Culture. *American Anthropologist* 56:801-824.

– (1957), Environment and Culture in the Amazon Basin: An Appraisal of the Theory of Environmental Determinism. In *Studies in Human Ecology.* Washington: The Anthropological Society of Washington.

– (1971), *Amazonia: Man and Culture in a Counterfeit Paradise.* Chicago: Aldine Publishing Company.

Meggers, B.J. & Evans, C. (1973), An Interpretation of the Cultures of Marajó Island. In Gross 1973:39-47.

Melatti, J.C. (1971), Nominadores e Genitores: um Aspecto do Dualismo Krahó. In Maybury-Lewis 1971a:347-353.

– (1979), The Relationship System of the Krahó. In Maybury-Lewis 1979a:46-79.

Menget, P. (1977), Adresse et référence dans la classification sociale Txicáo. In Albert *et al.* 1977:323-339.

Métraux, A. (1946), The Caingang. In Steward 1946a:445-475.

– (1948a), The Guaraní. In Steward 1948a: 69-94.

– (1948b), The Tupinambá. In Steward 1948a:95-134.

– (1948c), The Paressí. In Steward 1948a: 349-360.

– (1948d), Tribes of Eastern Bolivia and the Madeira Headwaters. In Steward 1948a:381-454.

Miller, J.G. (1965), Living Systems: Basic Concepts. *Behavioural Science* 10:193-237.

Moore, S.F. (1963), Oblique and Asymmetrical Cross-Cousin Marriage and Crow-Omaha Terminology. *American Anthropologist* 65:296-311.

Morey, R.V., Jr. (1972), Warfare Patterns of the Colombian Guahibo. In Avalos & Ravines 1972:59-68.

Morey, R.V., Jr. & Marwitt, J.P. (1978), Ecology, Economy, and Warfare in Lowland South America. In Browman, D.L., ed., *Advances in Andean Archaeology*, pp.247-258. The Hague: Mouton Publishers.

Morissette, J. & Racine, L. (1973), La Hiérarchie des *wamani:* essai sur la pensé classificatoire Quechua. In *Signes et Langages des Amériques*. Recherches Amérindiennes au Québec III:167-188.

Murdock, G.P. (1949), *Social Structure*. New York: The Free Press.

— (1965), Political Moieties. In *Culture and Society: 24 Essays by George Peter Murdock*, pp.332-347. Pittsburgh: University of Pittsburgh Press.

— (1981), *Atlas of World Cultures*. Pittsburgh: University of Pittsburgh Press.

Murphy, R.F. (1956), Matrilocality and Patrilineality in Mundurucú Society. *American Anthropologist* 58:414-434.

— (1960), *Headhunter's Heritage*. Berkeley: University of California Press.

— (1973), Social Structure and Sex Antagonism. In Gross 1973:213-224.

— (1979), Lineage and Lineality in Lowland South America. In Margolis & Carter 1979: 217-224.

Murphy, R.F. & Quain, B. (1955), *The Trumaí Indians of Central Brazil*. Monographs of the American Ethnological Society 24. Seattle: University of Washington Press.

Murphy, Y. & Murphy, R.F. (1974), *Women of the Forest*. New York: Columbia University Press.

Murra, J.V. (1968), An Aymara Kingdom in 1567. *Ethnohistory* 15:115-151.

Myers, T. (1983), Redes de Intercambio Tempranas en la Hoya Amazónica. *Amazonia Peruana* IV:8, pp.61-75.

Needham, R. (1958a), A Structural Analysis of Purum Society. *American Anthropologist* 60:75-101.

— (1958b), The Formal Analysis of Prescriptive Patrilateral Cross-Cousin Marriage. *Southwestern Journal of Anthropology* 14:199-219.

— (1960a), A Structural Analysis of Aimol Society. *Bijdragen tot de Taal-, Land-en Volkenkunde* 116:81-108.

— (1960b), Lineal Equations in a Two-Section System: A Problem in the Social Structure of Mota (Banks Island). *Journal of the Polynesian Society* 69:23-30.

— (1961), An Analytical Note on the Structure of Sirionó Society. *Southwestern Journal of Anthropology* 17:239-255.

— (1962), *Structure and Sentiment: A Test Case in Social Anthropology*. Chicago: The University of Chicago Press.

— (1963), Introduction. In Durkheim & Mauss 1963: vii-xlviii.

— (1964a), Descent, Category, and Alliance in Sirionó Society. *Southwestern Journal of Anthropology* 20:229-240.

— (1964b), The Mota Problem and Its Lessons. *Journal of the Polynesian Society* 73:302-314.

— (1966a), Age, Category, and Descent. *Bijdragen tot de Taal-, Land- en Volkenkunde* 122:1-35.

— (1966b), Terminology and Alliance I: Garo, Manggarai. *Sociologus* 16:141-157.

— (1967), Terminology and Alliance II: Mapuche; Conclusions. *Sociologus* 17:39-53.

— ed. (1971a), *Rethinking Kinship and Marriage*. A.S.A. Monographs 11. London: Tavistock Publications.

— (1971b), Introduction. In Needham 1971a: xiii-cxvii.

— (1971c), Remarks on the Analysis of Kinship and Marriage. In Needham 1971a:1-34.

— (1972), Prologo. In Suárez 1972:7-39.

— (1973), Prescription. *Oceania* 43:166-181.

— (1979), *Symbolic Classification*. Santa Monica: Goodyear Publishing Company.

Netherly, P.J. (1977), *Local Level Lords on the North Coast of Peru*. Ann Arbor: University Microfilms International.

Nimuendajú, C. (1939), *The Apinayé*. The Catholic University of America Anthropological Series 8. Washington: The Catholic University of America Press.

– (1942), *The Šerente*. Publications of the Frederick Webb Hodge Anniversary Publication Fund IV. Los Angeles: The Southwest Museum.

– (1946), *The Eastern Timbira*. Berkeley: University of California Press.

– (1948), The Cawahíb, Parintintin, and their Neighbours. In Steward 1948a: 283-298.

Nimuendajú, C. & Lowie, R.H. (1937), The Dual Organizations of the Ramkokamekra (Canella) of Northern Brazil. *American Anthropologist* 39:565-582.

Nordenskiöld, E. (1917), The Guaraní Invasion of the Inca Empire in the Sixteenth Century: An Historical Indian Migration. *The Geographical Review* IV:103-121.

Nugent, S.L. (1982), "Civilization," "Society," and "Anomaly" in Amazonia. In Renfrew, C. *et al.*, eds., *Theory and Explanation in Archaeology*, pp.231-240. New York: Academic Press.

Oberem, U. (1974), Trade and Trade Goods in the Ecuadorian Montaña. In Lyon 1974: 346-357.

Oberg, K. (1973), Types of Social Structure among the Lowland Tribes of South and Central America. In Gross 1973:189-210.

Ortiz, A. (1969), *The Tewa World: Space, Time, Being, and Becoming in a Pueblo Society*. Chicago: University of Chicago Press.

Ossio, J.M. (1978), El Simbolismo del agua y la representación del tiempo y el espacio en la fiesta de la Acequia de la comunidad de Andamarca. In Albert *et al.* 1978:377-396.

Palomino Flores, S. (1970), *El Sistema de oposiciones en la comunidad de Sarhua*. Unpublished thesis. Ayacucho: Universidad Nacional de San Cristobal de Huamanga.

– (1971), Duality in the Socio-Cultural Organization of Several Andean Populations. *Folk* 13:65-88.

Pollock, D.K. (1985), Looking for a Sister: Culina Siblingship and Affinity. In Kensinger 1985a:8-15.

Postal, P.M. & Eyde, D.B. (1963), Matrilineality Versus Matrilocality among the Sirionó: A Reply to Needham. *Bijdragen tot de Taal-, Land- en Volkenkunde* 119:284-285.

Price, D. (1985), Nambiquara Brothers. In Kensinger 1985a:16-19.

Radcliffe-Brown, A.R. (1952), *Structure and Function in Primitive Society: Essays and Addresses*. London:Cohen & West.

– (1953), Dravidian Kinship Terminology. *Man* 53:112.

Ramos, A.R. (1974), How the Sanumá Acquire Their Names. *Ethnology* XIII: 171-185.

Ramos, A.R. & Albert, B. (1977), Yanoama Descent and Affinity: The Sanumá/Yanomam Contrast. In Albert *et al.* 1977: 71-90.

Reichel-Dolmatoff, G. (1973), The Agricultural Basis of the Sub-Andean Chiefdoms of Colombia. In Gross 1973:28-36.

Reining, P., ed. (1972), *Kinship Studies in the Morgan Centennial Year*. Washington: The Anthropological Society of Washington.

Ribeiro, D. (1974), Kadiwéu Kinship. In Lyon 1974:167-182.

Ribeiro, D. & Wise, M.R. (1978), *Los Grupos etnicos de la Amazonia Peruana*. Comunidades y culturas peruanas 13. Lima: Instituto Linguistico de Verano.

Rivers, W.H.R. (1968), *Kinship and Social Organization*. London School of Economics Monographs on Social Anthropology 34. London: University of London/The Athlone Press.

Rivière, P.G. (1966a), Oblique Discontinous Exchange: A New Formal Type of Prescriptive Alliance. *American Anthropologist* 68:738-740.

– (1966b), A Note on Marriage with the Sister's Daughter. *Man* 1:550-556.

66c), Age: A Determinant of Social ıssification. *Southwestern Journal of ıthropology* 22:43-60.

– (1969), *Marriage among the Trio: A Principle of Social Organization.* Oxford: Clarendon Press.

– (1973), The Lowland South America Culture Area: Towards a Structural Definition. Paper presented at the 72nd Annual Meeting of the American Anthropological Association. New Orleans.

– (1977), Some Problems in the Comparative Study of Carib Societies. In Basso 1977:39-42.

– (1980), *Dialectical Societies* (Review Article). *Man* 15:533-540.

– (1984), *Individual and Society in Guiana: A Comparative Study of Amerindian Social Organization.* Cambridge: Cambridge University Press.

Rodrigues, A.D. (1974), Linguistic Groups of Amazonia. In Lyon 1974:51-58.

Rowe, J.H. (1974), Linguistic Classification Problems in South America. In Lyon 1974:43-50.

Sarmiento de Gamboa, P. (1908), *History of the Incas.* London: The Hakluyt Society.

Scheffler, H.W. (1966), Ancestor Worship in Anthropology: or, Observations on Descent and Descent Groups. *Current Anthropology* 7:541-551.

– (1970), *The Elementary Structures of Kinship* by Claude Lévi-Strauss: A Review Article. *American Anthropologist* 72:251-268.

– (1971), Dravidian-Iroquois: The Melanesian Evidence. In Jayawardena, C. & Hiatt, L., eds., *Anthropology in Oceania: Essays in Honor of H.I. Hogbin*, pp. 231-254. Sydney: Angus and Robertson.

– (1972), Systems of Kin Classification: A Structural Typology. In Reining 1972: 113-133.

– (1974), Kinship, Descent, and Alliance. In Honigmann, J.J., ed., *Handbook of Social and Cultural Anthropology,* pp.747-793. New York: Rand McNally.

Scheffler, H.W. & Lounsbury, F.G. (1971),

A Study in Structural Semantics: The Sirionó Kinship System. Englewood Cliffs: Prentice Hall.

Schneider, D.M. (1965), Some Muddles in the Models: or, How the System Really Works. In Banton 1965:25-85.

– (1972), What is Kinship All About? In Reining 1972:32-63.

– (1984), *A Critique of the Study of Kinship.* Ann Arbor: The University of Michigan Press.

Schwerin, K.H. (1972), Arawak, Carib, Gê, Tupí: Cultural Adaptation and Culture History in the Tropical Forest, South America. In Avalos & Ravines 1972:39-57.

– (1982), The Kin Integration System among Caribs. Paper presented at the 44th International Congress of Americanists. Manchester.

Seeger, A. (1977), Fixed Points on Arcs in Circles: The Temporal, Processual Aspect of Suyá Space and Society. In Albert *et al.* 1977:341-359.

– (1981), *Nature and Society in Central Brazil.* Cambridge: Harvard University Press.

Shapiro, J.R. (1974), Alliance or Descent: Some Amazonian Contrasts. *Man* 9:305-306.

– (1975), Alliance or Descent: Some Amazonian Contrasts. *Man* 10:624-625.

– (1984), Marriage Rules, Marriage Exchange, and the Definition of Marriage in Lowland South American Societies. In Kensinger 1984a:1-30.

– (1985), The Sibling Relationship in Lowland South America: General Considerations. In Kensinger 1985a:1-7.

Shapiro, W. (1966), Secondary Unions and Kinship Terminology: The Case of Avuncular Marriage. *Bijdragen tot de Taal-, Land- en Volkenkunde* 122:82-89.

– (1968), Kinship and Marriage in Sirionó Society: A Re-Examination. *Bijdragen tot de Taal-, Land- en Volkenkunde* 124: 40-55.

– (1970), The Ethnography of Two-Section Systems. *Ethnology* IX:380-388.

– (1971), Structuralism versus Sociology: A Review of Maybury-Lewis' *Akwe-Shavante Society. Mankind* 8:64-66.

Siskind, J. (1973), *To Hunt in the Morning.* New York: Oxford University Press.

Sorensen, A.P., Jr. (1973), South American Indian Linguistics at the Turn of the Seventies. In Gross 1973:312-341.

– (1984), Linguistic Exogamy and Personal Choice in the Northwest Amazon. In Kensinger 1984a:180-193.

Sperber, D. (1985), *On Anthropological Knowledge.* Cambridge: Cambridge University Press.

Steward, J.H., ed. (1946a), *Handbook of South American Indians I: The Marginal Tribes.* Bureau of American Ethnology Bulletin 143. Washington: Smithsonian Institution.

– ed. (1946b), *Handbook of South American Indians II: The Andean Civilizations.* Bureau of American Ethnology bulletin 143. Washington: Smithsonian Institution.

– ed. (1948a), *Handbook of South American Indians III: The Tropical Forest Tribes.* Bureau of American Ethnology Bulletin 143. Washington: Smithsonian Institution.

– (1948b), Tribes of the Montaña: An Introduction. In Steward 1948a:507-533.

– (1948c), The Witotoan Tribes. In Steward 1948a:749-762.

– (1948d), Culture Areas of the Tropical Forests. In Steward 1948a:883-899.

– ed. (1950), *Handbook of South American Indians VI: Physical Anthropology, Linguistics, and Cultural Geography of South American Indians.* Bureau of American Ethnology Bulletin 143. Washington: Smithsonian Institution.

Steward, J.H. & Faron, L.C. (1959), *Native Peoples of South America.* New York: McGraw-Hill Book Company.

Steward, J.H. & Métraux, A. (1948), Tribes of the Peruvian and Ecuadorian Montaña. In Steward 1948a:535-656.

Strathern, M. (1984), Marriage Exchanges: A Melanesian Comment. *Annual Review of Anthropology* 13:41-73.

Suárez, M.M. (1972), *Terminologia, alianza matrimonial y cambio en la sociedad Warao.* Serie Lenguas Indigenas de Venezuela. Caracas. (Also published in English, 1971, Terminology, Alliance, and Change in Warao society. *Nieuwe West-Indische Gids* 48:56-122.)

Tavener, C.J. (1973), The Karajá and the Brazilian Frontier. In Gross 1973:433-459.

Tax, S. (1937), Some Problems of Social Organization. In Eggan 1937:3-32.

Taylor, A.-C. (1982), The Marriage Alliance and Its Transformations in Jivaroan Societies. Paper presented at the 44th International Congress of Americanists. Manchester.

Taylor, K.I. (1977), Raiding, Dueling, and Descent Goup Membership among the Sanumá. In Albert *et al.* 1977:91-104.

Taylor, K.I. & Ramos, A.R. (1975), Alliance or Descent: Some Amazonian Contrasts. *Man* 10:128-130.

Thomas, D.J. (1971), Pemon Kinship Terminology. *Antropologica* 30:3-17.

– (1979), Pemon Zero Generation Terminology: Social Correlates. In Kensinger 1979a:63-80.

Torralba, P.A. (1981), Sharanahua. *Antisuyo* 4:37-83.

Trautmann, T.R. (1981), *Dravidian Kinship.* Cambridge: Cambridge University Press.

Turner, T.S. (1971), Northern Kayapó Social Structure. In Maybury-Lewis 1971a:365-371.

– (1979a), The Gê and Bororo Societies as Dialectical Systems: A General Model. In Maybury-Lewis 1979a:147-178.

– (1979b), Kinship, Household, and Community Structure among the Kayapó. In Maybury-Lewis 1979a:179-214.

Tylor, E.B. (1964), *Researches Into the Early History of Mankind and the Development of Civilization.* Chicago: The University of Chicago Press.

Vayda, A.P., ed. (1969), *Environment and Cultural Behaviour: Ecological Studies in Cultural Anthropology.* Garden City: The Natural History Press.

arin, J.A. & Villamarin, J.E. (1975), ship and Inheritance among the ɔana de Bogotá Chibcha at the Time of Spanish Conquest. *Ethnology* XIV:173-179.

Villas Boas, O. & Villas Boas, C. (1974), *Xingú: The Indians, Their Myths*. London: Souvenir Press.

Waddington, C.H. (1969), The Theory of Evolution Today. In Koestler, A. & Smythies, J.R., eds., *Beyond Reductionism: The Alpbach Symposium*, pp. 357-374. London: Hutchinson & Co.

Wagley, C. (1977a), *Welcome of Tears: The Tapirapé Indians of Central Brazil*. New York: Oxford University Press.

– (1977b), Time and the Tapirapé. In Albert *et al.* 1977:369-377.

Wagley, C. & Galvão, E. (1948), The Tapirapé. In Steward 1948a:167-178.

Webster, S.S. (1977), Kinship and Affinity in a Native Quechua Community. In Bolton & Mayer 1977:28-42.

Whitten, N.E., Jr. & Whitten, D.S. (1984), The Structure of Kinship and Marriage among the Canelos Quichua of East-Central Ecuador. In Kensinger 1984a:194-220.

Williams, F.E. (1932), Sex Affiliation and Its Implications. *Journal of the Royal Anthropological Institute* 62:51-81.

Yalman, N. (1962), The Structure of the Sinhalese Kindred: A Re-Examination of the Dravidian Terminology. *American Anthropologist* 64:548-575.

– (1965), Dual Organization in Central Ceylon? or The Goddess on the Tree-top. *Journal of Asian Studies* 24:441-457.

Zuidema, R.T. (1964), *The Ceque System of Cuzco: The Social Organization of the Capital of the Inca*. International Archives of Ethnography. Supplement to vol. 50. Leiden: E.J. Brill.

– (1965), American Social Systems and their Mutual Similarity. *Bijdragen tot de Taal-, Land- en Volkenkunde* 121:103-119.

– (1967), "Descendencia paralela" en una familia indígena noble del Cuzco. *Fénix* 17:39-62.

– (1969), Hierarchy in Symmetric Alliance Systems. *Bijdragen tot de Taal-, Land- en Volkenkunde* 125:134-139.

– (1977), The Inca Kinship System: A New Theoretical View. In Bolton & Mayer 1977:240-281.

— (1966c), Age: A Determinant of Social Classification. *Southwestern Journal of Anthropology* 22:43-60.